LAND ROVER 2·2A·3
OWNERS WORKSHOP MANUAL

By the Autobooks Team
of Writers and Illustrators

Land-Rover *Series 2, 2¼ Litre, Petrol 1959–61*

Land-Rover *Series 2A, Petrol, Diesel 1961–71*

Land-Rover *Series 3, Petrol, Diesel 1971–83*

BROOKLANDS BOOKS LTD.
P.O. BOX 146, COBHAM,
SURREY, KT11 1LG. UK
sales@brooklands-books.com

B-LR70WH

Printed in China

The following Autobook Workshop Manuals are currently available from Brooklands Books Ltd.

Alfa Romeo Giulia-Spider 1962-1978   OWM 724
BMW 1800 • 1800 TI 1964-1971   OWM 813
Citroen 19-20-21-23 1955-1975   OWM 742 and 954
Fiat X1/9 1974-1982   OWM 928
Land Rover Series 2 • 2A • 3 1959-1983   OWM 895
Lotus Elan 1962-1974   OWM 600
Mazda 808 • 818 1972-1979   OWM 877
Morgan Four 1936-1981   OWM 796
MGA & MGB 1955-1968   OWM 955*
MGB 1968-1981   OWM 935*
Sprite & Midget 1958-1980   OWM 745*
Opel GT   OWM 727
Porsche 356 1957-1965   OWM 827
Porsche 912 1965-1969   OWM 897
Reliant Scimitar 1968-1979   OWM 896
Toyota Celica 1600 1971-1977   OWM 804
Triumph Spitfire Mk.III, Mk.IV, 1500 1969-1980   OWM 711*
Triumph TR5 • 250 • TR6 1967-1975   OWM 826*
Volvo 1800 & 120 1960-1973   OWM 759 & 776
Volvo 164 1968-1975   OWM 782
VW Transporter 1954-1967   OWM 834

* Glovebox edition

ISBN 0 7136 2512 0

OWM 895

Contents

The Autobook, having been written and published in England, is produced using all English phrases, terms, spellings and component descriptions. Some of these do, of course, differ from those in general use in America and, therefore, in order to simplify the identification of components, the following glossary is provided.

Glossary

English	American	English	American
Aerial	Antenna	Layshaft (of gearbox)	Countershaft
Accelerator	Gas pedal	Leading shoe (of brake)	Primary shoe
Alternator	Generator	Locks	Latches
Anti-roll bar	Stabiliser or sway bar	Motorway	Freeway, turnpike, etc
Battery	Energizer	Number plate	License plate
Bodywork	Sheet metal	Paraffin	Kerosene
Bonnet (engine cover)	Hood	Petrol	Gasoline
Boot lid	Trunk lid	Petrol tank	Gas tank
Boot (luggage compartment)	Trunk	'Pinking'	'Pinging'
		Propeller shaft	Driveshaft
Bottom gear	1st gear	Quarter light	Quarter window
Bulkhead	Firewall	Retread	Recap
Cam follower or tappet	Valve lifter or tappet	Reverse	Back-up
Carburetter	Carburetor	Rocker cover	Valve cover
Catch	Latch	Roof rack	Car-top carrier
Choke/venturi	Barrel	Saloon	Sedan
Circlip	Snap-ring	Seized	Frozen
Clearance	Lash	Side indicator lights	Side marker lights
Crownwheel	Ring gear (of differential)	Side light	Parking light
Disc (brake)	Rotor/disk	Silencer	Muffler
Drop arm	Pitman arm	Spanner	Wrench
Drop head coupe	Convertible	Sill panel (beneath doors)	Rocker panel
Dynamo	Generator (DC)	Split cotter (for valve spring cap)	Lock (for valve spring retainer)
Earth (electrical)	Ground		
Engineer's blue	Prussian blue	Split pin	Cotter pin
Estate car	Station wagon	Steering arm	Spindle arm
Exhaust manifold	Header	Sump	Oil pan
Fast back (Coupe)	Hard top	Tab washer	Tang; lock
Fault finding/diagnosis	Trouble shooting	Tailgate	Liftgate
Float chamber	Float bowl	Tappet	Valve lifter
Free-play	Lash	Thrust bearing	Throw-out bearing
Freewheel	Coast	Top gear	High
Gudgeon pin	Piston pin or wrist pin	Trackrod (of steering)	Tie-rod (or connecting rod)
Gearchange	Shift	Trailing shoe (of brake)	Secondary shoe
Gearbox	Transmission	Transmission	Whole drive line
Halfshaft	Axleshaft	Tyre	Tire
Handbrake	Parking brake	Van	Panel wagon/van
Hood	Soft top	Vice	Vise
Hot spot	Heat riser	Wheel nut	Lug nut
Indicator	Turn signal	Windscreen	Windshield
Interior light	Dome lamp	Wing/mudguard	Fender

The Land-Rover

The Vehicle

The Series 2 Land-Rover, introduced in April 1958 with the new $2\frac{1}{4}$ litre petrol engine – a sturdy four cylinder OHV unit – was replaced by the Series 2A in September 1961 when the optional $2\frac{1}{4}$ litre diesel engine was introduced.

The vehicles are produced in two wheelbase lengths, 88 inch and 109 inch, and a more powerful 2.6 litre six cylinder engine was added as an option to the long wheelbase model in September 1966.

The Series 3 was introduced in October 1971 with a choice of the earlier engines, the 3.5 litre capacity V8 engine being added to the range in April 1980 and the 2.6 litre engine being discontinued from August 1980.

The vehicles have a sturdy box-section chassis, painted inside and out, and aluminium alloy non-corroding body construction.

Four wheel or two wheel drive is available on all models except the V8 engined vehicles which have a permanent four wheel drive.

The gearbox has four speeds and reverse. All forward speeds, from the introduction of Series 3, have synchromesh. The transfer box has two speed reduction on main gearbox output.

The suspension uses semi-elliptic, underslung road springs with double acting telescopic shock absorbers (dampers).

Steering is by recirculating ball, worm and nut.

Drum brakes are fitted front and rear and later models have dual braking systems, split front and rear, with a brake warning switch.

There are many body styles and many variants with an extensive range of optional equipment.

The Autobook

This do-it-yourself Workshop Manual has been specially written for the practical motorist who wishes to maintain his vehicle in first-class condition and to carry out the bulk of his own servicing and repairs.

Comprehensive step-by-step instructions and illustrations are given on most dismantling, overhauling and assembling operations in order to simplify what might have appeared a complicated job. Certain assemblies require the use of expensive special tools, the purchase of which would be unjustified. In other instances, techniques or testing facilities which are not available to an owner are essential. In these cases, information may be included but the reader is recommended to pass the unit or component to an authorised agent or to a specialist for attention.

The Autobook is divided into chapters, each chapter being sub-divided into numbered sections. Should it be necessary to refer to another part of the manual, all cross-reference details are included. The numerous drawings contained are intended for two purposes: (i) to indicate the detailed assembly of components and (ii) to simplify the text by being included in the appropriate position for direct reference.

Throughout the manual hints and tips are included which will be found invaluable and there is an easy to follow fault diagnosis at the end of each chapter.

Information which can be of great help to those who are not skilled motor mechanics is given in 'Hints on Maintenance and Overhaul' at the end of the manual and should be referred to before starting work.

Whilst every effort has been made to ensure that the information is correct, it is obviously not possible to guarantee complete freedom from errors or omissions.

Instructions may refer to the righthand or lefthand side of the vehicle or components. These are to be considered as if the observer is standing behind the car and looking forward.

The Saving

Considerable savings on garage charges can be made by the car owner performing his own repairs whenever possible. On completion of such repairs, the motorist can drive in safety and confidence knowing that the work has been carried out correctly and to his own complete satisfaction.

Workhorse for half the world, the Land-Rover can tackle every kind of terrain

CHAPTER 1

THE PETROL ENGINE

1:1 Description

The Autobook covers the Land-Rover normal control Series 2, 2A and 3 models. Petrol engines of 2¼ litres, 2.6 litres and 3.5 litres are available to choice and in this chapter all engines are dealt with. The same basic techniques are applicable to working on any engine but constructional details are varied. These are clearly described where necessary.

The 2¼ litre engine has a conventional cylinder block and head of cast iron with overhead inlet and exhaust valves. It is a rugged four-cylinder unit with a three bearing crankshaft or five bearing crankshaft from serial number 3600001A or 99100001A; the lower numbering applies to units with a cast crankshaft and higher numbering a forged shaft. Two compression ratios are available, either 7:1 or 8:1. A chain driven camshaft with a chain tensioner provides the means of operation for the valve gear.

The 2.6 litre engine is a six-cylinder of unusual layout. The cylinder block is of cast iron with an inclined top face which carries the aluminium alloy cylinder head. Overhead inlet and side exhaust valves are fitted, both operated from a chain driven camshaft. A hydraulic chain tensioner maintains the chain tension. The crankshaft is carried in seven main bearings and incor-porates a torsional vibration damper. This engine is also available with either one of two compression ratios, 7:1 or 7.8:1.

The 3.5 litre engine is an eight-cylinder V-type with cylinders arranged in two banks of four. The aluminium cylinder block is fitted with dry cylinder liners and carries the crankshaft in five main bearings. Two connecting rods run on each of the four crankpins. The single camshaft is located centrally above the crankshaft and is driven by an inverted tooth type chain and 2:1 chainwheels. The compression ratio is 8.13:1.

1:2 Working on the engine in situ

The only operation which entails the removal of either in-line engine from the chassis is for removal of the crankshaft; even the rear main bearing oil seal can be replaced without moving the engine. Obviously, work on the flywheel or clutch will involve gearbox removal or engine removal on the 3.5 litre. Most operations at the front of the engine demand the removal of the radiator grille panel and radiator, or radiator and front panel assembly after draining the coolant. If a major overhaul is contemplated, time can be saved if the engine is removed, therefore instructions for this are given in the next section.

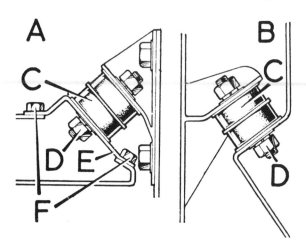

FIG 1 : 1 Engine mounting rubbers, 2¼ litre

Key to Fig 1 : 1
A Lefthand side mounting
B Righthand side mounting **C** Suspension rubbers
D Lower centre fixing **E** Support bracket, righthand side
F Support bracket fixings

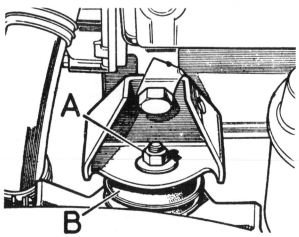

FIG 1 : 2 Engine mounting rubbers, 2.6 litre

Key to Fig 1 : 2 **A** Upper fixing **B** Suspension rubber

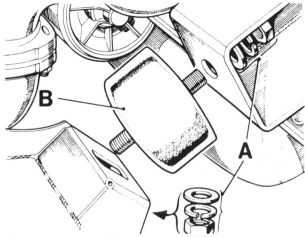

FIG 1 : 3 Engine mounting rubbers, 3.5 litre

Key to Fig 1 : 3 **A** Upper and lower fixings
B Suspension rubber

1 : 3 *Removing and replacing the engines*

(a) 2¼ litre :

1 Remove the bonnet panel, air cleaner (see **Chapter 3A**, **Section 3A : 4**), radiator and grille panel, or radiator and front panel assembly (see **Chapter 5**) after draining the coolant; remove the bellhousing cover where fitted. Disconnect the battery.

2 Remove the front floor, on early models, by undoing the locknuts below the four wheel drive and transfer gearlever knobs, then unscrewing the knobs to allow the floor plates to be unscrewed and lifted up.

3 Disconnect these items at the lefthand side of the engine: exhaust pipe, heater hoses, throttle link, cold start cables, leads from ignition coil, engine earth cable, engine mounting rubber upper fixing. See **FIG 1 : 1** for details of this mounting rubber.

4 Disconnect these items at the righthand side of the engine: fuel pipe at the pump inlet, battery lead at clip near the fuel pump, starter motor and dynamo or alternator leads, engine electrical leads at snap connectors or multi-plug adjacent to the dash, release the speedometer cable from its clip, disconnect the distributor vacuum pipe if necessary, then undo the engine mounting rubber upper fixing (see **FIG 1 : 1**).

5 Release the clutch fluid pipe and the electrical leads from their clips on the engine or dash panel.

6 If available, fit the special Rover lifting sling or else make up a substantial rope sling and pass it under and round the engine forward of the bellhousing and again forward of the sump but behind the crankshaft pulley. Connect to a properly suspended and tested lifting tackle, then just take the weight of the engine.

7 Lift the engine sufficiently to enable the righthand and lefthand mountings to be removed, then lower the engine to maintain alignment with the gearbox.

8 Place packing under the gearbox to support it, then undo all the bolts round the bellhousing. Move the clutch slave cylinder aside without disconnecting the fluid pipe.

9 Pull the engine forward to release the gearbox first motion shaft from the clutch, then hoist away.

10 As soon as possible, lower the engine to the floor and support safely or bolt to an engine stand. During these last two operations never allow any part of the person to be below the suspended load in case of a tackle failure.

11 Refit the engine generally in the reverse order of removal. Smear the splines of the primary pinion, the clutch centre and the withdrawal unit abutment faces with molybdenum disulphide grease such as Rocol MTS 1000.

12 Check the engine oil level and replenish as necessary.

13 Check the gearbox oil level.

14 Start the engine and check that the oil pressure warning light goes out. Check the coolant system for leaks.

15 Check and adjust, as necessary, the idle speed and the ignition timing.

16 Check and top up the coolant level, as necessary, when the engine is cold.

(b) 2.6 litre :

1 Carry out operations 1 and 2 as for the $2\frac{1}{4}$ litre engine. Remove the gearbox tunnel cover.
2 Disconnect the following items at the lefthand side of the engine: exhaust pipe, heat shield, starter motor leads, oil pressure switch leads and engine earth cable.
3 Disconnect the following items at the righthand side of the engine: heater hoses, ignition leads from coil, throttle linkage, speedometer cable, leads for cold start, coolant temperature and generator, brake servo hose, fuel feed pipe and cold start control cable. Where applicable, untape and remove the white wire from the throttle jack and remove the ignition coil from the bulkhead.
4 Fit a suitable lifting sling and connect to a lifting tackle. Just take the weight of the engine.
5 Remove the engine front mountings (see **FIG 1 : 2**).
6 Support the gearbox on substantial packing, then remove the bellhousing bolts.
7 Continue as for the $2\frac{1}{4}$ litre engine.

(c) 3.5 litre :

1 Remove the bonnet and disconnect the battery earth lead.
2 Drain the coolant system, remove the fan blades and cowl, then remove the radiator block (see **Chapter 5**).
3 Remove the air cleaner (see **Chapter 3A**).
4 Disconnect the heater hoses.
5 Disconnect the throttle cable from the lefthand carburetter and induction manifold.
6 Disconnect the vacuum pipe to the gearbox.
7 Disconnect the choke cable from the lefthand carburetter.
8 Disconnect the spill return pipe from the righthand carburetter.
9 Disconnect the vacuum pipe for the brake servo.
10 Disconnect the following leads, marking them for subsequent reconnection: from the alternator, choke thermostat switch, water temperature transmitter and ignition coil.
11 Unclip the engine harness and draw it clear.
12 Disconnect the lead from the oil pressure switch and the leads from the starter motor.
13 Disconnect the engine earth strap.
14 Disconnect the fuel supply pipe from the fuel pump.
15 Disconnect the exhaust pipes from the manifolds.
16 Remove all the fixings from the front mounting rubbers (see **FIG 1 : 3**).
17 Remove the coverplate from the bellhousing.
18 Remove the fixings securing the bellhousing to the engine.
19 Ensure that any ancillary items are disconnected.
20 Attach suitable lifting tackle and lift the engine just enough to remove the front mounting rubbers.
21 Draw the engine forward to release it from the bellhousing dowels and to clear the primary pinion from the clutch, then lift it clear.

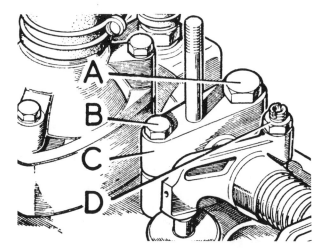

FIG 1 : 4   Rocker shaft mounting, $2\frac{1}{4}$ litre

Key to Fig 1 : 4   **A** Bracket to engine bolt
B Shaft to bracket bolt   **C** Rocker bracket   **D** Locknut

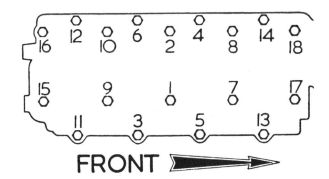

FIG 1 : 5   Cylinder head bolt sequence, $2\frac{1}{4}$ litre

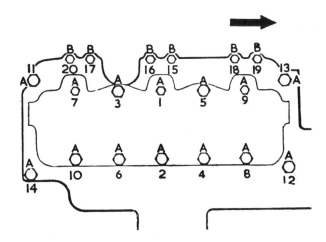

FIG 1 : 6   Cylinder head bolt sequence, 2.6 litre

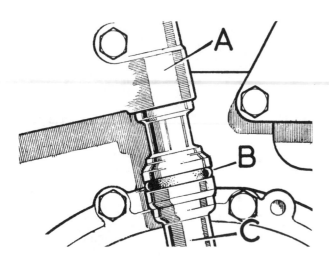

FIG 1 : 7   Seal between head and pump, 2.6 litre

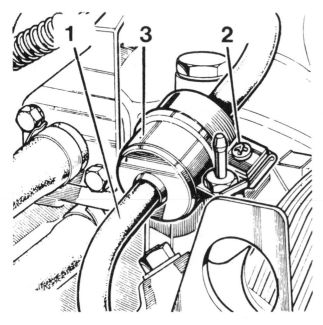

FIG 1 : 8   Engine breather filter, 3.5 litre

Key to Fig 1 : 8   1 Filter top hose   2 Filter clip
3 Breather filter

22 Refit the engine generally in the reverse order of removal, smearing the splines of the primary pinion, the clutch centre and the withdrawal unit with molybdenum disulphide grease such as Rocol MTS 1000 and using Unipart Universal jointing compound between the engine and gearbox joint faces and the vertical joint face of the bellhousing coverplate.

1:4 Removing and replacing the cylinder head

This operation can be conducted with the engine either in or out of the vehicle.

(a) 2¼ litre:

1 Remove the bonnet and air cleaner. Disconnect the battery.
2 Remove the rocker box cover.
3 Drain the coolant. A drain tap is situated at the side of the engine block as well as the one located below the radiator.
4 Disconnect or remove the following components at the righthand side of the engine: the distributor vacuum pipe, plug and coil high tension leads, plugs, fan shroud, oil gallery pipe and coolant bypass hose.
5 Disconnect or remove the following components at the lefthand side of the engine: top coolant hose, throttle linkage, cold start cables at carburetter, fuel pipe and exhaust pipe.
6 Now refer to **FIG 1 : 4**. Slacken the locknuts **D** and screw back the tappet adjusting screws until they all clear the pushrods. Undo bolts **A** and lift the rocker shaft clear of the cylinder head. Do not release bolts **B** unless the shaft and rockers are to be dismantled. Remove the assembly to a clean place.
7 Lift out the pushrods one at a time and identify them 1 to 8 from the front of the engine so that they can be replaced in the tappet seats from whence they were taken. Eight numbered holes in a strip of cardboard is a convenient and simple way of doing this.
8 Slacken the cylinder head bolts evenly in the reverse order to that shown in **FIG 1 : 5** until they can be screwed out by hand and removed. Lift off the cylinder head and discard the gasket.

To replace the cylinder head proceed as follows:

1 Make sure all components and particularly their mating surfaces are clean. Examine the threaded holes in the cylinder block into which the head bolts are screwed and see that no water or carbon is lying in them. This can cause a bolt to bottom instead of pulling down on the head, thus leading to a mysterious epidemic of blown gaskets.
2 If a non-retorque fabric type head gasket is being used, it must be fitted dry, without grease or any sealing compound. If a copper-asbestos gasket is being used, smear a little clean oil on the cylinder block face and both sides of a new head gasket. Fit the gasket with the word 'PETROL' uppermost, and replace the head. Assemble the head bolts finger tight. On later engines, plain washers are fitted between the head bolts and cylinder head.
3 Replace the pushrods, making sure that they are located in the spherical seats of the tappet slides.
4 Fit the rocker shaft and just nip the fixing bolts lightly.
5 Tighten all the cylinder head bolts in the order shown in **FIG 1 : 5**. Tighten each a little at a time, working round the sequence. The large bolts, ½ inch UNF, are tightened to 65 lb ft (8.9 mkg) torque and the smaller $\frac{5}{16}$ inch UNF bolts to 18 lb ft (2.4 mkg) torque. Do not exceed these figures.
6 It will be convenient now to set the tappet clearances. All valves, inlet and exhaust, are set to .01 inch (.25 mm). Screw each adjusting screw down into its pushrod until the feeler gauge is just held between the rocker foot and the end of the valve stem, then lock the adjusting nut.

7 Set the clearances in the following order commencing at No 1 valve at the front of the engine:
Set No. 1 with No. 8 valve fully open
Set No. 3 with No. 6 valve fully open
Set No. 5 with No. 4 valve fully open
Set No. 2 with No. 7 valve fully open
Set No. 8 with No. 1 valve fully open
Set No. 6 with No. 3 valve fully open
Set No. 4 with No. 5 valve fully open
Set No. 7 with No. 2 valve fully open

8 Replace the rocker cover, using a new gasket and tighten the nuts evenly.

9 Continue to reassemble the engine by reversing the dismantling operations. Refill the radiator and reconnect the battery.

10 Allow the engine to run up to proper operating temperature, then remove the sparking plugs and rocker cover and check the cylinder head bolts for correct torque loading as they may have slackened slightly.

(b) 2.6 litre:

1 Remove the bonnet, disconnect and remove the air cleaner, disconnect the battery, drain the radiator and remove the carburetter. Disconnect the control rods at the bellcrank.

2 Disconnect all the high tension cables, then undo the bolts holding the distributor clamp plate to the crankcase. Do not undo the clamp bolt or the timing will be lost. Lift out the distributor; there is no need to remove the short drive shaft.

3 Disconnect the rocker oil feed pipe at the rear of the cylinder head.

4 Disconnect the electrical leads for the mixture control light and temperature transmitter. Release the brake servo pipe.

5 Remove the top radiator and bypass hoses.

6 Remove the rocker cover from the head and slacken all the tappet screws.

7 Undo the cylinder head bolts in the reverse order to that shown in **FIG 1 : 6**, slackening each a little at a time. Lift off the cylinder head and discard the gasket. Also discard the O-ring between the water pump and cylinder head (see **FIG 1 : 7**). Lift out and identify the pushrods as described for the 2¼ litre (six only for this engine).

To replace the cylinder head proceed as follows:

1 Ensure the cleanliness of all components by applying the principles described for the 2¼ litre engine, particularly note the reference to the threaded holes.

2 Remove the side rocker cover so that the pushrods can be seated in their cam followers in their correct order.

3 Smear a new head gasket on both sides with clean engine oil and replace on the block with the side marked 'THIS SIDE UP' on top. It will help the assembly if two bolts with their heads sawn off are screwed into place to hold the gasket on the sloping block until the head is in place. Cut slots in these two bolts so that they can be unscrewed with a screwdriver.

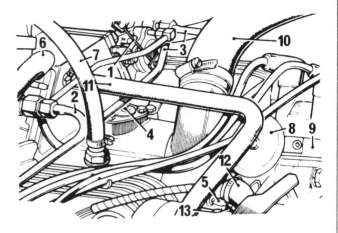

FIG 1 : 9 Induction manifold connections, 3.5 litre

Key to Fig 1 : 9   1 Carburetter choke cable   2 Fuel spill return pipe   3 Fuel supply pipe   4 Choke thermostat switch lead   5 Water temperature transmitter lead   6 Flame trap hoses   7 Brake servo vacuum pipe   8 Distributor vacuum unit   9 Distributor cap   10 Radiator return hose   11 Return hose   12 Thermostat bypass hose   13 Heater return pipe

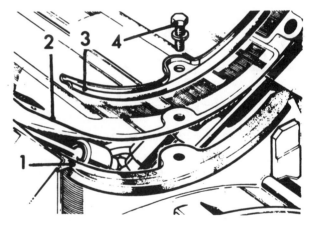

FIG 1 : 10   The induction manifold gasket, seals and clamps, 3.5 litre

Key to Fig 1 : 10   1 Seal   2 Gasket   3 Clamp   4 Clamp bolt

4 Replace the head and fit all the bolts. Connect the bypass hose or new O-seal, as necessary, at the same time.

5 Tighten the head bolts each a little at a time in the sequence shown in **FIG 1 : 6**. The bolts marked **A** are tightened to 50 lb ft (7 mkg) torque and those marked **B** to 30 lb ft (4 mkg).

6 Adjust the tappets, making sure that the screws are located in the pushrod ends. Screw the adjusting screws down until a .006 inch (.15 mm) feeler gauge is just held between the rocker foot and the end of the inlet valve stem, then lock the locknut.

7 Set the clearances in the following order, commencing at No. 1 valve at the front of the engine:
Set No. 1 with No. 6 valve fully open
Set No. 2 with No. 5 valve fully open
Set No. 3 with No. 4 valve fully open

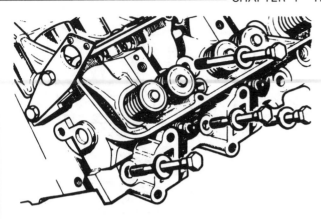

FIG 1 : 11   Cylinder head bolts, 3.5 litre

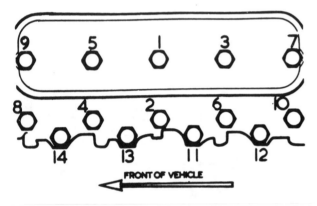

FIG 1 : 12   Bolt tightening sequence, 3.5 litre

Key to Fig 1 : 12
1, 3, 5 Long bolts
2, 4, 6, 7, 8, 9, 10 Medium bolts   11, 12, 13, 14 Short bolts

Set No. 4 with No. 3 valve fully open
Set No. 5 with No. 2 valve fully open
Set No. 6 with No. 1 valve fully open

8 Refit the side and top rocker covers, using new gaskets, then continue to reassemble the engine by reversing the dismantling procedure. Refill the radiator and reconnect the battery.
9 Run the engine up to operating temperature and recheck the torque loading of the cylinder head bolts, tighten where necessary.

(c) 3.5 litre:

1 Drain the cooling system (see **Chapter 5**).
2 Remove the air cleaner (see **Chapter 3A**).
3 Remove the engine breather filter (see **FIG 1 : 8**).
4 Disconnect the throttle cable from the carburetter and manifold.
5 Disconnect the choke cable, 1 in **FIG 1 : 9**, from the carburetter.
6 Disconnect the fuel spill return pipe 2 from the right-hand carburetter.
7 Remove the fuel supply pipe 3 from the carburetters.

8 Disconnect the lead 4 from the choke thermostat switch and, where fitted, the E.G.R. valve connections (see **Chapter 3A, Section 3A : 6**).
9 Disconnect lead 5 from the water temperature transmitter.
10 Disconnect the flame trap hoses 6 from the carburetters.
11 Disconnect the vacuum pipe 7 for the brake servo.
12 Disconnect the vacuum pipe for the gearbox.
13 Disconnect the vacuum pipe from the distributor 8.
14 Release the distributor cap 9.
15 Disconnect the heater hoses.
16 Disconnect the return hose 10 to the radiator.
17 Disconnect the return hose 11 from the top of the manifold.
18 Disconnect the thermostat bypass hose 12.
19 Disconnect the heater return pipe 13 from the manifold.
20 Remove the twelve manifold retaining bolts and lift off the manifold. Clean the bolt threads of old sealant without delay to preclude old sealant air-hardening and becoming difficult to remove.
21 Clean off coolant from the gasket 2 in **FIG 1 : 10** .
22 Remove the two bolts 4 and lift off the gasket clamps 3. Lift off and discard the gasket 2, remove and discard the gasket seals 1.
23 Remove the rocker covers and rocker shaft assemblies (see **Section 1 : 5**).
24 Disconnect the front exhaust pipes from their manifolds.
25 Remove the alternator
26 Slacken the cylinder head bolts evenly (see **FIG 1 : 11**).
27 Mark the heads for refitment to their original positions if both are being removed.
28 Remove the heads and discard the gaskets.
29 If necessary, remove the exhaust manifolds by tapping back the locking tabs and removing the securing bolts with lockwashers and, on later models, the washers.

Refitment is generally the reverse of the removal order with attention to the following points.

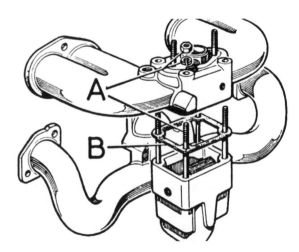

FIG 1 : 13   Separating the manifolds, 2¼ litre

Key to Fig 1 : 13   **A** Fixing nuts   **B** Joint washer

If the exhaust manifolds were removed, ensure that the mating faces of the manifold and cylinder head are clean and smooth and coat the manifold joint face with Foliac J166 or Moly Paul anti-seize compound. The plain washers are fitted between the manifold and lockplates.

Check that the faces of the block and head are clean and fit new head gaskets with the word 'TOP' uppermost. **DO NOT** use sealant. Locate the head on the block dowels, coat the cleaned threads of the cylinder head bolts with Thread Lubricant-Sealant 3M EC776 and immediately insert them into their correct locations (see **FIG 1 : 12**): the short bolts in positions 11 to 14, the long bolts in positions 1, 3 and 5, the medium length bolts in the remainder. Tighten the bolts a little at a time in the sequence shown; bolts 1 to 10 to a torque of 65 to 70 lb ft (9 to 9.6 mkg), the remainder to a torque of 40 to 45 lb ft (5.6 to 6.2 mkg). When all bolts have been tightened, re-check the torque settings.

1 : 5 *Decarbonization and attention to the valves*

(a) 2¼ litre :

Instructions for removing the cylinder head were given in **Section 1 : 4**. To decarbonize the engine and service the valve gear proceed as follows :

1 Attend to the cylinder block first. Plug all the waterways with pieces of rag or twists of newspaper of sufficient size so that they will not be pushed into the jacket and forgotten. This is vital. Examine the threaded holes in the block face and clean away any carbon or dry out any water. Blow into them to finally clean them, then put plugs of rag in as described for the waterways. With a flat scraper, clean the top face of the block thoroughly, then bring two pistons to top dead centre and scrape off the carbon. Use care during this operation so that the piston crowns are not damaged. A blunt penknife is the best tool to use. Under no circumstances use emerycloth or any abrasive to polish up the pistons or block. Turn the engine over to bring up the other two pistons and repeat the cleaning process. Wipe the bores free of carbon as the engine is turned. Do this several times. Cover the block with a piece of clean rag and attend to the head and rocker gear.

2 Unbolt the carburetter from the manifold and place to one side. The manifold can be separated, if necessary, by undoing the vertical bolts after it is removed from the cylinder head. This will be necessary if trouble is suspected with the mechanical 'hot spot' operation. Refer to **FIG 1 : 13** . If the 'hot-spot' bi-metallic spring has broken or the butterfly is hard to move, undo the screw in the counterweight and pull the counterweight, spring and adjusting plate from the spindle. Free the spindle or replace the spring, then reassemble the components in the reverse order to dismantling. The adjusting plate has several serrations which correspond to a setscrew fitted in the side of the manifold (see **FIG 1:14**). Remove the screw, then turn the adjusting plate so that the counterweight is only just sup-

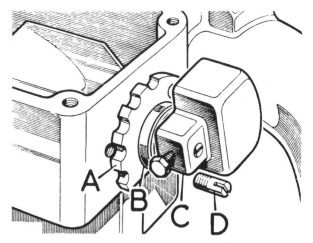

FIG 1 : 14   Adjusting the hot spot, 2¼ litre

Key to Fig 1 : 14   **A** Adjusting plate   **B** Bi-metal spring **C** Counterbalance weight   **D** Setscrew

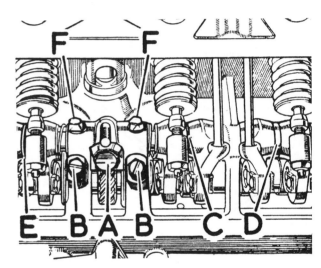

FIG 1 : 15   Rocker shaft locating screw, 2.6 litre

Key to Fig 1 : 15   **A** Oil feed bolt **B** Camshaft bearing locating screws   **C** Thin washer **D** Thick washer   **E** Medium washer   **F** Rocker shaft locating screws

ported by the spring. Replace the screw in the nearest serration. Fit the halves of the manifold together, using a new joint washer, but do not tighten the bolts until the manifold assembly is refitted to the cylinder head.

3 Remove the thermostat housing from the cylinder head.

4 Using a suitable spring compressor, remove all the valves and springs from the head, keeping them in sets identified to the position in the head from which they were removed.

5 Plug all the waterways and oil passages in the head, then remove all the carbon by the use of scrapers and wire brushes. Be careful not to score the valve seat faces.

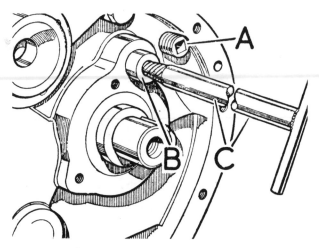

FIG 1 : 16   Rocker shaft extractor, 2.6 litre

Key to Fig 1 : 16   A Plug   **B** Shaft   **C** Extractor

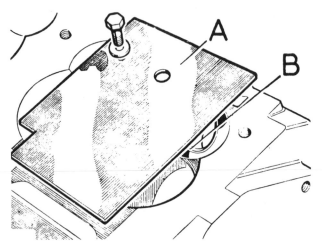

FIG 1 : 17   Protection plate, 2.6 litre

Key to Fig 1 : 17   A Plate   **B** Insert

6 Clean and polish the valves. It is permissible to spin the valves in an electric drill and use emerycloth for this but, again, do not damage the seating face.

7 Wipe the valves and valve guide bores clean and dry and then try each valve in its guide. The clearance between the inlet valve and its guide should not exceed .003 inch (.07 mm) and the exhaust .004 inch (.096 mm). If the clearance is excessive, check the valve stems for wear. Usually the guides will need replacing. If so, use piloted drifts and drive the guides out of the head. Fit new guides, again using piloted drifts and lubricate the guides and cylinder head bores before fitting. Special Rover drifts must be used both for removal and replacement. The tool part numbers are: inlet removal No. 274400, inlet replacement No. 601508 and exhaust removal No. 274401, exhaust replacement No. 600959.

8 After fitting new guides, the seats in the head must be recut to $30 + \frac{1}{4}$ deg. for the inlets and $45 + \frac{1}{4}$ deg. for the exhausts.

9 Examine the valve faces. If a noticeable ridge or distinct pitting is seen the valves must be refaced. This can only be done at a service station and should not be attempted if, by so doing, the valve will be brought to a knife edge.

10 If the valves can be reseated by lapping, smear a little abrasive paste on the face, insert in the head and oscillate to and fro using a suction cup tool. Every few strokes raise the valve and advance it half a turn or so to distribute the paste. Continue until a clear grey band shows all round the valve face and the head seating. Carefully clean away all abrasive paste and, when all the valves are completed, destroy any rag which may be contaminated.

11 Check that the valve springs are an interference fit between the inner and outer; if not, they must be renewed.

12 Clean all the components, then lubricate the valve stems with engine oil and insert them in their guides. With the aid of the spring compressor, replace the springs, caps and collets. Use new oil seals on each valve.

13 Complete the head assembly by fitting the thermostat and manifolds. Note that either a one piece or two piece joint washer is available for the manifold to head joint. Use whichever type was fitted originally. If the two piece type is fitted, the raised rings on the washers must go towards the head. Tighten the head to manifold bolts hard, then tighten the vertical bolts holding the manifolds together to 17 lb ft (2.3 mkg). Note that the two piece joint washers fit the inlet manifold only. The exhaust manifold is in metal to metal contact with the head.

14 Reassemble the engine as described in **Section 1 : 4**, making sure that all pieces of rag or paper are removed from the waterways and oilways.

(b) 2.6 litre:

This engine has the inlet valves only in the head, therefore, although the exhaust valves are in the cylinder block, they will be dealt with in this section. The inlet valve operation and most of the work necessary to service them and decarbonize the head is common to that described for the $2\frac{1}{4}$ litre engine with the following important differences.

1 The head is of light alloy and the valve seats are inserted. If a valve seat is badly burnt it must be ground away until it can be broken out and a new one pressed in. The head must be heated to 65°C (150°F) before doing this.

2 The seat insert must be recut to a $30 + \frac{1}{4}$ deg. angle.

3 Replace the valve guides if the clearance between a new valve stem and the guide exceeds .003 inch (.07 mm). Heat the head to 65°C (150°F) before removing or replacing guides. Use drift part No. 274400 or 274401 to remove the guides and drift part No. 601508 or 600959 to replace them.

4 Do not fit the O-rings to the valve guides until the valves are finally assembled. Pulling a valve out through the O-ring will destroy it.

To service the exhaust valves:

1 Remove all carbon from the block and pistons using the methods described for the $2\frac{1}{4}$ litre engine.

2 Remove the exhaust manifold and gaskets, then the side rocker cover and its joint washer.

3 Slacken each tappet screw right off and turn the engine until the rocker is on the low point of the cam. Commencing at No. 1 exhaust valve, insert the spring compressor and release the valve. Identify each set of valve components with the position in the engine from which they were removed. Be careful not to lose any of the split collets.

4 Clean up the valves and seats, then check the fit of the valve and the guides. If the clearance between a new valve and the guide exceeds .003 inch (.07 mm) a new guide should be fitted. If the seats are burnt beyond regrinding they must also be renewed.

5 To renew valve guides or seats, the side rocker shaft must first be removed. Proceed as follows :
(a) Remove the timing gear as detailed in **Section 1 : 6**.
(b) Remove the end plug from the front end of the rocker shaft.
(c) Remove the rocker shaft locating screws **F** (see **FIG 1 : 15**) and the oil feed bolt **A**.
(d) The shaft is in halves and can now be pulled out from the front and rear of the engine using the extractor part No. 262749. Lift the rockers, spacers and springs away, carefully noting their position ready for reassembly.

After the valve guides or seats have been attended to, the side rocker shaft can be replaced by reversing the dismantling procedure. It will be best to refit the rear half of the shaft first. Make sure the locating bolt holes are in line with the holes in the block. The extractor can be screwed into the shaft as a means of turning it into position. **FIG 1 : 16** shows the extractor in place in the shaft.

6 To remove a valve seat insert, first grind the insert with a cutting wheel to reduce its thickness as much as possible. Fit a protection plate over the cylinder block (see **FIG 1 : 17**) and break the insert out by using a chisel through the hole in the plate. The insert is very hard and fragments may fly off.

7 Drift the exhaust valve guide out by using drift part No. 274401 and driving it downwards.

8 Pull the new insert into place by using tool part No. 530625, then fit the protection plate again and leave in place for a few minutes in case the insert shatters. It is a wise precaution to wear goggles and keep all spectators away when working on these valve seat inserts. There is no need to heat the block or freeze the insert prior to fitting.

9 Lubricate a new valve guide and drift into position using drift part No. 600959.

10 The valve seat insert must now be ground to $45 + \frac{1}{4}$ deg. on its seating face using a power driven grinder. The insert is too hard to cut by hand tools.

11 Clean up or renew the valves, then lap them into the seats using the minimum of fine abrasive paste as described for the $2\frac{1}{4}$ litre engine.

12 Thoroughly clean all the components, lubricate the valve stems, then assemble to the cylinder block and fit the springs, caps and collets with the aid of the spring compressor.

13 At this point, the tappets should be adjusted to .01 inch (.25 mm) clearance. Start at No. 1 cylinder and

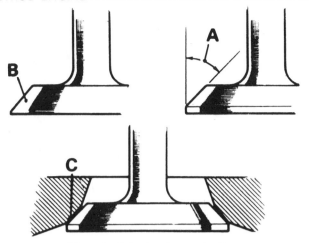

FIG 1 : 18   Valve head seats, 3.5 litre

Key to Fig 1 : 18   See text

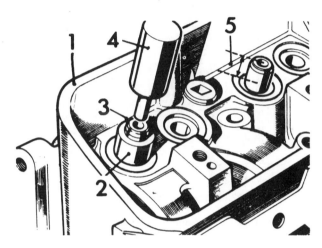

FIG 1 : 19   Fitting new valve guides, 3.5 litre

Key to Fig 1 : 19   1 Cylinder head   2 Distance piece 605774   3 New valve guide   4 Drift 600959   5 .75 in (19 mm)

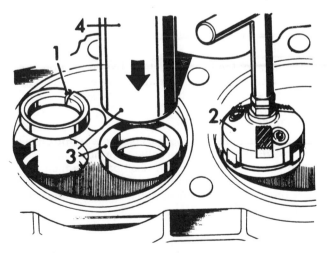

FIG 1 : 20   Fitting new valve seat inserts, 3.5 litre

Key to Fig 1 : 20   1 Old seat insert   2 Seat angle cutter   3 New seat insert   4 Press mandrel

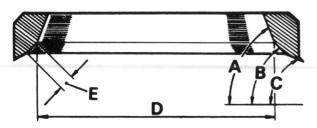

FIG 1 : 21   Valve seat data, 3.5 litre

Key to Fig 1 : 21   A 70 deg.   **B** 46 + ¼ deg.   **C** 20 deg.
D Inlet : 1.458 inch (37.03 mm) ; exhaust 1.240 inch (31.49 mm)
E .060 inch (1.50 mm)

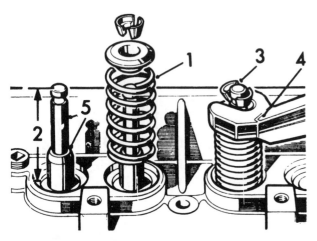

FIG 1 : 22   Fitting valves and springs, 3.5 litre

Key to Fig 1 : 22   1 Spring   2 See text   3 Collets
4 Spring compressor   5 Lubricate with engine oil

set each tappet in exactly the same sequence as described earlier for the inlet valves, i.e., No. 1 tappet with No. 6 valve fully open etc.

14 Replace the side rocker cover and continue to reassemble the engine as described in **Section 1 : 4**.

(c) 3.5 litre :

Removal of the head(s) is described in **Section 1 : 4**. When servicing a head, take great care not to damage the joint face.

Dismantling :

Using a suitable valve spring compressor (the official tool is 276102), remove the collets, springs and valves. Keep them identified to the positions in which they were fitted. Clean the combustion chambers with a soft wire brush. Clean the valves and the bores of the valve guides.

Valves :

Valves which are only slightly worn or pitted may be lapped to their seats. If this treatment is inadequate, the valves may be reground and the seats recut. Refer to **FIG 1 : 18**. The correct angle for the valve face **A** is 45°.

Reject any valve which has had to be ground to a knife-edge as at **B**. The valve to seat witness should be towards the outer edge as at **C**.

Valve guides :

Valve stems are slightly tapered. Valve guide bores are parallel. Stem to guide bore clearances are quoted in the **Technical Data** section of the **Appendix**. They differ between the inlet and the exhaust. Excessively worn guides should be removed using drift 274401 applied at their combustion chamber ends.

Replacement guides are .001 inch (.025 mm) larger than original guides to ensure an interference fit. Refer to **FIG 1 : 19**. Lubricate and fit new guides 3 using drift 4 (600959) and distance piece 2 (605774). Drive the guides into the heads until the drift bottoms on the distance piece. The dimension 5 for a fitted guide should be .750 inch (19 mm).

Valve seats :

Valve seat inserts which will not clean up without excessive recutting should be renewed. Replacement inserts are available in two oversizes: .010 inch (.25 mm) and .020 inch (.50 mm) larger on the outside diameter than standard to ensure an interference fit. Refer to **FIG 1 : 20**. Grind an old seat away until it is thin enough to be cracked and prised out. Heat the cylinder head evenly to approximately 65°C (150°F) and press in the new insert 3. If necessary, use cutter 2 on the valve seats. Seat diameters, angles and width are shown in **FIG 1 : 21**. If the seat width exceeds .078 inch (2.00 mm), it should be reduced to the specified width of .059 inch (1.5 mm) by the use of 20° and 70° stones in cutter 2 in **FIG 1 : 20**.

Fit the valves and check the dimension 2 in **FIG 1 : 22** from the valve stem tip to the valve spring seat surface. **This must not exceed** 1.875 inch (47.63 mm). If necessary, correct by grinding the end of the valve(s) or by fitting new parts.

FIG 1 : 23   Pushrods and tappets, 3.5 litre

Key to Fig 1 : 23   1 Pushrod   2 Tappet

Valve springs:

Check that the load required to compress the springs to the following specified length is within limits: 1.577 inch (40.05 mm) under a load of 70 lb ± 5% (31.78 kg ± 5%). Reject weak springs and obtain new replacements.

1 Identify each rocker shaft assembly and note which way round each is fitted. One end of each shaft is notched on one side only. Note that the notches are uppermost and that the notched end is forwards on the righthand bank and rearwards on the other. Note which is which.
2 Refer to **FIG 1 : 23**. Withdraw the pushrods 1 and tappets 2 and identify them to the positions to which they were fitted.
3 If a tappet cannot be withdrawn, it will be necessary to remove the camshaft as described in **Section 1:6** and withdraw the tappet downwards.
4 Refer to **FIG 1 : 24**. Dismantle a rocker shaft assembly by removing a splitpin 8 from one end. Withdraw the components and retain them in their correct sequence.

Pushrods:

Reject any pushrod which is bent or has a rough or damaged ball end or seat.

Hydraulic tappets:

Inspect the inner and outer surfaces of the bodies for blow holes, scoring etc. Reject tappets which are roughly scored or grooved or if blow holes through the wall could allow oil to leak from the lower chamber. The prominent wear pattern just above the lower end of the body is acceptable unless it is definitely grooved or scored. Inspect the cam contact surface and reject a tappet if this surface is excessively worn. **Tappets must rotate** and a round wear pattern is normal; a square pattern, indicating that the tappet has not been rotating, is not acceptable. Non-rotating tappets should be rejected and the relevant camshaft lobes should be specially suspected of being excessively worn. Reject tappets if the pushrod contact area is rough or damaged. Check that all new tappets rotate freely in their cylinder block locations.

Rocker arms:

Check that the pushrod and valve tip contact areas are smooth and undamaged. Note that there are two shapes of arms and, if replacements are required, check that the correct arms are obtained. If new arms are being fitted, ensure that the protective coating is removed from the oil feed hole and from the pushrod seat.

Rocker shafts:

Check that the rocker arm bearing areas are not excessively worn or scored and that the oil holes are clear.

Rocker covers:

If necessary, renew the rocker cover gaskets. Remove the old gasket and clean the mounting face with Bostik 6001 cleaner. Dry thoroughly. Apply an even film of

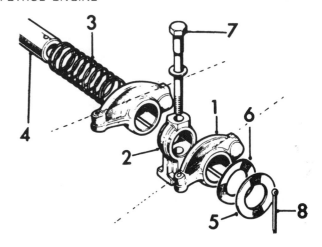

FIG 1 : 24   Rocker gear components, 3.5 litre

Key to Fig 1 : 24   1 Rocker arm   2 Bracket   3 Spring
4 Shaft 5 Plain washer 6 Wavy washer 7 Bolt 8 Splitpin

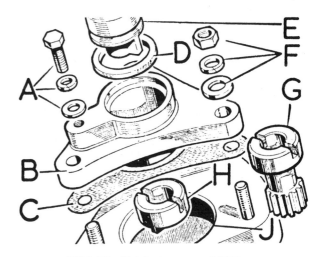

FIG 1 : 25   Distributor removal, 2¼ litre

Key to Fig 1 : 25   **A** Distributor fixings
B Distributor adaptor   **C** Joint washer   **D** Cork washer
E Distributor   **F** Adaptor fixings   **G** Top drive shaft, early engines   **H** Drive shaft coupling, later engines
J Vertical drive gear housing

Bostik 1775 impact adhesive to the rocker cover and gasket faces; allow the adhesive to become touch-dry before attaching the gasket. **The gasket fits one way round only and must be located and attached accurately first time.** Leave for at least 30 minutes before fitting the cover to the cylinder head. Short cover screws are fitted inboard and long ones outboard.

Tappet noise:

Tappets from which the oil has drained will be noisy until they become refilled. Running the engine at approximately 2500 rev/min for a few minutes should eliminate tappet noise.

Reassembly:

Refer to **FIG 1:22**. Lubricate the stems and guide bores 5 with engine oil. Check that dimension 2 does not exceed 1.875 inch (47.63 mm).

Fit and compress the valve springs 1, ensure they are correctly located, fit the collets 3, release the spring compressor and check that the collets are correctly seated.

Lubricate all working surfaces with engine oil. Use new splitpins 8 in **FIG 1:24**. Ensure that each rocker shaft assembly is the correct way round as noted on removal and that the notches are uppermost and the valve ends of the arms slope away from the brackets. The baffle plates are fitted to the front of the lefthand side and to the rear of the righthand side. Tighten bolts

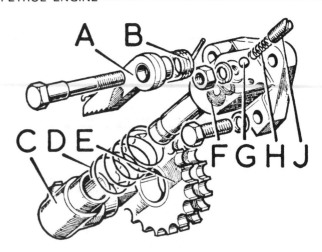

FIG 1:28   Details of chain tensioner, 2¼ litre

Key to Fig 1:28   **A** Ratchet   **B** Ratchet spring
C Cylinder   **D** Chain tensioner spring   **E** Idler wheel
F Piston   **G** Non-return valve   **H** Spring   **J** Plug

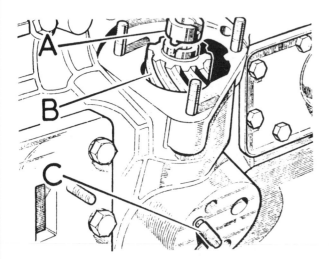

FIG 1:26   Distributor removal, 2¼ litre

Key to Fig 1:26   **A** Drive shaft coupling
B Vertical drive gear assembly   **C** Locating screw in oil filter location face

7 evenly and finally torque tighten them to 25 to 30 lb ft (3.5 to 4.0 mkg). The remaining operations are the reverse of the removal sequence.

1:6 Removing the timing gear and camshaft

(a) 2¼ litre:

It is not difficult to remove the camshaft and fit a replacement, but any attention to the camshaft bearings will be beyond the resources of an average private owner since special line boring or reaming equipment of a most expensive nature is essential. If the bearings are unserviceable the whole engine block should be stripped and sent to a Rover service agent equipped to carry out this work.

1 Dismantle the engine as described in **Section 1:4** but, in addition, remove the radiator and grille panel or, on later installations, the radiator and front panel assembly.
2 Remove the external oil filter and mounting.
3 Remove the distributor and its drive gear. **FIG 1:25** shows the method of removal for the distributor. Once this is lifted out, undo the grub screw (**C** in **FIG 1:26**) and remove the gear using a pair of small round nose pliers.
4 Remove the engine front cover by first slackening the generator or alternator fixings and removing the fan belt. Take off the generator or alternator adjusting link to gain access to the cover bolts, then remove the starter dog and driving pulley. A solid spanner and a sharp tap with a heavy hammer will start the dog unscrewing. Separate the bypass pipe from the thermostat housing, then undo all the cover fixing bolts including those at the sump flange and lift off the cover. Clean the cover and examine the crankshaft oil seal. If this is to be renewed, carefully lever the old seal out and press the new one in. Apply a smear of Hylomar PL 32/M jointing compound to the outside of the seal and

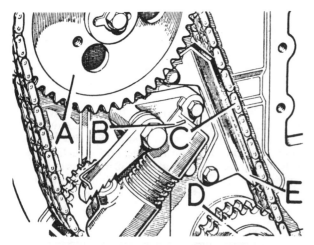

FIG 1:27   Chain tensioner in position, 2¼ litre

Key to Fig 1:27   **A** Camshaft wheel   **B** Ratchet spring
C Timing chain   **D** Crankshaft wheel   **E** Vibration damper

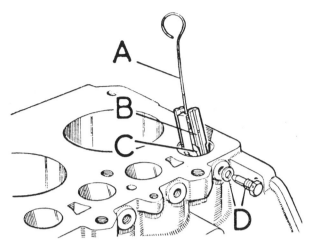

FIG 1:29 Removing tappets, 2¼ litre

Key to Fig 1:29 **A** Hook **B** Slide **C** Roller
D Locating bolt

press it in with the garter spring facing inwards (towards the engine block when assembled).

5 Undo the bolt (**B** in **FIG 1:27**) and remove the chain tensioner ratchet and spring. Compress the piston spring by hand and unbolt the tensioner from the block. Dismantle it and clean all components in clean fuel. Replace if undue wear is evident. Make sure the ball valve and seating are clean and in good condition. **FIG 1:28** shows the tensioner in detail.

6 Remove the chain vibration damper (**E** in **FIG 1:27**).

7 Remove the tappet locating bolts (**D** in **FIG 1:29**), then hook the tappet slides and rollers out. Lastly, remove the tappet guides as shown in **FIG 1:30**.

8 Lift off the timing chain, undo the bolt in the centre of the camshaft sprocket and pull the sprocket from the shaft. Use an extractor for this; do not lever the sprocket away from the block. Remove the thrust plate, then pull the camshaft gently forwards and out of the block, supporting it along its length to prevent the cam lobes from scoring the bearings.

(b) 2.6 litre:

This engine, unlike the 2¼ litre, will allow renewal of the camshaft bearings but it must be noted that the rearmost bearing can only be serviced when the engine is out of the chassis and the flywheel housing is removed.

1 Dismantle the engine as described in **Sections 1:4** and **1:5** (removal of side rocker shaft) but, in addition, remove the radiator and grille panel or, on later installations, the radiator and front panel assembly (see **Chapter 13**).

2 Remove the generator or alternator, fan belt, fan blades, distance piece and fan pulley. Undo the starter dog and remove the driving pulley. Undo the bolts and lift off the front cover, then remove the oil thrower from the crankshaft. Clean up the cover and, if necessary, replace the crankshaft oil seal as described for the 2¼ litre engine.

3 Refer to **FIG 1:31** and remove the plug **A**, where fitted, from the chain tensioner. With a ⅛ inch (3 mm)

Allen key, **B**, turn the adjuster clockwise until the spring loading is removed. Unbolt the tensioner and remove from the engine.

4 Undo the bolt in the centre of the camshaft chainwheel and, with a suitable extractor, pull the wheel from the camshaft and lift off the timing chain. Remove the camshaft thrust plate.

5 Remove the distributor as described in **Section 1:4**. Refer to **FIG 1:15**. The bolt marked **A** must be removed and the distributor vertical drive gear assembly withdrawn upwards.

6 Refer to **FIG 1:15** and remove the bolts **B**.

7 Screw a bolt, with a piece of plate or mild steel strip to make a handle to grip with, into the front end of the camshaft and gently pull the camshaft forward until the bearings are just clear of their housings. Lift the bearings off the shaft, keeping them in their correct pairs as indicated by the numbers stamped

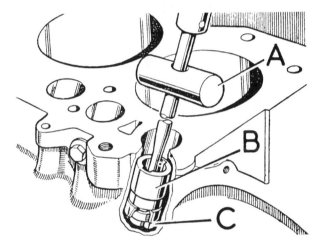

FIG 1:30 Removing tappet guides, 2¼ litre

Key to Fig 1:30 **A** Special tool **B** Guide **C** Adaptor

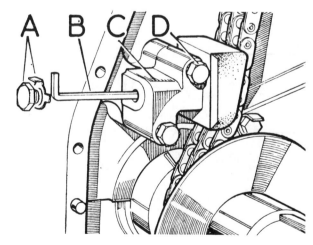

FIG 1:31 Chain tensioner, 2.6 litre

Key to Fig 1:31 **A** Plug and washer **B** Allen key
C Tensioner **D** Fixing bolts

on the end face. Continue to extract the shaft, supporting it along its length to prevent damage.

(c) 3.5 litre:

1 Referring to **Chapter 5**, drain the cooling system. Remove the fan cowl, blades and pulley. Turn the engine to TDC of No. 1 cylinder firing stroke.
2 Disconnect the bypass hose from the thermostat.
3 Disconnect the heater return hose from the water pump.
4 Disconnect the inlet hose from the water pump.
5 Release the alternator adjusting link from the water pump housing.
6 Disconnect the vacuum pipe from the distributor.

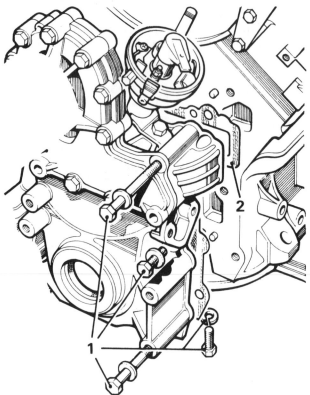

FIG 1 : 32 Timing gear cover, 3.5 litre

Key to Fig 1 : 32   1 Fixings (two in sump)   2 Washer

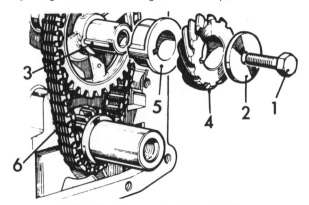

FIG 1 : 33 The camshaft drive, 3.5 litre

Key to Fig 1 : 33   1 Bolt   2 Washer   3 Key   4 Distributor drive gear   5 Spacer   6 Camshaft drive chain

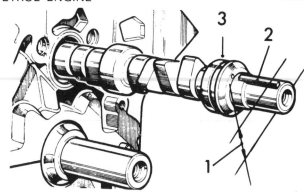

FIG 1 : 34 Removing the camshaft, 3.5 litre

Key to Fig 1 : 34   1 1.187 inch (30.15 mm) maximum
2 Key   3 Camshaft

7 Release the distributor cap, unclip the leads and move the cap aside.
8 Disconnect the low tension lead from the coil and the lead from the oil pressure switch.
9 Unscrew the starter dog and withdraw the crankshaft pulley and mud deflector.
10 Mark the distributor body relative to the centre line of the rotor arm and the body in line with the timing gear cover. Remove the distributor.
11 Remove the cover fixings, including two bolts from the sump (see **FIG 1 : 32**).
12 Withdraw the timing cover and discard the gasket.
13 Clean the retaining bolt threads before the sealant can air-harden.
14 Clean the cylinder block and cover joint faces and the bottom edge of the cover where it contacts the sump gasket after withdrawing the cover. If the units which remain attached to the cover are to be removed, refer to the relevant chapter or sectional texts for procedure descriptions.

With the timing cover removed, confirm that No. 1 piston is still at TDC of the firing stroke. Refer to **FIG 1 : 33**. Remove bolt and washer 1 and 2, withdraw the distributor drive gear 4 and the spacer 5. Withdraw both chainwheels complete with chain 6. **Do not rotate the engine if the rocker shaft assemblies are in position** or the valve gear and pistons will be damaged. If other operations require the engine to be rotated, **remove both rocker shaft assemblies.**

Renew worn or damaged chainwheels. Renew a chain which is worn or stretched.

Camshaft removal:

Remove both rocker shaft assemblies and all the pushrods and tappets. Remove the timing gear cover and the camshaft drive chain and chainwheels as described earlier. Carefully withdraw the camshaft as shown in **FIG 1 : 34**.

When inspecting the camshaft, check particularly any cam lobe on which it was found (see **Section 1 : 5**) that a non-rotating tappet was operating. Slight scuffing of cam lobe faces may be corrected by judicious stoning. Note that the space between the key 2 and the keyway in the camshaft drive gear acts as a lubrication oilway. Check that the overall dimension 1 over the shaft and key does not exceed 1.187 inch (30.15 mm).

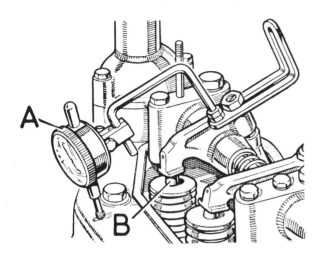

FIG 1:35 Checking valve opening, 2¼ litre

Key to Fig 1:35   **A** Dial gauge   **B** No. 1 exhaust valve

Timing cover oil seal:

Remove the fixings and withdraw the mudshield. Prise out the oil seal. Support the cover, front face uppermost, across the oil seal housing bore, on a suitable wooden block. Enter the oil seal, open side first, into the bore. Press in until the plain face is .062 inch (1.5 mm) approximately below the cover face. Replace the mudshield.

1:7 Replacing the timing gear and camshaft

(a) 2¼ litre:

1 Replace the camshaft, taking great care not to score the bearings as the shaft passes through them. Fit the thrust plate but do not bend up the locking tabs. Fit the chainwheel and see that the end float of the shaft lies between .0025 and .0055 inch (.06 and .13 mm). If not, select another thrust plate or grind one down. When correct, bend up the thrust plate bolt locking tabs.

2 Replace the tappet assemblies, cylinder head, pushrods and rocker shaft.

3 Retime the camshaft as follows:
(a) Note that there are two methods of timing: one is by marks on the flywheel and the other by a pointer on the timing cover. The flywheel type is described first.
(b) Remove the coverplate from the flywheel housing and turn the flywheel in the direction of engine rotation until the EP mark is in line with the pointer. Temporarily fit the chainwheel to the camshaft.
(c) See that No. 1 cylinder exhaust valve is fully closed and has .010 inch (.25 mm) tappet clearance.
(d) Fit a clock gauge as shown in **FIG 1:35**, then turn the chainwheel until the gauge shows the exact point when the valve is fully open. Fit the chain so that there is no slack on the driving side. If there is slack, refit the chainwheel in another position on the splines, recheck that the valve position has not

altered and try the chain on again. When correct, lock the chainwheel to the camshaft.
(e) To retime the camshaft if the engine has the pointer on the timing cover proceed as follows:
Rotate the crankshaft until the keyway for the crankshaft wheel is exactly vertical.
(f) Fit the camshaft chainwheel as shown in **FIG 1:36**, then replace the chain with no slack on the driving side and tighten the chainwheel fixing bolt.

4 Refit the timing chain tensioner as shown in **FIG 1:27**, then refit and adjust the vibration damper **E**, so that there is a maximum of .010 inch (.25 mm) clearance between it and the chain.

5 To assist in fitting the front cover, temporarily remove the stud from the cylinder block front face. Smear the new joint washers on both faces with grease and bolt the cover to the cylinder block. Replace the stud. Fit the bypass pipe to the thermo-

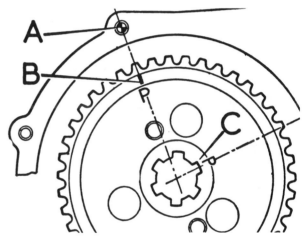

FIG 1:36 Camshaft chainwheel marking, 2¼ litre

Key to Fig 1:36   **A** Tapped hole in cylinder block
B Groove marked 'P'   **C** Fit spline P to camshaft key

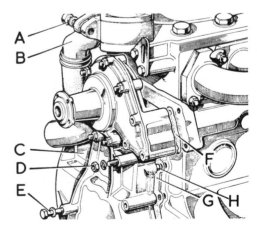

FIG 1:37 Front cover assembly, 2¼ litre

Key to Fig 1:37   **A** Bypass pipe bolt   **B** Bypass pipe
C Front cover **D** Generator link fixing **E** Front cover fixings
F Joint washer **G** Joint washer **H** Locating dowels, 2 off

stat housing. Replace the crankshaft pulley and starter dog. Tighten the dog to 150 lb ft (20.5 mkg). **FIG 1:37** shows the front cover assembly in detail.

6 Continue to rebuild the engine by reversing the dismantling procedure.

7 Retime the distributor as follows, referring to **Technical Data** of the **Appendix** to obtain the correct timing figures:

Rotate the engine until the appropriate timing marks are in alignment (see **FIG 1:38** or **1:39**) and both valves of No. 1 cylinder are closed. Insert the vertical drive shaft assembly as shown in **FIG 1:40**, locate the small hole in the drive gear bush through the oil filter location face and fit the grub screw (see **FIG 1:26**). Fit the short drive shaft coupling as shown in **FIG 1:41**. Replace the distributor with the vacuum unit facing to the rear, making sure the shaft key engages the slot in the short drive shaft,

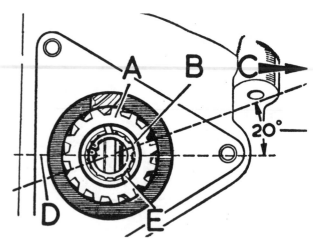

FIG 1:40   Fitting vertical drive gear, 2¼ litre

Key to Fig 1:40   **A** Vertical drive gear
B Master spline for locating drive shaft, early engines   **C** To front of engine   **D** Line parallel with engine centre line
E Offset slot for use with later type drive shaft coupling

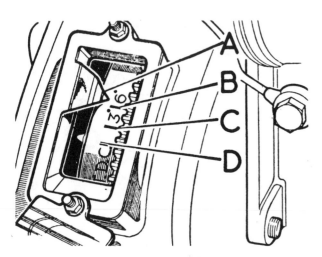

FIG 1:38   Flywheel timing marks, 2¼ litre

Key to Fig 1:38   **A** Pointer   **B** 6 deg. mark   **C** 3 deg. mark   **D** TDC mark

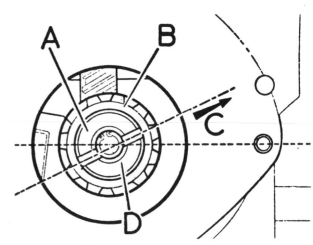

FIG 1:41   Fitting drive coupling, 2¼ litre

Key to Fig 1:41   **A** Top drive coupling
B Vertical drive gear   **C** No. 1 cylinder   **D** Narrow segment

and set the octane selector so that the fourth line from the left of the calibration markings is against the face of the distributor body. If all is well the contacts should just be separating. Slight adjustment can be made by loosening the clamp bolt. Check that the rotor arm is pointing to No. 1 cylinder. The exact timing point can be checked when the battery is reconnected. Put a 12-volt bulb between the distributor low tension terminal and earth. Switch the ignition on and turn the engine two revolutions in the direction of rotation. The bulb should light when the timing pointer comes into alignment with the appropriate mark.

8 Refit the external oil filter, replace the radiator and refill with coolant.

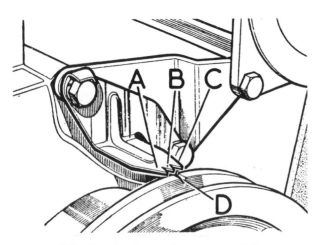

FIG 1:39   Front cover timing marks, 2¼ litre

Key to Fig 1:39   **A** 6 deg. point   **B** 3 deg. point
C TDC point   **D** Pulley mark

(b) 2.6 litre:

The camshaft bearings must be fitted dry. See that the correct pairs of bearings are assembled together and that the locating holes in the bearings are in alignment with the holes in the cylinder block.

1 Insert the camshaft just far enough to allow the skew gear to pass through the intermediate housing webs, then assemble the bearings to the camshaft. Put a distance piece temporarily between the middle pair of bearings so that it can be pulled out when the shaft is home. Squirt oil down the locating holes, then fit the retaining bolts. Fit the camshaft thrust plate, ensuring that the shaft has .0045 to .0065 inch (.11 to .16 mm) end float.

2 Refit the side rocker shafts, making sure that the locating screw holes are in correct alignment and replace the end plug.

3 Reassemble all the valve operating gear and time the camshaft as follows:

(a) Engine with markings on flywheel.

Proceed exactly as described for the equivalent $2\frac{1}{4}$ litre engine by placing the flywheel EP mark opposite the pointer and then turning the camshaft until the No. 1 cylinder exhaust valve is fully open as shown by the clock gauge.

Fit the chain and camshaft chainwheel, making certain that there is no slack on the driving side of the chain. The chainwheel can be adjusted on the camshaft to achieve this. Check the clock gauge reading to ensure that the camshaft has not moved, then tighten the chainwheel bolt and lock it.

(b) Engine with pointer on front cover.

Rotate the engine until the crankshaft keyway is exactly vertical.

Fit the chainwheel and chain as shown in **FIG 1:42**, ensuring that there is no slack on the driving side of the chain. Replace the camshaft chainwheel bolt, tighten and lock up.

4 Bolt the chain tensioner to the engine, then with the Allen key turn the sleeve clockwise until the head of

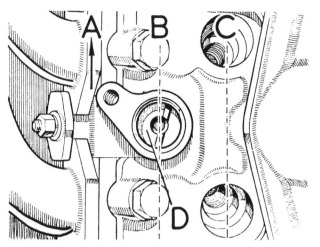

FIG 1:43   Position of distributor drive shaft, 2.6 litre

Key to Fig 1:43   A Front of engine   **B** Centre line parallel with plug holes   **C** Centre line through plug holes **D** Larger segment of drive

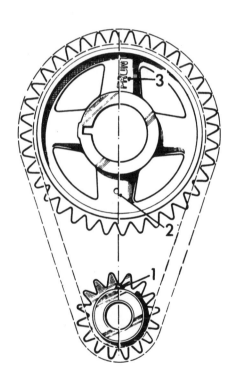

FIG 1:44   Camshaft drive marks, 3.5 litre

Key to Fig 1:44   1 Crankshaft wheel timing mark 2 Camshaft wheel timing mark   3 FRONT mark (fitted outwards)

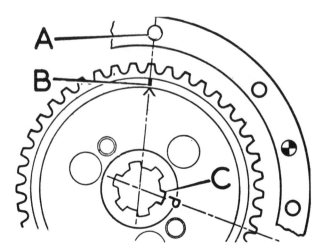

FIG 1:42   Front cover timing marks, 2.6 litre

Key to Fig 1:42   **A** Tapped hole in cylinder block **B** Groove in line with tapped hole   **C** Fit chainwheel spline **P** on to camshaft key

the tensioner moves forward against the chain. Never turn the sleeve anticlockwise. Replace the plug after removing the Allen key.

5 Replace the front cover, smearing grease on both faces of the new joint washer.

6 Fit the crankshaft pulley, tightening the starter dog to 200 lb ft (27.5 mkg). Replace the fan blades and

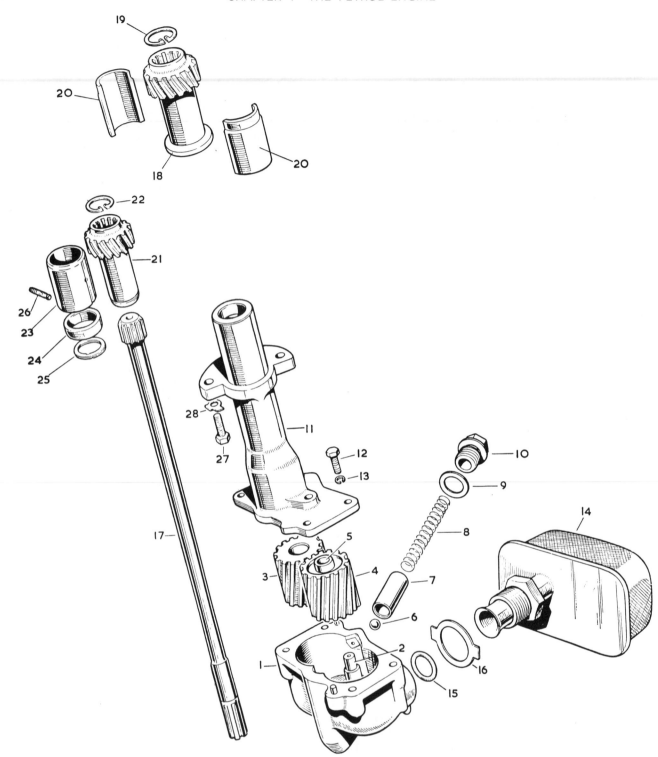

FIG 1:45 Oil pump, 2¼ litre

Key to Fig 1:45   1 Oil pump body   2 Spindle for idler gear   3 Oil pump gear, driver   4 Oil pump gear, idler
5 Bush for idler gear   6 Steel ball*   7 Plunger*   8 Spring*   9 Washer*   10 Plug*   11 Oil pump cover
12 Setbolt (⁵⁄₁₆ inch UNF x ⅞ inch long) (fixing cover to body)   13 Spring washer (fixing cover to body)   14 Oil filter for pump
15 Sealing ring (fixing oil filter to oil pump)   16 Lockwasher (fixing oil filter to oil pump)   17 Drive shaft for oil pump
18 Vertical drive shaft assembly   19 Circlip for drive shaft   20 Bush for drive shaft gear   21 Vertical drive shaft assembly
22 Circlip for drive shaft   23 Bush for drive shaft gear   24 Thrust washer for drive shaft   25 Retaining ring for washer and bush
26 Locating screw for drive shaft bush   27 Setbolt (⁵⁄₁₆ inch UNF x 1 inch long) (fixing oil pump to cylinder block)   28 Lockwasher (fixing oil pump to cylinder block)

* For oil pressure release valve

dynamo. Adjust the dynamo belt tension to between $\frac{5}{16}$ to $\frac{7}{16}$ inch (8 to 11 mm) free movement.

7 Turn the engine in the direction of rotation until the TDC mark on the flywheel or crankshaft pulley is opposite the pointer with both valves of No. 1 cylinder closed. Insert the distributor drive shaft and gear so that the short drive shaft eventually is positioned as shown in **FIG 1:43**. Fit the locating bolt.

8 Replace the distributor, engaging the key in the shaft with the slot in the drive shaft. Check that the rotor arm is in the No. 1 cylinder firing position and the distributor vacuum unit faces the front of the engine.

9 Rotate the engine forward two turns until the appropriate timing mark for the fuel to be used is in alignment with the pointer (flywheel or crankshaft pulley as applicable). Slacken the pinch bolt on the distributor clamp and rotate the distributor body until the points are just opening on the leading side of the cam. A test lamp can be used to obtain the exact point of break. Tighten the pinch bolt and replace the distributor cap.

10 Reverse the dismantling procedure for the assembly of the remaining items, then refill the radiator and reconnect the battery.

(c) 3.5 litre:

If the engine has not been rotated, refitment of the chain and chainwheels will be the reverse of the removal sequence. Refer to **FIG 1:44**. Note the timing marks 1 and 2 and the camshaft chain gear marking 3. Ensure that the distributor drive gear, 4 in **FIG 1:33**, is fitted with its annular groove face in contact with the flanged face of the spacer 5. Torque tighten bolt 1. If the engine has been rotated, follow the procedure described in operations 1, 2 and 3.

Lubricate all working surfaces with engine oil. Fit the camshaft and time its drive before refitting the rocker shaft assemblies. The camshaft timing procedure is as follows:

1 Set No. 1 piston at TDC, noting that, on completion of the timing operations, this will be the firing stroke. Temporarily fit the camshaft chainwheel with the FRONT marking outwards as shown in **FIG 1:44**.

2 Turn the camshaft until the timing mark 2 is at the 6 o'clock position. Withdraw the chainwheel without disturbing the camshaft. Fit the chainwheels to the chain with the timing marks 1 and 2 aligned and the FRONT mark 3 outwards.

3 Fit the wheels and chain. Fit the spacer, distributor drive gear, washer and retaining bolt (5, 4, 2 and 1 in **FIG 1:33**) as described earlier. Torque tighten the retaining bolt.

The timing gear cover may now be refitted. The procedure is basically the reverse of the removal sequence, noting the following:

Coat both sides of the new gasket 2 in **FIG 1:32** with Hylomar PL 32/M. Prime the oil pump. Set the distributor rotor arm approximately 30 deg. before its final marked position and fit the cover. Coat the threads of the cover securing bolts with Thread Lubricant Sealant 3M EC776. The remaining operations are the reverse of

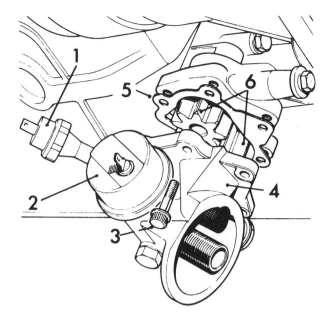

FIG 1:46 Components of the oil pump, 3.5 litre

Key to Fig 1:46   1 Oil pressure switch
2 Oil pressure transmitter   3 Pump cover retaining bolt
4 Pump cover   5 Gasket   6 Pump gears

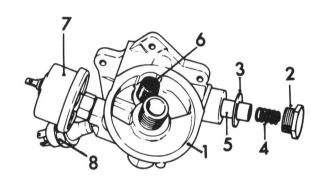

FIG 1:47 Components of the pump cover, 3.5 litre

Key to Fig 1:47   1 Pump cover   2 Plug   3 Washer
4 Spring   5 Relief valve   6 Bypass strainer   7 Oil pressure transmitter   8 Oil pressure switch

the removal sequence. Refer, as necessary, to the relevant chapter and sectional texts and, when the engine can be run, refer to **Chapter 4, Section 4:5** and check and adjust the ignition timing.

1:8 Servicing the oil pump and filters

(a) 2¼ litre:

The oil pressure at 2000 rev/min with a warm engine should be between 35 and 65 lb/sq inch. Any pressure much lower than this may denote trouble with the pump but there are many other possible causes including worn engine bearings. If it is decided to strip the pump, this can be done quite easily.

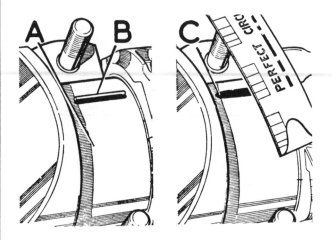

FIG 1:48 Checking big-end clearance, 2¼ litre

Key to Fig 1:48
A Journal
B Initial position of 'Plastigage'.   **C** Flattened 'Plastigage'
Measure width against scale on 'Plastigage' packet

1 Drain the oil from the sump, then remove the sump bolts and lower away. Clean the crankcase and sump joint faces.
2 Remove the two bolts holding the pump and pull the pump from the engine complete with its drive shaft. This will not upset the distributor timing.
3 Refer to **FIG 1:45** and strip and clean all the components.
4 Inspect the relief valve ball seating. If this is pitted it is possible to lap it in by the use of a spare ball soldered to a piece of tubing rotated by a hand drill. Use coarse abrasive paste to start with and finish with fine paste. Wash thoroughly afterwards.
5 Check and replace the gears if the end float exceeds .005 inch (.12 mm) for the steel gear and .006 inch (.15 mm) for the aluminium gear. Use a steel straightedge across the pump body and check with feeler gauges.
6 Measure the radial clearance between the gear teeth and the body, again using feeler gauges. This must not exceed .004 inch (.10 mm).
7 The backlash between the gears must not exceed .012 inch (.28 mm).
8 Reassemble the pump in the reverse order to dismantling, giving all moving parts a smear of clean oil. See that the plain portion of the drive gear bore is uppermost and use a little jointing cement between the pump body and shaft housing.
9 Reassemble to the engine: tighten the bolts using new locking tabs. Replace the sump and refill with clean oil. After 1000 miles (1600 km), recheck the sump bolts for correct torque. Slacken each bolt, in turn, approximately one flat, then retighten to 12 lb ft (1.65 mkg).

To renew the external oil filter, first place a receptacle below it to catch the oil which will drain out. Undo the hexagon at the base of the filter chamber and remove the chamber and filter. Discard the element and sealing ring. Wipe the chamber clean, fit a new element and sealing ring and replace on the housing. Tighten the hexagon.

(b) 2.6 litre:

The oil pressure at 2000 rev/min with a warm engine should be between 40 and 50 lb/sq inch.
1 To remove the pump, first drain the oil, then remove the sump.
2 At the side of the crankcase, just forward of the starter motor, will be seen a hexagon with a domed housing. Wipe all dirt away from around this, then unscrew carefully. This is the oil pressure relief valve and is not adjustable. Be careful not to lose the steel ball and spring when the hexagon housing comes free.
3 Immediately above this relief valve is another set-bolt and locknut. This locates the oil pump and when it is removed the pump can be withdrawn downwards.
4 Dismantle the pump by undoing the four bolts in the cover, then wash all the components and examine for wear. The replacement dimensions for end float, backlash and radial clearance are the same as those given for the 2¼ litre engine. Replace where necessary and rebuild the pump by reversing the dismantling process.
5 Replace the pump in the cylinder block and refit the locating bolt and the oil pressure relief valve.
6 Refit the sump using a new joint washer and refill with oil. After 1000 miles (1600 km), recheck the sump bolts for correct torque. Slacken each bolt, in turn, approximately one flat, then retighten to 12 lb ft (1.65 mkg).

The external oil filter is serviced in the same way as the one fitted to the 2¼ litre engine. The only small difference is that the bolt holding the filter element chamber is at the top of the chamber not the bottom.

(c) 3.5 litre:

The oil pressure at 2400 rev/min with a warm engine should be between 30 and 40 lb/sq in.

To dismantle the pump, refer to **FIG 1:46** and proceed as follows:

Remove the oil filter canister as described later, remove the leads from the pressure switch 1 and from the pressure transmitter 2, remove the cover retaining bolts 3, withdraw the cover 4, lift off the gasket 5 and remove and clean the gears 6. Refer to **FIG 1:47**. Remove and clean the plug 2, washer 3, spring 4, relief valve 5 and strainer 6.

With the gears fitted to the timing gear cover, place a straightedge across them and, using feelers, measure the clearance between the straightedge and the cover face. This should not be less than .0018 inch (.05 mm).

Reassemble the internal parts, fully packing the oil pump gear housing with petroleum jelly. No other grease must be used. Ensure that the petroleum jelly is forced into every cavity between the teeth of the gears. Unless the pump is fully packed, it may not prime itself when the engine is started. Renew the oil pump cover gasket. Torque tighten the cover retaining bolts and the relief valve plug.

Unscrew the canister, using a strap spanner if necessary. Discard the old sealing washer. Lightly lubricate the new washer and screw on the canister without delay so as to avoid the need to prime the pump. Screw on the canister until the seal touches the pump cover face. Tighten by hand a further half turn only. **Do not overtighten**.

After checking and replenishing, if necessary, the oil level, start the engine and ensure that the oil pressure warning light goes out. If not, the oil pump must be dismantled and primed as described earlier. Run the engine, check for leaks and, finally, when the engine has been stopped for a while, recheck the oil level.

1 : 9 Removing the clutch and flywheel

On either engine, on early models, this operation can be carried out without removing the engine from the vehicle. On later models, remove the front floor and seat base (see **Chapter 13**), move the gearbox rearwards or remove the engine as necessary. See **Chapter 6** for the method of removing the clutch.

(a) 2¼ litre:

To remove the flywheel once the clutch is taken off, release the locking tags, if fitted, and unscrew the setbolts. The flywheel is held by these eight bolts and a dowel. Once the bolts are removed, and the reinforcing plate on five main bearing engines, the flywheel can be pulled off the crankshaft.

If the flywheel face which contacts the clutch friction plate is scored it can be refaced by removing up to .030 inch (.76 mm) of metal. Do not exceed this amount and make sure that the clutch bolts and dowels were removed first so that the refacing extends right across the flywheel face. Minimum thickness on later models is 1.375 inch (34.72 mm).

To renew the starter ring gear, grip the flywheel vertically in a vice, then drill a $\frac{3}{16}$ inch (4 mm) hole through the ring at the root of a tooth so as to weaken the ring. Place a heavy cloth or sack over the gear, then drive a chisel down from the root of the tooth into the hole, thus breaking the gear. The cloth will prevent any pieces flying off unexpectedly.

Heat a new starter ring to between 220°C to 225°C (light straw colour) and then lay it on the flywheel. Have the square edge of the teeth against the flywheel flange. Allow to cool slowly and thus contract and grip the flywheel. Do not hasten the cooling.

The flywheel can be reassembled to the crankshaft once the ring has cooled. Make sure that the crankshaft boss and the flywheel register are clean. Tighten the bolts to 60 to 65 lb ft (8.5 to 9 mkg) or 100 lb ft (13.8 mkg) on five main bearing engines and bend up the locking tabs, if fitted. The flywheel must not run out of true more than .002 inch (.05 mm) at the edge of the friction plate surface.

(b) 2.6 litre:

To remove and service the flywheel of this engine, proceed in all respects as for the 2¼ litre three main bearing engine.

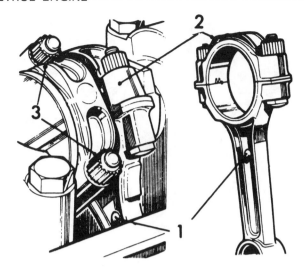

FIG 1 : 49   The connecting rods, 3.5 litre

Key to Fig 1 : 49   1 Domed boss   2 Connecting rod cap 3 Cap retaining nuts

The minimum thickness of the flywheel on later models is 1.204 inch (30.5 mm).

(c) 3.5 litre:

Remove the engine assembly as described in **Section 1 : 3**.

Remove the clutch assembly as described in **Chapter 6, Section 6 : 5**.

Measure the overall thickness and fit a new flywheel if this is less than 1.572 inch (39.93 mm). If the thickness is above this minimum, the rear face may, if necessary, be refaced by grinding after removing the dowels. Recheck that the overall thickness has not been reduced below the minimum specified.

An unserviceable ring gear may be removed by drilling through and breaking off, precautions being taken against flying fragments. Heat a new ring gear uniformly to 170° to 175°C (338° to 347°F) and, with the chamfered inner diameter towards the flywheel, fit it firmly and squarely. Allow the assembly to cool gradually.

The bolt holes are not symmetrical. Work diagonally when gradually tightening the bolts, then finally torque tighten them to 50 to 60 lb ft (7 to 8.5 mkg). The remaining operations are the reverse of the dismantling sequence.

1 : 10 The pistons and connecting rods

(a) 2¼ litre:

1 Strip the engine as described in **Sections 1 : 4** and **1 : 5** enough to remove the cylinder head. This can be done either in or out of the chassis. Drain the oil and remove the sump. All work on the pistons can now proceed without removing the engine.
2 Turn the crankshaft to bring two pistons to bottom dead centre. Mark the caps and connecting rods so

FIG 1:50 Removing the connecting rods and pistons, 3.5 litre

Key to Fig 1:50   1 Guide bolt 605351   2 Connecting rod

that they can be replaced in the right order in the engine and the right way round. Undo the two big-end nuts and remove the cap and bearing shell from each rod. Push the connecting rod and piston up the bore and remove from the top of the engine. Keep the components in their related sets including the bolts and nuts. Turn the crankshaft half a turn and repeat for the other two pistons.

3 If the engine is to be rebored, new pistons and correctly gapped rings will be supplied. If not, check the piston, ring and connecting rod as follows:

(a) Remove the rings carefully by using either the special pliers or the three legged device obtainable at any good accessory shop. In an emergency, cut three strips of tinplate about .5 inch (12.7 mm) wide and work these under the ring and move round until they are parallel to the length of the piston and spaced at 120 degrees from each other. Slip the ring up and off.

(b) Clean all carbon from the piston, being careful not to damage the grooves. Examine carefully for cracks or damage. Any area of heavy bearing showing on the sides of the piston denotes a bent connecting rod. Check and renew if necessary.

(c) Check the gudgeon pin fit in the piston and rod. There should not be more than .0005 inch (.012 mm) clearance between the pin and the rod and an interference fit in the piston. In practical terms, this means that with the components cold and dry the pin will just slide into the connecting rod bush but, to enter the piston, the latter must be heated to 55°C (132°F). On Series 3 models the gudgeon pin is a hand fit in the piston at room temperature. Note that, if the piston crown is marked with an 'X', the pin must be withdrawn and fitted at that side.

(d) To check the big-end fit on the crankpin, assemble the components with a piece of 'Plastigage' as shown in **FIG 1:48**. Full instructions for the use of 'Plastigage' are given on the packet. Tighten the big-end nuts to 35 lb ft (4.9 mkg) for bolts with machine cut threads or 25 lb ft (3.5 mkg) for rolled

thread bolts. The latter are identifiable by a drill centre at the threaded end. The clearance between the bearings and crankpin must not exceed .0025 inch (.063 mm) or be less than .00075 inch (.019 mm). The end float between the big-end and crankpin webs should lie between .007 to .012 inch (.20 to .30 mm).

(e) Push each piston ring into an unworn part of the cylinder bore and check the gap. This must be between .015 to .020 inch (.38 to .5 mm) for all rings. Use a piston to push the ring down so that it seats squarely in the bore.

(f) The side clearance between the rings and piston grooves should be .0018 to .0038 inch (.046 to .097 mm) for compression rings and .0015 to .0035 inch (.038 to .089 mm) for scraper rings.

4 Reassemble the pistons and connecting rods using new gudgeon pin circlips. It is important that if there is an 'X' on the piston crown that this goes towards the front of the engine. The oil spray hole in the rod always faces the camshaft. Fit the compression rings with the word 'TOP' or 'T' uppermost. The scraper ring can be fitted either way up.

5 Smear a little clean oil on the cylinder bore and on the outside of the piston. Assemble the piston ring clamp to the piston, first making sure that the ring gaps are spaced at 120 degrees. Enter the assembly from the top face of the cylinder block and push the piston gently through the clamp and into the bore. Refit the big end bearing, securing the cap with new nuts and tightening them to the torque given in paragraph 3 (d).

6 Rebuild the engine as described in previous sections.

(b) 2.6 litre:

All work on the pistons and connecting rods in this engine can be undertaken with the engine in the chassis.

Strip the engine as described previously and remove the connecting rods and pistons from the top of the cylinder bores as described for the 2¼ litre engine. The note concerning withdrawing the gudgeon pin from the side of the piston marked 'X' applies here. Check the components exactly as described for the 2¼ litre engine. The compression ring gap should be between .015 to .020 inch (.38 to .5 mm) and the scraper ring .015 to .033 inch (.38 to .8 mm).

The ring to piston groove clearance should be between .002 to .004 inch (.05 to .10 mm). Gudgeon pin and big-end clearances are also the same as for the 2¼ litre engine.

When reassembling the engine, use new gudgeon pin circlips and fit the connecting rod ensuring that the oil spray hole is to the same side as the bore number stamped on the piston crown. If no bore number is marked, fit the rod so that the oil spray hole is away from the camshaft. This is opposite to the instruction for the 2¼ litre engine. Use a piston ring clamp to assist the rings to enter the bore but, due to the sloping face of the cylinder block, careful work with the fingers is necessary to get the rings in without damage. Fit new big-end cap nuts, tightening them to 20 lb ft (2.8 mkg). Continue to assemble the engine as described in previous sections.

(c) 3.5 litre:

1 Remove the cylinder heads as described in **Section 1:4**. Remove the oil sump, oil pick-up pipe and strainer.

2 Remove the connecting rod cap retaining nuts. Remove the caps and identify them to their own connecting rods. Note that the rib on the edge of each cap is fitted on the same side as the domed boss 1 (see **FIG 1:49**) on the connecting rod and that the domed boss faces forwards on the righthand bank of cylinders and rearwards on the left. Screw guide bolts 605351 onto the connecting rod bolts as shown in **FIG 1:50**.

3 Push each connecting rod and piston up the cylinder bore and withdraw the assembly from the top. Retain each connecting rod and piston in sequence together with its own cap. Remove the guide bolts.

Gudgeon pins have an interference fit in the connecting rod little-ends and have to be pressed out under a hydraulic press of 8 tons capacity. If the same piston is to be refitted, mark which way round and in which bore it was located. Note also which way round the connecting rods were fitted. The domed bosses on the connecting rods will face each other on each crankpin.

Refer to **FIG 1:51**. Locate the piston and connecting rod 1 on tool 3 (lower part of tool 605350). Locate the upper part 4 of this tool on the gudgeon pin and, under a press 2, press out the gudgeon pin 5.

Remove the carbon deposits from the pistons, particularly from the ring grooves. With the pistons and the cylinder block at the same temperature, measure the bore and piston diameters at rightangles to the axes of the gudgeon pins and, in the case of the bores, 1.5 to 2.0 inch (40 to 50 mm) from the cylinder head face. The ranges of bore/piston acceptable clearances are quoted in the **Technical Data** section of the **Appendix**.

A single standard of oversize piston is available for fitting to standard bores. This is .0010 inch (.025 mm) oversize and the cylinder bores must be honed to give the specified running clearances.

There are two compression rings and one (composite) oil control ring. The top compression ring 1 in **FIG 1:52** is chrome parallel faced. The second compression ring 2 has an L-profile and is marked 'T' or 'TOP' to ensure that it will be fitted the correct way up. The composite oil control ring comprises three sections 3 and 4 as shown.

Using feeler gauges, check the ring gaps with the rings square in the upper part of the cylinder bore. Gap widths are quoted in the **Technical Data** section of the **Appendix**. Compression ring gaps which are below limits may be widened with a fine-cut file. If new piston rings are to be fitted, the cylinder bores must be deglazed by honing to a crosshatch finish. The clearance of the compression rings in their grooves should be within .002 to .004 inch (.05 to .10 mm).

Gudgeon pins must have an interference press fit with their connecting rod little-ends. Their clearance in

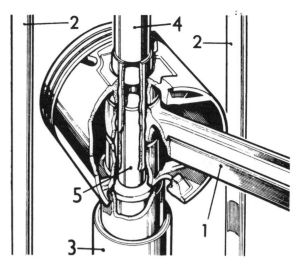

FIG 1:51   Removing a gudgeon pin, 3.5 litre

Key to Fig 1:51   1 Connecting rod   2 Press frame
3 Tool 605350 (lower section) 4 Tool 605350 (upper section)
5 Gudgeon pin

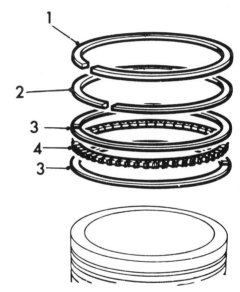

FIG 1:52   Piston rings, 3.5 litre

Key to Fig 1:52   1 Top compression ring   2 Second
compression ring   3 Oil control rail rings   4 Oil control
expansion ring

the piston bores should be within the range of .0002 to .0003 inch (.005 to .007 mm).

Do not attempt to salvage bent, twisted or damaged connecting rods, but obtain new replacements. Reject bearing shells which are scored or excessively worn. If a bearing failure has occurred, examine the crankpin for transfer of bearing metal and ensure that all oilways are clean and clear. Crankpins may be salvaged by regrinding undersize. Two non-standard sizes of big-end shells are available (see **Section 1:11**).

Connecting rod to crankpin clearances (and crankshaft journal to main bearing clearances) are best

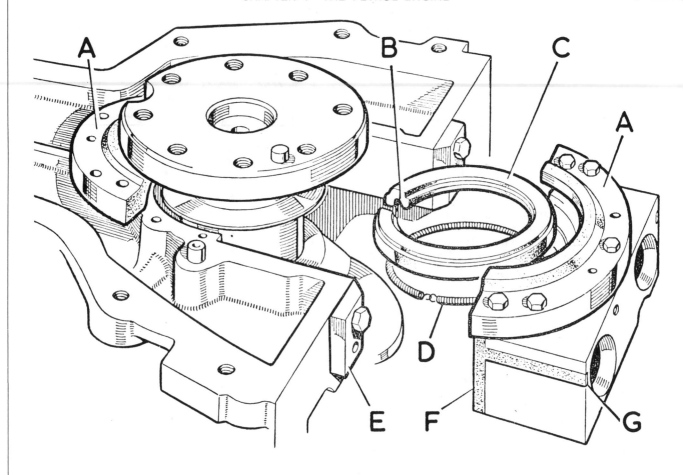

FIG 1 : 53   Rear main bearing oil seal, three main bearing type, 2¼ litre

Key to Fig 1 : 53   **A** Retainer halves   **B** Split line of seal to be towards top of engine when fitted   **C** Split oil seal
D Garter spring, hook and eye to be midway between split and hinge of oil seal when fitted   **E** Guides, part No. 270304, for
rear main bearing cap T-seals   **F** Trim these edges before fitting cap to prevent seal from folding   **G** Trim these ends when
cap is fitted to allow $\frac{1}{32}$ inch (.8 mm) protrusion

measured by using 'Plastigage', which is a proprietary plastic 'thread', as follows.

1 Select the diameter of 'Plastigage' which covers the clearance to be measured. Place a length of the 'thread' on the journal along its full width.

2 Fit the bearing shell and cap. Torque tighten the retaining nuts or bolts. The 'Plastigage' will be squeezed down to the clearance dimension of the bearing and its width will increase. **Do not turn the connecting rod or crankshaft while the 'Plastigage' is in position.**

3 Remove the bearing cap and shell and, using the 'Plastigage' scale provided with the 'thread', read off the clearances. The maximum width will indicate the minimum clearance and the minimum width the maximum clearance.

Refitment of the pistons and connecting rods is the reverse of the removal sequence. Fitment of the gudgeon pins requires a press and the same tooling set-up as for their removal (see **FIG 1 : 51**). Use guide bolts 605351, lubricate the piston rings, pistons and the cylinder bores with engine oil and use a piston ring compressing tool to enter the pistons into the bores.

Check that the bossed domes (see **FIG 1 : 49**) face each other on each crankpin and that the caps are fitted the correct way round. Lubricate the crankpins and big-ends. Torque tighten the cap retaining nuts. The end float between the connecting rod on each crankpin should be within .006 to .014 inch (.15 to .36 mm).

Refer to the relevant chapter and sectional texts for the remaining assembly operations which follow the reverse of the dismantling sequence.

1 : 11   The crankshaft and main bearings

(a) 2¼ litre :

To remove the crankshaft, the engine must be removed from the vehicle as described in **Section 1 : 3**. Secure the engine safely on an engine stand or on blocks on the floor. Drain the oil and remove the sump, oil pump, timing cover, timing chain, clutch, flywheel and flywheel housing. Undo the big-end nuts and remove the caps, keeping them in order. Push the pistons and rods a little way up the bores, out of the way, unless the cylinder head is off and it is intended to remove the pistons as well.

Now continue as follows :

1 Undo the main bearing cap bolts and remove the bearing caps, keeping them in order of removal.

2 Lift the crankshaft away and, on three main bearing engines, remove the oil seal from the rear of the crankshaft. Remove the oil seal retainer halves, on three main bearing engines, from the rear of the crankcase and the rear main bearing face.

3 To check the crankshaft bearing fit, first thoroughly clean and dry all the components, then lay the shaft back in the crankcase with the shell bearing top halves in position. Refit the bearing caps and bottom bearing shells using a piece of 'Plastigage' between each journal and bearing as described for checking big-end clearance. At the same time, refit the thrust bearings. Tighten the bearing cap bolts to 85 lb ft (11.75 mkg), then release and measure the 'Plastigage'. The clearance should be between .0008 and .00285 inch (.02 and .07 mm). Outside these limits, the shaft should be ground undersize and the equivalent new bearing shells fitted. Remove all traces of the 'Plastigage' and replace the bearings. Nip up the bolts, then lever the shaft forwards and back to check the end float. This should be between .002 and .006 inch (.05 and .15 mm). If it is greater, oversize thrust washers can be fitted, but make sure that the shaft remains centralized. The thrust washers must not be different one from the other by more than .003 inch (.8 mm).

4 The crankshaft is replaced by reversing the dismantling procedure, but pay special attention to the instructions which follow for renewing the rear main bearing oil seal. During all these operations great care must be taken to exclude all dirt and grit. Make very sure that the oilways in the crankshaft are absolutely clean before putting the shaft back. Any grinding dust left here will ruin a bearing in no time.

5 Assemble all the bearing top halves to the crankcase, apply a very slight smear of oil and then fit the thrust washers. Lay the shaft in the bearings and replace the front and centre lower bearing shells and bearing caps. Tighten the bolts finger tight. Rotate the shaft. Now refer to **FIG 1 : 53** for three main bearing engines. Carefully hook the garter spring **D** round the shaft as shown. Do not stretch it. Move it up against the oil thrower flange. Apply silicone grease MS4 to the shaft and both sides of the oil seal lip. Place the oil seal over the shaft with the recess towards the spring and oil thrower flange. This is clearly shown in **FIG 1 : 53**. Gently fit the spring into the seal recess, then move the seal to its running position on the shaft. Apply Hylomar PL 32/M sealing compound to the seal diameters of the two retaining plates **A**. Do not use trichlorethylene to degrease these plates. Wipe clean with a dry cloth before applying the Hylomar. Bolt the crankcase retaining plate to the crankcase, compressing the seal to assist assembly. Tighten the top three bolts hard, but leave the two nearest the split line finger tight. See that the split in the oil seal remains vertically towards the cylinder head. Bolt the other retainer to the main bearing cap in the same way. Fit the T-seals to the sides of the cap and just take their

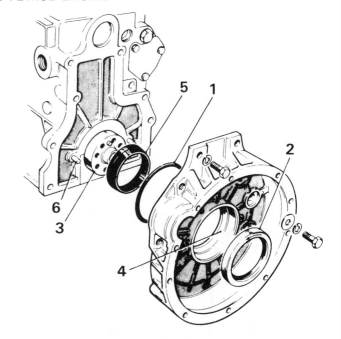

FIG 1 : 54   Rear main bearing oil seal, five main bearing, 2¼ litre

Key to Fig 1 : 54   1 O-ring   2 Oil seal   3 Oil seal journal   4 Seal housing bore   5 Seal guide, 18G 1344   6 Dowel

sharp edges off at positions **F** and **G** (see **FIG 1 : 53**). The two guides **E** are worth making up to assist the seals to slide into the crankcase. Apply the silicone grease to the T-seals. Now fit the bearing cap assembly, complete with bearing shell, and pull down until within $\frac{1}{32}$ inch (.8 mm) of fully home. Check that the seal has entered the retainer without damage. If all is well, continue to pull the cap down and tighten the bolts to 85 lb ft (11.75 mkg). Repeat for the centre and front bearing caps. Tighten the four bolts, two in each seal retainer, left slack. See that the shaft rotates freely.

6 On five main bearing engines, the rear oil seal is located in the flywheel housing (see **FIG 1 : 54**). Discard the O-ring 1 and oil seal 2. Ensure that the journal 3 is not damaged and is clean. Check that the seal housing 4 is clean and dry and free from burrs. Ensure that the seal outside diameter is clean and dry : do not touch the lip. Press in the seal, lip first, until it is flush or a maximum of .020 inch (.50 mm) below the outer face of the housing. When fitting the housing, fit the O-ring seal, lubricate the outside diameter of the seal guide 5 (18G 1344) and the seal journal 3 with concentrated 'Oildag' in a 25 per cent solution with clean engine oil. Place the guide on the crankshaft flange and, using the two dowels 6 to ensure initial squareness, fit the flywheel housing and remove the seal guide. The number five main bearing cap is fitted in the same manner as that used on three main bearing engines and new bolts must be used on all bearing caps.

7 Continue to rebuild the engine as described in earlier sections.

FIG 1 : 55   Removing the crankshaft, 3.5 litre

Key to Fig 1 : 55   1 Rear oil seal   2 Cruciform face seals   3 Location for jointing compound   4 End piece and rear main bearing cap   5 Rear cap retaining bolts   6 Pilot bearing   7 Main bearing caps   8 Flanged bearing shell   9 Connecting rod cap retaining nuts   10 Connecting rod big-end caps   11 Crankshaft   12 Main bearing cap retaining bolts

(b) 2.6 litre:

The instructions given for the $2\frac{1}{4}$ litre three main bearing engine apply exactly to this engine, with the following minor exceptions.

1 The bearing clearance should be between .0006 and .002 inch (.015 and .05 mm).
2 Tighten the bearing cap bolts to 75 lb ft (10 mkg).

(c) 3.5 litre:

1 Remove the engine as described in **Section 1 : 3**.
2 Remove the timing gear cover, timing chain and gears as described in **Section 1 : 6**.
3 Remove the clutch and flywheel as described in **Section 1 : 9**.
4 Remove the sump and strainer.
5 Withdraw the connecting rod caps and lower bearing shells.
6 Refer to **FIG 1 : 55**. Withdraw the main bearing cap retaining bolts 5 and 12. Remove the main bearing caps 4 and 7. Keep them identified to their locations. Withdraw seal 1. Lift out the crankshaft.
7 Withdraw the main bearing shells from the block. If the original bearing shells are to be refitted, keep them identified to their other halves.

Reject bearing shells which are scored or excessively worn. If a bearing failure has occurred, inspect the journal for transfer of metal and check that the oilways in the crankshaft and in the block are clear and clean (this will also apply if there has been a big-end failure). Note that the centre bearing shells 8 are flanged. They control the axial float of the crankshaft. The rear bearing cap and end piece 4 are integral and the assembly carries cruciform side face seals 2 (see also **FIG 1 : 56**) and the lower half of the rear seal 1 location.

If cylinder bores have been honed either to deglaze their surfaces for new piston rings or to resize to suit oversize pistons, the block must be thoroughly cleaned and the oilways flushed through with clean engine oil.

Main bearing to crankshaft journal clearances are best measured by using 'Plastigage' as described in **Section 1 : 10**. Crankpins and main journals may be reground to suit the non-standard big-end and main bearing sizes. Refer to the **Technical Data** section of the **Appendix** for the acceptable range of clearances.

1 Locate the upper bearing shells in the block and check that the oilways align. Lubricate the shells and shaft journals with engine oil and lift the shaft into position.

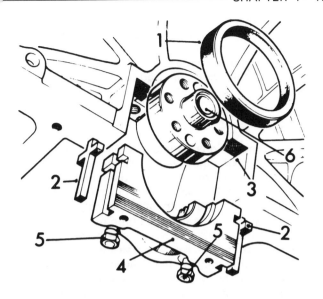

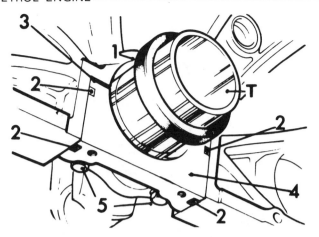

FIG 1:56   Crankshaft rear bearing cap and oil seal, 3.5 litre

Key to Fig 1:56   1 Rear seal   2 Cruciform face seal
3 Location for jointing compound   4 End piece and
rear main bearing cap   5 Rear cap retaining bolts
6 Crankshaft

FIG 1:57   Fitting the rear oil seal, 3.5 litre

Key to Fig 1:57   1 Rear oil seal   2 Cruciform face seals
3 Location for jointing compound   4 End piece and rear
main bearing cap   5 Rear cap retaining bolts
T Guide tool RO 1014

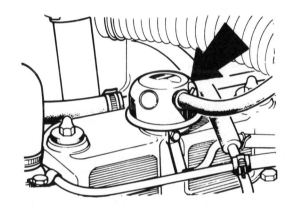

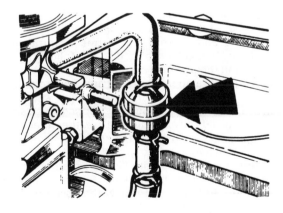

FIG 1:58 Engine breather filter (above) and crankcase ventilation flame trap (below), 2¼ and 2.6 litre

2 Lubricate the lower bearing shells and fit all shells and caps except that at the rear (4 in **FIG 1:55**). Fit the cap retaining bolts, but leave them slack. Align the thrust faces of the centre bearing by tapping the crankshaft with a mallet forwards and rearwards. Torque tighten the bearing retaining bolts for these caps.

3 Refer to **FIG 1:56**. Fit new cruciform side face seals 2. Do not cut them to length. They must protrude approximately .062 inch (1.59 mm) beyond the cap parting line. Apply Hylomar PL 32/M jointing compound to the rearmost half of the cap parting face or to the equivalent face of the cylinder block as shown at 3 in **FIGS 1:56** and **1:57**.

4 Lubricate and fit the rear cap 4. Fit bolts 5, but leave them slack. Check that the cap is fully home and squarely seated. Tension the cap bolts 5 equally by one quarter turn and then back each off by one full turn.

5 Lubricate the rear seal journal. Refer to **FIG 1:57** and use guide tool **T** (RO 1014), which must also be lubricated, to fit a new rear seal 1 without, at any time, handling the lip seal. Keep the outside diameter of the seal clean and dry. Push it home fully, withdraw the guide tool and torque tighten the rear cap retaining bolts.

6 Using a dial gauge against the rear of the crankshaft, check that the axial float is within .004 to .008 inch (.10 to .20 mm). The remaining sequence is the reverse of the removal operations 1 and 2. Refer to the relevant sectional and chapter texts.

1:12 Reassembling a stripped engine

In the previous sections, full instructions have been given for the reassembly of each major unit including static timing procedures for three main bearing 2¼ and

2.6 litre engines. Timing procedures for later type engines are given in **Chapter 4, Section 4:5**. No difficulty should be experienced in reassembling an engine if the operations are worked through in sequence. Utter cleanliness is essential; clean out all oil galleries and drillings using lint free rag or pipe

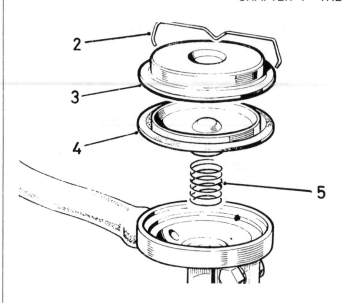

FIG 1:59 Crankcase emission valve, 2¼ and 2.6 litre

Key to Fig 1:59   2 Clip   3 Cover   4 Diaphragm
5 Spring

cleaners. Be careful not to leave a piece of rag stuck in an oilway.

Always use new locking tabs or washers and gaskets. Do not exceed the stated torque figures for bolts and nuts as bolts can be easily stretched and weakened.

1:13 Emission control equipment

Crankcase ventilation:

Crankcase fumes are vented into the induction system to be burnt with the fuel/air mixture in the normal combustion process.

A number of different layouts are employed according to model and market, but the principle remains the same. Maintenance is confined to the following filter cleaning and replacement at specified mileages.

The engine breather filter for 2¼ and 2.6 litre engines (see **FIG 1:58**) contains a gauze which should be washed in clean petrol, dried and dipped in clean oil. Shake off surplus oil and refit. The breather filter for 3.5 litre engines is shown in **FIG 1:8** and must be renewed at specified mileages.

A flame trap is incorporated in the breather hose on some models (see **FIG 1:58**). Unclip the hose from each end of the flame trap and renew the assembly complete.

The crankcase emission valve which is shown in **FIG 1:59** should be removed for inspection and cleaning from time to time.

Disconnect the two hosepipes and remove the securing nut and bolt. Withdraw the valve unit.

Release the spring clip and remove the top cover. Lift out the diaphragm, plunger and spring.

Clean all the parts **except the diaphragm** in methylated spirits and examine them for damage or corrosion.

Replace the spring in the body and then fit the diaphragm onto the spring, ensuring that it is seating correctly.

Fit the cover and secure with the clip.

Warm up the engine and adjust the carburetter if necessary.

Air pump:

To meet regulations in force in some countries, an air pump is fitted which delivers air to the exhaust manifold through an air rail. Air pump drive belt tension is correct when the belt deflects by ¼ inch (6 mm) under thumb pressure at the centre of its longest run. Adjust, if necessary, by slackening the pump mounting bolts, moving the pump and retightening the bolts.

The check valve, fitted at the air rail end of the air hose to prevent pump damage in the event of a backfire or belt failure, can be checked by removing and blowing through it. Do not use an air line. Air should pass from the hose end towards the air rail and not in the reverse direction. Renew the valve if faulty.

Checking and repairing the air pump, if necessary, will have to be entrusted to a suitably equipped service station.

Exhaust gas recirculation (EGR):

The nitric content in the exhaust is reduced, at peak combustion temperatures, by recirculating controlled quantities of exhaust gas. There is no recirculation at idle or full load, only at part load, dependent on the signal from the induction vacuum source and the production setting.

The EGR valve can be recognised by the lagged outlet pipe.

Testing the EGR valve:

1 Bring the engine to normal operating temperature.
2 Ensure that the choke is fully off.
3 The valve should open and close with changes in engine speed and should close instantly on closing the throttle. Care should be taken when checking as the valve gets very hot.

1:14 Fault diagnosis

(a) Engine will not start

1 Battery discharged
2 Starter jammed in mesh or defective
3 Ignition faults
4 Carburetter fault
5 Lack of fuel
6 Incorrect 'hot spot' adjustment

(b) Engine starts but stops at once

1 Faulty electrical connection
2 Lack of fuel

(c) Engine will not idle

1 Incorrect carburetter setting
2 Fuel pump faulty
3 Ignition timing incorrect or ignition fault
4 Burnt valve
5 Blown cylinder head gasket
6 Choked exhaust system

(d) Engine misfires on acceleration

1 Faulty distributor contact breaker
2 Coil or capacitor faulty
3 Defective sparking plug
4 Carburetter air leak or punctured diaphragm

(e) Engine misfires

1 Air leak in exhaust system
2 Defective valves
3 Ignition timing retarded
4 Carburetter air leak
5 Valve timing incorrect

(f) Engine knocks

1 Ignition too far advanced
2 Slack tappets
3 Worn bearings
4 Excessive carbon

(g) Engine runs erratically

1 Incorrect ignition timing
2 Faulty fuel pump
3 Sparking plug defective
4 Stuck valve or incorrect tappet clearance
5 Leaking exhaust system

(h) Lack of power

1 Incorrect ignition timing
2 Low compression, worn cylinders or burnt valves
3 Binding brakes
4 Clutch slip

NOTES

CHAPTER 2

THE DIESEL ENGINE

2 : 1 Description

This engine is offered as an alternative to the petrol engines described in **Chapter 1**. The compression ratio is 23 : 1 and fuel is injected into the cylinders by C.A.V. Pintaux injectors. The pistons are of light alloy with a swirl inducing recess in the crown. Overhead valves are driven from a camshaft situated high up on the side of the engine which is, in turn, driven by chain and jockey wheel from the crankshaft. A distributor type rotary fuel pump is fitted and the fuel system has four fuel filters to ensure cleanliness of the delivery to the injectors.

A high capacity, spur gear oil pump is driven from the engine camshaft. This pump has a strainer submerged in the oil sump and an external fullflow filter unit with a replacement element.

To assist in starting from cold, heater plugs are fitted to each cylinder. Operation of these is controlled by the starting key which has a 'heater plug' position. The key is held in this position for about 10 seconds before turning on to the starter motor position.

The high compression ratio of diesel engines makes heavy demands on the starter and a heavy duty pre-engaged type is fitted. To cope with the current requirements heavy duty batteries are provided.

2 : 2 Working on the engine in situ

All components, except the crankshaft and main bearings, can be conviently worked on with the engine installed in the vehicle. For a major overhaul, however, where the engine is to be extensively reconditioned, it will be found quicker in the long run to remove it.

In most operations carried out with the engine in place, removal of the grille and radiator, or radiator and front panel assembly on later models, will simplify matters considerably.

For the operator who has no access to suitable lifting tackle, the following operations are possible without removing the engine : decarbonization and attention to the valves, renewal of the hot plugs, injectors and push-rod tubes, camshaft and tappet renewal, pistons, big-end bearing renewal, rocker shaft overhaul. The oil pump and strainer can also be worked on from below as can the clutch and flywheel if the gearbox is removed. Accessories such as the water pump, thermostat, starter, dynamo or alternator, injection pump and vibration damper, where fitted, are all easily accessible.

When working on the engine in the vehicle, if the engine is being run for test or any reason, make sure that an oil bath air cleaner, if fitted, is fixed safely in the vertical position. Should the cleaner be loose and tip sideways, it is possible for oil to be drawn in with the air and act as excess fuel. The engine will then overspeed out of control and serious damage can result.

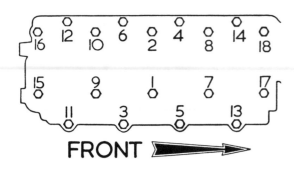

FIG 2:1 Cylinder head bolt sequence

Key to Fig 2:1 $\frac{1}{2}$ inch bolts 90 lb ft (12.5 mkg)
$\frac{5}{16}$ inch bolts 18 lb ft (2.4 mkg)

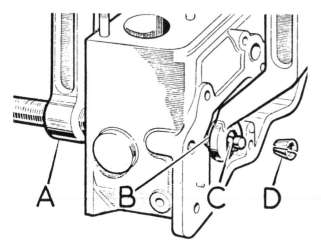

FIG 2:2 Removing the valves

Key to Fig 2:2 A Compressor tool **B** Spring **C** Valve
D Split collets

2:3 *Removing the engine*

1 Remove the spare wheel from the bonnet, if fitted, disconnect the bonnet support stay, then lift the bonnet as high as possible and slide sideways out of the hinges. Some differences exist between the early and later installations so some operations listed may not be relevant.

2 Disconnect the air cleaner and hose.

3 Disconnect the battery leads and remove the battery.

4 Drain the coolant by undoing one tap below the radiator and one at the lefthand side of the cylinder block.

5 Disconnect the front lamp leads at the snap connectors and earth terminal. Now pull the wiring clear to the front of the engine.

6 Detach the top radiator hose at the header tank and the bottom hose from the water pump. Undo the fan blades if necessary and allow them to rest on the cowl. Remove them when the radiator and grille

panel, or radiator and front panel assembly, is removed.

7 Remove the bolts securing the front apron, then the bolts securing the grille to the front crossmember and wings. Lift the radiator, grille panel and head-lamps assembly upwards and forwards clear of the vehicle.

8 Loosen the bolts securing the front exhaust pipe and disconnect the exhaust pipe from the manifold.

9 Disconnect the heater pipes, if fitted, at the engine side of the dash.

10 Disconnect the wiring from the starter motor, generator or alternator, oil pressure warning switch, water temperature transmitter and the glow plug (heater) lead from the resistance on the dash. Disconnect the engine earth cable.

11 Disconnect the fuel pipe to the fuel pump and distributor pump and the fuel pipe from the spill pipe to the fuel filter. Plug all ports and lay the pipes away in a clean place to avoid the ingress of dirt.

12 Remove the accelerator rod, then the cut-off cable from the steady bracket on the engine and from the lever on the injection pump. If a brake servo is fitted, disconnect the vacuum hose.

13 If available, fit the Rover engine sling to the engine or otherwise make up a suitable rope sling to pass beneath the engine. With suitably safe tackle, just take the strain of the weight of the engine. Check any improvized sling for proper location.

14 Remove the front floor and gearbox cover from the body.

15 From below the vehicle, support the weight of the gearbox on substantial wooden blocks; do not use house bricks. Alternatively, insert a piece of timber 1 inch (25 mm) thick between the gearbox and crossmember.

16 Remove the nuts and washers securing the gearbox to the flywheel housing. Remove the clutch slave cylinder without disconnecting the supply pipe and move to one side.

17 Remove the engine front supports and gently pull it forward to clear the gearbox input shaft. Make sure all is clear, then carefully hoist the engine from the vehicle.

18 At this point it is convenient to drain the oil from the sump before mounting the engine on a stand or supporting it on the floor for further work.

Installing the engine is generally the reverse of the removal procedure with attention to the following points:

Clean the engine and bellhousing mating faces and coat them with Hylomar PL 32 sealant.

Smear the splines of the primary pinion, the clutch centre and the withdrawal unit abutment faces with molybdenum disulphide grease such as Rocol MTS 1000.

Prime the fuel system (see **Chapter 3B**).

Replenish engine and gearbox lubricating oil.

On starting the engine, check that the oil pressure warning light goes out and check the coolant system for leaks.

Adjust engine speed settings if necessary.

When the engine is cold, check and top up the coolant level.

2:4 Removing the cylinder head

This operation can be performed with the engine either in or out of the vehicle. If in the vehicle, remove the bonnet, disconnect the battery and drain the coolant. Now proceed as follows:

1 Remove the air cleaner and flexible pipe complete.
2 Disconnect the breather hose from the rocker cover. Unscrew the dome nuts securing the rocker cover and lift the cover clear.
3 Remove the rocker shaft pedestal securing bolts, then fit the inverted rocker cover to the rocker bracket studs and remove the assembly using the top cover as a retainer.
4 Withdraw the pushrods, keeping them in their correct order for refitting.
5 Disconnect, on early installations, the pipes from the main fuel filter; the pipe from the filter to the injection pump must be removed completely to prevent distortion.
6 Remove, on early installations, the bolts securing the filter to the support bracket of the engine, detach the heater plug earth lead and withdraw the filter.
7 Disconnect the fuel 'bleed back' pipe from the injector nozzle and from the union nut on the main fuel return pipe. Remove the fuel pipes, injection pump to nozzles. Fit blanking plugs or caps to the injection pump outlet unions, to the fuel lift pump outlet, to the fuel return pipe union and to the injector nozzle inlet and outlet unions.
8 Remove the injector nozzle securing nuts and remove the nozzle assemblies.
9 Disconnect the leads and take out the heater plugs.
10 Remove the top coolant hose and the thermostat bypass hose. If a brake servo is fitted, disconnect the vacuum pipe and the butterfly control rod from the induction manifold.
11 Disconnect the oil feed pipe from the rear of the cylinder head, righthand side, and the front exhaust pipe from the manifold. Disconnect heater hoses if fitted.
12 Loosen the cylinder head bolts evenly in the reverse order to that shown in **FIG 2:1**, then remove them completely and lift the head clear. Discard the cylinder head gasket.
13 Remove the inlet and exhaust manifolds and the thermostat if necessary.

2:5 Servicing the cylinder head and valves

1 Remove the valves with a valve spring compressor as shown in **FIG 2:2**. Lay out the valves, springs, caps and collets so that if it is desired to refit them they will be in order of removal. Remove the seals from the valve guides.
2 Clean all carbon from the cylinder head using a blunt scraper; make sure no carbon particles fall into the waterways by plugging these with rag or screws of newspaper. Be sure all these plugs are removed at the proper time. This operation is important because it is possible for a piece of hard carbon to fall from a waterway when the head is being replaced and lodge on the head gasket, thereby spoiling the seal.

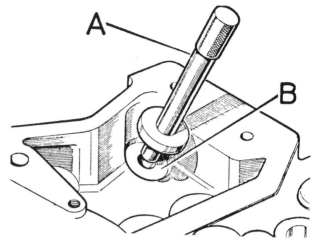

FIG 2:3 Removing pushrod tubes

Key to Fig 2:3　　A Drift　　B Tube

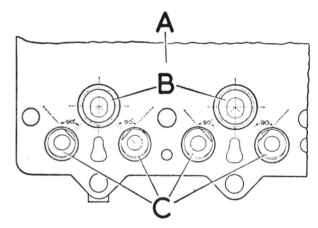

FIG 2:4 Position of pushrod tubes

Key to Fig 2:4　　A Head　　B Hot plug　　C Pushrod tubes

3 Clean all carbon from the valves, but do not touch the seating face. Try the valves in their guides. If the clearance between the valve stem and the guide exceeds .004 inch (.096 mm), the parts are worn. Measure the valve stem; inlet valve stems should measure .3112 – .0005 inch (7.90 – .013 mm) and exhaust valves .3415 – .0005 inch (8.67 – .013 mm). If the valves are within these limits yet slackness is apparent between the valve and guide, new guides must be fitted.
4 Drift the guides from the head using Rover drifts, part Nos. 274400 and 274401, inlet and exhaust respectively. Remove and scrap the seals.
5 To fit new guides it is necessary to use drifts, part Nos. 600959 for the exhausts and 601508 for the inlets. Early type guides with internal oil seal grooves have three packing washers under the exhaust guide head and two packing washers under the inlet guide head. Later type guides for external oil seals do not require packing washers. Lubricate the outside diameter of a guide with engine oil and carefully drift into position.

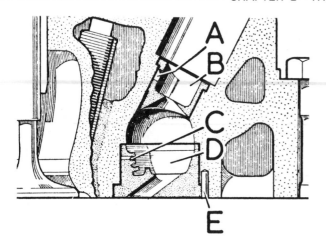

FIG 2:5   View of injector shroud and hot plug

Key to Fig 2:5   **A** Hole positioned towards head centre line
B Shroud   **C** Swirl holes   **D** Hot plug   **E** Locating peg

6 If new guides have been fitted it will be necessary to recut the valve seats in the cylinder head to ensure concentricity with the guide. Remove the hard surface of the existing seating with a piece of emerypaper, then recut the seats to an angle of 45 + $\frac{1}{4}$ deg. both inlet and exhaust. Special cutting tools, Rover part Nos. 274413 and 274414, inlet and exhaust, are available for this operation.

When cutting the seats, do not apply excessive pressure to the tool as this may cause it to judder and ruin the seat.

7 If the old valves are to be used again, check them for concentricity of the seat to the stem by applying a little engineer's blue to the cylinder head seating and then refitting the valve and rotating it one turn. Marking all round the valve shows all is well. If not, the safest course is to fit a new valve. The old valve can be refaced on a valve trueing machine provided this does not reduce the face to a knife edge.

8 The new or reground valves should be lapped into their seats using grinding paste. Smear a little paste on the valve face, insert it in the cylinder head and, by applying a suction cup tool to the valve, oscillate the valve back and forth several times, raise the valve from its seat, move it forwards a third of a turn and repeat the grinding process. Do this three or four times, pausing to re-distribute the paste, then remove the valve, being careful not to touch the ground surface. If a grey band of contact shows all round the valve face and the cylinder head seat, all is well and the process can be repeated on the next valve. If contact is not obtained, repeat the grinding and again examine the faces. If proper contact is not obtained this time, re-examine the valve for truth and the cylinder head seat for concentricity with the valve guides. Do not carry on grinding interminably. Wipe all traces of grinding paste from the head with clean rag, being careful to destroy this rag and anything else which may be contaminated with abrasive once the lapping is completed. Wash the valves in petrol and wipe dry.

9 To assemble the valves, first fit a new rubber seal to each valve guide, smear a little engine oil on the valve stem and insert it in the guide. On later engines, fit the oil seals fitted with springs to the inlet valve guides and the oil seals with external projectors to the exhaust valve guides. Replace the springs, caps and cotters with the aid of the spring compressor. Note that the springs are an interference fit in each other. If they are slack they must be scrapped. A red stripe is painted on springs suitable for the later type guides with external oil seals. It is recommended that the whole assembly, comprising exhaust valves, guides and springs, is fitted in place of the earlier types, although later type springs can be fitted provided the packing washers are removed.

Pushrod tubes:

Leaks sometimes develop at these, thereby necessitating renewal. Proceed as follows:

1 Drift out the defective tubes as shown in **FIG 2:3** using Rover drift, part No. 274399. When the tubes are removed they are scrap.

2 Fit new tubes, complete with sealing rings, by pressing them into the head from the head face. Smear them well with silicone MS4 compound beforehand. Ensure that the chamfers on the tubes and in the cylinder head are in full contact and that the flat on the tube is at right angles to a line drawn between the centre of the pushrod tube and the centre of the hot plug (see **FIG 2:4**).

Injector shrouds:

In order to renew the injector shrouds it is necessary to remove the hot plugs. **FIG 2:5** clearly shows the construction.

1 Remove the hot plugs by inserting a copper drift through the injector shroud aperture and tap evenly round the inside of the hot plug.

2 If the injector shrouds are tight, drift them out towards the injector bore, then carefully clean the combustion chamber.

3 The hole in the side of the shroud is for manufacturing purposes only but can be used as a guide when fitting new ones.

4 Smear a little engine oil on the new shroud and insert in the cylinder head with the hole pointing towards the centre of the head. Drift into position using tool part No. 274399.

5 Replace the hot plugs by tapping gently with a hide-faced hammer. Check with a dial indicator to see that they do not protrude more than .001 inch (.025 mm) above the head face and are not recessed below the face more than .002 inch (.05mm). If the plugs are loose in the head, retain them temporarily with a little grease.

The rocker shaft:

1 To strip the shaft, remove all the components and lay them out in order as shown in **FIG 2:6**.

2 If necessary, press the bushes from the rockers and press new ones in. Make sure the oil holes are in alignment. Ream the new bushes to .53 + .001 inch (13.5 + .02 mm).

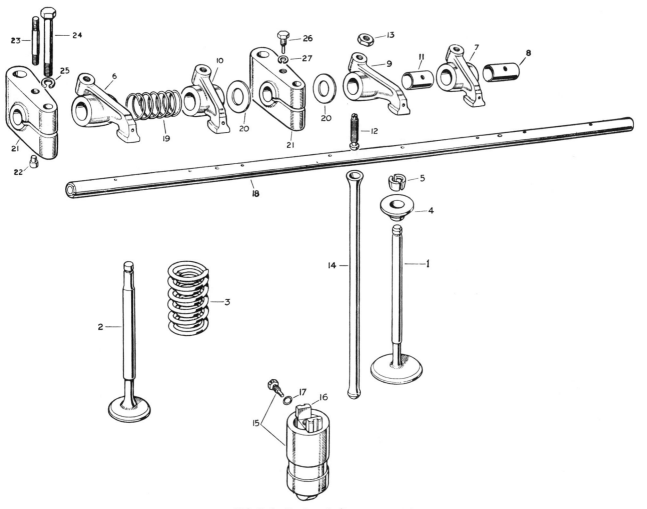

FIG 2:6   Rocker shaft arrangement

Key to Fig 2:6   1 Inlet valve   2 Exhaust valve   3 Valve spring, inner and outer   4 Valve spring cup
5 Split cone for valve, halves   6 Valve rocker, exhaust lefthand   7 Valve rocker, exhaust righthand
8 Bush for exhaust valve rocker   9 Valve rocker, inlet lefthand   10 Valve rocker, inlet righthand   11 Bush for
inlet valve rocker   12 Tappet adjusting screw   13 Locknut for tappet adjusting screw   14 Tappet pushrod
15 Tappet, tappet guide, roller and setbolt assembly   16 Tappet   17 Copper washer for tappet guide setbolt
18 Valve rocker shaft   19 Spring for rocker shaft   20 Washer for rocker shaft   21 Rocker bracket
22 Locating dowel for rocker bracket   23 Stud for rocker bracket   24 Setbolt ($\frac{5}{16}$ UNF x 2 inch long) (fixing
rocker bracket to cylinder head)   25 Spring washer (fixing rocker bracket to cylinder head)   26 Locating screw
(for rocker shaft at bracket)   27 Spring washer (for rocker shaft at bracket)

3 To reassemble the shaft, fit an intermediate bracket to the shaft and engage locating screw (26 in **FIG 2:6**). Continue to assemble as shown in **FIG 2:6**, noting particularly that the rockers are 'handed'.

2:6 *Decarbonizing*

Most of the work called for under this heading has been covered in the previous section with the work described in 'Servicing the cylinder head'. There remains, however, the piston crowns to deal with. Turn the engine over to bring two pistons to TDC. Plug the waterways and the pushrod apertures with rag or paper, being careful to remove all these when work is complete. Scrape all the carbon from the piston crowns and in the swirl recesses with a blunt tool, being careful

not to damage the surfaces. Turn the engine over and deal with the other two pistons. Wipe any carbon particles from the cylinder bores, turning the engine over several times until the bores are clean. On no account use abrasive paper in an attempt to polish the pistons.

2:7 *Replacing the cylinder head*

1 If a non-retorque fabric type cylinder head gasket is being used, it must be fitted dry, without grease or any sealing compound. If a copper-asbestos type gasket is being fitted, obtain a new gasket and coat both sides sparingly with a jointing cement such as Hylomar SQ32M. Place the gasket on the cylinder block with the word 'DIESEL' uppermost. Carefully place the cylinder head assembly on the gasket and

loosely fit all the cylinder head bolts except those which hold the rocker shaft pedestals. Five main bearing engines and later three main bearing engines have plain washers fitted between the cylinder head bolts and the cylinder head.

2 Replace the pushrods in their original positions, making sure that their lower ends are correctly located in the tappets.

3 Locate the rocker shaft assembly on the cylinder head, ensuring that the pushrods are seating on the rocker adjusting screws. Fit the pedestal bolts but do not tighten at this stage.

4 Now tighten all the cylinder head bolts in the order shown in **FIG 2:1**. All the $\frac{1}{2}$ inch bolts must be tightened to 90 lb ft (12.5 mkg) whilst the $\frac{5}{16}$ inch bolts must be tightened to 18 lb ft (2.4 mkg). Work round the sequence a little at a time, trying to keep the pressure as even as possible.

5 Do not turn the engine over until all excess slack is eliminated from the tappets. Check each rocker for movement and take up the slack, turn the engine over half a turn and again check the tappets. Do this several times. This is important because excess slack can allow the pushrod to lift out of the spherical seat and onto the tappet slide. Further movement will then damage the pushrod.

6 The tappets can now be adjusted to their proper running clearance. This is .010 inch (.25 mm) with the engine hot or cold. Turn the crankshaft in the direction of rotation until No. 8 valve from the front of the engine is fully open. Check the clearance for No. 1 valve as shown in **FIG 2:7**, using a feeler gauge, spanner and screwdriver. The complete sequence for setting tappets is as follows:

Set No. 1 tappet with No. 8 valve fully open
Set No. 3 tappet with No. 6 valve fully open
Set No. 5 tappet with No. 4 valve fully open
Set No. 2 tappet with No. 7 valve fully open
Set No. 8 tappet with No. 1 valve fully open
Set No. 6 tappet with No. 3 valve fully open
Set No. 4 tappet with No. 5 valve fully open
Set No. 7 tappet with No. 2 valve fully open

7 Complete the reassembly of the head by replacing the rocker cover and refitting the heater plugs. The injectors must also be replaced. Proceed as follows:

Smear a new copper joint washer with grease and fit one to each injector. Insert a new corrugated sealing washer into each injector nozzle recess in the head with its raised portion upwards (see **FIG 2:8**). Locate the injectors in the head and tighten the clamping nuts to 6 to 8 lb ft (.8 to 1.0 mkg). Do not overtighten. Connect the injector feed pipes and spill pipes and tighten all the pipe unions. Tighten the heater plugs to 25 lb ft (3.4 mkg).

8 Replace the manifolds, using new gaskets where required, and complete the assembly by reversing the dismantling process.

Start and run the engine until it reaches normal operating temperature.

Remove the rocker cover and, while the engine is hot, check/tighten the $\frac{1}{2}$ in UNF cylinder head bolts in the order shown in **FIG 2:1** to 90 lb ft (12.5 mkg).

2:8 Removing the timing gear and camshaft

To obtain access to the camshaft, it is necessary to remove the timing cover and chain. If the engine is installed in the vehicle, first remove those items which are in the way. Refer to **Section 2:3** and carry out operations 1 to 9. If the engine is out of the vehicle, ignore **Section 2:3**. From here onwards the situation of the engine does not affect the work.

Remove the cylinder head as described in **Section 2:4**, being careful to store all the injection equipment in a dustproof place. Now proceed as follows:

1 Slacken the generator/alternator mounting brackets and remove the fan belt and adjusting link.

2 Remove all the pipes from the injection pump and disconnect the throttle and cut-off controls. Blank off all the pump apertures either with the proper aluminium plugs or with adhesive tape to prevent the ingress of foreign matter.

3 Undo the securing nuts and washers, then lift the pump upwards and clear of the engine.

4 The rear tappet chamber cover and fuel lift pump can now be removed as one unit. Take off the forward tappet chamber cover and oil filler pipe.

5 Undo the bolts retaining the water pump and remove the pump and joint washer.

6 Unscrew the starter dog and pull off the vibration damper (if fitted): remove the key. The starter dog will probably be jammed tight. To remove it, use a ring spanner and strike the handle sharply with a hammer.

7 The tappet assemblies must now be removed complete. First remove the guide locating bolts from the side of the cylinder block, then with a piece of hooked wire lift out the roller and brass slide. Do not allow the guide to move or the roller may fall into the camshaft chamber. Keep the assemblies in order. Refer to the instructions given in **Chapter 1** for the $2\frac{1}{4}$ litre petrol engine. The construction is the same.

8 The vertical drive shaft gear can be lifted out as shown in **FIG 2:9** after removing the locating screw from the external filter adaptor joint face. The split bush may be removed by tapping to release the dowels. Do not remove the aluminium plug in the gear unless absolutely necessary. A new plug must always be fitted if the old one is removed. This assembly is similar to the one described in **Chapter 1** for the $2\frac{1}{4}$ litre petrol engine.

9 Undo the bolts and lift off the timing case front cover. The timing gear will appear as shown in **Chapter 1, FIG 1:27**. Remove the tensioner ratchet securing bolt and withdraw the ratchet and spring. Compress the tensioner spring, undo the securing bolts and lift off the tensioner. The timing chain will now be slack enough to lift off. Undo the bolt in the centre of the camshaft chainwheel. The chainwheel may pull off the shaft easily but a special puller may be necessary. This can be made up from a piece of

mild steel with three bolts in it. The two outer ones are screwed into the holes in the wheel and the centre one is then tightened against the end of the shaft, thus pulling the wheel free. If the wheel is very tight, put a piece of brass on the end of the shaft to avoid damaging the thread.

10 The thrust plate bolts must now be removed and the thrust plate lifted away. Tabwashers are deleted on later engines. The camshaft will be free to come forward out of the engine. Do this very gently, supporting the shaft through the side apertures so that the intermediate bearings are not damaged.

2:9 Replacing the timing gear and camshaft

Refer to **FIG 2:10**. This shows all the component parts quoted in this section.

It is possible to replace bearings, but these are supplied undersize when new and have to be line reamed in position. The tools needed are specialized and expensive: therefore, this is definitely a job for a Rover service station.

If a new camshaft is being fitted, make sure that it is marked 'DIESEL' between No. 1 and 2 cams.

To reassemble the timing gear proceed as follows:

1 Smear a little clean engine oil on all the camshaft bearing surfaces, then introduce it carefully into the engine. Support it until it is home in the rear bearing.

2 Fit the thrust plate and tighten the bolts, but do not bend up the locking tags, if fitted, until the end float has been checked. Use a dial indicator and see that the shaft has between .0025 and .0055 inch (.06 and .13 mm) of float. If it is not within these limits, fit a new thrust plate. Bend up the locking tags if fitted.

3 Check the tappet assemblies for wear and replace where necessary. Smear each guide with oil and replace in the block, making sure that the locating hole in the guide lines up with the screw hole in the block. Gently lower the roller into the guide, do not drop it in. Make sure the chamfer on the inside diameter faces to the front of the engine. Replace the tappet slide, also with the word 'FRONT' towards the front of the engine. Screw the locating bolt in with the fingers to make sure that it enters the hole in the guide. Continue until all the tappets are assembled. Tighten the locating bolts and then wire them together in pairs using 20 SWG iron wire.

4 Clean and examine the tensioner, replace any worn components, lubricate with engine oil and reassemble.

5 If the rubber on the chain vibration damper is grooved, fit a new damper.

6 Fit the camshaft chainwheel to the shaft, but do not fit the bolt at this stage.

7 Replace the cylinder head, pushrods and rockers as described in **Section 2:7**.

8 Turn the crankshaft in the direction of rotation until the EP mark on the flywheel is in line with the timing pointer.

9 Fit a dial indicator to No. 1 cylinder exhaust valve, as shown in **Chapter 1, FIG 1:35**. Turn the camshaft in the direction of rotation until the cam has nearly

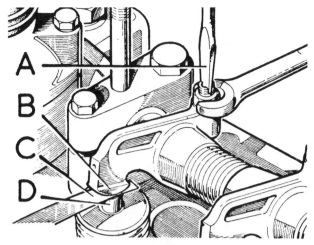

FIG 2:7 Setting the tappet clearance

Key to Fig 2:7   **A** Screwdriver   **B** Rocker
C Feeler gauge   **D** Valves

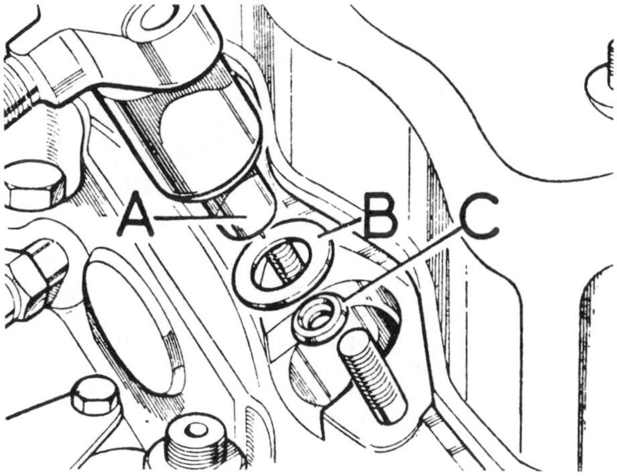

FIG 2:8 Fitting fuel injectors

Key to Fig 2:8   **A** Injector   **B** Copper washer
C Steel washer, raised position uppermost

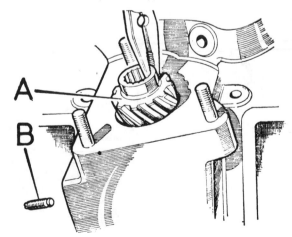

FIG 2:9 Removing the vertical drive shaft gear

Key to Fig 2:9   **A** Gear   **B** Locating screw housed in tapping at oil filter face

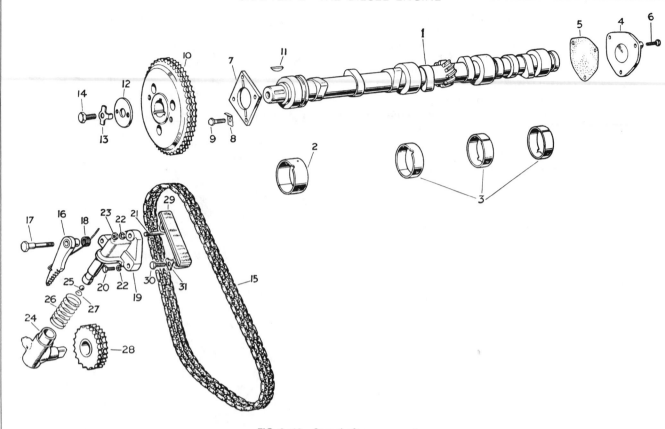

FIG 2:10 Camshaft components

Key to Fig 2:10 1 Camshaft 2 Bearing complete for camshaft, front 3 Bearing complete for camshaft, centre and rear 4 Rear end cover for camshaft 5 Joint washer for cover 6 Setbolt ($\frac{1}{4}$ inch UNF x $\frac{7}{8}$ inch long) (fixing cover to block) and spring washer 7 Thrust plate for camshaft 8 Locker (fixing thrust plate to cylinder block) 9 Setbolt ($\frac{1}{4}$ inch UNF x $\frac{3}{4}$ inch long) (fixing thrust plate to cylinder block) 10 Chainwheel for camshaft 11 Key locating camshaft chainwheel 12 Retaining washer (fixing chainwheel to camshaft) 13 Locker (fixing chainwheel to camshaft) 14 Setbolt ($\frac{3}{8}$ inch UNF x $\frac{7}{8}$ inch long) (fixing chainwheel to camshaft) 15 Camshaft chain ($\frac{3}{8}$ inch pitch x 78 links) 16 Ratchet for timing chain adjuster 17 Special bolt fixing ratchet and piston to block 18 Spring for chain adjuster ratchet 19 Piston for timing chain adjuster 20 Setbolt ($\frac{5}{16}$ inch UNF x $1\frac{1}{4}$ inch long) (fixing piston to cylinder block) 21 Stud ($\frac{5}{16}$ inch UNF) (fixing piston to cylinder block) 22 Spring washer (fixing piston to cylinder block) 23 Nut ($\frac{5}{16}$ inch UNF) (fixing piston to cylinder block) 24 Cylinder for timing chain adjuster 25 Steel ball ($\frac{7}{32}$ inch) for non-return valve 26 Spring for chain tensioner 27 Retainer for steel ball 28 Idler wheel for timing chain 29 Vibration damper for timing chain 30 Setbolt ($\frac{1}{4}$ inch UNF x $\frac{1}{2}$ inch long) (fixing damper to cylinder block) 31 Locking plate (fixing damper to cylinder block)

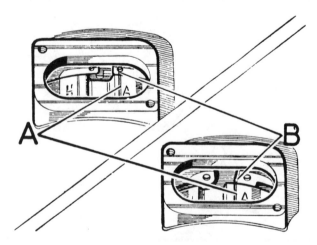

FIG 2:11 Early type pump, timing marks

Key to Fig 2:11 A Mark on pump rotor or circlip straightedge B Scribed mark

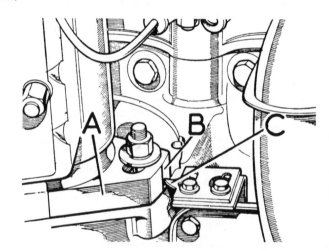

FIG 2:12 Later type pump, timing marks

Key to Fig 2:12 A Flange B Timing mark C Pointer

fully opened No. 1 exhaust valve. Note the indicator reading and mark the chainwheel and timing case at this position. Turn the camshaft further onwards until the indicator again shows the same reading. Make another mark on the chainwheel exactly between the other two marks. This is the place where the valve is fully open. Turn the camshaft back until the centre mark on the wheel is opposite the mark on the timing case.

10 Fit the chain vibration damper, then fit the chain with no slack on the driving side. It may be necessary to remove and reposition the chainwheel to obtain this condition. Do not turn the camshaft; watch the dial indicator as a check.

11 Refit the tensioner assembly and ratchet. Allow the jockey wheel to take up the slack in the chain.

12 Turn the crankshaft back against the direction of rotation half a turn, then slowly turn forwards to the EP mark. Check the dial indicator reading to see that No. 1 exhaust valve is fully open. If not, repeat item 10 by moving the camshaft chainwheel to another spline. When all is well, remove the dial indicator and fit the chainwheel bolt with a new locking tag and tighten up.

13 Replace the oil seal in the timing case cover as described for the $2\frac{1}{4}$ litre petrol engine (see **Chapter 1**), if necessary. Smear a little engine oil on the inner surface of the seal. Using all new joint washers, fit the timing case cover and bolt up evenly.

14 Fit the vibration damper (or crankshaft pulley) and starter dog. Continue to reassemble the engine by reversing the dismantling procedure. For instructions regarding refitting and timing the injection pump see the next section.

2:10 Timing the injection pump

The flywheel is marked with 15 deg. and 16 deg. markings. These give the position at which injection begins. The setting for Series 3 models is 13 deg. BTDC.

Early pumps have internal timing marks (see **FIG 2:11**), while the later type pump has an external mark (see **FIG 2:12**).

The 16 deg. mark is for the early type pump and the 15 or 13 deg. mark is for the later type pump.

Proceed to set the timing with the greatest precision and care possible.

1 Turn the crankshaft forwards until No. 1 piston is ascending on the compression stroke. Turn on slowly and align the appropriate timing mark with the pointer. If the crankshaft is turned too far, do not turn back. Continue turning forwards until No. 1 piston is again on the compression stroke, then again align the mark and pointer. Always look squarely at the pointer so that no errors of vision occur. These can put the timing out by as much as 2 deg.

2 Mesh the driving gear assembly with the camshaft so that the master spline is approximately 20 deg. from the centre line of the engine (front end, see **FIG 2:13**). Lock the split bearing bush in position with the grub screw.

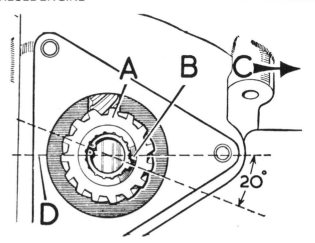

FIG 2:13 Setting the vertical drive gear

Key to Fig 2:13   **A** Drive gear 20 deg. angle to engine centre line   **B** Master spline at **C** Front of engine   **D** Line parallel with engine centre line

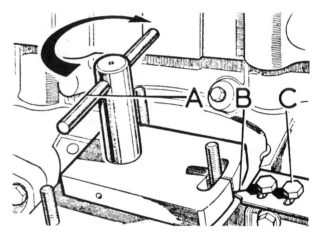

FIG 2:14 Timing gauge

Key to Fig 2:14   **A** Gauge in position   **B** Pointer **C** Bolts retaining pointer

3 Remove the inspection cover on the injection pump (early type) and rotate the spindle in the direction of rotation until the line marked 'A' on the driving plate, lines up with the mark on the timing ring (see **FIG 2:11**).

4 Fit the pump to the engine. With a mirror, look through the pump inspection aperture and make the final adjustment by turning the pump body to align the timing ring with the 'A' mark. While doing this, hold the pump drive plate and thus the skew gear against the drive side of the camshaft gear so that backlash does not upset the positioning.

5 Check the timing by turning the engine forwards until the 'A' mark on the pump driven plate aligns with the mark on the timing ring. If not, repeat the timing operation. Checking by this method will magnify any error. If correct, lock up all the pump fixings and replace the inspection cover.

6 If a later type pump with the external timing mark is being fitted, the special timing gauge part No. 605836 is essential. Set the engine flywheel to the

15 or 13 deg. mark, then insert the drive gear as described earlier and illustrated in **FIG 2 : 13**. Insert the timing gauge, as shown in **FIG 2 : 14** and twist in a clockwise direction to remove any backlash. Hold in this position, slacken the bolts (see **FIG 2 : 14**) and adjust the pointer **B** to align with the mark on the gauge. Tighten the bolts **C**. Remove the gauge and drop the short drive shaft in, locating it on the master spline. Rotate the pump shaft to line up with the master spline on the short drive shaft, then fit the pump to the engine. Rotate the pump body until the timing mark (see **FIG 2 : 12**) lines up with the pointer, then tighten the pump fixings. Check the timing by rotating the engine as described for the earlier type pump.

7 Prime the fuel system (see **Chapter 3B, Section 3B : 4**.

2 : 11 Servicing the oil pump and filters

If low oil pressure is traced to a defective pump, it is best to fit an exchange pump if possible, rather than to attempt to recondition the unit. However, some improvement may be made by fitting new gears if the gear chamber is undamaged.

To remove the pump, drain off the engine oil and remove the sump. Undo the two securing bolts and lower the pump, complete with driving shaft, down and away from the engine. Lift out the driving shaft, unscrew the securing nut and take off the filter gauze assembly (see **Chapter 1, FIG 1 : 45**). Undo the bolts holding the upper casing to the lower body, tap them gently apart and remove the gears. The idler gear spindle may be removed if necessary. Unscrew the relief valve plug and release the spring, plunger and ball.

Wash all the parts in clean petrol and dry off. Assemble the gears in the gear chamber and check the radial clearance between the tips of the gear teeth and the chamber wall. This must not exceed .004 inch (.10 mm). Lay a straightedge across the gear chamber face and measure the end float of the gears with feeler gauges. This should be between .002 and .005 inch (.0508 and .127 mm) for steel gears or .003 and .006in (.0762 and .1524mm) for aluminium gears. If these clearances are exceeded, try fitting new gears. If this does not correct the measurement, a new pump is needed.

To assemble the pump, lubricate the gears and place in the gear chamber, plain portion of the drive gear uppermost. Smear a little Hylomar sealant between the gear chamber face and the upper body, or gasket on later models, and bolt together. Fit the relief valve ball, plunger, spring and plug. Insert the longer end of the splined shaft into the pump and locate in the driving gear.

With the inlet port facing to the rear of the engine, offer the pump and driving shaft up into place and fit and tighten the securing bolts. Fit a new tabwasher and seal to the filter gauze pipe, position the filter square with the sump bottom and tighten the nut. Bend up the tab on the washer.

Refit the sump and refill with oil.

To renew the external oil filter element, place a drip tray beneath the filter housing and unscrew the bolt at the base of the filter housing, on early models, then unscrew the bolt at the base of the filter container.

Withdraw the container and discard the element. Wash the container in petrol, wipe dry, then, on early models, fit new inner and outer sealing rings, or, on later models, the large rubber washer, insert a new element, then replace and bolt up the container.

2 : 12 Removing and replacing the clutch and flywheel

For this operation the engine must either be out of the vehicle or the gearbox must be removed as described in **Chapter 7**. If access to the clutch only is required, it is not necessary to remove the seat base nor completely remove the gearbox: proceed with the gearbox removal but only withdraw the gearbox rearward approximately 5 inch (130 mm).

Mark the clutch coverplate and flywheel so that the plate can be refitted in its correct position on reassembly.

Undo the bolts holding the coverplate to the flywheel, working diametrically opposite each time and easing off the pressure gradually. Lift off the coverplate and driven (friction) plate. Note which way round the driven plate was assembled. The flywheel retaining bolts can now be removed after the locking tags are released and the flywheel will then pull off the dowel and can be lifted clear.

The bush for the primary pinion can be drifted out of the flywheel and a new one pressed in. It must be reamed in position to .878 inch (22.3 mm) on Series 2 and 2A engines. On Series 3 engines it should be reamed to .8755 to .8757 inch (22.237 to 22.242 mm).

If the starter gear teeth on the flywheel are damaged the flywheel will have to be machined, if an early type engine, and a ring gear fitted.

If a later type engine with a shrunk on ring gear, proceed as detailed for the 2¼ litre petrol engine (see **Chapter 1**).

Sometimes the pressure face of the flywheel has become scored. This can be faced off, provided that not more than .03 inch (.76 mm) of metal is removed. On later models, the minimum thickness of the flywheel is 1.455 inch (36.957 mm).

Replace the flywheel, making sure that the crankshaft boss and the flywheel register are clean. Tighten the bolts to 60 to 65 lb ft (8.5 to 9.0 mkg) and lock with new locking tabs. The flywheel should not run out of true by more than .002 inch (.05 mm) measured on the friction face.

Reassemble the clutch by reversing the dismantling process, making sure that the friction plate is centralized and fitted the right way round. Tighten the clutch cover to flywheel bolts to 22 to 25 lb ft (3.0 to 3.5 mkg), working diagonally round to avoid distorting the cover.

2 : 13 The pistons and rods

These can be removed with the engine either in or out of the chassis.

Proceed to gain access to them by removing the sump and cylinder head as described in earlier sections.

Turn the crankshaft until two big-ends are at BDC. Undo the big-end cap nuts and remove the cap. The cap will be numbered on one face to correspond with numbering on the rod. This identifies the crankpin (1 to 4) and shows which way round the caps must be refitted. Push the connecting rod up the bore and extract the piston and rod from the top of the cylinder block. Repeat for the other pistons and rods.

With the piston and rod assembly removed from the engine, remove the gudgeon pin circlips from the piston and push the gudgeon pin out towards the side marked 'X', on early engines, on the piston crown.

Check the fit of the little-end bush on the gudgeon pin. There should be a maximum of .0006 inch (.015 mm) clearance with the pin cold and dry. In practice, the pin should slide in without any perceptible side shake. If renewal of the bush is necessary, press out the old bush by using a vice and a distance piece. The new bush can be pressed in by the same method, making sure that the oil holes are in alignment. Ream the bush carefully to size on a proper jig. There must be no make-shift methods used or the piston will not be in proper alignment with the rod.

Check that the connecting rod or cap has not been filed by bolting the rod and cap together without bearings, then slackening one nut right off. There must be no clearance between the cap and rod at this side.

Check the connecting rod big-end bearing nip by assembling the rod and cap with the bearing shells which it is intended to use. Tighten the bolts, then slacken one nut right off. There should now be a clearance of between .002 and .004 inch (.05 and 1 mm) on early engines or .004 and .008 inch (.10 and .20 mm) on later engines on this side. This can be adjusted by selective assembly of the bearing shells as these are available in slightly varying thicknesses. Do not file the rod or cap.

The pistons must be cleaned of all carbon and oil deposit if it is intended to use them again. Clean the crown thoroughly, paying particular attention to the swirl recess. Remove the piston rings by slipping an old feeler gauge under one end and working the ring over it and onto the land of the piston. Alternatively, a simple three-legged device can be purchased cheaply at any accessory shop which makes this operation easy. Clean all carbon from the ring groove, using a piece of broken ring as a scraper. Do not remove any metal from the piston while doing this.

Examine the piston skirt for heavy marking. If this has occured at top and bottom on opposite sides, suspect a bent connecting rod and check accordingly.

The fit of the piston in the cylinder bore must be checked. In the absence of a more accurate method, insert a long length of .004 inch (.10 mm) feeler gauge stock in the bore and insert the piston as shown in **FIG 2:15**. The piston must be upside down and the gudgeon pin axis must be in line with the crankshaft. If the piston and bore are fit for further service, the piston should become a tight fit when the bottom of the skirt enters the bore.

Check the piston ring gaps by entering each ring in the bore and then square it up by pushing a piston down behind it. Make sure the ring is in an unworn part of the bore when checking. The top ring must have a gap of .014 to .019 inch (.35 to .5 mm), the second and third compression rings .010 to .015 inch (.25 to .4 mm)

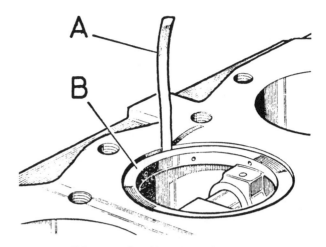

FIG 2:15 Checking piston clearance

Key to Fig 2:15   A Feeler gauge **B** Piston in cylinder bore

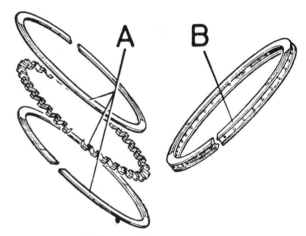

FIG 2:16 Scraper rings

Key to Fig 2:16   A Later type. Fit above gudgeon pin only **B** Early type. Fit above or below gudgeon pin

and the early type one-piece scraper ring should be .010 to .015 inch (.25 to .40 mm). The later three-piece scraper ring gap should be .015 to .045 inch (.4 to 1.14 mm). The side clearance in the groove should lie between .0025 to .0045 inch (.06 to .011 mm) for all rings, except late type scraper rings which must have .0015 to .0025 inch (.04 to .064 mm).

When fitting rings to the piston, make sure that the second and third compression rings are fitted with the side marked 'T' uppermost. The top ring and the scraper can be fitted either way up.

It will be seen that the pistons have a second scraper ring groove at the bottom of the skirt. This is not used.

The later type three-piece scraper ring can be fitted as a replacement for the earlier one-piece ring, but it must never be fitted in the groove below the gudgeon pin. Assemble it to the piston by first winding in one rail followed by the expander with its ends butted in line with the gudgeon pin. Take great care that the ends do not overlap. See that the coloured paint on each end of the expander is visible when the ring is fitted. Fit the second rail, position the rail gaps approximately 1 inch (25.4 mm) to the left of the butted ends of the expander. **FIG 2 : 16** shows the two types of scraper ring.

Check the gudgeon pin fit in the piston. With the pin cold and dry, it should be an interference fit, but capable of being fitted by hand pressure when the piston is warmed. On Series 3 models the gudgeon pin should be a hand fit in the piston at room temperature.

To reassemble the pistons and connecting rods, first fit the rings, correctly gapped as described earlier in this section, then fit the connecting rod to the piston with the oil spray hole in the rod on the same side as the V-shaped swirl recess in the piston crown. Push the gudgeon pin home, on early engines, from the side of the piston marked 'X' and secure with new circlips. Never re-use circlips in pistons. Make sure they have seated in their grooves properly.

Fit a ring compressor to the piston and insert the piston and rod assembly in the cylinder bore from the top face of the block. The swirl recess in the piston crown must face the camshaft side of the engine. Gently tap the piston down through the compressor and into the bore, using a piece of soft wood. Fit the big-end bearing shells and big-end caps and, using new nuts, tighten the nuts to 25 lb ft (3.5 mkg). All components should be lightly lubricated with engine oil before assembly.

Complete the reassembly of the engine by replacing the sump and cylinder head. Refill the sump with engine oil.

2 : 14 *The crankshaft and main bearings*

For attention to these components, the engine must be removed from the vehicle. The cylinder head, sump, timing chain, connecting rods, oil pump, flywheel and clutch must be taken off and the engine secured with the crankshaft uppermost.

To remove the shaft, undo all the bearing cap bolts and remove the caps; make sure that all are properly marked for reassembly. If the bearing shells are likely to be replaced, keep them with their appropriate bearings. Lift out the shaft.

This crankshaft cannot be reconditioned for diesel engines. If the shaft journals are worn oval or scored, a new crankshaft of standard size should be fitted.

Remove the rear oil seal retainer halves from the crankcase and rear main bearing.

Before fitting the new shaft or replacing the old one, make sure that everything is clean and dry. Pay particular attention to the oilways in the shaft. Wash them through with petrol from a good force feed gun and dry off with compressed air.

First check the main bearing nip. Fit the front main bearing cap without shells and torque the bolts to 100 lb ft (13.8 mkg); slacken one side only and check that there is no clearance at the joint face. If there is a clearance, a complete new cylinder block must be fitted. Repeat for the centre and rear main bearing caps. Fit the shells to the crankcase and bearing caps, then bolt up to a torque of 100 lb ft (13.8 mkg). Slacken one bolt right off and with a feeler gauge see that between .004 to .006 inch (.1 to .15 mm) clearance exists between the cap and crankcase on the side which has the slackened bolt. Do

this to each bearing. The clearance can be adjusted by selective assembly of bearing shells as they are available in slightly varying thicknesses.

When the nip has been correctly adjusted, remove the bearing caps and fit new standard size thrust bearings to each side of the centre main bearing. Lay the crankshaft in place, but do not lubricate at this stage.

Refit the bearing caps and shells and bolt up evenly. Check that the crankshaft will turn freely by hand. It should resist rotation when a .0025 inch (.06 mm) shim paper is placed between any bearing shell and crankshaft journal. Plastigage can also be used to measure journal clearances as described in **Chapter 1, Sections 1 : 10** and **1 : 11**. Adjust by selective assembly of bearing shells.

Using a dial indicator, check the crankshaft end float. It should lie between .002 and .006 inch (.05 and .15 mm). If not, fit suitable oversize thrust bearings. Make sure that the crankshaft remains central by not allowing the variation in thrust bearing thickness at either side to exceed .003 inch (.07 mm). Remove the crankshaft. The rear main bearing oil seal is fitted in exactly the same way as the seal for the $2\frac{1}{4}$ litre three main bearing petrol engine. Refer to **Chapter 1** for details.

Tighten the bearing bolts hand tight and rotate the shaft to make sure it is free. If correct, then proceed to pull the bolts on all the main bearings up to 100 lb ft (13.8 mkg) gently and evenly, rotating the shaft from time to time to check for freedom of movement.

When the engine has run for a while, oil leakage can sometimes occur past the neoprene seals in the sides of the rear main bearing cap. To avoid having to strip the engine completely, remove the sump and, with a square section drift, ram the neoprene seals up in their grooves as far as they will go. Insert a short piece of seal in each groove, leaving the new piece protruding below the cap face by $\frac{1}{32}$ inch (.8 mm). Replace the sump and pull the sump bolts up tight.

2 : 15 *Reassembling a stripped engine*

All dismantling and reassembly operations have been given in preceding sections, so it is simply a matter of taking the various operations in the proper sequence. Before starting work, a complete set of gaskets, special washers, circlips, splitpins and locking tags must be obtained. Never attempt to replace any of these items once used. Make sure that all oilways are clear and clean and have their running surfaces lubricated with engine oil as assembly proceeds.

Commence by fitting the crankshaft, connecting rods, pistons and flywheel. It is necessary to fit the flywheel at this stage as the markings on its periphery will be needed to time the camshaft and injection pump. Fit the camshaft and the oil pump, then bolt the sump on. Turn the engine right way up and fit the tappets, then the cylinder head, pushrods and rocker gear. Time the camshaft and fit the chain, tensioner and rocker gear. Replace the water pump and timing cover. Press the pulley on to the crankshaft and lock with the starter dog. Fit the clutch and injection pump.

The engine can now be replaced in the vehicle and the thermostat, water pump, generator/alternator, heater plugs, injectors and piping added. Replace the rocker cover after the tappet clearances have been set.

2:16 *Fault diagnosis*

(a) Engine will not start

1 Incorrect starting procedure
2 Starter motor defective
3 Batteries discharged
4 Heater plug circuit broken
5 Foreign matter in fuel system
6 Supply of fuel to injectors restricted
7 Insufficient compression
8 Injector setting incorrect
9 Injector auxiliary spray hole blocked

(b) Engine stalls

1 Slow-running incorrectly adjusted
2 Incorrect tappet clearance
3 Injector setting incorrect
4 Injector auxiliary spray hole blocked
5 Insufficient compression

(c) Reduced power and rough running

1 Broken valve spring
2 Incorrect tappet clearance
3 Burnt valve
4 Broken piston rings
5 Uneven compression

6 Injectors burnt, nozzle valve not seating
7 Incorrectly timed injection pump
8 Fuel supply restricted
9 Injectors loose in cylinder head
10 Fuel pump delivery insufficient

(d) Engine overheats

1 Defective cooling system
2 Defective lubrication system
3 Defective injectors
4 Incorrect injection pump timing
5 Restricted fuel supply

(e) Low oil pressure

1 Defective pump
2 Relief valve not seating
3 Worn bearings
4 Wrong grade or insufficient oil

(f) Black smoke from exhaust

1 Defective injector
2 Injection pump wrongly timed

(g) White vapour from exhaust (hot engine)

1 Coolant leaking into combustion chamber

NOTES

CHAPTER 3A

THE PETROL FUEL SYSTEM

3A:1 Description

Four types of carburetter are fitted to the petrol engined vehicles described in this book. The $2\frac{1}{4}$ litre engines are fitted with either a Solex or Zenith type, the 2.6 litre models have the Stromberg or SU and the 3.5 litre has a twin Zenith-Stromberg installation. Reference to the illustrations in this chapter will make clear the type of carburetter with which a particular vehicle is equipped. The $2\frac{1}{4}$ litre engines have a mechanical fuel pump and the 2.6 litre and 3.5 litre have an electric pump. The fuel filter is incorporated in the design of the mechanical pump, but the double entry electric pump feeds a separate filter in the engine compartment as does the later electric pump which also incorporates a renewable filter in the body: this pump cannot be dismantled except for cleaning the filter.

3A:2 The fuel pumps and filters

(a) Mechanical:

In this section refer to **FIG 3A:1**, noting particularly that components for the early and later type pumps are shown.

To dismantle the pump, proceed as follows:

1 Undo the retainer 11 and remove the sediment bowl 10, gasket 9 and filter 8.

2 Mark the top and bottom halves of the body, then undo the screws 2 and separate the parts.

3 Remove the valve retainer 6 and pull out the valves 5. **Particularly note which way up each one is fitted.** On later models the valves are staked into the body. Scrape away the staking to remove the valves.

4 Ease the diaphragm 12 from the rim of the lower body, then depress it slightly in the centre and turn either way through 90 deg. when it will be pushed clear by spring 13.

5 Prise out the oil seals 14, 15 or 27, 28.

6 To release the rocker arm 24, remove pin 21 or 30. The later pin is held by the retainers 31.

Inspect all parts carefully and wash in clean fuel. Obtain a service kit and renew the diaphragm, oil seals and sediment bowl gasket. If the valves are suspect, these should also be replaced.

To rebuild the pump, carry out the following operations:

1 Replace the rocker arm and pivot pin. If a late type pump, peen the retainers into the pump body.

2 Fit new oil seals and peen the housing flange over the retainer in at least three places.

3 Hold the pump body with the rocker arm downwards and the diaphragm return spring in place. Position the diaphragm over the spring with the flattened end of its rod in line with the slot in the link. Push downwards, then turn to engage with the link.

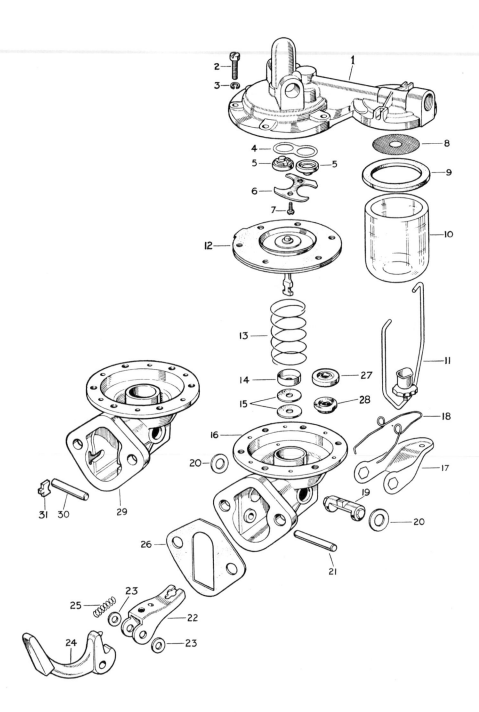

FIG 3A : 1   Mechanical fuel pump

Key to Fig 3A : 1   1 Top cover   2 Securing screws   3 Spring washer   4 Valve gasket   5 Valves   6 Retainer for valves
7 Screw for retainer   8 Gauze filter disc   9 Cork sealing gasket   10 Sediment bowl   11 Bowl retainer   12 Diaphragm
assembly   13 Diaphragm spring   14 Oil seal retainer, early type   15 Sealing washers, early type   16 Pump body, early type
17 Hand priming lever   18 Return spring for hand lever   19 Hand rocker   20 Cork washers   21 Rocker arm pivot pin, early type
22 Operating link   23 Plain washers   24 Rocker arm   25 Return spring   26 Joint washer   27 Oil seal retainer, latest type
28 Oil seal, latest type   29 Pump body, latest type   30 Rocker arm pivot pin, latest type   31 Retainer for pivot pin, latest type

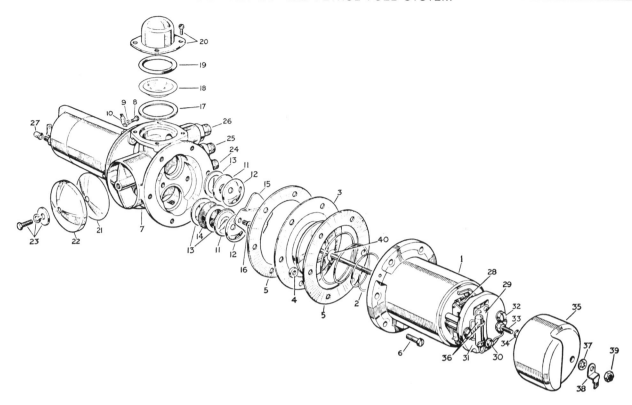

FIG 3A:2 Electric fuel pump

Key to Fig 3A:2   1 Magnet housing   2 Spring for armature   3 Diaphragm   4 Roller   5 Joint washer
6 Securing screw, body to housing   7 Body   8 Special screw (earth connection)   9 Spring washer (earth connection)
10 Lucar blade (earth connection)   11 Melinex valve assembly   12 Valve cap   13 Sealing washer   14 Fuel filter
15 Clamp plate   16 Clamp plate screws   17 Sealing ring for outlet air bottle   18 Diaphragm for outlet air bottle   19 Rubber
sealing ring   20 Outlet air bottle, dome and screw   21 Joint washer for inlet air bottle   22 Cover for inlet air bottle
23 Securing screw and washers   24 Union, main fuel supply   25 Union, main fuel supply   26 Union for outlet pipe
27 Nylon protection cap   28 Contacts rocker assembly   29 Spring blade contact   30 Anchor screw   31 Moulded endplate
32 Retaining screw for endplate   33 Terminal screw   34 Composition washer   35 End cover   36 Condenser and clip
37 Shakeproof washer   38 Lucar blade   39 Nut   40 Impact washer for armature

4 Replace the valves

5 Put the top cover over the lower body, aligning the marks made when dismantling. Fit the screws but do not tighten. By means of the priming lever, depress the diaphragm fully, now tighten all the screws. If this is properly done, the diaphragm edges will be flush with the pump joint faces. If not, slacken the screws and repeat the operation.

6 Replace the filter and sediment bowl, using the new gasket. Do not overtighten the retainer nut.

To test the pump, immerse it in a bath of clean paraffin and operate the rocker arm several times. Empty the pump, then place a finger over the inlet port. Operate the rocker arm again for several strokes, then remove the finger. A distinct suction sound should be heard. Repeat for the outlet side. This time, air pressure should be felt for 2 or 3 seconds after the rocker arm has stopped operating. Again hold the finger over the outlet and build up pressure; immerse the pump in the paraffin and look for air bubbles round the diaphragm joint.

(b) Electric, double entry:

In this section refer to **FIG 3A:2**; both ends of the pump are similar so the overhaul instructions apply to each.

To dismantle this pump, proceed as follows:

1 Remove the end cover 35.

2 Mark the magnet housing 1 and body 7, then remove the screws 6 and gently pull the components apart.

3 Unscrew the diaphragm 3 in an anticlockwise direction, taking care not to lose the eleven rollers 4.

4 Remove the diaphragm complete with spring and gaskets.

5 Remove the contact 29, then the terminal screw 33 and nut.

6 Remove the endplate 31 and capacitor (condenser) 36.

7 Remove the contact pivot pin from the mechanism.

8 Remove the lead washer and terminal screw from the end cover. If the main body and valves require attention, continue as follows:

9 Remove the outlet air bottle dome 20 and items 17, 18 and 19, keeping them in order for reassembly.

10 Remove items 23, 22 and 21 from the inlet air bottle.

11 Remove the clamp plate 15 and gently ease out the valve assemblies, keeping them carefully in order for reassembly.

Inspect all components for damage and renew all diaphragms, gaskets and, if necessary, the contact points. If these latter items are burnt, suspect that the capacitor has broken down and renew it.

Proceed to reassemble the pump as follows:

1 Fit a new joint washer 21, then secure the dome 22 with screw 23.
2 Fit a new diaphragm 18 and secure with items 17, 19 and dome 20.
3 Replace the valves in the order shown in **FIG 3A : 3** and in the location shown in **FIG 3A : 4**.
4 Fit the contact assembly to the endplate using a new lead washer. Replace the components in the reverse order to dismantling.
5 Fit the spring 2 (see **FIG 3A : 2**), large end towards the diaphragm as illustrated. Fit the impact washer 40.

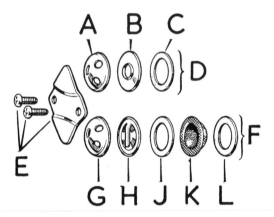

FIG 3A : 3   Order of valve component assembly

Key to Fig 3A : 3   **A** Retaining cap   **B** Disc valve
C Cork washer   **D** Outlet valve assembly
E Clamp plate and screw   **F** Inlet valve assembly
G Retaining cap   **H** Disc valve   **J** Cork washer
K Filter   **L** Cork washer

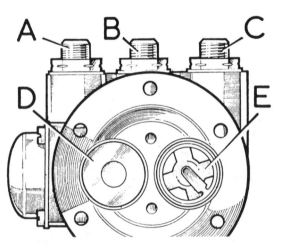

FIG 3A : 4   Location of valves

Key to Fig 3A : 4   **A** Outlet   **B** Righthand inlet
C Lefthand inlet   **D** Outlet valve   **E** Inlet valve

FIG 3A : 5   Checking contacts

Key to Fig 3A : 5   **A** Contact blade   **B** Gauges, .030 inch (.75 mm) minimum clearance

6 Screw the diaphragm assembly 3 into position by not more than six turns, then fit the eleven rollers around the armature.
7 Hold the assembly horizontally in the left hand, then push the armature in firmly with the right hand. If the contact breaker throws over, screw the armature (diaphragm) in until it just fails to do so, then unscrew one-sixth of a turn at a time until it will just throw over. Do not jerk the assembly. Now unscrew a further two-thirds of a turn.
8 Replace the assembly on the pump body but do not tighten the screws yet. Hold the points in contact, then insert a matchstick under one of the white fibre rollers. Now pass a current through the pump; this will actuate the armature and stretch the diaphragm. While in this condition, tighten the screws.
9 Hold the contact blade against the pedestal and bend the blade until a .030 inch (.75 mm) feeler will slide between the contact stops as illustrated in **FIG 3A : 5**. Refit the cover.

To test the pump, see that it will lift fuel (either petrol or paraffin) 3 feet from a supply tank, priming itself promptly. Block the outlet; the action should cease for at least 15 seconds.

(c) Electric, single entry:

1 Disconnect the fuel inlet pipe from the pump and blank the end of the pipe.
2 Release the end cover from the bayonet fixing, using a suitable spanner.
3 Withdraw the filter and clean by using a compressed air jet from the inside of the filter.
4 Remove and clean the magnet in the end cover.
5 Replace the magnet in the centre of the end cover and reassemble in the reverse order of dismantling, using a new gasket for the end cover if necessary.

(d) Main filter element:

1 Unscrew the centre bolt and withdraw the filter bowl.

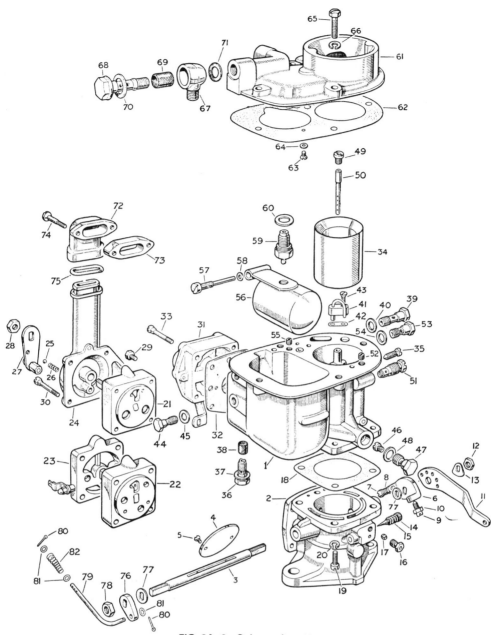

FIG 3A : 6 Solex carburetter

Key to Fig 3A : 6   1 Carburetter body   2 Throttle chamber   3 Spindle for throttle   4 Butterfly for throttle
5 Special screw fixing butterfly   6 Throttle abutment plate   7 Special screw for slow-running adjustment   8 Spring for
slow-running adjustment   9 Special screw for throttle stop   10 Locknut for throttle stop   11 Throttle lever   12 Nut fixing
throttle lever   13 Lockwasher for nut   14 Special screw for mixture control   15 Spring for mixture control   16 Screwed union
for suction pipe   17 Olive for suction pipe   18 Joint washer for throttle chamber   19, 20 Fixing chamber to carburetter body
21 Starter body and valve, without starter heater element   22 Starter body and valve complete, with starter heater element
23 Heater element for starter   24 Cover for starter   25 Ball for starter valve   26 Spring for starter valve   27 Lever for starter
28 Nut fixing starter lever   29 Special bolt fixing starter cable   30 Special screw fixing starter body   31 Accelerator pump
complete   32 Joint washer for pump   33 Special screw fixing pump   34 Choke tube   35 Special screw fixing choke tube
36 Non-return valve   37 Fibre washer for valve   38 Filter gauze for non-return valve   39 Jet, accelerator pump
40 Fibre washer for jet   41 Pump injector   42 Joint washer for pump injector   43 Special screw fixing injector
44 Economy jet (blank)   45 Joint washer for blank jet   46 Main jet   47 Main jet carrier   48 Fibre washer for carrier
49 Correction jet   50 Emulsion tube   51 Pilot jet   52 Jet air bleed   53 Starter jet, petrol   54 Fibre washer for jet
55 Economy jet   56 Float   57 Spindle for float   58 Copper washer for spindle   59 Needle valve complete
60 Fibre washer for valve   61 Top cover for carburetter   62 Joint washer for top cover   63, 64 Joint washer to top cover
fixings   65, 66 Top cover to body fixings   67 Banjo union   68 Special bolt for union   69 Filter gauze for union
70 Large fibre washer   71 Small fibre washer   72 Elbow for top cover   73 Distance piece, elbow to top cover
74 Screw fixing elbow to top cover   75 Rubber sealing washer, elbow to starter cover   76 Lever for accelerator pump rod
77 Special washer for lever   78 Nut fixing lever to spindle   79 Control rod for accelerator pump   80 Splitpin for
control rod   81 Plain washer for control rod   82 Spring for control rod

3A:3 *The carburetters*

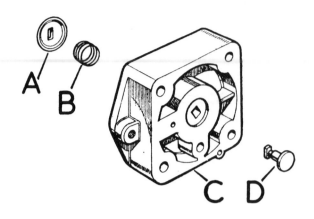

FIG 3A:7 Pump body assembly

Key to Fig 3A:7 A Economy valve washer **B** Valve spring
C Body **D** Valve

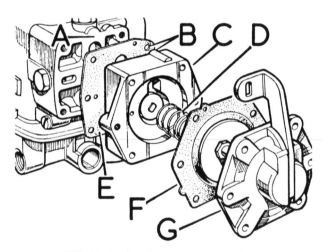

FIG 3A:8 Accelerator pump complete

Key to Fig 3A:8   **A** Carburetter body
B Location peg and hole for pump body to gasket
C Pump body   **D** Pump spring   **E** Pump body gasket
F Pump membrane assembly   **G** Top pump cover

2 Remove the small sealing ring and discard the element.
3 Withdraw the large sealing ring from the underside of the filter body.
4 Reassemble using new sealing rings and a new element with the small hole downwards.

(e) In-line filter:

1 Disconnect the fuel pipes from each end.
2 Slacken the clip and withdraw the unit.
3 Fit the new filter with the end marked 'IN' towards the fuel pump, using the nuts and olives supplied. If the filter is marked with an arrow, the filter must be fitted with the arrow pointing away from the pump.

(a) 2¼ litre engine, Solex carburetter:

In this section refer to **FIG 3A:6**.

To dismantle the carburetter, remove components in the following order:
1 Detach the cover 61, removing elbow 72 if necessary.
2 Remove the joint washer 62.
3 Unscrew the valve 59 and remove complete with washer 60.
4 Remove the screw 14, then detach chamber 2 from body 1. Remove gasket 18.
5 Make light marks on the throttle butterfly and choke wall, then remove the two screws from the spindle, remove the butterfly and withdraw the throttle spindle.
6 Remove screws 30 and detach the starter unit. Note that this may or may not have the heater assembly 23 fitted.
7 Remove the float 56 from the body, then items 41, 34, 49, 50, 39, 53, 51, 36 and 47 in that order.
8 Detach the accelerator pump by removing the screws 33.

Inspect all parts for damage, particularly the throttle spindle bore for ovality and the float for punctures. If either of these are found, renew the parts concerned. Do not clean out any jets or fuel passages with wire or metal tools. Nothing more than an air jet should be necessary. Examine the accelerator pump diaphragm for pin holes and renew if any are present. Use all new seals and gaskets when rebuilding.

Rebuilding the carburetter:

This is a reversal of the dismantling procedure, but refer to **FIG 3A:7** to see that the economy valve is held in place by turning washer **A** through 90 deg. **FIG 3A:8** shows the complete accelerator pump assembly. When replacing the butterfly, see that the marks made when dismantling are in alignment.

Tuning the carburetter for slow-running:

1 Set the mixture control screw one and a half turns from fully in.
2 Screw the slow-running throttle stop screw one turn further in after contacting the abutment.
3 Run the engine up to normal temperature, then adjust the mixture control screw to give even idling. Adjust the slow-running screw to give an engine idling speed of 500 rev/min. Do not try to make the engine idle at a lower speed as stalling on acceleration is almost certain to occur.

(b) 2¼ litre engine, Zenith carburetter:

In this section refer to **FIG 3A:9**.

This carburetter operates on very similar principles to the Solex previously described. The main difference lies in the starting arrangements. The Solex had a separate starting carburetter, sometimes fitted with a heater, whereas the Zenith relies on a simple strangler valve in the air intake to induce a rich mixture.

To dismantle the carburetter, undo the screws 43 and 44 holding the top cover 36 to the body 1 and lift off the

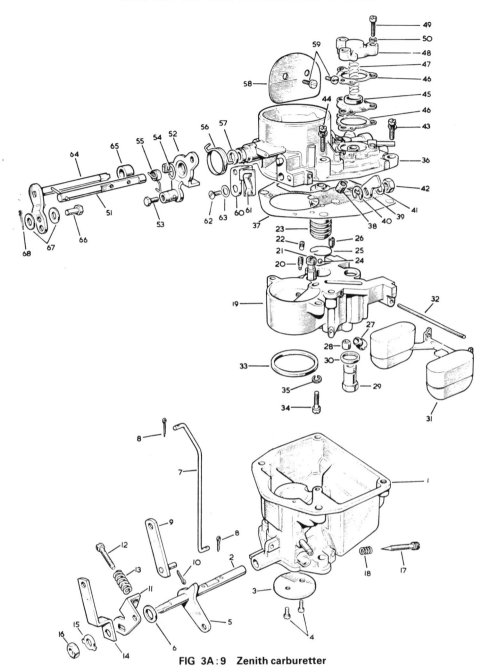

FIG 3A:9   Zenith carburetter

Key to Fig 3A:9   1 Carburetter main body   2 Throttle spindle   3 Butterfly for throttle   4 Special screw fixing butterfly
5 Floating lever on throttle spindle   6 Plain washer on spindle for floating lever   7 Interconnecting link, throttle to choke
8 Splitpin fixing link to levers   9 Relay lever, throttle to accelerator pump   10 Splitpin fixing relay lever to floating lever
11 Throttle stop and fast-idle lever   12 Special screw for throttle stop   13 Spring for throttle stop   14 Throttle lever
15 Lockwasher for throttle levers   16 Special nut for throttle levers   17 Volume control screw   18 Spring for control screw
19 Emulsion block   20 Pump jet   21 Pump discharge valve   22 Plug for pump jet   23 Piston for accelerator pump
24 Ball for piston   25 Circlip for piston   26 Slow-running jet   27 Main jet   28 Enrichment jet   29 Needle valve
30 Special washer (2 mm)   31 Float   32 Spindle for float   33 O-ring, emulsion block to body   34 Special screw (fixing
emulsion block to body)   35 Spring washer (fixing emulsion block to body)   36 Top cover for carburetter   37 Gasket for top cover
38 Ventilation screw (3.0) for choke   39 Internal pump lever   40 Retaining ring for pump lever   41 Shakeproof washer
(fixing pump lever)   42 Special nut (fixing pump lever)   43 Screw and spring washer, short (fixing top cover to main body)
44 Screw and spring washer, long (fixing top cover to main body)   45 Diaphragm for carburetter   46 Gasket for diaphragm
47 Spring for diaphragm   48 Cover for diaphragm   49 Screw (fixing diaphragm cover)   50 Spring washer (fixing diaphragm
cover)   51 Spindle and pin for choke lever   52 Lever and swivel for choke   53 Screw for choke lever swivel
54 Circlip fixing choke lever to top cover   55 Small spring for choke lever   56 Large spring for choke lever   57 Plain washer
for choke spindle   58 Butterfly for choke   59 Special screw fixing butterfly   60 Bracket and clip for choke cable
61 Clip for choke bracket   62 Special screw (fixing choke bracket to top cover)   63 Shakeproof washer (fixing choke bracket to
top cover)   64 Spindle and lever for accelerator pump   65 Spacing washer for pump spindle   66 Pin (fixing relay lever
to pump lever)   67 Plain washer (fixing relay lever to pump lever)   68 Splitpin (fixing relay lever to pump lever)

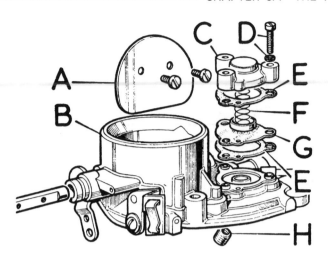

FIG 3A:10   Top cover details

Key to Fig 3A:10
B Carburetter top cover   C Economy valve diaphragm cover
D Diaphragm cover fixings   E Diaphragm gaskets
F Diaphragm spring   G Diaphragm assembly
H Ventilation jet
A Choke butterfly disc

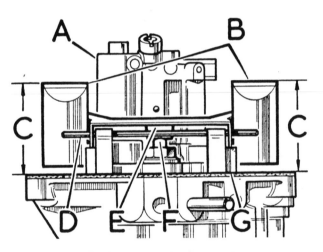

FIG 3A:11   Checking float setting

Key to Fig 3A:11
B Highest points on floats
(33 mm)   D Hinge pin
F Needle valve   G Gasket
A Emulsion block
C Dimension to be 1⅛ inch
E Central tongue on float carrier

top cover. Detach the emulsion block 19 from the top cover, being careful not to drop the accelerator pump assembly. Lift off the float assembly. If the throttle butterfly 3 or strangler valve 58 are to be removed, mark them as described for the Solex carburetter. Pay particular attention to the economy valve assembly on the top of the cover. This is released when screws 49 are removed. Do not stretch or damage the spring 47. Note that at the base of the accelerator pump bore is a ball valve retained by a circlip. It is not necessary to remove this.

Clean and inspect all parts as described for the Solex carburetter, noting the warning against poking metal objects through jets or fuel passages. Particularly carefully inspect the economy diaphragm 45 and its gaskets 46. If the diaphragm has the slightest pinhole or the gaskets are cracked, a mysterious and annoying flat spot will appear whenever the throttle is opened, which can become bad enough to stall the engine. It is a wise plan to replace this diaphragm whenever the carburetter is given a major service.

Rebuilding the carburetter:

Use all new gaskets and seals, being careful to position the O-ring 33 in the emulsion block 19 correctly. Proceed by reversing the dismantling process, making sure that the butterfly valves are aligned with the marks made when dismantling. See that the economy valve diaphragm and gaskets have the air hole aligned with the hole in the carburetter cover. **FIG 3A:10** shows the assembly in detail. Set the float level as follows: position the float assembly and emulsion block on the top cover held upside down as shown in **FIG 3A:11**. The dimension **C** must be adjusted by bending the tongue **E**, not by altering the float carrier arms. Check the fast-idle interconnection by closing the strangler valve (58 in **FIG 3A:9**) fully and then seeing if a .040 inch (1.25 mm) diameter drill can just pass between the throttle butterfly edge 3 and the choke tube. Bend link 7 until this condition exists. On Series 3 models, use a .055 inch (1.40 mm) drill for this test.

Tuning the carburetter for slow-running (basic carburetter only):

Adopt the methods recommended for the Solex carburetter, i.e. adjustment of the throttle stop screw and mixture control screw.

(c) 2.6 litre engine, Stromberg carburetter (Zenith type 175CD2S):

In this section refer to **FIG 3A:12**.

This carburetter operates on very different principles from those described so far. It is known as a variable choke device since the manifold depression controls the position of the air valve and fuel metering needle.

To dismantle this carburetter, first remove the damper 3, top cap 1, spring 12 and diaphragm air valve assembly 8, 9 and 10. If necessary, undo screw 17 and pull out needle 16. Undo the screws 61 and 62 and lift off the float chamber 59. Unscrew the jet assembly from the body. This assembly consists of items 47 to 56 inclusive. These can be dismantled for cleaning if necessary. Remove the float. Detach the throttle butterfly 20 and the cold start unit, items 35 to 46. **Do not** remove the discs from the spindle 35.

Clean and examine all components, being careful to use only clean rag to clean the diaphragm. See that the float is not punctured and that the throttle spindle bores are not worn oval.

To rebuild the carburetter, commence with the cold start assembly, position the components as shown in **FIG 3A:13** and assemble to the carburetter body, then fit the butterfly. Note the position of the throttle control return spring, shown as **A** in **FIG 3A:14**. Continue by

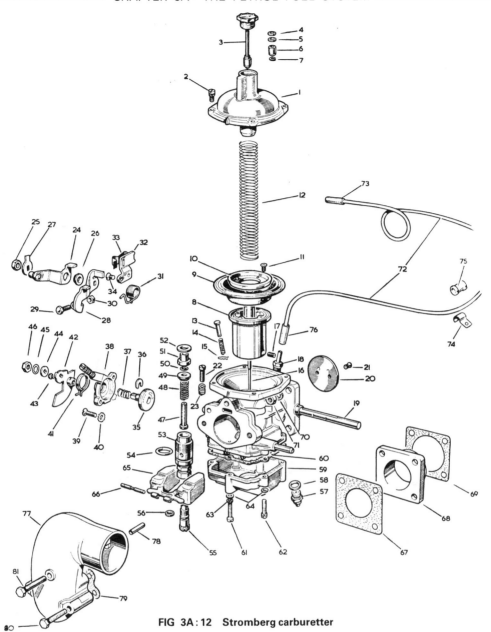

FIG 3A : 12   Stromberg carburetter

Key to Fig 3A : 12   1 Top cover for carburetter   2 Special screw and washer fixing top cover   3 Damper and oil cap assembly
4 Special washer, upper   5 Special washer, lower   6 Bush for damper   7 Retaining ring, for damper   8 Air valve,
shaft and diaphragm assembly   9 Diaphragm   10 Retaining ring for diaphragm   11 Special screw fixing retaining ring
12 Return spring for air valve   13 Lifting pin for air valve   14 Spring for lifting pin   15 Spring clip for lifting pin
16 Metering needle   17 Locking screw for metering needle   18 Ignition adaptor   19 Throttle spindle   20 Butterfly for throttle
21 Special screw fixing butterfly   22 Throttle stop screw   23 Spring for stop screw   24 Throttle lever   25 Special nut
(fixing throttle levers)   26 Special washer (fixing throttle levers)   27 Tabwasher (fixing throttle levers)
28 Throttle stop and fast-idle screw   29 Special screw for throttle stop   30 Locknut for throttle stop   31 Throttle return spring
32 Bracket and clip for choke cable   33 Clip for choke bracket   34 Special screw fixing choke bracket   35 Cold start spindle
36 Special washer for starter spindle   37 Cold start spring   38 Cover for cold start   39 Special screw (fixing cover)
40 Shakeproof washer (fixing cover)   41 Return spring for cam lever   42 Cam lever for cold start
43 Clamping screw for cam lever swivel   44 Spacing washer (fixing cam lever to cold start spindle)   45 Shakeproof washer
(fixing cam lever to cold start spindle)   46 Special nut (fixing cam lever to cold start spindle)   47 Jet orifice
48 Spring for jet orifice   49 Guide bush for jet orifice   50 O-ring for jet orifice   51 Bush for jet orifice
52 Special washer for jet orifice   53 Carrier for jet orifice   54 O-ring for carrier   55 Adjusting screw for jet orifice
56 O-ring for adjusting screw   57 Needle valve   58 Washer for needle valve   59 Float chamber   60 Gasket for float chamber
61 Special screw, long (fixing float chamber) 62 Special screw, short (fixing float chamber) 63 Plain washer (fixing float chamber)
64 Plain washer (fixing float chamber)   65 Float and arm   66 Spindle for float   67 Joint washer for carburetter
68 Adaptor for carburetter   69 Joint washer for adaptor   70 Spring washer (fixing carburetter and adaptor to cylinder head)
71 Nut ($\frac{5}{16}$ inch UNF) (fixing carburetter and adaptor to cylinder head)   72 Suction pipe, carburetter to distributor
73 Rubber sleeve, suction pipe to adaptor   74 Clip for suction pipe (on engine)   75 Rubber grommet for clip (on engine)
76 Rubber sleeve, suction pipe to carburetter   77 Air inlet elbow assembly   78 Adaptor for top breather hose
79 Joint washer for inlet elbow   80 Setbolt ($\frac{5}{16}$ inch UNC x $2\frac{1}{2}$ inch long) (fixing elbow to carburetter)   81 Setbolt ($\frac{5}{16}$ inch
UNC x 3 inch long) (fixing elbow to carburetter)

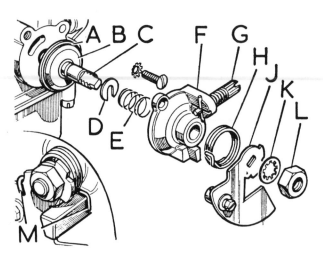

FIG 3A : 13   Cold start assembly

Key to Fig 3A : 13   A Cold start outer disc   **B** Cold start inner disc   **C** Cold start spindle   **D** Spring retaining clip **E** Cold start spring   **F** Cover for cold start   **G** Clamping screw for cam lever swivel   **H** Return spring for cam lever **J** Cam lever for cold start   **K** Shakeproof washer **L** Locknut   **M** Return spring location

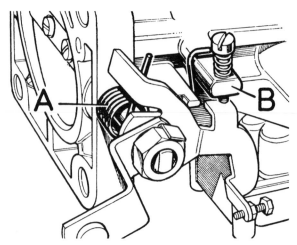

FIG 3A : 14   Throttle return spring position

Key to Fig 3A : 14   A Return spring   **B** Carburetter body

assembling the float chamber, checking the float position as illustrated in **FIG 3A : 15**. Fit new O-rings to the jet components and assemble in the order shown in **FIG 3A : 16**. Assemble the diaphragm to the air valve and fit the metering needle with its shoulder level with the surface of the air valve. Assemble the air valve very carefully to the carburetter body, ensuring that the metering needle enters the jet orifice. If necessary, unclamp the jet assembly to allow the needle to enter easily. The jet must now be centralized with the needle.

Proceed as follows :

Fit the air valve return spring and carburetter top cover and tighten the screws. See that the air valve moves easily.

Lift the air valve fully and tighten the jet assembly fully, then slacken off half a turn.

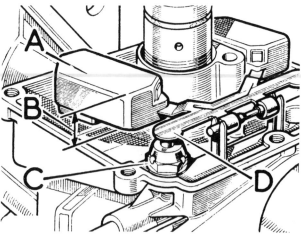

FIG 3A : 15   Float level adjustment

Key to Fig 3A : 15   **A** Float   **B** Needle valve **C** $\frac{5}{8}$ inch (16 mm)   **D** Tag

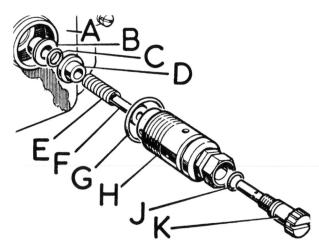

FIG 3A : 16   Jet assembly

Key to Fig 3A : 16   **A** Carburetter body, throttle orifice **B** Bushing for jet orifice   **C** O-ring for bushing for jet orifice **D** Guide bush   **E** Spring for jet orifice   **F** Jet orifice **G** O-ring for jet carrier   **H** Carrier for jet orifice **J** O-ring for jet orifice   **K** Adjusting screw for jet orifice

Allow the air valve to fall; the needle will enter the orifice and thus centralize it. If necessary, gently push the air valve down by inserting a pencil in the dashpot at the top of the cover. Slowly tighten the jet assembly, checking all the time that the air valve falls freely by raising it a $\frac{1}{4}$ inch (6 mm) and releasing it. It must drop firmly onto the bridge. When all is well, fill up the dashpot with SAE.20 engine oil to within a $\frac{1}{4}$ inch (6 mm) of the rod in which the damper operates.

Fit and secure the damper assembly.

Tuning the carburetter for slow-running (basic carburetter only) :

1 Remove the air cleaner and the damper assembly (see **FIG 3A : 12**, item 3).

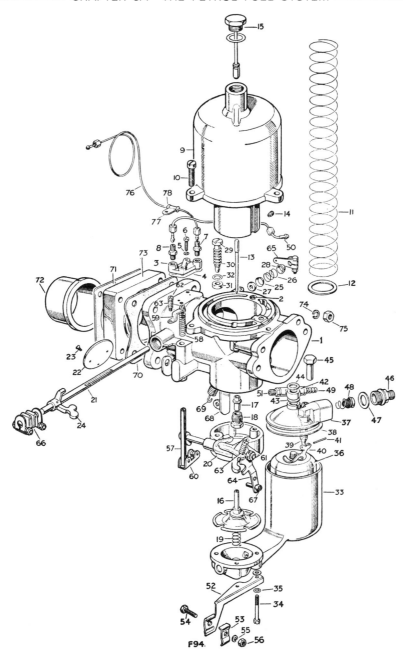

FIG 3A:17 SU carburetter

Key to Fig 3A:17   1 Carburetter body   3 Adaptor, ignition and weakening device   4 Gasket for adaptor
5 Shakeproof washer (fixing adaptor)   6 Screw (fixing adaptor)   7 Union for ignition pipe   8 Union for economizer pipe
9 Suction chamber and piston complete   10 Special screw fixing suction chamber   11 Spring for piston (yellow)
12 Thrust washer for suction chamber   13 Needle, SS   14 Special screw fixing needle   15 Oil cap complete   16 Jet complete
17 Jet bearing   18 Jet screw   19 Jet spring   20 Jet housing complete   21 Throttle spindle   22 Throttle butterfly
23 Screw for throttle butterfly   24 Throttle stop   25 Gland washer for throttle spindle, brass   26 Spring for throttle spindle gland
27 Gland washer for throttle spindle, langite   28 Retainer cap for gland washer   29 Slow-running adjusting valve
30 Gland spring for slow-running   31 Gland washer for slow-running, rubber   32 Brass washer for slow-running
33 Float chamber   34 Bolt (fixing float chamber)   35 Shakeproof washer (float chamber)   36 Float (fixing float chamber)
37 Lid for float chamber   38 Joint washer for float chamber lid   39 Needle valve and seat   40 Lever for float   41 Pin for lever
42 Banjo (on float chamber)   43 Fibre washer for banjo (on float chamber)   44 Aluminium washer for banjo (on float chamber)
45 Cap nut fixing banjo (on float chamber)   46 Double-ended union for carburetter   47 Washer for union
48 Filter and spring for carburetter body   49 Economizer union for rubber tube   50 Pipe for economizer   51 Union for
economizer pipe   52 Choke bracket   57 Sliding rod, roller and cam shoe   58 Spring for sliding rod   59 Top plate
61 Bottom stop screw   62 Top stop screw   63 Spring for stop screw   64 Cold start lever   65 Lever for throttle return spring
68 Bracket for throttle return spring   69 Throttle return spring   70 Joint washer for carburetter   71 Joint washer for
distance piece   72 Liner for manifold   73 Distance piece for carburetter   74 Spring washer (fixing carburetter and distance
piece to cylinder head)   75 Nut ($\frac{5}{16}$ inch UNF) (fixing carburetter and distance piece to cylinder head)   76 Suction pipe,
complete   77 Clip for suction pipe on engine   78 Rubber grommet for clip on engine

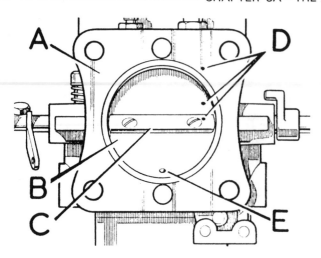

FIG 3A:18 Alignment marking of butterfly

Key to Fig 3A:18   **A** Body   **B** Butterfly   **C** Spindle
D Marks   **E** Hole in butterfly

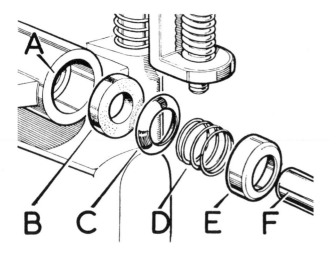

FIG 3A:19 Spindle gland

Key to Fig 3A:19   **A** Body   **B** Langite gland washer
C Brass gland washer   **D** Spring   **E** Retainer
F Spindle

2 Hold the air valve 8 down on the bridge in the throttle bore.

3 Screw up the jet adjustment screw 55 until the jet 47 contacts the air valve. Turn the screw back three turns.

4 Run the engine up to operating temperature, then adjust the throttle stop screw 22 until the engine idles at 500 rev/min. Adjust the jet screw 55 until the engine speed and note is smooth and regular.

5 To check the setting, lift the air valve 8, by $\frac{1}{32}$ inch (.8 mm). If the engine speeds up, the mixture is too rich; if it stops, too weak. When correct, the speed will remain constant or fall very slightly. To enrich the mixture, unscrew the jet screw 55; to weaken it, screw the screw into the body.

6 When the adjustment is correct, replace the damper and air cleaner.

7 The fast-idle (choke) adjustment is made by operating the choke fully and adjusting screw 29 in lever 28 until the engine runs at 1000 to 1200 rev/min. Push the choke in and check that screw 29 now clears lever 42.

(d) 2.6 litre engine, SU carburetter:

In this section refer to **FIG 3A:17**.

This carburetter operates on a similar principle to the Stromberg in that variations in manifold depression raise and lower the air valve and fuel metering needle. The same care must be taken to centralize the jet.

To dismantle the carburetter, remove oil cap and damper rod 15, then undo screws 10 and remove the suction chamber and piston 9 as a unit. Gently ease the piston from the chamber and remove spring 11 and washer 12.

Slacken the screw 14 and remove the metering needle 13. Remove the union 46 and gauze filter from the float chamber lid, then undo cap nut 45 and remove banjo 42. The lid 37 and washer 38 will now lift off. Take out the float and then release the pin 41. This will free the fork 40 and the needle valve 39 can be released.

Now release screws 34 and the float chamber can be separated from the carburetter body. The spring 19, jet 16 and jet housing 20 can now be removed. Undo screw 18 and take out jet bearing 17. Remove items 29 to 32. Remove return spring lever 65, then carefully mark the butterfly 22 as illustrated in **FIG 3A:18**. Close the split ends of the screws 23, remove them, push the butterfly out of the slot and slide the spindle 21 out of the body. Prise the gland assemblies, items 25 to 28, from each side of the body and all the necessary dismantling is completed.

Clean and inspect all the components, paying particular attention to the diaphragm surrounding the jet, the throttle spindle bores and all joint faces. Obtain a set of gaskets and seals, then proceed to rebuild the carburetter as follows:

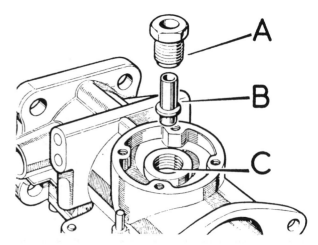

FIG 3A:20 Fitting jet bearing

Key to Fig 3A:20   **A** Jet screw   **B** Jet bearing
C Body

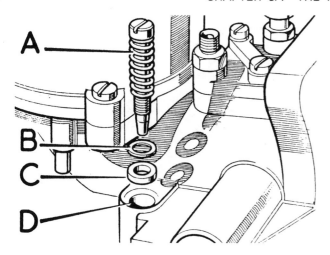

FIG 3A:21   Slow-running valve

Key to Fig 3A:21   **A** Slow-running screw and spring
B Brass washer   **C** Gland washer   **D** Body

1 Insert the throttle into the body from left to right as viewed from the air intake. Assemble the new gland components as shown in **FIG 3A:19**, using a piece of tube to tap the retainer **E** home.

2 Remove the spindle and reinsert from right to left. Assemble a new gland in the opposite side of the body.

3 Assemble the butterfly to the alignment marks made when dismantling. Insert the two screws, but only tighten just enough to hold the butterfly. Snap the butterfly shut to centralize it, then tighten the two screws. When satisfied that the butterfly is completely closing the bore when the spindle is rotated, spread the ends of the screws to prevent loosening.

4 Refit the throttle return spring lever, but do not tighten.

5 Refit the needle to the piston with the shoulder on the needle flush with the face of the piston. Insert the piston into the suction chamber and rotate it, watching to see that the needle is not bent.

6 Fit the jet bearing 17 and jet securing screw 18 into the body as shown in **FIG 3A:20**, but do not tighten the screw yet.

7 Place the piston in the carburetter body, replace the washer and spring, then fit the suction chamber over these items and tighten the screws.

8 Invert the carburetter and insert the jet and diaphragm assembly 16. Gradually tighten the jet securing screw 18, making sure that the jet 16 does not move off centre and bind on the needle 13.

9 Remove the jet and diaphragm assembly 16, then fit the jet housing 20. Replace the jet and diaphragm, aligning the holes in the jet and the jet housing.

10 Fit spring 19, float chamber 33 and choke bracket 52. Do not fully tighten screws 34 at this stage. Operate choke lever 64 to extend the diaphragm to its furthest travel, then tighten the screws 34.

11 Turn the carburetter back up the right way and lift the piston as high as possible by hand, then allow it to fall. It should come to rest with a distinct 'click'. If

not, the jet is binding on the needle and operations 8 to 10 must be repeated.

12 Fit the slow-running valve as shown in **FIG 3A:21**, screwing the screw right in at this stage.

13 Assemble the needle valve and float fork as shown in **FIG 3A:22**, bending the fork at **B** to obtain dimension **D** using a $\frac{7}{16}$ inch (11 mm) bar as a gauge.

14 Replace the float and float chamber lid complete with its union and banjo assembly.

The carburetter may now be replaced on the engine and adjusted as follows:

1 Hold the piston down on the bridge in the throttle bore, then unscrew the stop screw 61 until free play can just be felt at the lever. Screw the screw back in one and a half turns.

2 Run the engine up to operating temperature.

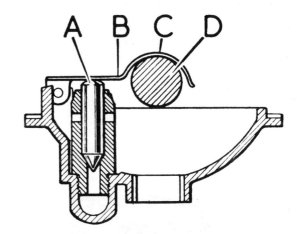

FIG 3A:22   Setting float level fork

Key to Fig 3A:22   **A** Valve   **B** Point at which fork may be bent   **C** Fork   **D** $\frac{7}{16}$ inch (11 mm) bar

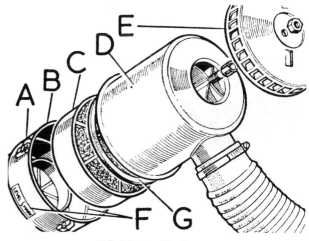

FIG 3A:23   Air cleaner

Key to Fig 3A:23   **A** Clips   **B** Oil container
C Wire mesh unit   **D** Air cleaner body   **E** Intake cap
F Level mark   **G** Washer

3 Adjust screw 62 until the engine idles at 500 rev/min. While adjusting screw 62, minor movements of stop screw 61 should be made until the engine note is even and regular.

4 Tighten the return spring bracket 65.

To check this adjustment, lift the piston $\frac{1}{32}$ inch (.8 mm). If the engine speed rises, the mixture is too rich; if it falls greatly, too weak. When correct, the speed will remain constant or fall only slightly. Move screw 61 to correct the mixture if necessary.

3A : 4 *The air cleaner*

(a) 2¼ litre engine:

Remove the air cleaner intake elbow from the carburetter, release the fixing strap and lift out the cleaner complete with hose and elbow.

Dismantle the cleaner by releasing the clips (**A** in **FIG 3A : 23**), drain the oil from the container **B** and withdraw the wire mesh unit **C**. Wash all components in clean petrol and allow to dry. Refill with clean oil and reassemble by reversing the dismantling process.

Replace on the engine and tighten all fixings.

(b) 2.6 litre engine:

Proceed exactly as for the 2¼ litre engine.

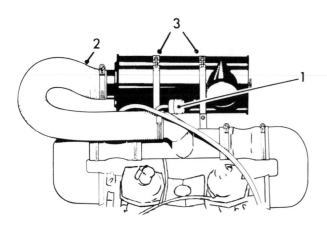

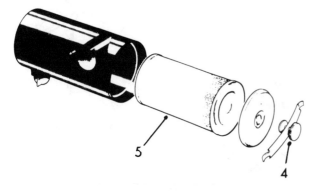

FIG 3A : 24   Air cleaner, 1st type, 3.5 litre engine

Key to Fig 3A : 24   1 Breather filter   2 Air hose
3 Straps   4 End clamp   5 Element

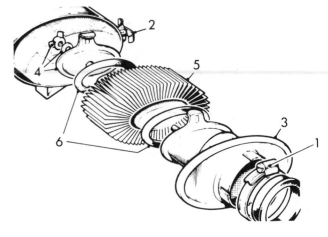

FIG 3A : 25   Air cleaner, 2nd type, 3.5 litre engine

Key to Fig 3A : 25   1 Hose clips   2 Endplate clips
3 Endplate   4 Nut, washer, retaining plate   5 Element
6 Sealing washers

(c) 3.5 litre engine:

One of two types of air cleaner may be fitted.

On the type shown in **FIG 3A : 24**, disconnect the engine breather filter 1, release the air hose 2 from the cleaner, release the straps 3 and remove the cleaner. Release the clamp 4 and remove the endplate. Withdraw the filter element 5.

Fit a new filter element and reverse the removal procedure.

On the type shown in **FIG 3A : 25**, release the hose clips 1 on each side of the cleaner and withdraw the air cleaner elbows. Detach the vacuum pipes and air intake temperature control hose. Withdraw the cleaner from the retaining posts while, at the same time, disconnecting the hose from the engine breather filter. Release the endplate clips 2, withdraw the endplate 3, remove the wingnut, washer and retaining plate 4, then withdraw the elements 5.

Renew the elements and fit new sealing washers 6, then reverse the removal procedure.

3A : 5 *Evaporative loss control*

As part of the measures taken to reduce the pollution caused by noxious emissions into the atmosphere, the system described in this section is designed to eliminate petrol fumes from the storage tank.

The principle is shown diagrammatically in **FIG 3A : 26** from which it may be seen that the evaporative emissions from the fuel tank are led by the pipe 2 into an expansion tank 3 from which a further pipe 4 leads to a charcoal filled adsorption container 1 situated in the engine compartment. At the side of this container there is an air inlet pipe 5 open to the atmosphere, and from the top a pipe 6 leads to the carburetter air cleaner through a flame trap.

Normal fuel tank breathing is through the air inlet pipe 5. Fumes from the tank or expansion chamber are fed into the charcoal container where they are adsorbed on the charcoal. At times of high vacuum in the inlet tract a quantity of air will be inhaled through the pipe 6 and air inlet 5 which purges the trapped emissions into the engine.

The function of the expansion tank is simply to provide an overflow reservoir for fuel expanding in high ambient temperatures. As the overflow pipe is at the bottom of the expansion tank, any fuel here will run back to the main tank as fuel is consumed.

Under normal conditions the charcoal container should be replaced at the specified maintenance intervals, but if any liquid fuel has entered, shown by weeping at the air inlet pipe, it should be replaced immediately. **Do not attempt to cleanse the container.**

When fitting a new container, note that the open inlet pipe faces inboard and towards the rear.

3A:6 *Exhaust emission control*

As a further measure towards the elimination of pollution, certain changes have been made to carburation characteristics and the ignition timing procedure.

On $2\frac{1}{4}$ litre petrol engines a modified Zenith carburetter known as the 36IVE is used and has a number of points of difference from the standard model.

The main enrichment jets have a cadmium plated finish to give special flow characteristics. They are not interchangeable with similar size jets having a natural finish.

In order to weaken the excessively rich mixture drawn into the engine on overrun with closed throttle, a vacuum operated 'throttle prop' device is fitted. Under the high manifold depression obtaining at these times a trigger valve, connected to the inlet manifold by a pipe, is operated and relays the depression to a vacuum servo which in turn operates a rod link to the throttle butterfly and opens it by a small amount.

This condition is maintained until the manifold depression drops when the trigger valve closes and the throttle is allowed to return to its closed position.

A fuel cut-off valve, solenoid operated, which cuts off the idle bypass and progression chambers when the ignition is switched off, is fitted to prevent running-on. This has been found of advantage as the idle speed has been increased to 750 to 800 rev/min to increase the airflow under closed throttle conditions.

The fuel cut-off is preset and must not be adjusted.

An additional fuel filter (see **Section 3A:2**) is fitted between the carburetter and the pump on the righthand side of the engine. This is a sealed unit and the complete unit must be renewed at the stipulated maintenance intervals.

The accelerator pump linkage is set in its maximum position with the throttle relay lever in the hole in pump lever nearest to the pump spindle.

Slow-running adjustment:

This must be carried out when the ignition timing is correctly set as described in **Chapter 4, Section 4:7**. Refer to **FIG 3A:27**.

Bring the engine up to normal working temperature, then unlock the mixture screw 2, turn it gently by hand until it is fully in, then screw back three-quarters of a turn.

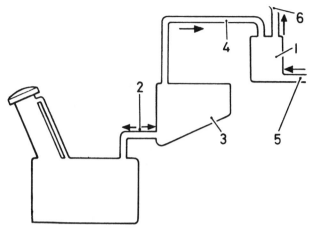

FIG 3A:26 Evaporative loss control

Key to Fig 3A:26
1 Charcoal container   2 Pipe
3 Expansion tank   4 Pipe   5 Air inlet
6 Pipe to carburetter

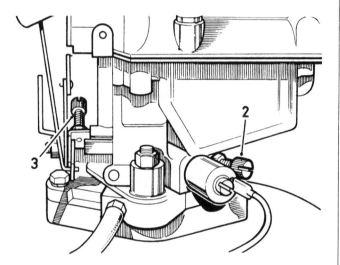

FIG 3A:27 Slow-running adjustment, Zenith 35 IVE

Key to Fig 3A:27   2 Mixture control screw
3 Throttle stop screw

Adjust the throttle stop screw 3 to obtain an engine speed of 800 rev/min, then reset screw 2 for the highest speed at this throttle setting.

Using the throttle stop screw, bring the speed back to 800 rev/min and lock the screw, temporarily.

Weaken the mixture by turning the mixture screw clockwise to obtain 750 rev/min and then turn the screw back a quarter turn and lock.

Finally, reset the throttle stop screw to give as near to 800 rev/min without exceeding this figure and lock it.

Tamper-proof carburetters:

These carburetters may be identified by the tamper-proof sealing tube fitted around the slow-running adjustment screw.

The purpose is to more stringently control the air/fuel mixture and, consequently, the exhaust gas emissions.

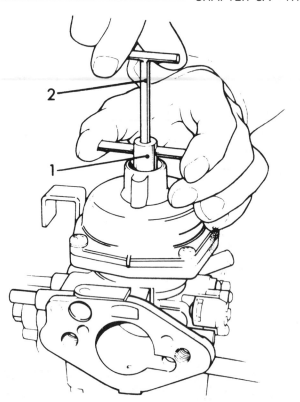

FIG 3A : 28 The fuel mixture adjusting tool S353

Key to Fig 3A : 28 1 Outer tube 2 Inner tube

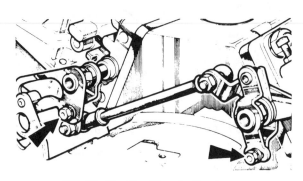

FIG 3A : 29 Throttle adjusting levers

The only readily accessible external adjustment is to the throttle settings for fast-idle speed and, on later carburetters, this requires a special tool.

Unauthorized breaking of tamper-proof devices, carburetter adjustments or the fitting of incorrectly related parts may render the owner or repairer liable to legal penalties according to local territory legislation.

Whenever adjustments are made, an approved type of CO meter and a tachometer must be used to ensure that the final exhaust gas analysis falls within legal limits.

2¼ litre :

Using an approved CO meter and tachometer to the manufacturers' instructions, proceed as already described and check that the CO emission is within the legal limits for the territory ; usually about 4 per cent.

3.5 litre :

The carburetters fitted to this engine operate in the same manner as the Stromberg carburetter described in **Section 3A : 3(c)** but with additional units.

A temperature compensator opens progressively with increasing engine temperature to maintain a correct mixture.

A throttle bypass valve is set to open at a predetermined manifold depression to admit a supply of air during deceleration in order to avoid the over-rich mixture normally present at this time.

Covers are provided over certain parts of the carburetter to prevent alteration of factory calibrations.

The jet adjuster is inside the air valve, making it impossible to alter the fuel mixture without having the special tool S353. Additionally, the slow-running adjustment screws are sealed off with a factory-fitted tube to prevent tampering by anyone other than a fully qualified mechanic using the proper equipment necessary to carry out any adjustment apart from altering the idle speed. It is, therefore, advisable that the vehicle be taken to an authorized service station whenever tuning, balancing or mixture and carbon monoxide checks are necessary. The details given next are for these adjustments and checks provided that the tool S353, an exhaust gas analyzer and an airflow meter are available.

To dismantle the carburetters, work on one carburetter at a time to prevent an interchange of parts and follow the instructions in **Section 3A : 3(c)** except for the jet assembly which is a one-piece unit pressed into the carburetter body.

Idle speed and balance, Australian vehicles :

1 Check that the throttle controls move freely. Check that the throttles are closed when the accelerator pedal is released, but start to open with a minimum depression of the pedal.

2 Accurate engine speed is essential, so check the ignition timing and automatic advance mechanism. The sparking plugs must be in good condition and the engine mechanically sound.

3 The engine must be at normal operating temperature, so run it for at least five minutes after the thermostat opens.

4 Remove the air cleaner and disconnect the throttle linkage so that each carburetter runs independently.

5 Using an airflow meter (carburetter balancer), check to ensure that air flow is the same for both carburetters. If necessary, turn the idle speed adjusting screw on each carburetter by a small amount to achieve a balance.

6 Check the idle speed with the aid of a tachometer. Turn the idle speed adjusting screws by equal amounts to obtain the correct idle speed given in **Technical Data**.

7 Increase the engine speed to 1600 rev/min and check the balance between the two carburetters. If necessary, turn the idle speed adjusting screws on both carburetters by small amounts to achieve a balance once more.

8 Allow the engine to return to the normal idling speed and recheck the airflow balance.

9 Refit the throttle linkage between the carburetters. It is important to note that whenever carburetter tuning is carried out, the engine should be 'cleared out' by increasing engine speed to 2000 rev/min for one minute and then returning to normal idle to continue the tuning operation. This procedure should be repeated at intervals of three minutes throughout the tuning operation.

Checking and adjusting the CO level :

The carbon monoxide (CO) level present in the exhaust gases can be checked and, if necessary, altered to conform with exhaust emission regulations for the territory concerned. Generally, the level should not exceed 4 per cent.

1 Disconnect and plug the outlet hose from the air pump.

2 Ensure that the idling speed is correct as detailed in the preceding instructions.

3 Fit an exhaust gas analyzer in accordance with the manufacturer's instructions. Check the CO reading.

4 Should the CO reading vary by a large amount from the permitted limits, adjust the mixture as shown in **FIG 3A : 28**. Fit the tool S353 after removing the piston damper from the top of the carburetter. Ensure that the tool outer tube engages positively in the air valve (the two lugs in the outer tube must engage the slots in the air valve). Hold the outer tube steady to prevent damage to the air valve diaphragm and fit the inner tool so that the hexagon end engages the jet adjuster at the base of the air valve.

5 Hold the outer tube and turn the inner tool as necessary to alter the fuel mixture setting. Turning the inner tool (and jet adjuster) clockwise will enrich the mixture, whilst turning it anticlockwise will weaken it.

6 Repeat the preceding step to alter the mixture by an equal amount on the second carburetter.

7 Recheck the CO reading, noting the warning given previously regarding 'clearing out' the engine once every three minutes during all tuning operations.

8 Continue adjusting the mixture by small and equal amounts on both carburetters until the correct CO reading is obtained.

9 Top up the carburetter dampers with the correct oil to within about .5 inch (12 mm) from the top of the damper tube. Refit the damper caps and recheck the CO reading, adjusting the mixture once more if necessary.

10 On completion, remove the analyzer, refit the air cleaner and recheck the idling speed as detailed earlier. Refit the air pump outlet hose.

Idle speed and balance, other areas :

The following tools are essential for adjusting the carburetters : carburetter balancer 605330 and adjust-

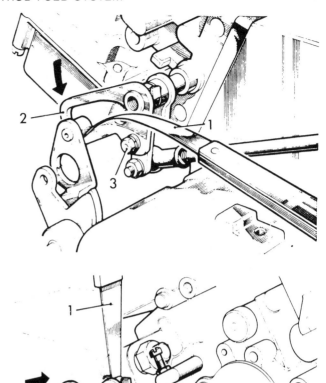

FIG 3A : 30   Adjusting throttle linkage

Key to Fig 3A : 30   1 Feeler gauge   2 Throttle lever
3 Adjusting lever screw   4 Linkage   5 Adjusting lever screw

ing tool MS80. If these are not available, the work should be entrusted to an authorized service station.

1 Carry out operations 1 to 3 as for Australian vehicles.

2 Remove the air cleaner and slacken the screws securing the throttle adjusting levers on both carburetters (see **FIG 3A : 29**).

3 Check and adjust the idle speed as necessary. A special tool is required for this operation if a tamper-proof sleeve is fitted.

4 Check the mixture on each carburetter separately by lifting the air valve .03 inch (.8 mm). If the engine speed increases immediately, the mixture is too rich ; if it decreases immediately, the mixture is too weak.

5 Remove the piston damper plug and insert tool MS80, locating the outer sleeve of the tool in a machined slot to prevent the air valve twisting. Turn the inner tool clockwise to enrich the mixture or anticlockwise to weaken it. When the mixture is

FIG 3A:31 Adjusting fast-idle

Key to Fig 3A:31 1 Cold start adjuster 2 Fast-idle
adjusting screw 3 Cold start cam 4 Feeler gauge
5 Locknut

correct, lifting the air valve by the stated amount
will make little or no difference.

6 Zero the gauge on the tool 605330 and place it onto
the carburetter adaptors, ensuring that there are no
air leaks. If the engine stalls or there is a considerable decrease in speed, the mixture is too rich; if
there is an increase in speed, the mixture is too
weak. If necessary, remove the tool, readjust the
mixture and refit the tool.

7 Check the gauge reading. With the pointer in the
'zero' sector, no adjustment is necessary.

8 If the gauge pointer moves to the right, decrease the
air flow through the lefthand carburetter by
unscrewing the throttle stop screw or increase the
air flow through the righthand carburetter by screwing in the throttle stop screw. Reverse the procedure if the pointer moves to the left.

9 Correct the idle speed if necessary, maintaining the
gauge pointer in the 'zero' sector.

10 Remove the tool. With the mixture setting and
balance correctly adjusted, the difference in engine
speed will be within 25 rev/min.

11 Fit an approved CO meter to the manufacturer's
instructions and check the exhaust emission which
should not exceed 4 per cent or any other level fixed
by local territory legislation.

12 Put a .006 inch (.15 mm) feeler 1 (see **FIG 3A:30**) between the underside of the roller on the countershaft
lever and the throttle lever on the lefthand carburetter.

13 Apply pressure to the throttle lever 2 to hold the
feeler.

14 Tighten the screw 3 and withdraw the feeler.

15 Place the same feeler between the left leg of the fork
on the adjusting lever and the pin on the throttle
lever on the righthand carburetter.

16 Apply pressure to the linkage 4 to hold the feeler.

17 Tighten the screw 5 and withdraw the feeler.

18 Refit the air cleaner.

Fast-idle adjustment:

The fast-idle adjustment is preset on the lefthand carburetter and should not normally require adjustment.
If necessary, remove the lefthand carburetter.

1 Set the cold start adjuster 1 (see **FIG 3A:31**) fully
outward.

2 Slacken the fast-idle adjusting screw 2.

3 Hold the cam 3 in the maximum position.

4 Adjust the screw 2 against the cam 3 until there is a
gap of .024 to .026 inch (.61 to .66mm) between the
top edge of the butterfly and the barrel wall.

5 Use feeler gauges or a No. 72 drill (.65 mm) 4 to
measure the gap at the top edge of the butterfly.

6 Secure the locknut 5 without disturbing the
adjustment.

7 Refit the carburetter.

An alternative method may be used for an approxi-
mate setting at temperatures above 10°F.

Set the fast-idle screw against the cam to give an
engine speed of 1000 to 1200 rev/min when the choke
warning light just goes out.

On some later carburetters a special tool supplied to
authorized service stations may be necessary to adjust
the fast-idle speed setting.

Cold start adjuster:

At starting temperatures down to 0°F, turn the spring-
loaded adjuster 1 (see **FIG 3A:31**) so that the peg is at
right angles to the slot and leave in this position. At
lower temperatures, turn the adjuster until the peg is in
the slot.

3A:7 *Setting the throttle control*

This operation is described in **Chapter 3B**.

3A:8 *Fault diagnosis*

(a) Difficult cold starting
Solex, Zenith, SU and Stromberg:

1 Insufficient choke
2 Fast-idle adjustment incorrect
3 Float level too low
4 Flooding

(b) Difficult hot starting
Solex, Zenith, SU and Stromberg:

1 Choke sticking on
2 Blocked air filter
3 Float level too high
4 Zenith only, internal leakage
5 SU only, jet tube stuck down

(c) Erratic slow-running
Solex, Zenith, SU and Stromberg:

1 Float level too low
2 SU only, piston sticking
3 Solex and Zenith only, incorrect setting
4 SU and Stromberg, incorrect jet setting
5 All types, air leaks

6 SU and Stromberg, no oil or too thick an oil in the damper

(d) Poor acceleration

1 Zenith only, acceleration pump sticking or ball valves not seating or stuck
2 Solex only, pump diaphragm leaking, linkage incorrectly adjusted, non-return valve blocked, accelerator jet blocked, discharge tube ball valve stuck
3 SU and Stromberg, no oil or oil too thin in damper or piston sticking

(e) High fuel consumption

Solex, Zenith, SU and Stromberg:

1 Blocked air cleaner
2 Wrongly adjusted carburetter
3 Float level too high
4 Worn jets and needle
5 Choke sticking on
6 SU and Stromberg only, wrong type of needle
7 Solex and Zenith only, accelerator linkage wrongly adjusted

NOTES

CHAPTER 3B

THE DIESEL FUEL SYSTEM

3B:1 Description

Great care must be taken when dealing with direct injection fuel systems to eliminate dirt and grit. For this reason all diesel Land-Rovers are fitted with at least three, and export models four, filters between the tank and injection pump. Reference to **FIG 3B:1** will clearly show the location of the filters and also the pipe layout. It will be seen that fuel is lifted from the tank by a diaphragm type mechanical pump via a filter in the tank, thence through one or two more filters to the injection pump. A fine gauze filter is also fitted in the injection pump head. The high pressure fuel is led to the injectors from the pump with overspill being carried back to the tank. The injection pump is of the distributor type and no attempt can be made to overhaul it by anyone other than a competent service engineer equipped with a great deal of specialized equipment. Any failure of this unit invariably means obtaining an exchange pump from a Rover dealer. The same applies to the nozzle assemblies; it is quite impossible to dismantle these and reset them without special equipment and knowledge.

3B:2 Maintenance

No maintenance is required by either the injection pump or nozzles. Maintenance of the system must be confined to keeping the filters clean. In this connection, if the main filter element sludges up in an unreasonably short time this is due to an excess of wax in the fuel and the supplier should be consulted. Never draw fuel from a storage tank at its lowest point, impurities will always collect here.

Remember that the engine must never be run even for a few moments without coolant. The injectors will overheat and be ruined.

3B:3 The fuel filters

Reference to **FIGS 3B:2** and **3B:3** will clearly show the layout of the filters and other pipes and components. Particularly note that the early layout has a bowl filter on the lift pump while the later layout has a sedimentor.

(a) Lift pump bowl filter:

To clean this filter, undo the nut holding the glass bowl up to the casting, swing the retainer aside and lower the bowl. Clean the bowl and filter gauze and refit. Use a new cork gasket between the bowl and casting.

(b) Main filter, early type:

Refer to **FIG 3B:4**.
To renew the element proceed as follows:

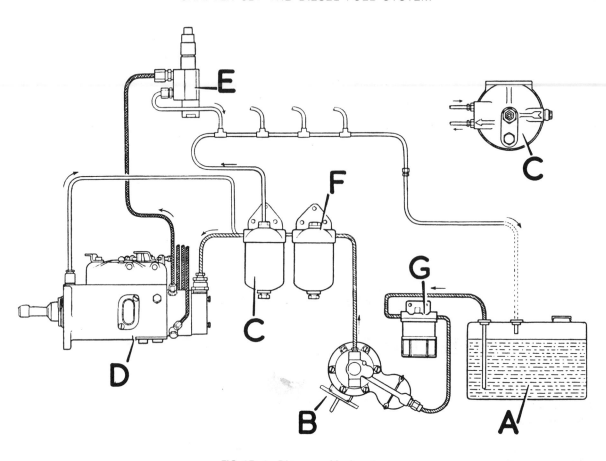

FIG 3B:1   Diagram of fuel system

Key to Fig 3B:1   **A** Fuel tank   **B** Fuel pump   **C** Main filter   **D** Injection pump   **E** Injection nozzle
F Additional filter (early export models)   **G** Sedimentor (latest export models)   //////// Low pressure delivery
xxxxxxx High pressure delivery   ==== Excess fuel spillback

1 Slacken plug **N** and allow the fuel to drain into a suitable container.
2 Disconnect the bleed back pipe from the top of the filter.
3 Support the container **J** and undo cap nut **B**.
4 Remove the container **J** and oil seals **C** and **F**.
5 Discard the element, then wash the container thoroughly in clean fuel. See that the centre spindle is clean and that the drain hole in the plug **N** is clear.
6 Renew ring **K** if any doubts exist about its condition. Renew seals **C** and **F**.
7 Fit a new element and replace the container **J**, tightening cap nut **B**.
8 Reconnect pipes, tighten the drain plug **N** and prime the system.

(c) Main filter, late type:

Refer to **FIG 3B:5**.

The late type filter can be identified by the black nylon fuel pipes and the fact that it is attached to the dash, not the engine. The filter element forms part of the filter body, thus the engine cannot be run without an element in position.

To renew the element, support the holder **C** and undo bolt **A**. Discard the element and wash the holder **C** in clean fuel. Renew the rubber washers in the top of the filter and in the element holder **C**.

Push a new element on to the filter top spigot with the perforations in the element to the top. Fit holder **C** and tighten bolt **A**. Prime the system.

An additional main filter is mounted beside the filter just described if the vehicle is intended for export. **FIG 3B:6** shows the layout. A paper element is fitted but the instructions for renewing it are identical to those given for the main filter, late type.

(d) Sedimentor:

Latest vehicles are fitted with a sedimentor which removes the larger droplets of water and foreign matter from the fuel. This device is illustrated in **FIG 3B:7**. Occasionally slacken drain plug **E**, allow water to escape and tighten the plug when clean fuel emerges. Priming the system is not necessary after doing this.

To clean the unit, first disconnect pipe **B** and support it above the supply tank level. Support bowl **D** and undo bolt **A**. Clean all parts in petrol. Fit new seals and replace the bowl and element. Tighten bolt **A** and connect pipe **B**. Prime the system as described in **Section 3B:4**.

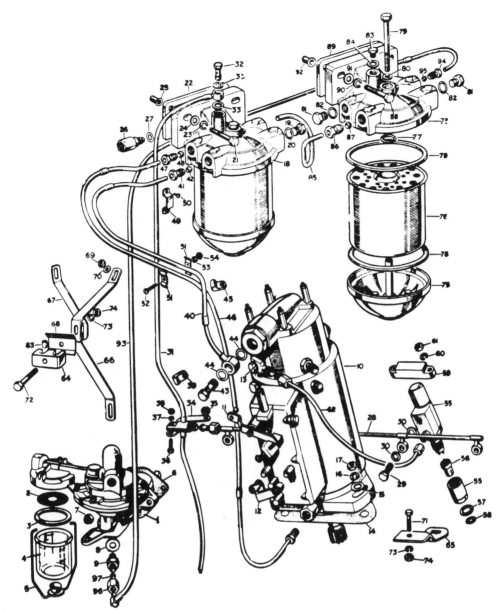

FIG 3B : 2   Layout of early type system

Key to Fig 3B : 2   1 Fuel pump, mechanical   2 Filter for sediment bowl   3 Washer for sediment bowl   4 Sediment bowl
5 Retainer   6 Joint washer   7 Self-locking nut   8 Joint washer for mechanical pump inlet and outlet
9 Union for mechanical pump inlet and outlet   10 Distributor pump   11 Accelerator control lever for distributor pump
12 Stop lever for distributor pump   13 Joint washer for injection pipe, distributor pump end   14 Joint washer
15-17 Distributor pump to cylinder block fixings   18 Fuel filter   19 Plug for filter   20 Joint washer   21-25 Filter to dash fixings
26 Non-return valve for filter   27 Joint washer   28 Leak-off pipe   29 Banjo bolt (fixings, leak-off pipe to injector)
30 Washer (fixings, leak-off pipe to injector)   31 Fuel pipe, spill return to tank   32 Banjo bolt (fixing spill return pipe to filter)
33 Joint washer (fixing spill return pipe to filter)   34 Bracket for leak-off pipe   35 Locknut fixing bracket to injector stud
36-38 Spill return pipe to bracket on injector stud fixings   39 Clip   40 Fuel pipe, filter to distributor pump
41 Nut (fixing pipe to filter)   42 Olive (fixing pipe to filter)   43 Banjo bolt (fixing pipe to distributor pump)
44 Joint washer (fixing pipe to distributor pump)   45 Clip, fixing pipe to distributor pump   46 Fuel pipe, distributor
return to filter   47 Nut (fixing pipe to non-return valve at filter)   48 Olive (fixing pipe to non-return valve at filter)
49 Clip   50 Drive screw (fixing distributor pump feed and return pipes together)   51 Double pipe clip (fixing distributor
pump feed and return pipes together)   52-54 Pipes and clips fixings   55 Injector   56 Nozzle   57 Copper joint washer
for injector   58 Steel joint washer for injector   60, 61 Injector to cylinder head fixings   62 Injector pipe to No. 2 cylinder
63 Damper for injector pipe   64 Shroud   65 Bracket for shroud   66 Support strap for shroud   67 Steady strap for shroud
68 Backplate for shroud   69, 70 Fixings, straps to injector studs   71-74 Fixings, shroud and dampers to backplate, strap and
support bracket   75 Fuel filter*   76 Element*   77 Small seal for element*   78 Large seal for element*   79 Special centre
bolt for filter*   80 Washer for centre bolt*   81 Plug for fuel filter*   82 Joint washer*   83 Plug for fuel filter, top, leak-off*
84 Joint washer for leak-off plug*   85 Transfer pipe, extra filter to basic filter*   86 Nut (fixing pipe to filter)*
87 Olive (fixing pipe to filter)*   88-92 Filter to dash fixings*   93 Fuel pipe, pump to filters*   94 Nut (fixing pipe to filter)*
95 Olive (fixing pipe to filter)*   96 Nut (fixing pipe to filter)*   97 Olive (fixing pipe to filter)*

*Additional fuel filter

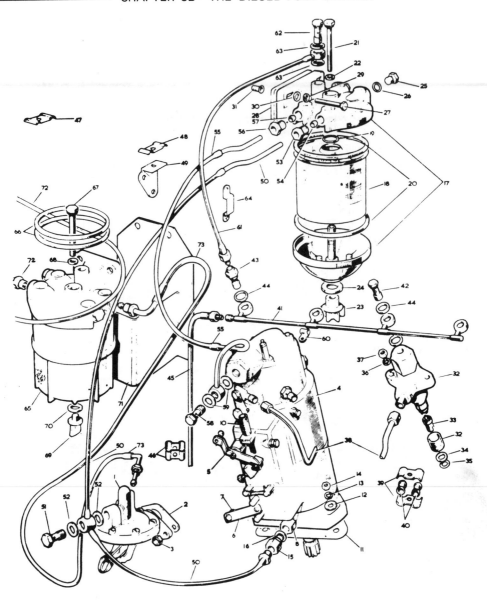

FIG 3B:3 Layout of late type system

Key to Fig 3B:3 1 Fuel pump, mechanical   2 Joint washer, fuel pump to cylinder block   3 Self-locking nut, fixing fuel pump
4 Distributor pump   5 Accelerator control lever for distributor pump   6 Stop lever for distributor pump   7 Swivel clamp
for stop lever, for distributor pump   8 Union, fuel pipe connection for distributor pump   9 Joint washer for injector pipe,
distributor pump end   10 Sleeve for control lever stop screw   11 Joint washer for distributor pump   12 Plain washer
(fixing distributor pump to cylinder block)   13 Spring washer (fixing distributor pump to cylinder block)   14 Nut ($\frac{5}{16}$ inch UNF)
(fixing distributor pump to cylinder block)   15 Non-return valve for distributor pump   16 Joint washer for non-return valve
17 Fuel filter   18 Element for fuel filter   19 Small seal for element   20 Large seal for element   21 Special centre bolt
for filter   22 Washer for centre bolt   23 Nylon drain plug for filter   24 Rubber seal for drain plug   25 Plug for filter
26 Joint washer for plug   27 Bolt ($\frac{5}{16}$ inch UNF x $1\frac{1}{8}$ inch long) (fixing filter to dash)   28 Distance plate (fixing filter to dash)
29 Spring washer (fixing filter to dash)   30 Plain washer (fixing filter to dash)   31 Rivnut ($\frac{5}{16}$ inch UNF) (fixing filter to dash)
32 Injector complete   33 Nozzle for injector   34 Copper joint washer for injector   35 Steel joint washer for injector
36 Spring washer (fixing injectors to cylinder head studs)   37 Nut ($\frac{5}{16}$ inch UNF) (fixing injectors to cylinder head studs)
38 Injector pipe to No. 2 cylinder   39 Clamping plate for injector pipe grommet   40 Grommet for injector pipe   41 Spill
rail pipe complete   42 Banjo bolt for No. 1, 2 and 3 injectors (fixing spill rail pipe to injectors)   43 Banjo union for No. 4 injector
(fixing spill rail pipe to injectors)   44 Joint washer for banjo bolt (fixing spill rail pipe to injectors)   45 Fuel pipe,
spill return to tank   46 Double clip, clamping feed and return pipes together   47 Double clip, fixing feed and return pipes to
chassis sidemember   48 Double clip for feed and return pipes   49 Bracket for clip   50 Fuel pipe, mechanical pump and
distributor pump to filter   51 Banjo bolt (fixing fuel pipe to mechanical pump)   52 Joint washer (fixing fuel pipe to
mechanical pump)   53 Nut (fixing pipe to filter)   54 Olive (fixing pipe to filter)   55 Fuel pipe (filter to distributor pump)
56 Nut (fixing pipe to filter)   57 Olive (fixing pipe to filter)   58 Banjo bolt (fixing pipe to distributor pump)   59 Joint washer
(fixing pipe to distributor pump)   60 Clip (fixing fuel pipe to distributor pump)   61 Fuel pipe filter to spill rail at No. 4 injector
62 Banjo bolt (fixing fuel pipe to filter)   63 Joint washer (fixing fuel pipe to filter)   64 Double clip, fixing fuel pipes to
bulkhead   65 Sedimentor   66 Seal for sedimentor   67 Special centre bolt for sedimentor   68 Washer for centre bolt
69 Drain plug for sedimentor   70 Rubber seal for drain plug   71 Mounting bracket for sedimentor   72 Fuel pipe, tank
to sedimentor   73 Fuel pipe, sedimentor to mechanical pump

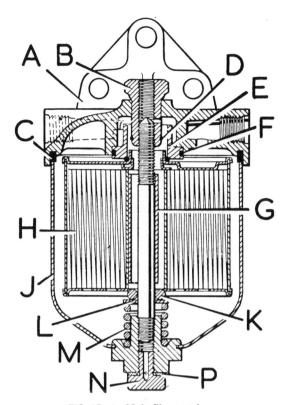

FIG 3B:4 Main filter, early type

Key to Fig 3B:4   **A** Housing cover   **B** Cap nut
C Oil seal   **D** Circlip   **E** Sealing ring   **F** Oil seal
G Location sleeve   **H** Element   **J** Container   **K** Seal
L Plain washer   **M** Spring   **N** Drain plug   **P** Washer

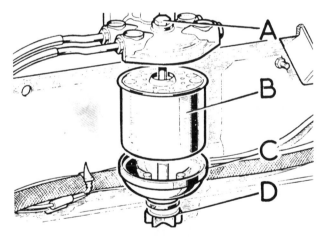

FIG 3B:5 Main filter, late type
Key to Fig 3B:5   **A** Retaining bolt   **B** Element
C Holder   **D** Water drain plug

3B:4 Priming the system

When any disconnection has been made in the system or if the tank level has run low, the system must be primed as follows:

(a) Early type filter:

1 Slacken the air vent screw (**B** in **FIG 3B:8**), on the top of the engine filter, then operate the hand priming

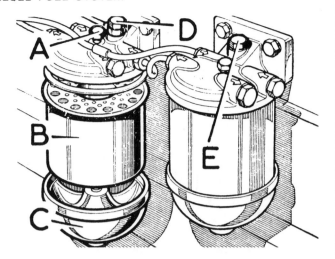

FIG 3B:6 Twin filters, export models

Key to Fig 3B:6   **A** Retaining bolt   **B** Element
C Holder   **D** Bleed pipe   **E** Vent screw

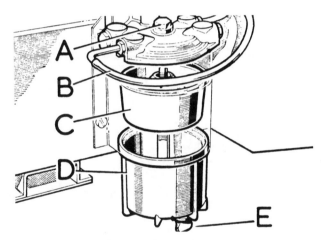

FIG 3B:7 Fuel sedimentor

Key to Fig 3B:7   **A** Retaining bolt   **B** Inlet pipe
C Element   **D** Bowl   **E** Water drain plug

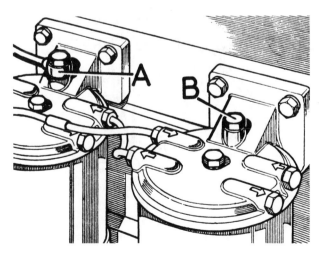

FIG 3B:8 Filter air vent

Key to Fig 3B:8   **A** Bleed pipe   **B** Air vent screw

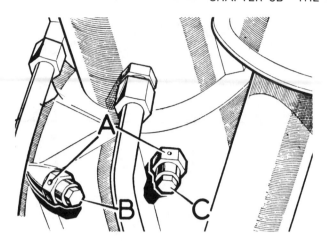

FIG 3B:9   Injector pump air vents

Key to Fig 3B:9   **A** Fuel orifice   **B** Distributor air vent
C Distributor control cover air vent

lever on the mechanical pump until fuel free from bubbles emerges. Tighten the screw. Operate the priming lever a few more times to clear the air into the bleed pipe.

2 Release the air vent screw (**B** in **FIG 3B:9**) on the injection pump and operate the hand priming lever until fuel free of bubbles emerges. Retighten the screw.

3 Release the air vent screw (**C** in **FIG 3B:9**) and repeat operation 2.

4 Start the engine and check for leaks.

(b) Late type filter or filter and sedimentor:

Proceed exactly as for the early type filter but slacken both the bleed pipe **A** and vent screw **B** (see **FIG 3B:8**) in turn.

Ensure that the fuel lift pump lever is on the bottom of the cam, otherwise the hand priming lever may be ineffective and prevent priming of the system.

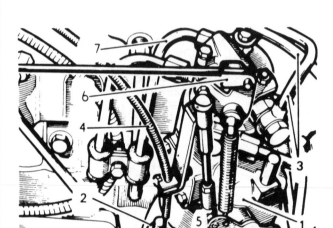

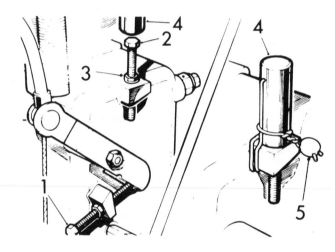

FIG 3B:11   Speed control screws

Key to Fig 3B:11   1 Slow-running control screw
2 Maximum control screw   3 Locknut   4 Screw collar
5 Seal

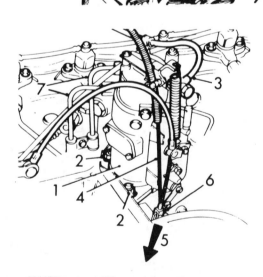

FIG 3B:10   Removing the injector pump

Key to Fig 3B:10   1 Distributor pump   2 Mounting nuts
3 Fuel pipes   4 Engine stop cable   5 Stop lever return spring   6 Accelerator linkage   7 Injector fuel pipe

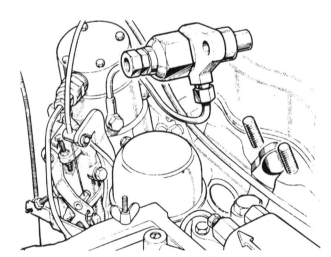

FIG 3B:12   Testing a nozzle assembly

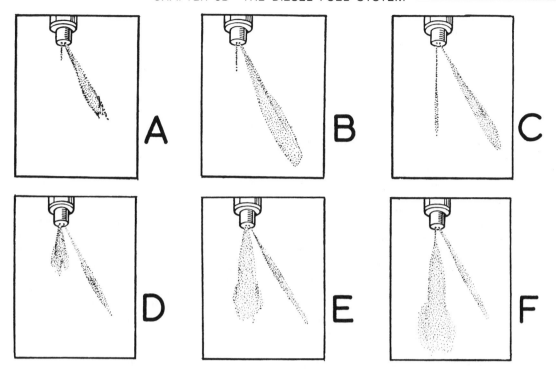

FIG 3B : 13   Nozzle spray forms, starting to running conditions, A to F

3B : 5 *The fuel lift pump*

This pump is identical in operation to the mechanical fuel pump fitted to the 2¼ litre petrol engine. Refer to **Chapter 3A** for servicing instructions.

3B : 6 *The injection pump*

No servicing of this unit is possible. In the event of failure, an exchange must be made at a Rover dealer.

To remove the distributor injection pump, proceed as follows, referring to **FIG 3B : 10**.
1 Disconnect the battery earth lead.
2 Disconnect the engine stop cable 4 and the stop lever return spring 5.
3 Disconnect the accelerator linkage at the securing clip 6.
4 Disconnect the fuel pipe 7 from the distributor pump and the injectors. Also disconnect the fuel inlet and outlet pipes 3 at the distributor pump.
5 Undo the mounting nuts 2 and remove the pump.

Refitting the distributor to obtain the correct timing is covered in **Chapter 2, Section 2 : 10**. After obtaining the correct timing, reconnect the pipes and controls as shown in **FIG 3B : 10** and prime the system as described in **Section 3B : 4**.

When fitting a new or exchange distributor pump, the slow-running and maximum control screw will require setting. The slow-running screw may be supplied loose and should be fitted as shown in **FIG 3B : 11**.

Adjust the slow-running control screw to obtain an engine speed of 590 ± 20 rev/min. If a revolution meter is not available, adjust the screw to obtain the lowest engine speed consistent with smooth, even running.

Screwing the screw inwards will increase the engine speed and vice versa. When the correct adjustment is obtained, tighten the locknut.

Adjustment of the maximum control screw may not be required. Where the screw is sealed, as shown in **FIG 3B : 11**, this indicates that adjustment has been carried out and that the setting should not be altered. Correct adjustment will allow a maximum engine speed of 4200 ± 20 rev/min. This may be checked by road testing the

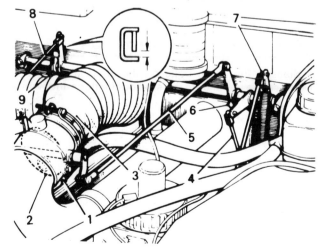

FIG 3B : 14   **Diesel models with servo-assisted brakes**

Key to Fig 3B : 14   1 Non-return valve   2 Butterfly valve
3 Rubber hose   4 Hand throttle   5 Manifold butterfly
linkage   6 Pinch bolt   7 Accelerator linkage
8 Distributor pump linkage   9 Pinch bolt

vehicle, the road speed equivalent of 4200 rev/min being 48 mile/hr (77 km/hr) in third gear. When adjustment is correct, tighten the locknut and fit the screw collar. Wire lock and seal the screw collar as shown in **FIG 3B : 11**.

3B : 7 *The injector nozzle assemblies*

These assemblies cannot be serviced by the private owner, but it is possible to check and test them on the vehicle so as to isolate any particular defective one.

To make a quick check if a nozzle is suspected of causing loss of power and irregular running, loosen the fuel feed pipe union on each injector in turn whilst the engine is idling and again at 1000 rev/min.

If the nozzle has been operating properly, there will be a reduction in rev/min accompanied by obvious roughness, but a faulty nozzle will make little or no difference when the feed pipe is loosened.

To test the nozzles on the vehicle, first remove the fuel spill gallery pipe complete, then disconnect the fuel feed pipe between the pump and nozzle to be tested. Remove the nozzle from the engine and reconnect to the pump so that the spray pattern can be observed (see **FIG 3B : 12**). Loosen the feed pipe unions to the remaining nozzles. Turn the engine over on the starter and watch the spray pattern of the nozzle under test. Very little fuel should issue from the main spray hole, but a fine spray should be ejected from the auxiliary spray hole. If the fuel is ejected as a liquid jet or issues from the main hole, then the nozzle must be replaced by an overhauled exchange assembly. **FIG 3B : 13** shows the development of nozzle spray forms from starting to running conditions.

It is extremely dangerous to allow diesel fuel spray to contact the skin, since the high injector pressure enables the fuel oil to penetrate the skin and it may poison the blood which can be fatal.

3B : 8 *The air filter*

This was described in **Chapter 3A**.

3B : 9 *Setting the throttle controls*

Slacken the pinch bolts on the cross-shaft levers. Depress the pedal onto the stop on the floor and, while holding the throttle linkage in the fully open position, tighten the pinch bolts. If necessary, adjust the pedal limiting stops to permit full and unrestricted throttle opening.

Diesel models with servo-assisted brakes obtain the required vacuum via a non-return valve fitted to the induction manifold downstream of a butterfly valve. The linkage must be set so that the butterfly valve opens slightly in advance of the fuel distributor pump linkage during acceleration, otherwise overfuelling will result. Move the engine speed hand control to the idle position. Remove the rubber hose from the manifold and check that the butterfly valve is fully closed. There should then be a clearance as shown in **FIG 3B : 14** between the front arm of the cross-shaft lever and the fuel distributor pump link. If necessary, slacken the pinch bolt and move the lever to obtain this clearance.

After removing the non-return valve from the manifold it may be checked as follows.

Do not use high pressure air to check the valve, but use the mouth and blow down the hose connector. Air should pass freely in this direction. It should not be possible to blow through in the opposite direction. Renew the valve if it is faulty.

3B : 10 *Fault diagnosis*

(a) Engine will not idle

1 Slow-running control screw incorrectly set
2 Injector nozzle faulty

(b) Reduced power and rough running

1 Fuel starvation. Check at each nozzle by loosening feed pipe union
2 Injector nozzle faulty or not seated in cylinder head
3 Injector nozzle overheated
4 Injection pump timing incorrect

(c) Engine overheats

1 Check 1 in (b)
2 Injector nozzle faulty
3 Injection pump timing incorrect

(d) Black smoke from exhaust

1 Injector nozzle faulty
2 Injection pump timing incorrect

CHAPTER 4

THE IGNITION SYSTEM

4:1 Description

The petrol engines described in this manual rely on the same design of distributor for the ignition systems. The only minor differences are to the cam and the cap. The unit incorporates automatic timing control by centrifugal mechanism and a vacuum operated unit. A micrometer adjustment is provided on some models to enable fine alterations to the ignition point to be made by hand. Such alterations can compensate for changes in engine condition or for the use of various grades of fuel.

The weights of the centrifugal device fly out against the tension of small springs as engine speed rises. This movement advances the contact breaker cams relative to the distributor driving shaft to give advanced ignition. The vacuum unit is connected by a small-bore pipe or pipes to the inlet manifold. Depression in the manifold operates the vacuum unit, the suction varying with engine load. At small throttle openings, with no load on the engine, there is a high degree of vacuum in the manifold, causing the vacuum unit to advance the ignition. When hill-climbing on large throttle openings, the much reduced vacuum ensures that the unit will retard the ignition. The various elements of the two automatic controls can be seen in **FIG 4:1** as items 8, 9 and 10.

4:2 Routine maintenance

Refer to **FIG 4:1**, other models are similar, and remove distributor cap 2. Pull rotor 5 squarely off the end of cam spindle 13. Now lubricate the cam spindle. Add only a few drops of oil to the felt pad or to the recess and do not remove the screw. There is a clearance provided for the oil to make its way downwards.

Squirt a few drops of oil to lubricate the centrifugal advance mechanism, but take great care to avoid letting oil get onto the contact breaker plate or the points 6. Smear a little grease or engine oil on the cam. Apply the tiniest drop of oil to the contact breaker pivot.

On Lucas sliding contact distributors, using Shell Retinax or equivalent grease, lubricate the underside of the heel actuator 1 (see **FIG 4:2**). Also, using the same grease, lubricate the actuator ramps and contact breaker heel ribs 2. In addition, grease the fixed pin and actuator fork 3.

Adjusting the contact breaker points:

Refer to **FIG 4:3** and slacken screw **C**. Adjust the points to the correct gap of .014 to .016 inch (.35 to .40 mm) as measured with a feeler gauge. It will be necessary to turn the engine until one of the cams has opened the points to the fullest extent so that the gap is

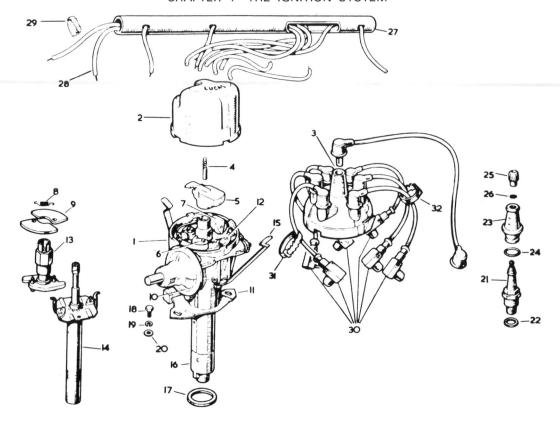

FIG 4:1 Exploded view of distributor, Mk2, 2A

Key to Fig 4:1   1 Distributor body   2 Distributor cap, early type   3 Distributor cap, later type   4 Brush and spring for cap
5 Rotor arm   6 Contact points   7 Condenser   8 Auto advance spring, set   9 Auto advance weight   10 Vacuum unit
11 Clamping plate   12 Baseplate for contact breaker   13 Cam   14 Shaft and action plate   15 Clip for cover   16 Driving dog
17 Cork washer for distributor housing   18 Setbolt ($\frac{1}{4}$ in UNF x $\frac{9}{16}$ in long) (Fixing distributor to cylinder block)   19 Spring washer
(Fixing distributor to cylinder block)   20 Plain washer (Fixing distributor to cylinder block)   21 Sparking plug
22 Washer for plug   23 Cover for sparking plug   24 Rubber sealing ring for plug cover   25 Cable nut   26 Washer for cable nut
27 Ignition wire carrier   28 Sparking plug lead set   29 Cable cleat securing No. 1 plug lead and coil leads
30 Spark plug plastic covers   31, 32 Cleats

measured at the position of maximum opening. Do not alter the gap unless it varies considerably from the suggested setting.

The Lucas sliding contact and Ducellier distributors fitted to the $2\frac{1}{4}$ litre five main bearing engines, or the distributor fitted to the 3.5 litre engine, can use the foregoing to set the static position, but final settings must be made dynamically as described in **Section 4:7**.

Cleaning the contact points:

If the contact points are dirty or pitted they must be cleaned by polishing them with a fine carborundum stone, taking care to keep the faces flat and square. Afterwards, wipe away all dust with a cloth moistened in fuel. The contacts may be dismantled to assist cleaning. If the moving contact is removed from its pivot, check that it is not sluggish. If it is tight, polish the pivot pin with a strip of fine emerycloth, clean off all dust and apply a tiny spot of oil to the top of the pin. If a spring testing gauge is available, the contact breaker spring should have a tension of 20 to 24 oz measured at the points.

4:3 Ignition faults

If the engine runs unevenly, set it to idle at a fast speed. Taking care not to touch any metal part of the sparking plug leads, pull off the insulated sleeves, thereby disconnecting each plug in turn. Disconnecting a plug which is firing properly will make the uneven running more pronounced. Disconnecting a plug in a cylinder which is not firing will make no difference.

Having located the faulty cylinder, hold the lead carefully to avoid shocks so that the metal end is about $\frac{3}{16}$ inch away from the cylinder head. A strong regular spark shows that the fault might lie with the sparking plug. Remove and clean it or, alternatively, substitute it with a new plug.

If the spark is weak and irregular, check that the lead is not perished or cracked. If it appears to be defective, renew it and try another test. If there is no improvement, remove the distributor cap and wipe the inside clean and dry. Check the carbon brush 4 in **FIG 4:1**. It should protrude from the moulding and be free to move against the pressure of the internal spring. Examine the surface inside the cap for signs of 'tracking', which can be seen as a thin black line between the electrodes or to some metal part in contact with the cap. This is caused by sparking and the only cure is to fit a new cap.

Testing the low-tension circuit:

Before carrying out electrical tests, confirm that the contact breaker points are clean and correctly set. Then proceed as follows:

1 Disconnect the thin cable from the **CB** terminal on the coil and from the side of the distributor. Connect a test lamp between the two terminals. Turn the engine over slowly. If the lamp lights when the contacts close and goes out when they open, the low-tension circuit is in order. If the lamp fails to light, the contacts are dirty or there is a break or loose connection in the low-tension wiring.

2 If the fault lies in the low-tension circuit, switch on the ignition and turn the crankshaft until the contact points are fully open. Refer to the wiring diagrams in **Technical Data** and check the circuit with a 0-20 voltmeter. If the circuit is in order, the meter should read approximately 12 volts.

3 Battery to control box terminal **A**. Connect the voltmeter between terminal **A** and earth. No reading indicates a faulty cable or loose connection.

4 Control box. Connect the meter between the other auxiliary terminal **A1** and earth. No reading indicates a broken or loose connection.

5 Control box auxiliary terminal **D** to terminal **IGN** on ignition switch. Connect the meter between terminal **IGN** and earth. No reading indicates a damaged cable or loose connection.

6 Ignition coil. Disconnect the cable from terminal **CB** and connect the meter between this terminal and earth. No reading indicates a fault in the primary winding of the coil and a replacement coil must be fitted. If the reading is correct, remake the connection to the coil.

7 Ignition coil to distributor. Disconnect the thin cable from the side terminal on the distributor and connect the meter between the end of this cable and earth. No reading indicates a damaged cable or loose connections.

8 Contact breaker and capacitor. Connect the meter across the contact breaker points. No reading indicates a faulty capacitor.

Capacitor:

The best method of testing a capacitor (condenser) is by substitution. Disconnect the original capacitor and connect a new one between the low-tension terminal on the side of the distributor and to earth.

If a new capacitor is needed, fit one complete with bracket, but, if necessary, unsolder the original bracket and solder it on the new capacitor using as little heat as possible. Capacitor capacity is .18 to .22 microfarad.

4:4 Removing and dismantling the early distributor

Use **FIG 4:1** for reference. Before removing the distributor, turn the crankshaft until the rotor arm 5 is pointing to the brass segment in the cap which is connected to No. 1 cylinder plug lead at the front of the

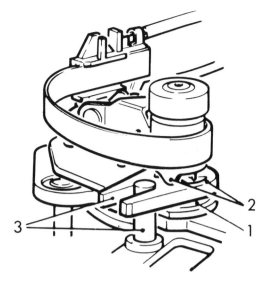

FIG 4:2 Additional lubrication of sliding contact distributor

Key to Fig 4:2   1 Underside of the heel actuator
2 Actuator ramps and contact breaker heel ribs   3 Fixed pin and actuator fork

engine. This will provide a datum for replacement. Provided the pinch bolt in the clamp plate 11 is not loosened, the distributor can be removed and replaced without disturbing the ignition timing. Do not turn the crankshaft after this.

1 Remove the cap 2 and disconnect the cable from the low-tension terminal. Disconnect the suction pipe from vacuum unit 10. Remove the bolts securing the clamp plate 11 to the housing in the crankcase and withdraw the distributor.

2 Pull off the rotor arm. Remove the nut which holds assembly 6 and lift off the insulating bush, terminal tags, moving contact and spring assembly and the washer. The fixed contact plate can then be lifted off.

3 Remove the two screws securing the baseplate and unhook the flexible link coming from the vacuum unit.

4 Before further dismantling, note the relative positions of the rotor arm driving slot at the top of item 13 and the driving dog 16 which is offset and can only engage its driving spindle in one position. Then, when the cam assembly is fitted to the centrifugal weights during reassembly, the timing will not be 180 deg. out.

5 Take out the cam retaining screw recessed in the rotor arm housing on the end of the spindle. Remove the springs 8 and lift off the cam. Take out the weights 9.

6 To release the vacuum unit, remove the circlip at the adjusting nut end. Unscrew the knurled nut, remove the friction spring and withdraw the unit from the body.

7 Check all parts for wear and service the cap and contact breaker by following the instructions in **Section 4:2**. If the shaft 14 is slack in the body, drive out the parallel pin, pull off dog 16 and withdraw the spindle. Press out the old bush. Immerse the new bush in thin engine oil for 24 hours and press it into the body.

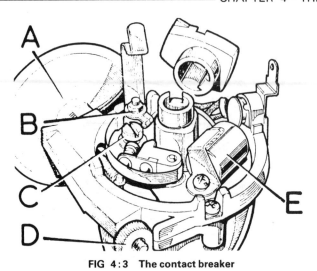

FIG 4:3   The contact breaker

Key to Fig 4:3   **A** Micrometer scale   **B** Terminal screw
C Contact adjustment screw   **D** Micrometer adjusting nut
E Capacitor

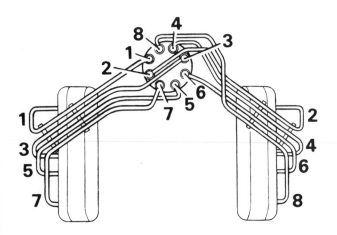

FIG 4:4   Correct fitting of HT leads, 3.5 litre engines

Reassembly is the reversal of dismantling, but note the following points:
1 Lubricate the parts of the centrifugal advance mechanism, the distributor shaft and that part of the shaft which accepts the cam with thin engine oil.
2 Turn the vacuum control adjusting nut to its half way position. Engage the cam driving pins with the centrifugal weights so that, when seen from above, the small offset of the driving dog is on the right and the driving slot for the rotor arm is at the six o'clock position.
3 Fit the distributor in its housing and turn the rotor arm until the driving dog engages. Provided the crankshaft has not been turned, the rotor arm should finish up pointing to No. 1 cylinder segment in the cap. Replace the plug leads in the firing order of 1, 3, 4, 2 or 1, 5, 3, 6, 2, 4 ($2\frac{1}{4}$ or 2.6 litre engine). Distributor rotation is anticlockwise when viewed from above. If the clamping plate has been moved, resulting in lost timing, refer to the next section.

4:5 *Timing the ignition*

If the engine has been dismantled and the ignition timing disturbed, refer to **Chapter 1** for retiming instructions for both the $2\frac{1}{4}$ and 2.6 litre three main bearing engines (see **Section 1:7(a)** and **(b)**).

$2\frac{1}{4}$ litre five main bearing engines and 3.5 litre engine distributors are dealt with in **Section 4:7**.

4:6 *Sparking plugs*

Inspect, clean and adjust sparking plugs regularly. The inspection of the deposits on the electrodes is particularly useful because the type and colour of the deposit gives a clue to the conditions inside the combustion chamber and is, therefore, most helpful when tuning.

Remove the sparking plugs by loosening them a couple of turns and then blowing away loose dirt from the plug recesses with compressed air or a tyre pump. Store them in the order of removal.

Examine the gaskets. If they are about half their original thickness they may be used again.

Examine the firing end of the plugs to note the type of deposit. Normally, it should be powdery and range from brown to greyish tan in colour. There will also be slight wear of the electrodes and the general effect is one which comes from mixed periods of high-speed and low-speed driving. Cleaning and resetting the gap is all that will be required. If the deposits are white or yellowish, they indicate long periods of constant-speed driving or much low-speed driving. Again, the treatment is straightforward.

Black, wet deposits are caused by oil entering the combustion chamber past worn pistons, rings or down valve stems. Sparking plugs of a type which run hotter may help to alleviate the problem, but the cure is an engine overhaul.

Dry, black, fluffy deposits are usually the result of running with a rich mixture. Incomplete combustion may also be a cause and this might be traced to defective ignition or excessive idling.

Overheated sparking plugs have a white, blistered look about the centre electrode and the side electrode may be badly eroded. This may be caused by poor cooling, wrong ignition timing, or sustained high speeds with heavy loads.

Have the sparking plugs cleaned on an abrasive-blasting machine and tested under pressure after attention to the electrodes. File these until they are clean, bright and parallel. Set the electrode gap to .025 inch. Do not try to bend the centre electrode. The spark plug gap for Series 3 models should be .029 to .032 inch.

Before replacing the plugs, clean the threads with a wire brush. Do not use a wire brush on the electrodes. If it is found that the plugs cannot be screwed in by hand, run a tap down the threads in the cylinder head. Failing a tap, use an old sparking plug with crosscuts down the threads. Finally, tighten the plugs to a torque of 30 lb ft. If a torque wrench is not available, tighten with a normal box spanner through half a turn.

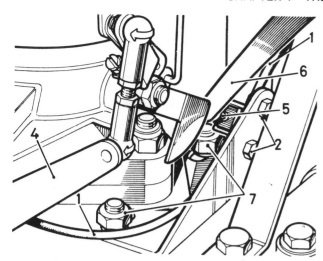

FIG 4:5   Throttle controlled vacuum switch adjustment

Key to Fig 4:5   1 Vacuum pipes   2 Switch retaining bolts
4 Throttle linkage   5 Switch plunger   6 .003 inch
feeler gauge   7 Bracket mounting nuts

Sparking plug leads:

To fit new leads, insert the cable after smearing the
socket with silicone grease to prevent water from entering. Push the lead right home and then secure it with
the screw. To fit the high-tension cable to the ignition
coil, slip the knurled terminal over the cable first. Then
bare about $\frac{1}{4}$ inch of the wires and thread them through
the brass washer removed from the old cable. Fan out
the wires over the face of the washer to hold it in place.
Screwing the terminal nut into the coil socket will hold
the cable firmly.

On 3.5 litre engines, the leads must be fitted as shown
in **FIG 4:4** to avoid cross-firing. When pushing leads
onto plugs, ensure that the ferrules within the shrouds
are firmly seated on the plugs. Shroud ends should be
within .25 inch (6 mm) of the metal body of the plugs.

4:7 Emission control

Special distributors provide retarded ignition at low
engine speeds while retaining the normal advance
facility at higher speeds. However, when the throttle is
shut from high engine speeds, a retarded setting is
needed and is achieved by fitting a throttle controlled
vacuum switch.

Refer to **FIG 4:5**. The switch is inserted in the vacuum
line between the inlet manifold and the distributor
retard capsule. A throttle operated cam governs the
switch progressively from open to closed.

At the open position (switch plunger out), the switch
closes off the vacuum line, opens the distributor capsule to atmosphere and allows the ignition to advance.

At the closed position (switch plunger in), the switch
opens the vacuum line to the capsule and the ignition is
retarded.

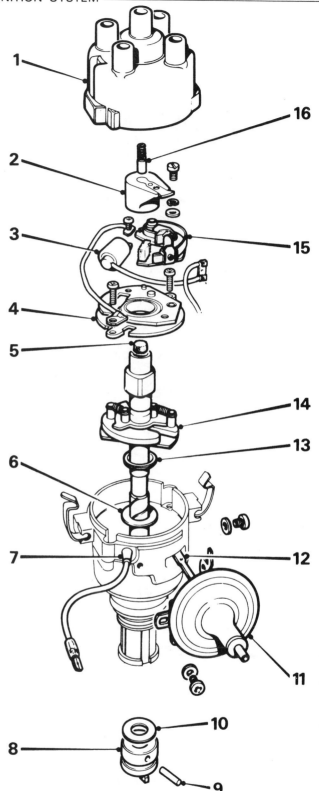

FIG 4:6   Components of a Lucas distributor

Key to Fig 4:6   1 Distributor cap   2 Rotor arm
3 Condenser (capacitor)   4 Baseplate assembly   5 Felt pad
6 Steel washer   7 Low-tension lead   8 Drive dog
9 Retaining pin   10 Thrust washer   11 Vacuum unit
12 Operating arm   13 Spacer   14 Automatic advance
mechanism   15 Contact set   16 Pick-up brush

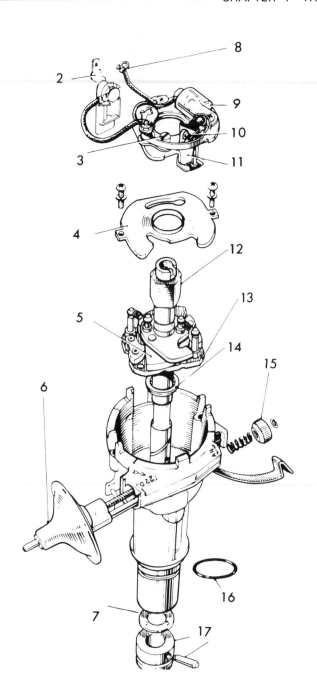

FIG 4 : 7   Components of the 25D6 distributor

Key to Fig 4 : 7   2 Low-tension terminal   3 Fixed contact plate securing screw   4 Contact breaker baseplate   5 Centrifugal timing control weights   6 Vacuum timing control   7 Thrust washer   8 Contact breaker earth connector   9 Capacitor   10 Contacts   11 Contact breaker moving plate   12 Cam   13 Action plate   14 Distance collar   15 Micrometer adjustment nut   16 Oil seal washer   17 Dog and pin

Adjusting the vacuum switch:

First ensure that the throttle linkage is fully in the idle position, then push the switch plunger fully in and hold.

Measure the clearance between the plunger and the cam on the throttle linkage. This must be .003 inch (.076 mm).

If necessary, adjust by loosening the mounting bracket nuts and moving the switch and bracket complete in the required direction.

Ignition timing:

To ensure compliance with any exhaust emission regulations it is essential that the timing is set dynamically. This requires the use of a tachometer and a stroboscopic lamp. The static timing may be used as an initial setting, but this is not acceptable as a final setting. The timing mark for the engine appears either with a multiple pointer and a single mark on the pulley or a single pointer with a scale of marks on the crankshaft pulley.

Make sure that the vacuum switch is correctly set and that all pipes are sound and correctly fitted. Connect a stroboscopic lamp to No. 1 sparking plug in accordance with the maker's instructions.

Set the engine idle speed to as near 500 rev/min as possible without exceeding this figure or 650 rev/min on 3.5 litre. Set the vernier adjustment on the distributor, where fitted, to the fully advanced position.

Slacken the distributor clamp bolt and carefully rotate the distributor to synchronise the light at the setting given in **Technical Data**. Secure the clamping bolt and check the timing.

Later 2¼ litre, three main bearing engine distributor:

Servicing:

1 Remove the distributor as already described.
2 Remove the rotor arm 2 (see **FIG 4 : 6**) and felt pad 5 from the cam spindle.
3 Push the low-tension lead and grommet 7 into the distributor.
4 Remove the contact set 15.
5 Remove the capacitor 3.
6 Remove the baseplate 4 complete with the low-tension lead after disengaging the operating arm 12.
7 Remove the vacuum advance unit 11.
8 Drift out the drive dog rollpin 9 and remove the dog 8 and thrust washer 10.
9 Remove the shaft complete with automatic advance mechanism 14, steel shim 6 and nylon spacer 13. Do not dismantle the advance mechanism other than renewing the springs if the automatic advance has not been operating correctly.
10 Check all parts for damage or excessive wear and renew if necessary. Certain items are only renewed as complete assemblies. If there is excessive side movement in the shaft bearings, the distributor must be renewed complete. The shaft assembly must be renewed completely if there is any wear or damage in the moving parts or on the cam. The automatic advance springs should be renewed if there is any sign of weakness. The baseplate assembly must be renewed if the spring between the

plates is damaged or if the plates do not move freely. Renew the distributor cap if there is any sign of 'tracking' or cracks. Clean off any carbon deposits on the electrodes. Check the high-tension brush for freedom of movement and the rotor for damage, electrode security, burning or 'tracking' and renew as necessary.

11 Use Rocol MP (Molypad) grease when refitting the shaft. Ensure that the nylon spacer 13 and steel washer 6 are fitted as shown in **FIG 4:6**.

12 Fit the thrust washer 10. Using a new rollpin 9, fit the drive dog so that the tongues are parallel to the rotor arm and to the left of its centreline when the rotor arm points upwards. If a new shaft is being fitted, drill through the hole in the drive dog while pushing the shaft from the cam end and holding the drive dog and washer firmly against the distributor body.

13 The remaining procedure is a reversal of the disassembly. Adjust the contacts as described in **Section 4:2** and add one drop of oil to the cam shaft felt pad.

Later 2.6 litre engine distributor:

Servicing:

There are three variants in use. Variations can include a cap screen cover and/or an external adjuster or neither.

The following instructions apply to all.

Dismount the distributor as described earlier and refer to **FIG 4:7**.

1 Spring back the clips and remove the moulded cap. Pull off the rotor arm. Take careful note of the relative position of parts as they are dismantled. Remove the screen if fitted.

2 Remove the nut, insulating bush, capacitor lead, low-tension lead, moving contact spring and insulating washer from the spring anchor pin and the moving contact and insulating washer from the pivot pin.

3 Remove screw 3 and lift off the fixed contact plate. Remove the capacitor 9 and earth lead 8. If the vacuum unit has only one connection, disconnect the spring between the unit and the baseplate and remove the baseplate. If the vacuum unit has two connections, push the baseplate downward, disconnect the unit arm and remove the baseplate.

4 **Before further dismantling, note the relative positions of the rotor arm driving slot above the cam and the driving dog 17 which is offset and can only engage the drive shaft in one position.** Then, when the cam assembly is refitted to the centrifugal weights at reassembly, the timing will not be 180 deg. out.

5 Remove the cam retaining screw and remove the cam 12. Remove the springs and automatic timing control weights.

6 Remove the circlip at the adjusting nut end, if applicable, to release the vacuum unit. Remove the adjusting nut 15 and spring and withdraw the vacuum unit 6. Where no external adjuster is fitted, drive out the rollpin from the distributor body and withdraw the vacuum unit.

7 Check the parts for wear, the moulded cap for 'tracking', the condition of the points and the tension of the moving contact spring which should be 18 to 24 oz measured at the points. Examine the high-tension leads.

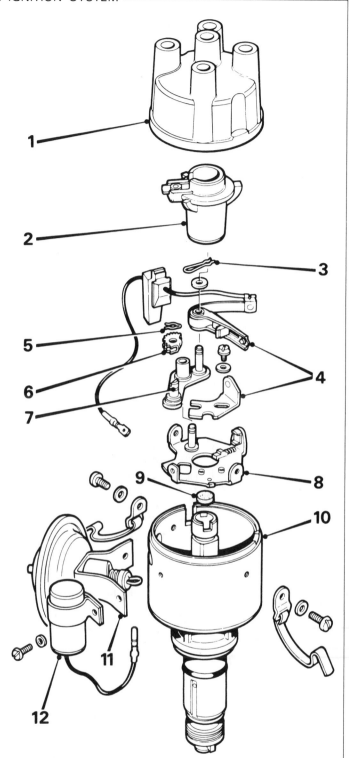

FIG 4:8   Components of Ducellier distributor

Key to Fig 4:8

	1 Distributor cap	2 Rotor arm
3 Retaining clip	4 Contact set	5 Retaining clip
6 Serrated cam	7 Eccentric 'D' post	8 Baseplate
9 Felt pad	10 Distributor body	11 Vacuum unit
12 Condenser		

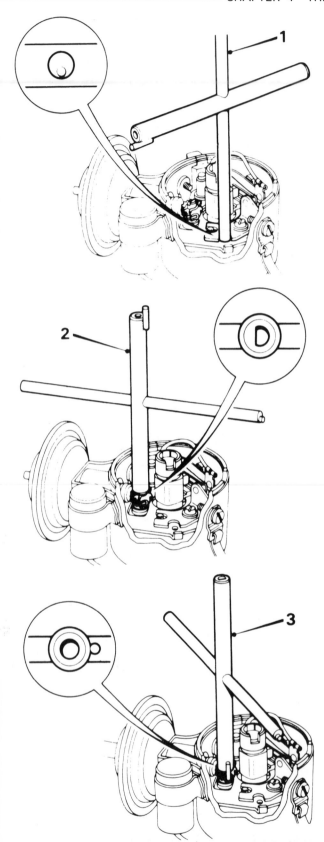

Reassembly is the reverse of the dismantling procedure.

1 Lubricate the parts of the automatic timing control, the bearing and cam spigot with thin engine oil.
2 Turn the vacuum control adjustment to mid-position.
3 Fit the distributor to its housing and turn the rotor arm to engage the driving dog.

2¼ litre, five main bearing engine distributor:

Lucas sliding contact type:

Follow the instructions given for the later Lucas distributor; additional lubrication has been covered in **Section 4 : 2, FIG 4 : 2.**

Ducellier distributor:

Servicing:

1 Remove the distributor.
2 Pull off the rotor arm 2 (see **FIG 4 : 8**).
3 Remove the felt pad 9 from the cam.
4 Remove the screws retaining the capacitor 12 and vacuum unit 11.
5 Remove the spring clip 5 from the eccentric 'D' post 7.
6 Mark the position of the serrated cam 6 in relation to the spring seat of the vacuum unit operating link.
7 Disengage the vacuum unit operating link and the serrated cam from the eccentric 'D' post.
8 Remove the vacuum unit.
9 Remove the contact breaker retaining clip 3, the locking screw and remove the contact breaker set.
10 Remove the remaining screw from the baseplate 8 and, taking care to retain the nylon pressure pad and spring, lift out the baseplate.
11 Examine all parts for damage or excessive wear and renew as necessary. Excessive side play in the shaft or wear in the advance mechanism will necessitate renewal of the distributor.
12 Lubricate the centrifugal weight pivot posts and lightly smear the cam, pressure pad and contact pivot post with Retinax 'A' or equivalent grease.
13 The remaining operations are a reversal of the dismantling procedure, aligning the marks made on the serrated cam and vacuum unit operating link when fitting to the eccentric 'D' post. Make a preliminary setting of the contact gap (see **Technical Data**). Place the felt pad in the cam and add one drop of engine oil.
14 Refit and adjust the distributor as already described.

The drive dog is a loose fit on the drive shaft to ensure correct alignment.

If the distributor has been removed to enable other work to be carried out and is being refitted without any servicing, it can be refitted in a similar manner to the Lucas distributor. After servicing, it is essential to have special tool 18G 1308, a timing light and a vacuum pump available to set the dwell angle, the dwell variation and the vacuum advance all as given in **Technical Data**. If the equipment is available, proceed as follows.

1 Carry out the refitting procedure for the Lucas distributor (see **Section 4 : 4**).
2 Check the dwell angle at idle speed with the vacuum pipe disconnected.

FIG 4 : 9 Ducellier distributor setting using tool 18G 1308

Key to Fig 4 : 9   1 Adjusting the dwell angle   2 Adjusting the dwell variation   3 Setting the vacuum advance

3 If adjustment is necessary, slacken the contact locking screw (see **FIG 4 : 8**) and use special tool 18G 1308 as shown at 1 in **FIG 4 : 9** to move the fixed contact plate as required.

4 Check the dwell angle at 2000 rev/min, vacuum pipe disconnected. It should be within the tolerance given in **Technical Data**. Variation outside the tolerance indicates a mechanical fault in the distributor.

5 Connect the vacuum pipe, increase engine speed to 2000 rev/min and release the accelerator. Check the dwell variation. Adjust, if necessary, by rotating the eccentric 'D' post (7 in **FIG 4 : 8**) using tool 18G 1308 as shown at 2 (see **FIG 4 : 9**). Setting the dwell for minimum variation may alter the basic setting. Recheck at idle speed and adjust the timing if necessary.

6 If the vacuum unit has been renewed or the distributor dismantled, connect a vacuum pump to the vacuum unit and run the engine at idle speed, insert a timing light between the end of the low-tension lead from the side of the distributor and a good earth.

7 Slowly increase the vacuum and note the point at which the vacuum advance starts (see **Technical Data**). Adjustment of the serrated cam (6 in **FIG 4 : 8**), one tooth at a time, using tool 18G 1308 as shown at 3 in **FIG 4 : 9** will alter the point at which the vacuum advance starts.

8 Remove equipment, tighten the clamp plate bolt and connect the vacuum unit pipe.

9 The remaining operations are a reversal of the removal procedure.

3.5 litre, V8 engine distributor :

Servicing :

1 Remove the distributor (see **Chapter 1, Section 1 : 6**).

2 Unclip and remove the cap.

3 Withdraw the rotor arm and felt pad.

4 Remove the contact spring or remove the nut and lift off the insulating bush together with the low-tension and capacitor leads.

5 Remove the Quickafit contact set.

6 Remove the capacitor.

7 Remove the dwell angle adjuster screw and spring.

8 Remove the centrifugal advance coverplate earth lead.

9 Remove the vacuum unit and grommet.

10 Remove the contact breaker baseplate.

11 Remove the centrifugal advance coverplate.

12 Remove the springs carefully from the centrifugal advance unit.

13 Remove the screw inside the cam and lift off the cam shaft.

14 Remove the weights.

15 Drive out the pin and remove the drive gear and tabwasher.

16 Examine all parts for wear or damage and renew as necessary.

Reassembly is a reversal of the dismantling operations.

Locate the vacuum unit link with the Quickafit contacts before the unit is secured to the body.

Do not stretch the centrifugal unit springs.

Finally, set the points to .014 to .016 inch (.35 to .40 mm).

Refit the distributor as detailed in **Chapter 1, Section 1 : 7** and set the static timing, **before starting the engine**, by the basic lamp timing method.

Set the idle speed to 650 rev/min.

Using suitable electronic equipment, set the dwell angle as follows.

1 Set the selector knob to the 'calibrate' position.

2 Adjust the calibration knob to give a zero reading on the meter.

3 Couple up the Tach-dwell meter to the engine, following the manufacturer's instructions.

4 Set the selector knob to the '8-cylinder' position and the Tach-dwell selector knob to 'dwell'.

5 Using the hexagon headed adjustment screw on the side of the distributor body, adjust the dwell angle to 26 deg. to 28 deg. The '4-cylinder' position can be used, if necessary, but, in this case, adjust to 52 deg. to 56 deg. Uncouple the meter.

Carry out a dynamic timing check as already described.

4 : 8 *Fault diagnosis*

(a) Engine will not fire

1 Battery discharged

2 Distributor contact points dirty, pitted or maladjusted

3 Distributor cap dirty, cracked or 'tracking'

4 Carbon brush inside distributor cap not touching rotor

5 Faulty cable or loose connection in low-tension circuit

6 Distributor rotor arm cracked

7 Faulty coil

8 Broken contact breaker spring

9 Contact points stuck open

(b) Engine misfires

1 Check 2, 3, 5 and 7 in (a)

2 Weak contact breaker spring

3 High-tension plug and coil leads cracked or perished

4 Sparking plug(s) loose

5 Sparking plug insulation cracked

6 Sparking plug gap incorrectly set

7 Ignition timing too far advanced

NOTES

CHAPTER 5

THE COOLING SYSTEM

5 : 1 *Description*

The engines covered in this manual have a pressurized cooling system. The natural thermo-syphon action of the water is augmented by a centrifugal impeller mounted at the cylinder block end of the fan spindle. The impeller receives water from the bottom tank of the radiator and passes it through the cylinder block. From here it rises into the cylinder head(s) until it reaches a thermostat valve which prevents cold water passing to the top tank of the radiator. The water is then recirculated through the engine until it is hot enough to open the thermostat valve, thus giving a quick warm up. The hot water in the top tank of the radiator falls through the finned core where it is cooled. The passage of the cooling air past the core is assisted by the action of the fan.

A spring-loaded valve in the radiator filler cap or, on 3.5 litre, in the expansion tank pressurizes the system and so increases the temperature at which the water boils. Note that early models are pressurized to 10 lb/sq inch (.7 kg/sq cm) and later models to 9 lb/sq inch (.6 kg/sq cm). As the coolant temperature falls, a vacuum is created and a valve opening at 1 lb/sq inch (.07 kg/sq cm) is incorporated in all filler caps.

On 3.5 litre models, the radiator filler plug must not be removed when the engine is hot: the pressure in the system could cause personal injury from the plug or scalding from the hot coolant.

It is essential to note that the diesel engine must not be run, even for a few seconds, without coolant in it. Lacquer formation on the injectors would ruin them almost at once. The wisest precaution to take if the diesel cooling system is drained is to disconnect the batteries so that the heater plugs and starter motor are inoperative; failing this, at least attach a label to a prominent place in the driving cab stating that the system has been drained and the engine must not be started until it is refilled.

5 : 2 *Maintenance of cooling system, all models*

It is a good plan to inspect the cooling system at the same time that the oil level is checked. **Do not remove filler caps when the coolant is hot.** If the cap must be removed, protect the hands with a pad of cloth, turn the cap to the first stop and release all pressure before removing the cap. See that the water level in the radiator reaches the bottom of the filler neck on $2\frac{1}{4}$ or 2.6 litre engines or halfway up the expansion tank on 3.5 litre engines, that the hoses are not cracked or perished, the drain taps or plugs are properly closed and that no water leaks are visible. Check the fan belt tension; on $2\frac{1}{4}$ litre petrol and diesel engines there should be $\frac{5}{16}$ to $\frac{7}{16}$ inch (8 to 11 mm) slack between the fan and the crankshaft pulleys and the same on the 2.6 litre petrol engine. To adjust the tension, slacken the generator pivot bolts and the bolt on the adjusting link, move the generator as necessary, then tighten the bolts.

Adjust the belt tension of models fitted with an alternator in place of the generator to the following figures. For the $2\frac{1}{4}$ litre engine the belt should deflect .25 to .375 inch (6.5 to 9.5 mm) midway between the fan and alter-

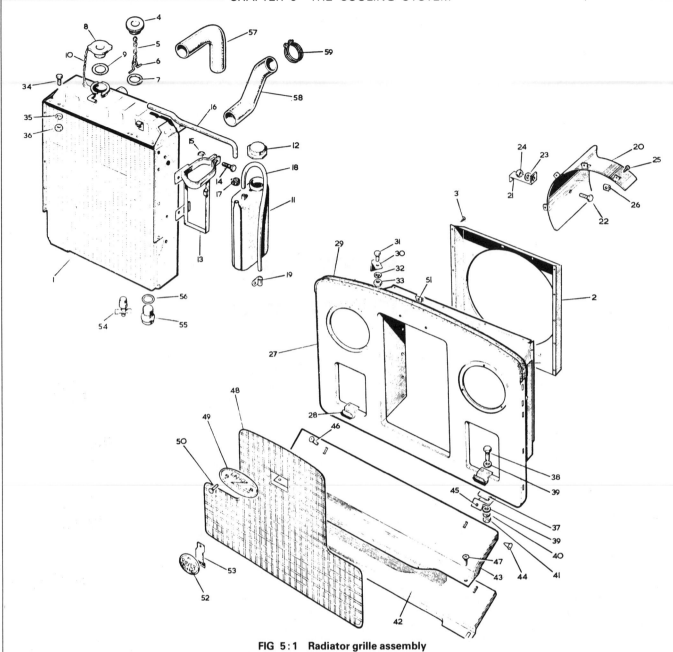

FIG 5:1   Radiator grille assembly

Key to Fig 5:1   1 Radiator block assembly   2 Fan cowl   3 Drive screw for cowl   4 Filler cap   5 Filler cap chain   6 Retainer for chain   7 Filler cap joint washer   8 Filler cap with overflow bottle provision   9 Joint washer   10 Chain for filler cap   11 Overflow bottle for radiator   12 Cap for overflow bottle   13 Carrier bracket for overflow bottle   14 Bolt ($\frac{1}{4}$ inch UNF x $\frac{7}{8}$ inch long) (clamping bottle to carrier)   15 Self-locking nut ($\frac{1}{4}$ inch UNF) (clamping bottle to carrier)   16 Hose, radiator to overflow bottle   17 Clip, fixing hose   18 Flexible pipe, overflow bottle outlet   19 Clip, fixing outlet pipe   20 Shroud for fan cowl   21 Steady strip for shroud   22 Bolt ($\frac{1}{4}$ inch UNF x $\frac{5}{8}$ inch long) (fixing steady strip to shroud)   23 Spring washer (fixing steady strip to shroud)   24, 25, 26 Shroud fixings   27 Radiator grille panel complete   28 Support clip for grille mesh   29 Bonnet rest strip, 35 inch long   30 Protection plate for headlamp   31 Bolt ($\frac{1}{4}$ inch UNF x $\frac{5}{8}$ inch long) (fixing plate to grille panel)   32 Spring washer (fixing plate to grille panel)   33 Nut ($\frac{1}{4}$ inch UNF) (fixing plate to grille panel)   34 Bolt ($\frac{1}{4}$ inch UNF x $\frac{5}{8}$ inch long) (fixing radiator block to grille panel)   35 Spring washer (fixing radiator block to grille panel)   36 Nut ($\frac{1}{4}$ inch UNF) (fixing radiator block to grille panel)   37 Rubber buffer (fixing grille panel and front apron bracket to chassis frame)   38 Bolt ($\frac{5}{16}$ inch UNF x 1$\frac{1}{2}$ inch long) (fixing grille panel and front apron bracket to chassis frame)   39 Plain washer (fixing grille panel and front apron bracket to chassis frame)   40 Spring washer (fixing grille panel and front apron bracket to chassis frame)   41 Nut ($\frac{5}{16}$ inch UNF) (fixing grille panel and front apron bracket to chassis frame)   42 Front apron panel (alternatives)   43 Front apron panel (alternatives)   44 Rubber buffer for front apron panel   45 Securing bracket for panel   46 Fixings, apron panel to brackets   47 Fixings, apron panel to chassis   48 Grille for radiator   49 'Land Rover' nameplate   50 Drive screw (fixing nameplate and grille to grille panel)   51 Spire nut (fixing nameplate and grille to grille panel)   52 'Diesel' badge, where applicable   53 Fixing bracket for badge – Rivet (fixing bracket and badge to grille – Lockwasher (fixing bracket and badge to grille)   54 Drain tap for radiator   55 Drain plug for radiator   56 Joint washer for plug   57 Hose for radiator, top   58 Hose for radiator, bottom   59 Radiator hose clips

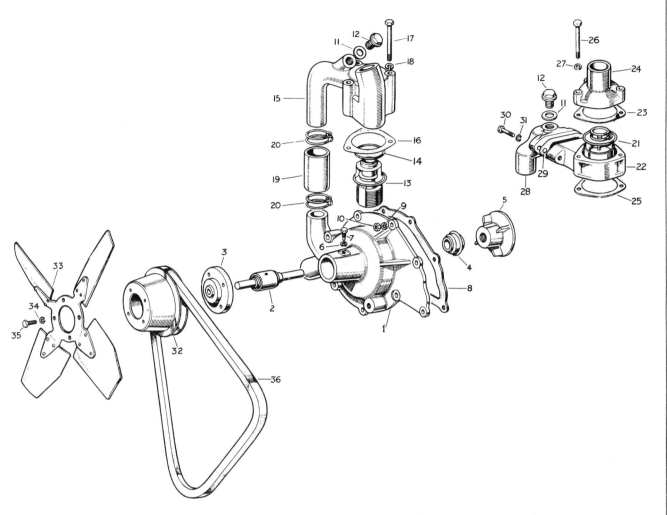

FIG 5 : 2   2¼ litre, petrol and diesel, pump layout

Key to Fig 5 : 2   1 Water pump casing   2 Pump spindle and bearing   3 Hub for fan   4 Carbon ring and seal unit
5 Impeller for pump   6 Spring washer (locating bearing casing)   7 Special setbolt (locating bearing casing)   8 Joint washer
for water pump   9 Spring washer (fixing water pump to front cover)   10 Nut (fixing water pump to front cover)
11 Joint washer (for heater return in water outlet pipe)   12 Plug (⅜ inch BSP) (for heater return in water outlet pipe)
13 Thermostat   14 O-ring, thermostat to water outlet pipe   15 Water outlet pipe, thermostat to radiator
16 Washer for outlet pipe   17 Setbolt (¼ inch UNF x 2½ inch long) (fixing outlet pipe to cylinder head)   18 Spring washer
(fixing outlet pipe to cylinder head)   19 Hose for bypass pipe   20 Clip for hose   21 Thermostat   22 Thermostat housing
23 Joint washer for thermostat housing, upper   24 Water outlet pipe, thermostat to radiator   25 Joint washer for
thermostat housing, lower   26 Setbolt (¼ inch UNF x 2½ inch long) (fixing thermostat housing and outlet pipe to cylinder head)
Setbolt (¼ inch UNF x 2¾ inch long) (fixing thermostat housing and outlet pipe to cylinder head)   27 Spring washer (fixing
thermostat housing and outlet pipe to cylinder head)   28 Thermostat bypass pipe   29 Joint washer for bypass pipe
30 Setbolt (5/16 inch UNF x 1 inch long) (fixing bypass pipe to thermostat housing)   31 Spring washer (fixing bypass pipe to
thermostat housing)   32 Fan pulley   33 Fan blade   34 Spring washer (fixing fan blade and pulley to hub)   35 Setbolt (¼ inch
UNF x ¾ inch long) (fixing fan blade and pulley to hub)   36 Fan and dynamo belt

nator pulleys. For the 2.6 litre engine fitted with an alternator, deflection is the same as for the earlier models.

On 3.5 litre engines, the deflection should be .5 ±.06 inch (11 to 14 mm).

Flushing the system :

The cooling system should be drained and flushed at least once or twice a year in the following manner :
1 Remove the radiator cap or plug, as applicable, and open the drain taps or plugs. Allow the coolant to drain away.

2 Place a hose in the radiator filler and fill the system ; adjust the flow to equal that draining from the taps.
3 Run the 2¼ or 2.6 litre engine for a few minutes.
4 Stop the engine, close the taps and refill the system to the bottom of the radiator filler neck on 2¼ or 2.6 litre engines.
5 On 3.5 litre engines, using prepared solution, fill the radiator and fit the filler plug and washer. Add water to the expansion tank up to half full and fit the expansion tank filler cap.
6 Run the engine until the thermostat opens, indicated by the top radiator hose becoming hot.

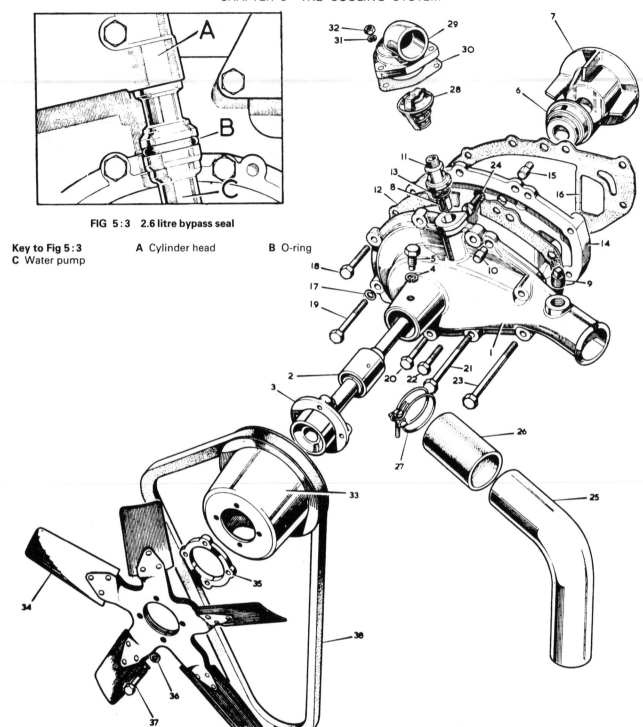

FIG 5:3   2.6 litre bypass seal

Key to Fig 5:3   **A** Cylinder head   **B** O-ring
C Water pump

FIG 5:4   2.6 litre petrol engine, pump layout

Key to Fig 5:4   1 Water pump assembly   2 Spindle and bearing complete   3 Hub for fan blade   4 Spring washer (locating bearing in casing)   5 Special setbolt (locating bearing in casing)   6 Carbon ring and seal   7 Impeller for pump
8 Tube for thermostat bypass   9 Plug ($\frac{3}{8}$ inch BSP) for heater adaptor hole in casing   10 Dowel for water pump casing
11 Connector, bypass to water pump   12 Joint washer for water pump   13 Rubber seal, pump to cylinder head
14 Adaptor for water pump   15 Dowel for adaptor   16 Joint washer for adaptor   17 Spring washer *   18 Setbolt
($\frac{1}{4}$ inch UNF x 1 inch long) *   19 Setbolt ($\frac{1}{4}$ inch UNF x 1$\frac{5}{8}$ inch long) *   20 Setbolt ($\frac{1}{4}$ inch UNF x 1$\frac{1}{8}$ inch long) *   21 Setbolt
($\frac{1}{4}$ inch UNF x 2$\frac{1}{4}$ inch long) *   22 Setbolt ($\frac{1}{4}$ inch UNF x $\frac{7}{8}$ inch long) *   23 Setbolt ($\frac{1}{4}$ inch UNF x 2$\frac{3}{4}$ inch long)   24 Special
'Wedgelok' screw *   25 Inlet pipe for water pump   26 Hose, water inlet pipe to pump   27 Clip, hose to pump   28 Thermostat,
wax type   29 Outlet pipe to radiator   30 Joint washer for water outlet pipe   31 Spring washer (fixing pipe to cylinder head)
32 Nut ($\frac{1}{4}$ inch UNF) (fixing pipe to cylinder head)   33 Pulley for fan   34 Fan blade   35 Distance piece for fan blade
36 Spring washer (fixing pulley and blade to hub)   37 Setbolt ($\frac{1}{4}$ inch UNF x 1$\frac{1}{4}$ inch long) (fixing pulley and blade to hub)   38 Fan belt

*Fixing water pump and adaptor to block

7 Allow the engine to cool, check the coolant level and top up as necessary.

Frost precautions:

Only high quality inhibited glycol based solutions (containing no methanol) suitable for cast iron or aluminium engines, as applicable, should be used as antifreeze. For temperatures from −18°C, use one part of antifreeze to two parts of water or, for lower temperatures, equal parts. See the **Technical Data** section for the capacities of the various cooling systems. To add the antifreeze, first check that all the cooling system connections are in good order; antifreeze has a much more 'searching' action than plain water. Drain and flush the system, then add 1 gallon ($4\frac{1}{2}$ litres) of clean water, add the antifreeze and top up with water. Run the engine until the thermostat opens and the solution circulates through the radiator core. When the engine is cool, recheck the coolant level and top up if necessary. If possible, always use soft water in the cooling system. In hard water areas, or areas where the water has a salt content, distilled or rain water should be used.

In areas where no frost precautions are necessary, add three fluid ounces of Marston Lubricants SQ 36 Coolant Inhibitor concentrate to each gallon of water.

5:3 *The water pumps*

Petrol engines:

(a) $2\frac{1}{4}$ litre:

FIG 5:1 shows the layout and this applies to the diesel engine as well. The later type semi-sealed system is illustrated.

The pump can be removed without taking off the radiator; in this case, proceed as follows:
1 Partly drain off the coolant (into a clean container if it is an antifreeze solution).
2 Remove the shroud from the fan cowl.
3 Slacken the generator mounting bolts and push the generator inwards, remove the belt, then remove the generator adjusting link, fan blades and pulley.
4 Detach the bottom hose from the radiator and the bypass hose from the pump.
5 Undo the nuts and withdraw the pump. **FIG 5:2** shows the assembly in detail.

(b) 2.6 litre:

Proceed exactly as for the $2\frac{1}{4}$ litre engine except where a viscous fan with plastic fan blades is fitted in which case the radiator must be removed before removing the fan belt, fan blades and pulley/viscous coupling. Note that as there is no bypass hose, the pump must be tilted slightly to compress the O-ring at the bypass port on top of the pump (see **FIG 5:3** for detail of the assembly). **FIG 5:4** shows the complete pump unit.

(c) 3.5 litre:

1 Drain the coolant (see **Section 5:2**).
2 Slacken the pivot and link bolts and move the alternator towards the engine, then remove the drive belt.
3 Remove the fixings from the fan cowl and move the cowl towards the engine.

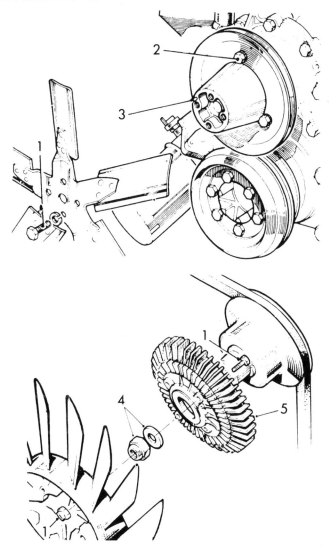

FIG 5:5 Fan blades and pulley, 3.5 litre engine. Top, standard type. Bottom, viscous coupling type

Key to Fig 5:5   1 Fan blade fixings   2 Pulley fixings
3 Pulley   4 Coupling nut and washer   5 Viscous coupling

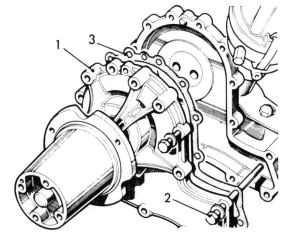

FIG 5:6 Water pump, 3.5 litre engine

Key to Fig 5:6   1 Pump   2 Long bolts   3 Joint washer

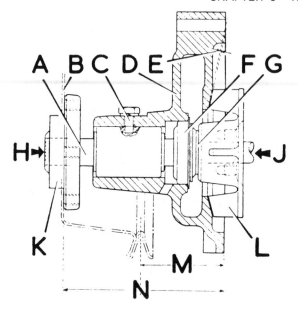

FIG 5:7   2.6 litre, sectioned view of pump

Key to Fig 5:7   **A** Pump spindle and bearing   **B** Fan belt pulley   **C** Bearing location bolt and washer   **D** Water pump body   **E** Dimension, .025 inch (.63 mm)   **F** Carbon ring and seal assembly   **G** Carbon seal faced towards impeller   **H** Support here when fitting impeller   **J** Support here when fitting hub   **K** Fan hub   **L** Impeller   **M** Dimension, 1.820 inch (46.2 mm)   **N** Dimension, 3.820 inch (97.0 mm)

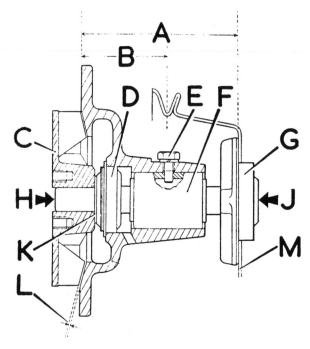

FIG 5:8   2¼ litre, sectioned view of pump

Key to Fig 5:8   **A** Dimension, 3.510 inch (89.15 mm)   **B** Dimension, 1.930 inch (49.0 mm)   **C** Impeller   **D** Carbon ring and seal assembly   **E** Locating bolt   **F** Pump spindle and bearing assembly   **G** Fan hub   **H** Support here when fitting hub   **J** Support here when fitting impeller   **K** Carbon seal faced towards impeller   **L** Dimension, .025 inch (.63 mm)   **M** Fan belt pulley

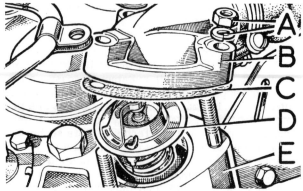

FIG 5:9   Thermostat mounting, 2.6 litre petrol engine

Key to Fig 5:9   **A** Outlet pipe fixing   **B** Outlet pipe   **C** Washer   **D** Thermostat   **E** Cylinder block

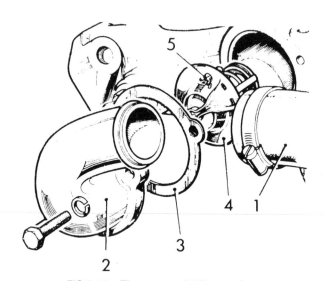

FIG 5:10   Thermostat, 3.5 litre engine

Key to Fig 5:10   **1** Hose   **2** Outlet elbow   **3** Joint washer   **4** Thermostat   **5** Jiggle pin

4   Remove the fan blade fixings 1 (see **FIG 5:5**) and remove the fan blades.
5   Lift out the fan cowl.
6   Remove the pulley fixings 2 and lift off the pulley 3 or remove the coupling fixing 4 and lift off the coupling 5 and pulley.
7   Release the alternator adjusting link from the pump.
8   Disconnect the inlet hose from the pump.
9   Remove the water pump bolts (see **FIG 5:6**) and withdraw the pump 1.
10   Clean the threads of the four long bolts 2 without delay before the old sealant can air harden.

Servicing the pumps, 2¼ and 2.6 litre petrol engines:

Exchange pumps can be obtained, but it is also possible to obtain new bearings and seals. If it is intended to replace the bearings or seals, refer to **FIGS 5:7** and **5:8** and proceed as follows:
1   Remove the bearing location bolt.

2 With a press or heavy vice and suitable distance rings to support the pump casing, press the spindle through the pump casing, thus removing the fan pulley hub as well as the bearings, spindle and impeller.

3 Cut the seal from the spindle and support the impeller. Press out the spindle.

4 Examine the spindle and bearing assembly; it need not be renewed if the bearing is not slack and the spindle not excessively corroded. This may be the case where a defective seal causing a water leak has been the reason for stripping the pump. Clean any corroded part of the spindle and paint with chlorinated rubber primer or good quality aluminium paint. If a steel deflector washer is fitted to the spindle, check that there is .018 inch (.46 mm) clearance between it and the bearing face.

5 Put a few drops of thick oil in the location hole in the bearing.

6 Press the spindle and bearing assembly into the front of the pump body with the longer end of the spindle leading. Locate with the setbolt and washer.

7 Support the spindle and press on the fan pulley hub to the dimensions shown in **FIG 5:7** or **5:8** as appropriate.

8 Turn the pump over and support the spindle at the front. Press the impeller onto the spindle, again referring to **FIG 5:7** or **5:8** as appropriate.

Replacing the 2¼ and 2.6 litre pumps:

This is a reversal of the removal process, but be sure to use all new joint washers. It will be found easier to fit the belt if it is engaged in the fan pulley groove before the fan and pulley are bolted to the pump spindle.

Replacing the 3.5 litre pump:

Refitting is a reversal of the removal procedure, using a new joint washer 3 (see **FIG 5:6**) and smearing the threads of the four long bolts with Thread Lubricant-Sealant 3M EC776. Tighten $\frac{7}{16}$ inch AF bolts to 6 to 8 lb ft (.8 to 1 mkg) and $\frac{1}{2}$ inch AF bolts to 20 to 25 lb ft (2.8 to 3.5 mkg). Adjust the fan belt tension (see **Section 5:2**) and refill the coolant system.

The 2¼ litre diesel engine:

Removal, servicing and replacement of this pump follow the same general lines as those described for the 2¼ litre petrol engine.

5:4 *The thermostat*

(a) 2¼ litre, petrol and diesel engines:

To remove the thermostat, refer to **FIG 5:2**. Partly drain off the coolant, then remove the top radiator hose. Remove the water outlet pipe 15 or 24 and lift out the thermostat 13 or 21. The differences are accounted for by the use of the bellows or wax filled types.

Replacement is a reversal of this procedure, but make sure that all new joint washers are used.

(b) 2.6 litre petrol engine:

To remove the thermostat, refer to **FIG 5:9**. Proceed as for the 2¼ litre engines by partly draining the coolant,

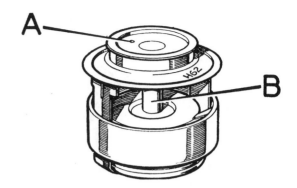

FIG 5:11   Bellows type thermostat

Key to Fig 5:11   **A** Bleed hole to prevent air locks
B Operating valve

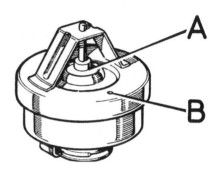

FIG 5:12   Wax filled thermostat

Key to Fig 5:12   **A** Operating valve   **B** Bleed hole
to prevent air locks

removing the top hose and the outlet pipe **B**. The thermostat **D** will then lift out. Replacement is a reversal of the removal process, but make sure that all new joint washers are used.

(c) 3.5 litre engine:

Drain off enough coolant to clear the induction manifold. If the engine is fitted with an air intake temperature control, release the air intake and move it to one side. Disconnect the hose 1 (see **FIG 5:10**) to the radiator. Remove the outlet elbow 2 and joint washer 3, then withdraw the thermostat 4. Replacement is a reversal of the removal procedure, ensuring that the jiggle pin 5 is uppermost (12 o'clock) and using a new joint washer 3.

To test a thermostat:

Obtain a container of water which can be heated to near boiling point. Support the thermostat in the water so that it does not touch the bottom or sides of the container. Raise the water temperature and, with the aid of a thermometer, check the opening point of the thermostat. For the 2¼ litre petrol and diesel engines the temperature should be:

Bellows type:

Commence to open between 161°F (71.7°C) and 168°F (75.6°C).

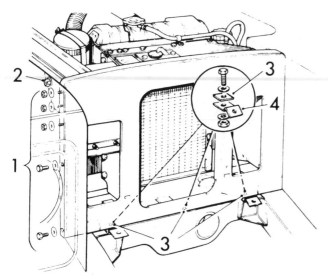

FIG 5:13 Radiator and front panel removal, Series 3

Key to Fig 5:13   1 Front panel fixings   2 Prop bracket bolt   3 Front panel to crossmember fixings 4 Front valance brackets

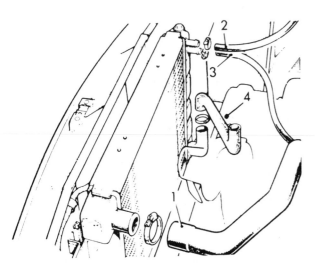

FIG 5:14 Radiator block, 3.5 litre engine

Key to Fig 5:14   1 Top hose   2 Expansion tank hose 3 Induction manifold hose   4 Bottom hose

Wax type:

Commence to open between 159°F (70.6°C) and 167°F (75°C).

For the 2.6 litre petrol engine the temperature should be:

Commence to open between 161°F (71.7°C) and 170°F (76.7°C).

For the 2.6 litre Series 3 petrol engine the temperature should be:

Commence to open between 167°F (75°C) and 176°F (80°C).

The 3.5 litre engine thermostat should commence opening between 173°F (78°C) and 182°F (83°C).

If the opening point is much different to these figures, the unit must be renewed. Similarly, a thermostat which remains open even when cold must also be renewed.

FIGS 5:11 and **5:12** show the difference between the bellows type and the wax filled thermostat.

5:5 Radiator and front panel assembly, Series 3

1 Remove the bonnet and battery, then drain the radiator and cylinder block.
2 Remove the grille and the front valance.
3 Working from the wheel arch, remove the five nuts and bolts securing the front panel to the righthand front wing, see 1 in **FIG 5:13**; this will include the two nuts and bolts retaining the prop bracket. Slacken the third nut and bolt 2 retaining the prop bracket to facilitate alignment of holes when refitting.
4 Remove the five nuts securing the front panel to the lefthand wing and remove the studs.
5 Release the top hose from the radiator.
6 Remove the nut securing the cowl to the battery tray.
7 Make a note of cable colour codes before disconnection, to facilitate reconnection, then disconnect the harnesses from the front panel. The earth lead is secured by the centre bolt. Disconnect the harness from the lefthand side and withdraw the harness from the righthand side. Disconnect the righthand harness from the lefthand section at the centre of the radiator aperture and withdraw the cables through the grommets.
8 Remove the three nuts and bolts 3, making a note of the number and position of the rubber packing pieces to ensure correct alignment on reassembly. Retrieve the two brackets 4.
9 Pull the assembly forward and disconnect the bottom hose from the pump. Withdraw the assembly.

Reassembly is a reversal of the removal operations, ensuring that the drain plugs are refitted, or taps closed, the rubber packing pieces are refitted in their original positions and all harnesses are refitted as noted on removal. On completion, refill the cooling system.

5:6 Radiator block, 3.5 litre

1 Drain the cooling system.
2 Release the fan cowl fixings and move the cowl towards the engine.
3 Disconnect the top hose 1 (see **FIG 5:14**).
4 Disconnect the expansion tank hose 2.
5 Disconnect the induction manifold hose 3.
6 Disconnect the bottom hose 4 from the radiator.
7 Remove the top radiator fixings.
8 Withdraw the radiator from the rubber mounted spigots.

Reassembly is a reversal of the removal operations.

5:7 *Fault diagnosis*

(a) External leakage

1 Loose hose clips
2 Defective hose
3 Damaged radiator
4 Defective water pump seal
5 Loose core plug
6 Damaged gasket

(b) Internal leakage

1 Defective cylinder head gasket
2 Cracked cylinder bore
3 Loose cylinder head bolts

(c) Poor circulation

1 Restriction in system, collapsed hose
2 Insufficient coolant

3 Inoperative water pump
4 Slack fan belt
5 Inoperative thermostat

(d) Overheating

1 Poor circulation
2 Dirty oil and sludge in engine
3 Choked radiator core
4 Incorrect ignition or injection pump timing
5 Incorrect valve timing
6 Low oil level
7 Tight engine
8 Choked exhaust system
9 Binding brakes
10 Excessive idling

(e) Overcooling

1 Defective thermostat

NOTES

CHAPTER 6

THE CLUTCH

6:1 Description

The clutch unit is a Borg and Beck single dry plate type operated by a hydraulic mechanism. Early vehicles are equipped with a coil spring cover unit, but later vehicles have the diaphragm spring cover. This latter unit cannot be overhauled and, in the event of failure, must be exchanged for a new one at a Rover Service Agent. The latest vehicles are also fitted with a hydrostatic operating mechanism which requires no adjustment throughout the life of the clutch. Instructions for setting this mechanism are included in this chapter.

6:2 Adjustment of pedal travel

This operation should be carried out regularly if the early non-hydrostatic mechanism is fitted to ensure that all the free play is not taken up, thereby allowing spring pressure to load the release bearing, giving rise to clutch slip as the friction plate wears. It must also be done whenever the clutch unit or any parts of the mechanism are removed and overhauled. This applies to both early and late type mechanisms. **FIG 6:1** illustrates the early mechanism and **FIG 6:2** the later (hydrostatic) mechanism.

First, check and, if necessary, adjust the pedal position and master cylinder free movement as shown by **FIG 6:3**. Adjust screw **A** until dimension **E** is appropriate to the type of mechanism. Now slacken locknuts **B** and rotate pushrod **C** until $\frac{1}{16}$ inch (1.5 mm) play is apparent at dimension **D**; tighten the locknuts. This will give $\frac{5}{16}$ inch (8 mm) free movement at the pedal pad.

Early models:

Refer to **FIG 6:4**, slacken locknut **C** and rotate pushrod **B** on the slave cylinder until the pedal free travel, measured at the pedal pad, increases from $\frac{5}{16}$ inch (8 mm) to $1\frac{1}{2}$ inch (38 mm). Tighten the locknut.

Late models, hydrostatic mechanism:

Hold the cranked operating lever on the clutch crossshaft down to ensure that all backlash in the mechanism is absorbed. Refer to **FIG 6:5**. Slacken nut **E** and turn nut **D** until dimension **C** is obtained. Lock nut **E**. Never loosen nut **D** on the shaft **B**; it must always be hard against the end of the thread.

Note that, with this hydrostatic mechanism, the pedal free travel remains at $\frac{5}{16}$ inch (8 mm). Any 'riding' of the clutch will cause rapid wear as the mechanism

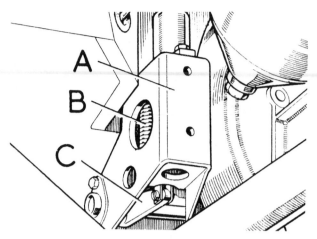

FIG 6:1   Early type mechanism

Key to Fig 6:1   A Support bracket   **B** Return spring
C Straight operating lever

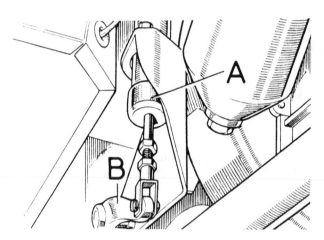

FIG 6:2   Later type mechanism

Key to Fig 6:2   A Slave cylinder   **B** Cranked operating lever

begins to operate immediately this small amount of free play disappears.

6:3 *Bleeding the hydraulic system*

During this operation, maintain the level of fluid in the reservoir by adding Unipart Universal Brake Fluid or other brake fluid having a minimum boiling point of 500°F (260°C) and complying with FMVSS 116 DOT 3 or SAE J1703, as work proceeds. If the reservoir is integral with the master cylinder, keep the fluid level up to the marking on the side of the reservoir; if the reservoir is separate from the master cylinder, keep the fluid level above the top of the inner reservoir.

Remove the front floor or gearbox tunnel, as necessary, to gain access to the slave cylinder, then attach a length of rubber or plastic tubing to the bleed screw as shown in **FIG 6:6**. Immerse the lower end of the tubing in a glass jar containing a little clean fluid. Slacken the bleed screw and pump the clutch pedal, pausing at the

end of each stroke. When no more bubbles appear from the tubing, tighten the bleed screw at the beginning of a downwards stroke at the pedal. Remove the tubing and replace the floor. Do not re-use fluid bled from the system.

6:4 *Servicing the hydraulic system*

(a) The master cylinder:

Removal of the master cylinder is a straightforward disconnecting operation, but it is a little more difficult on lefthand steering vehicles than righthand steering ones. On lefthand steering vehicles, the lefthand front wing must be removed and also the whole pedal bracket and its fixings. This allows the clutch pedal, bracket and master cylinder to come out as one assembly. On righthand steering vehicles, it is only necessary to remove the top cover from the pedal bracket before undoing the bolts holding the master cylinder and releasing the pushrod from the pedal trunnion. When the hydraulic pipes are released, take great care to prevent dirt entering them. It is best to wrap adhesive tape right over the end until ready for reassembly.

For overhauling the master cylinder, a kit of seals and rubbers is obtainable. Note that it does not matter whether or not the master cylinder has an integral or

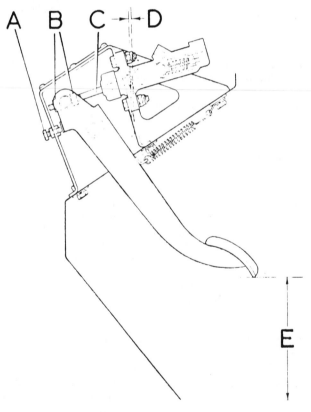

FIG 6:3   Pedal and master cylinder settings

Key to Fig 6:3   A Pedal position setting bolt   **B** Master cylinder pushrod locknuts   **C** Master cylinder pushrod **D** Free play $\frac{1}{16}$ inch (1.5 mm)   **E** Models with non-hydrostatic clutch mechanisms: $6\frac{1}{4}$ inch (158 mm)   Models with hydrostatic clutch mechanisms: $5\frac{1}{2}$ inch (140 mm)

separate reservoir. The internal components are identical. In all operations connected with hydraulic components, exercise the most scrupulous cleanliness. Cover the bench with newspaper and discard it as it becomes soiled. Wipe the external surfaces of components as clean as possible before dismantling, then wash everything in Girling cleaning fluid or clean new hydraulic fluid after dismantling. Inspect the surfaces of the cylinder bore and the piston for wear, scores or discolouration. If any of these are present, scrap the component.

Refer to **FIG 6 : 7**. Pull off dust cover **E**, release circlip **D** and then extract pushrod **P** and washer **C**. Very gently tap the casting on a piece of soft wood until the piston **N** and all the valve components slip out of the cylinder bore. Raise prong **L** on the spring retainer and pull away from the piston. Slip the valve stem **J** from the keyhole slot in **L** and the valve assembly can be dismantled.

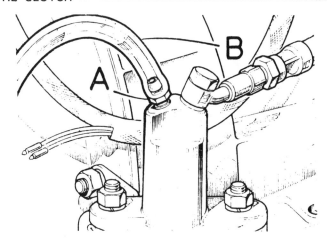

FIG 6:6 Bleeding the hydraulic system

Key to Fig 6:6   A Bleed screw   B Tubing

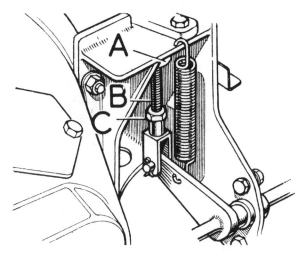

FIG 6:4 Slave cylinder adjustment, early type

Key to Fig 6:4   A Slave cylinder   B Pushrod
C Locknut

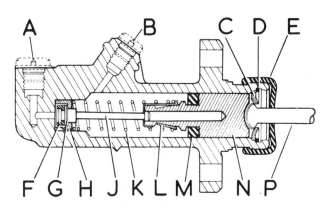

FIG 6:7 Sectioned view of master cylinder

Key to Fig 6:7   A Inlet port   B Outlet port   C Spring washer   D Circlip   E Dust cover   F Valve seal   G Spring washer   H Valve spacer   J Valve stem   K Return spring   L Spring retainer   M Piston seal   N Piston   P Pushrod

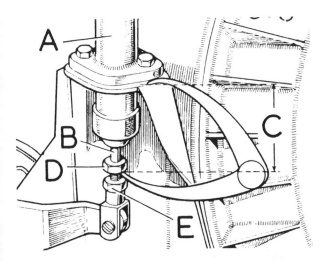

FIG 6:5 Slave cylinder adjustment, later type

Key to Fig 6:5   A Slave cylinder   B Pushrod   C 2½ inch (73.4 mm). Check dimension with calipers as shown   D Nut must be at end of pushrod thread   E Locknut for pushrod

Discard all the rubber components, then clean and inspect the remainder. If all is well, proceed to rebuild as follows :

1 Smear all the seals with Castrol Girling rubber grease and lubricate all other sliding surfaces with clean hydraulic fluid.

2 Fit the valve assembly as shown in **FIG 6 : 8**, paying particular attention to the detail given in **FIG 6 : 9**.

3 Replace the valve stem through the keyhole in the retainer, fit the piston seal as shown in **FIG 6 : 10**, then replace the retainer, locking the prong under the piston head.

4 Slide the piston and valve assembly into the previously lubricated cylinder and fit the pushrod, washer and circlip.

5 Liberally smear the inside of the dust cover with rubber grease and refit to the cylinder.

Replace the cylinder on the vehicle by reversing the dismantling procedure. Connect the hydraulic pipes and refill the system with fluid. Bleed the system as described in **Section 6 : 3**.

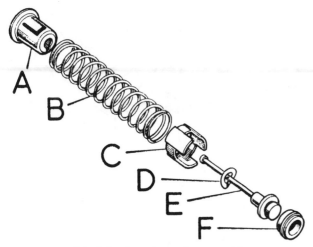

FIG 6:8   Complete valve assembly

Key to Fig 6:8   A Spring retainer   **B** Spring   **C** Valve spacer   **D** Spring washer   **E** Valve stem   **F** Valve seal

If it is required to remove the clutch only, on 2¼ or 2.6 litre engines, it is not necessary to remove the seat base and the gearbox. Just move the gearbox about 5 inches (127 mm) to the rear to gain access to the clutch fixings.

Removal:

Remove the front floor. Remove or detach the gearbox as described in **Chapter 7, Section 7:2** on 2¼ or 2.6 litre engines. On 3.5 litre models, remove the engine (see **Chapter 1, Section 1:3**).

Mark the position of the clutch cover in relation to the flywheel, then remove the six securing bolts and withdraw the clutch assembly. The clutch plate is released during this operation.

Remove the flywheel securing bolts and lift off.

When refitting the flywheel to the crankshaft, tighten up the bolts, on 2¼ or 2.6 litre engines, to 60 to 65 lb ft (8.3 to 9.0 mkg), but do not lock until the runout has been checked. This must not exceed .002 inch (.05 mm). For later models and 3.5 litre engines, refer to **Chapter 1, Section 1:9**.

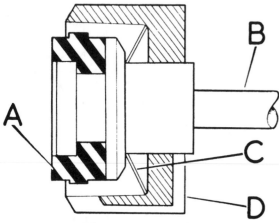

FIG 6:9   Valve seal detail

Key to Fig 6:9   A Valve seal   **B** Valve stem   **C** Spring washer   **D** Valve spacer

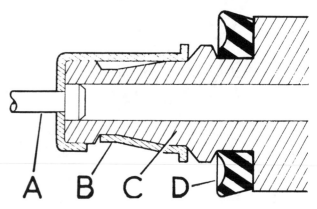

FIG 6:10   Piston seal detail

Key to Fig 6:10   A Valve stem   **B** Prong engaged **C** Piston   **D** Seal

(b) The slave cylinder:

Removal of the slave cylinder only involves undoing the holding bolts, disconnecting the pushrod and the hydraulic pipe. The remarks concerning cleanliness apply with equal force to this component.

To strip the slave cylinder, refer to **FIG 6:11**. Pull off the rubber dust cover and remove circlip **E**. The components can be gently jarred out of the body.

Clean and examine the unit as described for the master cylinder. Assemble the unit with new seals in the order shown in **FIG 6:11**. Note that the smaller end of the spring goes towards the piston.

Replace the unit on the vehicle by reversing the dismantling process and then carry out the bleeding operation (see **Section 6:3**).

6:5 *Servicing the clutch unit*

Refer to **FIG 6:12**. Note that items 24 to 32 show the early coil spring unit and items 33 and 34 the later diaphragm spring unit.

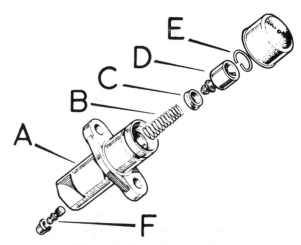

FIG 6:11   View of slave cylinder

Key to Fig 6:11   A Cylinder   **B** Spring   **C** Piston seal **D** Piston   **E** Circlip   **F** Bleed nipple

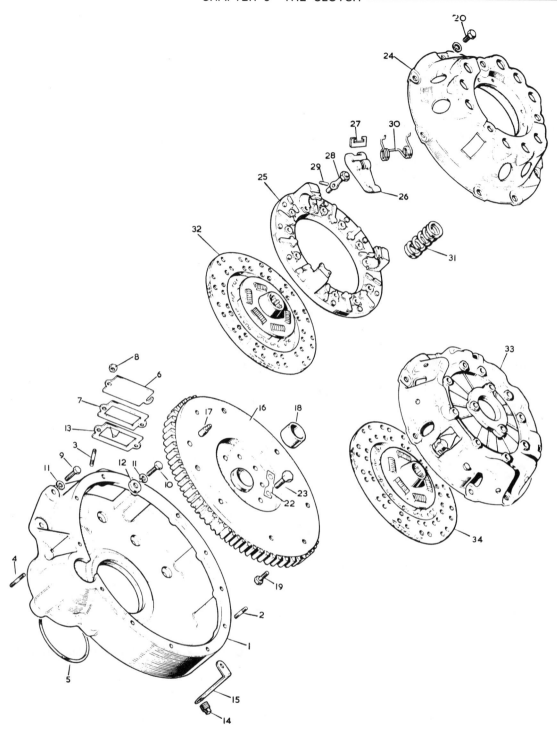

FIG 6:12 Clutch assembly

Key to Fig 6:12   1 Flywheel housing   2 Stud fixing flywheel housing to bellhousing   3 Stud fixing inspection cover
4 Stud for starter motor   5 Sealing ring for flywheel housing   6 Inspection coverplate (early type engines)   7 Joint washer
for coverplate   8 Nut fixing coverplate   9 Bolt   10 Bolt   11 Spring washer   12 Plain washer   13 Indicator for engine
timing (early type engines)   14 Drain plug for housing   15 Stowage bracket for drain plug. On later engines the plug is stowed
in a blind tapping in the flywheel housing   16 Flywheel assembly   17 Dowel locating clutch coverplate   18 Bush for primary
pinion   19 Special fitting bolt fixing clutch coverplate   20 Setbolt   21 Spring washer   22 Locker   23 Special setbolt
24 Coverplate for coil spring type clutch   25 Pressure plate   26 Release lever   27 Strut for release lever   28 Eyebolt and
nut for release lever   29 Pin for release lever   30 Anti-rattle spring for release lever   31 Clutch coil spring (9 off)   32 Clutch
driven plate   33 Diaphragm spring type clutch, fitted to 2.6 litre engines and later 2¼ litre diesel engines. Optional equipment on
2¼ litre petrol engines   34 Clutch driven plate

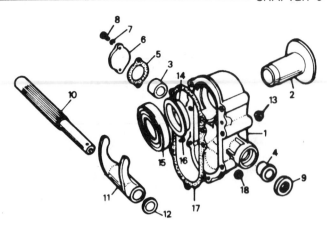

FIG 6:13 Series 2 and 2A clutch withdrawal mechanism

Key to Fig 6:13 1 Housing 2 Withdrawal sleeve
3 Bush 4 Bush 5 Joint washer 6 Coverplate
7, 8 Coverplate fixings 9 Oil seal 10 Cross-shaft
11 Operating fork 12 Thrust washer 13 Nut 14 Bush
for sleeve 15 Thrust bearing 16 Dowel 17 Gasket
18 Nut

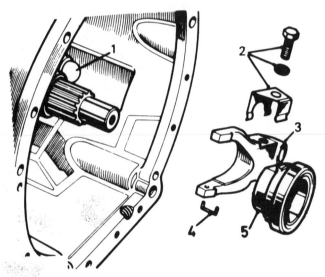

FIG 6:14 Series 3 clutch withdrawal mechanism

Key to Fig 6:14 1 Pivot 2 Spring clip 3 Release
lever 4 Staple 5 Release bearing and sleeve

Dismantling:

If the friction lining is worn down to within .02 inch (.5 mm) of the rivet heads or is oil stained, scored, badly glazed or burnt, it must be renewed. Exchange plates are available. If the flywheel face is scored, this may have up to .030 inch (.75 mm) of metal removed. The pressure plate 25 (**FIG 6:12**) on coil spring clutches may have up to .010 inch (.25 mm) of metal removed for the same reason.

If it is decided to remove the coil spring pressure plate from the cover, first mark the plate cover and release levers to facilitate reassembly. Hold the cover and plate compressed under a press, then remove the three release lever adjusting nuts. Gently free the press,

then lift off the cover and coil springs. Dismantle the levers, taking careful note of the sequence of lever, eyebolt, pin and anti-rattle spring so that they will be reassembled in the proper order.

After machining the pressure plate, reassemble the plate, levers and cover by reversing the dismantling process. Smear a little high melting point grease on all bearing surfaces of the levers.

To set the release lever height, hold the cover down on a surface plate with $\frac{3}{8}$ inch (9.5 mm) packing between the pressure plate and the surface plate. Do not use a friction plate for this as it is not sufficiently accurate. This holding down can only be accomplished if a press is available. Set a scribing block to 1.665 inch (42 mm) from the surface plate and adjust the nuts on the eyebolts until the ends of the release levers just contact the scriber. Stake the adjusting nuts to prevent movement. Release the press.

Replacing:

The clutch unit is replaced on the flywheel by reversing the dismantling process, but note that a mandrel made to fit the crankshaft bush bore and the bore of the friction plate is essential so that the friction plate is centralized and held until the cover bolts are tightened. Note that the longer side of the central boss of the friction plate is fitted facing away from the engine or with the side marked '**Flywheel side**' towards the flywheel. This applies to all engines, petrol and diesel. Tighten the coverplate bolts to 22 to 25 lb ft (3 to 3.5 mkg) on all $2\frac{1}{4}$ or 2.6 litre engines or 35 to 38 lb ft (4.9 to 5 mkg) on 3.5 litre engines.

If wear is suspected in the release bearing on 2 or 2A models, first undo the connecting tube from the release cross-shaft, then undo the bolts holding the clutch withdrawal unit to the bellhousing. The unit will then pull forward from the bellhousing. Drive the cross-shaft out of the operating fork, then press the bearing off the sleeve. Renew the bearing and reassemble by reversing the dismantling process. Always fit a new oil seal to the cross-shaft and a new joint washer between the unit and the bellhousing, otherwise oil can leak from the gearbox. Tighten the $\frac{1}{4}$ inch BSF nuts to 10 lb ft (1.4 mkg) and the $\frac{5}{16}$ inch BSF nuts to 15 lb ft (2 mkg) holding the unit to the bellhousing.

6:6 *Clutch withdrawal mechanism*

On Series 2 and 2A units this mechanism is incorporated with the primary pinion cover of the gearbox. Removal of the assembly is dealt with in **Chapter 7, Section 7:3**.

Remove the cross-shaft coverplate and drive out the cross-shaft. This will release the operating fork thrust washer and thrust spring (not shown in **FIG 6:13**). Press the withdrawal sleeve from the bearing.

If any of the bushes require renewal, this operation should be entrusted to a suitably equipped garage as the bushes must be reamed after fitting.

When inserting the cross-shaft, position the withdrawal shaft by placing a $\frac{7}{16}$ inch (11 mm) diameter bar between the withdrawal sleeve flange and the housing. Insert the shaft with the linkage connecting hole in line with the withdrawal sleeve axis.

Series 3 models have the clutch release mechanism shown in **FIG 6 : 14**. The release bearing and sleeve 5 can be withdrawn after removing the staple 4. After unbolting the spring clip 2, the release lever can be removed.

6:7 *Fault diagnosis*

(a) Grabbing clutch

1 Faulty operating mechanism
2 Glazed friction linings
3 Oil on friction linings
4 Loose engine mountings

(b) Slipping clutch

1 Check 1, 2 and 3 at (a)
2 Worn linings
3 Broken coil springs

(c) Dragging clutch

1 Check 1, 2 and 3 at (a)
2 Crankshaft bush binding on pinion shaft
3 Distorted clutch cover

(d) Clutch judder

1 Check 1, 2, 3 and 4 at (a)
2 Worn transmission shafts

NOTES

CHAPTER 7

THE GEARBOX AND TRANSFER GEARBOX

7:1 Description

The transmission of power from the engine is achieved by a unique gearbox/transfer box assembly. From the clutch, the drive is first taken to the main four speed gearbox. At the rear of the gearbox, a transfer box is attached which transmits the drive through an idler to the propeller shaft drive units. Two further controls are possible due to this arrangement. The idler wheel has two gears of different diameters and, by means of a sliding gear on the output shaft, a high or low ratio can be added to the four speeds of the main gearbox. The forward output shaft drives the front wheels and this can be connected or disconnected by means of a dog clutch on the output shaft to give 2 or 4 wheel drive.

The main gearbox on Series 3 models differs from earlier models, incorporating synchromesh on all four forward gears.

7:2 Removing the gearbox

2¼ and 2.6 litre models:

1 Remove the front floor and front seat base.
2 Remove the drain plugs from the main and transfer gearboxes and drain the oil.
3 Disconnect both propeller shafts. Disconnect any gearbox-driven optional equipment (see **Chapter 14**).
4 Release the handbrake expander rod from the relay levers, then remove the lever and relay mechanism. Remove the cross-shaft on lefthand drive vehicles.
5 Disconnect the speedometer cable at the gearbox.
6 Remove the fixing bolts from the two rear mountings. If necessary on certain models, move the exhaust pipe aside and, also on certain models, disconnect the engine earth strap. A tie rod may be fitted between the gearbox and chassis: if applicable, release it at the bellhousing.
7 Disconnect the clutch cross-shaft, where applicable, then release the clutch cylinder bracket and withdraw the bracket, cylinder and cross-shaft assembly. Where applicable, remove the clutch slave cylinder from the bellhousing.
8 Jack up the engine and place a 1 inch (25 mm) block of wood between the flywheel and the chassis.
9 Put a sling round the gearbox and take the strain on suitable lifting tackle.
10 Remove the nuts securing the bellhousing to the flywheel cover and slide the gearbox gently backwards away from the engine. Lift clear of the vehicle.

To refit, reverse the removal process, smearing the splines of the primary pinion, the clutch centre and the

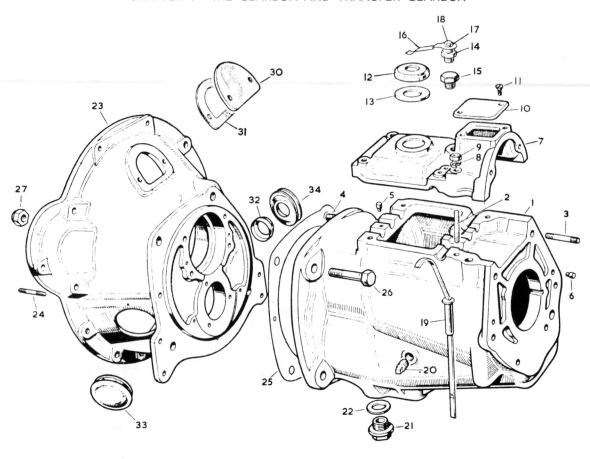

FIG 7 : 1   Main gearbox casing

Key to Fig 7 : 1 1 Gearbox casing assembly 2 Stud or bolt for top cover and gearchange plate   3 Stud, short, for transfer casing
4 Stud for bellhousing   5 Dowel locating top cover   6 Dowel locating transfer casing   7 Top cover for gearbox   8, 9 Fixings
for top cover, used with stud   10 Inspection coverplate for selectors   11 Setscrew fixing coverplate   12 Oil filler cap (early
gearboxes)   13 Joint washer for cap (early gearboxes)   14 Plug for retaining spring and cap (early gearboxes)   15 Plug
retaining selector spring (late gearboxes)   16 Retaining spring for cap (early gearboxes)   17, 18 Fixings for spring (early
gearboxes)   19 Oil level dipstick (early gearboxes)   20 Oil level filler plug   21 Drain plug for gearbox   22 Washer for plug
23 Bellhousing assembly   24 Stud for withdrawal race housing   25 Joint washer, bellhousing to gearbox   26, 27 Fixings for
gearbox casing   30 Top cover for bellhousing   31 Rubber seal for top cover   32 Centre for dust cover (early gearboxes)
33 Grommet for bellhousing hole   34 Grommet for bellhousing shaft

withdrawal unit abutment faces with Rocol MV3 or
Rocol MTS 1000 grease. It will be of help to engage top
gear so that the primary pinion can be turned by rotating the transmission brake drum. By this means the
primary pinion shaft can be slowly rotated to align with
the clutch driven plate splines.

3.5 litre models :

The vehicle must be raised and safely supported to
gain working space beneath the vehicle. The recommended procedure is to remove the gearbox from
beneath the vehicle. A suitable cradle will be necessary
to support the gearbox and withdraw it to the rear.

1 Disconnect the battery and release the handbrake.
2 Remove the bolts and lift out the gearlever.
3 Remove the seat base centre panel.
4 Release the breather pipes.
5 Remove all bellhousing bolts that can be reached
   from above. Move the air cleaner, if necessary, and

displace the speedometer cable and clutch pipe
from their brackets.
6 Drain the oil from the boxes if necessary.
7 Remove the detachable crossmember.
8 Remove the front exhaust pipes and also the branch
   pipe.
9 Mark the flanges and disconnect the propeller
   shafts from the gearbox. Move them aside.
10 Disconnect the speedometer cable.
11 Disconnect the handbrake cable at the transmission
   brake clevis pin, 'P' clip and remove the adjuster
   bracket bolts.
12 Disconnect the transfer gearlever linkage.
13 Detach the clutch slave cylinder and move it clear of
   the gearbox.
14 Remove the bellhousing coverplate.
15 Support the gearbox on a suitable hydraulic cradle.
16 Remove the bolts from the gearbox chassis mountings.

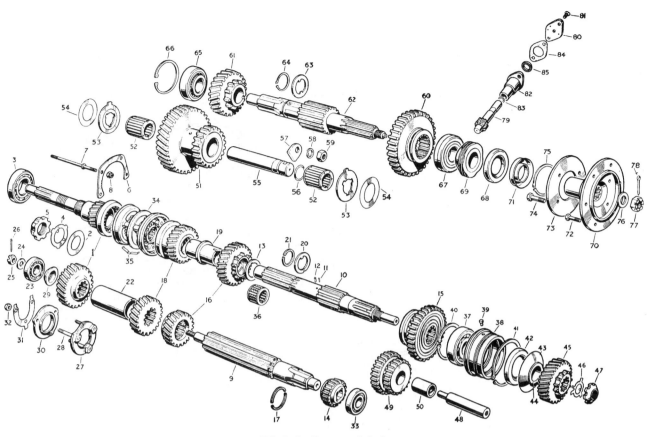

FIG 7:2 Gears and shafts

Key to Fig 7:2 1 Primary pinion and constant gear   2 Shield for primary pinion   3 Ballbearing for primary pinion   4, 5 Fixings for bearing   6-8 Fixings for bearing   9 Layshaft   10 Mainshaft   11 Peg for 2nd gear thrust washer   12 Peg for mainshaft distance sleeve   13 Thrust washer for 2nd speed gear   14 1st speed layshaft gear   15 1st speed mainshaft gear   16 2nd speed layshaft and mainshaft gear   17 Splitring for 2nd speed layshaft gear (early gearboxes)   18 3rd speed layshaft and mainshaft gear   19 Distance sleeve for mainshaft   20 Thrust washer for 3rd speed mainshaft gear   21 Spring ring fixing 2nd and 3rd mainshaft gears   22 Sleeve for layshaft   23 Bearing for layshaft, front   24-26 Fixings for bearing to layshaft   27 Bearing plate assembly for layshaft   28 Stud for bearing cap   29 Distance piece for layshaft   30 Retaining plate for layshaft front bearing   31, 32 Fixings for cap and bearing   33 Bearing for layshaft, rear   34 Synchronizing clutch   35 Detent spring for clutch   36 Roller bearing for mainshaft   37 Ballbearing for mainshaft   38 Housing for mainshaft bearing, rear   39 Peg, housing to casing   40 Circlip, bearing to housing   41 Circlip, housing to casing   42 Oil seal for rear of mainshaft   43 Oil thrower for mainshaft   44 Distance piece, rear of mainshaft   45 Mainshaft gear for transfer box   46, 47 Fixings for gear   48 Shaft for reverse gear   49 Reverse wheel assembly   50 Bush for reverse wheel   51 Gear, intermediate   52 Roller bearing for intermediate gear   53 Thrust washer for intermediate gear   54 Shim for intermediate gear   55 Shaft for intermediate gear   56 Sealing ring for intermediate gear   57 Retaining plate for shaft   58, 59 Fixings for plate   60 Low gearwheel   61 High gearwheel   62 Output shaft, rear drive   63 Thrust washer for high gearwheel   64 Circlip fixing washer to shaft   65 Bearing for output shaft, front   66 Circlip fixing bearing to case   67 Bearing for output shaft, rear   68 Oil seal for output shaft   69 Speedometer worm complete   70 Flange for output shaft, rear drive   71 Mudshield for flange   72 Fitting bolt for brake drum   73 Retaining flange for brake drum bolts   74 Fitting bolt for propeller shaft   75 Circlip retaining bolts and flange   76-78 Fixings for flange   79 Speedometer pinion   80 Retaining plate for pinion   81 Screw fixing plate to housing   82 Sleeve for pinion   83 Sealing ring for sleeve   84 Joint washer for sleeve   85 Oil seal for pinion

17 Disconnect the differential actuator leads and vacuum hoses, marking them for correct reassembly.

18 Check that all pipes, cables and wires have been released.

19 Remove the remaining bellhousing bolts.

20 Support the engine sump.

21 Draw the gearbox rearwards until it disengages from the engine, lower it and move it clear.

Refitting is, generally, the reverse of the removal procedure, smearing the splines of the primary pinion, the clutch centre and the withdrawal unit abutment faces with Rocol MTS 1000 grease and the gearbox joint faces with Unipart Universal jointing compound. Torque tighten the bellhousing bolts to 25 lb ft (3.5 mkg). Apply jointing compound to the coverplate and seal and to the joints between the bellhousing, cylinder block and rear main bearing cap. Torque tighten the coverplate bolts to 8 lb ft (1 mkg). On completion, check the oil level in the main and transfer gearboxes and replenish as necessary.

7:3 *The main gearbox, 2¼ and 2.6 litre models*

Reference should be made to **FIGS 7:1, 7:2** and **7:3**.

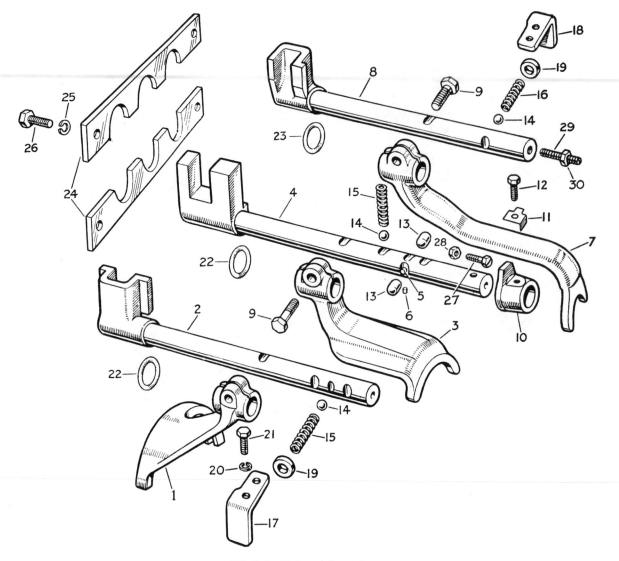

FIG 7 : 3 Main gearbox selectors

Key to Fig 7 : 3   1 Selector fork, 3rd and 4th speed   2 Shaft for fork, 3rd and 4th speed   3 Selector fork, 1st and 2nd speed
4 Shaft assembly for fork, 1st and 2nd speed   5 Interlocking pin   6 Peg fixing interlocking pin   7 Selector fork, reverse
8 Shaft for fork, reverse   9 Setbolt fixing forks to shafts   10 Stop for 2nd speed   11, 12 Fixings for stop   13 Interlocking
plunger   14 Steel ball for selectors   15 Selector spring, forward   16 Selector spring, reverse   17 Retaining plate lefthand
(for selector springs, side) 18 Retaining plate righthand (for selector springs, side) 19 Rubber grommet (for selector springs, side)
20, 21 Fixings for retaining plates   22 Seal for selector shafts   23 Seal for reverse shaft   24 Retaining plate for sealing ring
25, 26 Fixings for retaining plate   27 Setbolts (in cover for 2nd gear stop)   28 Locknut (in cover for 2nd gear stop)
29 Adjustable stop for reverse selector shaft   30 Locknut for stop

To dismantle the main gearbox :

1 Drain the oil from the main and transfer gearboxes.
2 Remove the main gearchange lever assembly, then the reverse stop hinge.
3 Remove the transfer box and front output shaft housing complete.
4 Remove the connecting tube from the clutch cross-shaft and the grommets from the bellhousing apertures.
5 Remove the primary pinion cover from the bell-housing. On Series 2 and 2A models this cover houses the clutch withdrawal mechanism.
6 Remove the oil filler cap.

7 Remove the plug 14 (see **FIG 7 : 1**), withdraw the spring and pack the hole with grease. This prevents the selector ball falling into the box when the cover 7 is removed.
8 Refer to **FIG 7 : 3**. Remove the plates 17 and 18, then remove the selector springs 15 and 16 and the two balls 14.
9 Refer to **FIG 7 : 1**. Remove plate 10 and the bolts which hold the cover 7 to the transfer box casing.
10 Remove the cover 7 and detach the selector ball in the cover from the grease holding it in place. Remove the locking plungers 13 (see **FIG 7 : 3**). Undo the nut 28 and bolt 27 and remove the second

speed gear stop 10 (see **FIG 7:3**). This stop is not fitted on Series 3 gearboxes.

11 Remove the selector shafts on Series 2 and 2A models as follows. Select first gear by moving the centre selector to the rear; remove the reverse gear selector by lifting and turning the selector shaft one quarter of a turn to the left. Move the first/second selector to neutral and lift it out; repeat for the third/fourth selector. The selectors can now be removed from their shafts by undoing the pinch bolts.

On Series 3 models proceed as follows. Select third gear by moving the righthand selector to the rear; lift, turn and withdraw the third/fourth selector shaft. Withdraw the first/second selector shaft followed by the reverse selector shaft.

12 Remove the transfer gearlever from the side of the bellhousing. So that the layshaft cannot rotate, engage fourth and second gears simultaneously. Remove the nut or bolt from the front of the layshaft. Remove the nut 47 in **FIG 7:2** from the rear of the mainshaft after undoing the tab washer. Then remove the tab washer, shim washer if fitted, transfer gear 45 and oil thrower 43.

13 Remove the bellhousing, noting the position of the two special fixing nuts which are fitted diagonally opposite one another. Tap the layshaft out of its bearing when removing the bellhousing so that it remains in the gearbox. Remove the primary pinion from the bellhousing. On Series 2 and 2A models, this is secured by the nut 5 which has a lefthand thread. On Series 3 models, the pinion is secured by a circlip on the shaft.

14 Remove the constant gear 1 from the layshaft.

15 Remove the fixings for the main and layshaft bearings in the bellhousing, items 6, 30 and 31, and press out the bearings.

16 Remove the synchronizing clutch unit 34 from the mainshaft, then withdraw the complete layshaft.

17 On Series 2 and 2A models, the layshaft can be dismantled. Remove the distance sleeve 22, the gears 18 and 16. Remove the splitring 17. Press off the rear bearing 33 and the first speed gear 14. The gears on Series 3 models are integral with the layshaft.

18 Drive the mainshaft forward out of the gearbox.

19 Remove the first speed gear 15. The rear part of the Series 3 mainshaft is dismantled as follows, referring to **FIG 7:4**. Remove the thrust washer 1, first speed gear 2 and bush 4. Withdraw the rear cone of the synchronizer assembly 3, followed by the synchronizer assembly 5 and the synchronizer front cone.

20 Prise out the spring ring 21 in **FIG 7:2** and discard it. Remove the thrust washer 20 and the gear 18. Remove the sleeve 19 and gear 16. Remove the pegs 11 and 12 and the thrust washer 13.

21 Take out the circlip 41 and tap out the housing 38 from the rear, thus releasing the peg 39. Remove the oil seal 42 and the circlip 40 and the bearing 37 can be pressed out of the housing.

22 Warm the gearbox and position it with the rear face upwards. Tap the rear face with a mallet. The inner race of the layshaft bearing should fall out. On some gearboxes two holes are provided so that the race can be drifted out. The reverse idler gear and shaft should be removed, while the gearbox is warm, by driving the shaft out to the rear.

23 The first/second speed synchronizer fitted to Series 3 models should be dismantled while the assembly

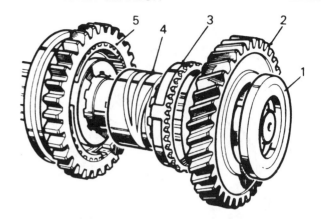

FIG 7:4   **Rear components of Series 3 mainshaft**

Key to Fig 7:4   1 Thrust washer   2 First speed gear
3 Rear cone of synchronizer   4 Bush   5 Synchronizer

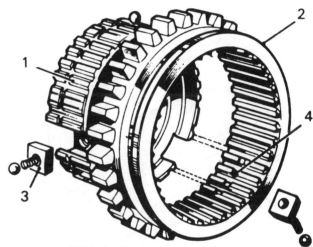

FIG 7:5   **First/second synchronizer**

Key to Fig 7:5   1 Inner member   2 Outer member
3 Block with spring and ball   4 Ball retaining groove

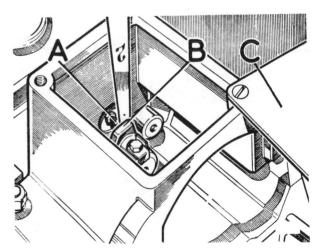

FIG 7:6   **Adjusting second speed stop**

Key to Fig 7:6   A Bolt   B Stop   C Cover

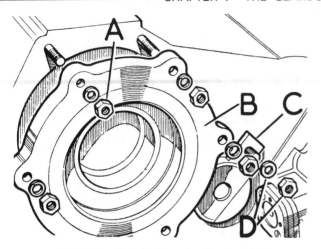

FIG 7:7   Mainshaft rear bearing housing

Key to Fig 7:7   A Fixing nuts   **B** Housing   **C** Retainer
for intermediate shaft   **D** Retainer fixings

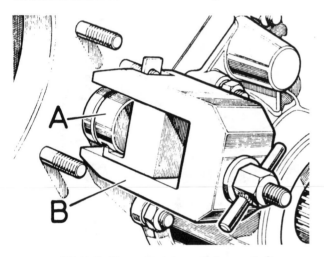

FIG 7:8   Removing intermediate gearshaft

Key to Fig 7:8   **A** Shaft   **B** Special tool

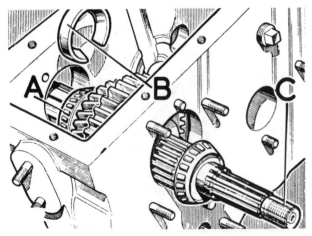

FIG 7:9   Removing front bearing outer race

Key to Fig 7:9   **A** Front bearing   **B** Packing piece
C Protection cap

is enclosed in a cloth so that no parts are lost. The
parts are shown in exploded form in **FIG 7:5**.

To rebuild the main gearbox:

1. Wash all components and inspect thoroughly. Discard any gears heavily pitted or marked. Discard
any slack or rough bearing, likewise any shaft with
the splines damaged. Note that the constant, second and third speed gears are only supplied as
mated pairs. Use all new circlips.

2. Drive a new layshaft outer bearing element into the
rear of the casing. The casing may need warming
first. Note that the lipped edge must be to the rear.

3. Check the fit of the reverse gear on its shaft. If necessary, have the bush renewed by a Rover agent.
Warm the casing before driving the shaft home.

4. Press the mainshaft rear bearing 37 into its housing
38 and secure with circlip 40. Press the oil seal 42
into the other end of the housing, knife edge
inwards.

5. Smear the outer diameter of the bearing housing
with jointing compound and push the complete
bearing housing into the casing and secure with
circlip 41. (Fit peg 39 first).

6. Replace the thrust washer 13; do not fit peg 12 at
this stage. Slide on sleeve 19, slot to the rear,
together with the second speed gear 16, cone to the
rear. Place the third speed gear 18 on the sleeve and
secure with the thrust washer 20 and the old spring
ring 21.

7. Press the third speed gear 18 hard against the
sleeve shoulder when the end float of gear 16, measured between the gear and the shoulder, should be
.004 to .007 inch (.10 to .18 mm). The end float of
gear 18 should be the same when gear 16 is pressed
hard against the sleeve shoulder. If the end float is
insufficient, a new sleeve is needed; if excessive,
the end of the sleeve may be rubbed down.

8. Remove the spring ring, take off the gear, then
replace the sleeve, thrust washer and old spring
ring. The sleeve should have an end float of .001 to
.008 inch (.03 to .20 mm). Various thicknesses of
thrust washer are available to achieve this.

9. When the end floats are correct, fit the peg 11, thrust
washer 13, peg 12, gears 16 and 18 on sleeve 19 and
slide sleeve 19 on the mainshaft, large slot to the
rear. Slide washer 20 on the shaft with its groove in
line with the small slot in sleeve 19. Secure with a
new spring ring.

10. On Series 2 and 2A models, slide gear 15 onto the
mainshaft and then press the shaft through the rear
bearing. On Series 3 models, proceed as follows.
Refer to **FIG 7:5**. Try fitting the inner member to the
outer member of the first/second synchronizer,
aligning the detent spring bores and ball retaining
grooves. Remove the inner and try again after rotating it first 120 deg. and then 240 deg. from the first
position. Note which position gives the best sliding
fit. Fit the block, springs and balls to the inner
member and slide into the outer member while
retaining the parts by hand. Refit the front synchronizing cone, the synchronizer unit, the rear synchronizing cone, the gear bush and thrust washer to
the rear of the mainshaft. Check that there is .002 to

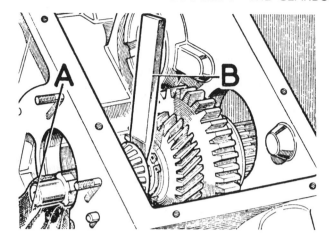

FIG 7:10   Removing front bearing inner race

Key to Fig 7:10   **A** Rag to protect casing   **B** Mild steel chisel-edged drift

.007 inch (.05 to .18 mm) clearance between the thrust washer and bush. Remove the thrust washer, fit the first gear and replace the thrust washer with its stepped face outwards. Press the shaft through the rear bearing.

11 Reassemble the Series 2 and 2A layshaft as follows. Slide the layshaft first speed gear 14 onto the rear of the layshaft 9 with the chamfered end of the teeth to the front. Fit the splitring 17 and slide gear 16, flange forwards, over the ring. Ensure that the ring is properly seated in the shaft 9. Slide gear 18 onto the layshaft with its flange forwards, followed by sleeve 22, constant gear and distance piece 29. Press bearing 23 onto the shaft and lock by means of nut 25 and washer 24.

12 Should the gears have any end float, fit a different thickness of distance piece 29. These are made in three thicknesses: .312 inch (7.9 mm), .332 inch (8.4 mm) and .352 inch (8.91 mm). When the end float is removed, take off the nut and washer, distance piece and constant gear from the shaft.

13 Fit the rest of the assembly in the casing, engaging the constant mesh gears.

14 Now assemble the primary pinion shaft 1 by pressing bearing 3 on until it abuts the shoulder. On Series 2 and 2A models, secure by fitting washer 2 and 4, and the lock-up nut 5. Bend up the tab of washer 4. On Series 3 models, fit the distance washer and old circlip and check the end float. Fit a new distance washer of suitable thickness if the end float is not minimal and secure it with a new circlip.

15 Press the primary shaft and bearing assembly into the previously warmed bellhousing and secure with retaining plate 6.

16 Press the layshaft front bearing 23 into the bellhousing simultaneously with operation 15. Fit retaining plate parts 27, 28, 30, 31 and 32.

17 Check the synchronizing unit spring 35 and renew if necessary. The springs should be replaced if a force less than 15 to 20 lb (6.5 to 9 kg) is sufficient to operate the synchronizer unit.

18 Fit the synchronizing clutch assembly 34 to the mainshaft with its recessed portion towards gear 18.

19 Place the needle roller bearing 36 on the mainshaft, then place the gear 1 and distance piece 29 on the layshaft 9. Offer the bellhousing to the gearbox casing, meshing the constant gears 1. Use a new joint washer between the bellhousing and the gearbox, then bolt them together.

20 Select top and second speeds together to lock the gears. Fit the nut 25 and washer 24 to the layshaft and tighten. Fit a new splitpin 26.

21 Fit the oil thrower 43, distance piece 44 and gear 45, splined flange rearwards, to the rear of the mainshaft and lock with washer 46 and nut 47.

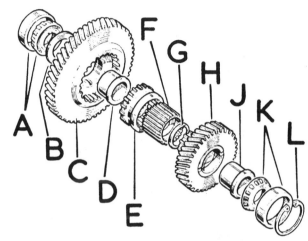

FIG 7:11   High and low speed gear assembly

Key to Fig 7:11   **A** Bearing for output shaft, rear   **B** Thrust washer for low gearwheel   **C** Low gearwheel   **D** Bush for low gearwheel   **E** Outer member for transfer change speed   **F** Inner member for transfer change speed   **G** Thrust washer for high gearwheel   **H** High gearwheel   **J** Bush for high gearwheel   **K** Bearing for output shaft, front   **L** Circlip fixing bearing

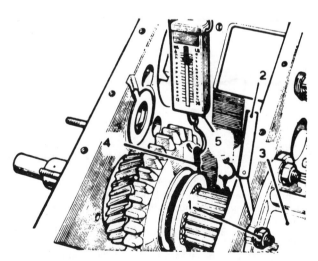

FIG 7:12   Setting the output shaft bearing preload

Key to Fig 7:12   1 Speedometer housing nuts   2 Feeler gauge   3 Speedometer housing   4 Nylon cord   5 Spring balance

22 The selector mechanism can now be replaced. Refer to **FIG 7:3** unless otherwise stated. Fit new rubber sealing rings 22 to the shafts 2 and 4. Fit the selectors 1 and 3 to their shafts 2 and 4. Fit the stop 10 to shaft 4. The stop 10 is not fitted to Series 3 models. Fit the cork seal 23 and selector 7 to the shaft 8.

23 Reverse the dismantling procedure to refit the selectors and locking plungers 13.

24 Fit the top cover.

25 Replace the reverse and third/fourth balls 14 and springs 15. The reverse spring is the stronger of the two. Fit the rubber grommets 19 and plates 17 and 18. Replace the first/second ball and spring, then retain with the screwed plug 14 (see **FIG 7:1**).

26 Refer to **FIG 7:6** and adjust the stop bolt so that there is .002 inch (.05 mm) clearance between the bolt head and the stop on the shaft when second speed is selected. The reverse stop bolt cannot be adjusted until the transfer box has been fitted.

27 Replace the clutch withdrawal mechanism in the bellhousing, refit the transfer box and front output housing complete, refit the gearchange mechanism.

28 Refill with the correct oil when the box is fitted to the vehicle.

29 With reverse gear selected, check that a clearance of .002 inch (.05 mm) exists between the end of the reverse selector shaft and the stop bolt. Slacken the locknut and adjust the stop bolt if required.

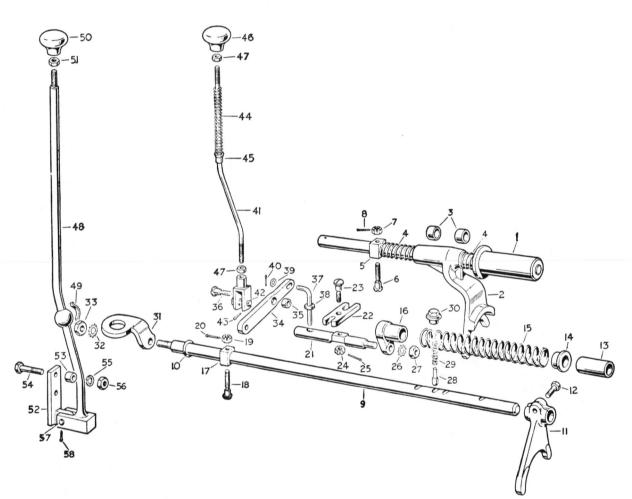

FIG 7:13   Transfer and front wheel drive controls

Key to Fig 7:13   1 Selector shaft, four wheel drive   2 Selector fork complete, four wheel drive   3 Bush for selector fork   4 Spring for selector fork   5 Block for selector shaft   6-8 Fixings for block   9 Selector shaft, transfer gearchange   10 Sealing ring for transfer gearchange shaft   11 Selector fork, transfer gearchange   12 Setbolt fixing fork   13 Distance tube for transfer selector shaft   14 Locating bush for selector shaft spring   15 Spring for gearchange selector shaft   16 Connector, gearchange to pivot shaft   17 Block for selector shaft   18-20 Fixings for block   21 Pivot shaft for selector shafts   22 Coupling, selector shafts to pivot   23-25 Fixings for coupling   26, 27 Fixings for pivot shaft   28 Plunger for transfer selector shaft   29 Spring for plunger   30 Plug   31 Link for selector shaft   32, 33 Fixings for link   34 Lever assembly, four wheel drive   35 Bush for lever   36 Special bolt, lever to housing   37 Locking pin, four wheel drive lever   38 Sealing ring, four wheel drive locking pin   39, 40 Fixings for locking pin   41 Selector rod, four wheel drive   42 Clevis complete for rod   43 Splitpin for clevis   44 Spring for selector rod   45 Special bush for spring   46 Control knob for rod   47 Locknut for knob and clevis   48 Transfer gearchange lever complete   49 Spring for transfer gearchange lever   50 Knob for gearchange lever   51 Locknut for knob   52 Bracket for gearchange lever   53 Distance piece for bracket   54-56 Fixings for bracket   57, 58 Fixings for gearlever

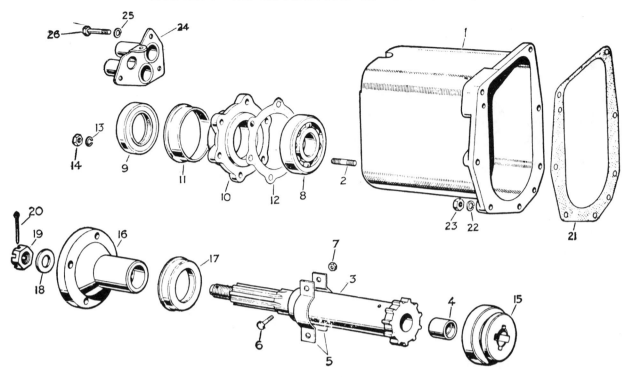

FIG 7:14 Front output shaft and housing

Key to Fig 7:14 1 Output shaft housing assembly 2 Stud for oil seal retainer 3 Front output shaft assembly 4 Bush for shaft 5 Oil thrower for output shaft 6, 7 Fixings for oil thrower 8 Bearing for front output shaft 9 Oil seal for shaft 10 Retainer for oil seal 11 Mudshield for retainer 12 Joint washer for retainer 13, 14 Fixings for retainer 15 Locking dog, four wheel drive 16 Flange for transfer shaft 17 Mudshield for flange 18-20 Fixings for flange 21 Joint washer for transfer housing 22, 23 Fixings for housing 24 Dust coverplate for selector shafts 25, 26 Fixings for dust cover

7:4 The transfer box, 2¼ and 2.6 litre models

In this section, refer to **FIG 7:2**.

The transfer box can be removed without removing the main gearbox. To do this, carry out the preliminary operations of obtaining access as described in **Section 7:2**.

From here, the operations are the same whether the gearbox is in the vehicle or out on the bench.

1 Remove the drive flange 70 (see **FIG 7:2**), complete with the brake drum. Disconnect the transfer gearlever and the handbrake lever.

2 Jack up the rear of the engine and insert a 1 inch (25 mm) wooden block between the flywheel housing and the chassis, then remove the transfer box bottom cover and take off the intermediate shaft retaining plate 57 (see **FIG 7:2**) by undoing the nut and extracting the stud.

3 Remove the mainshaft rear bearing housing (see **FIG 7:7**) or power takeoff unit if fitted.

4 Refer to **FIG 7:8**. The intermediate shaft must be extracted by the use of Rover extractor Part No. 605862 while supporting the intermediate gear by hand.

5 With the shaft 55 (see **FIG 7:2**) extracted, the gear cluster 51 can be removed from the bottom of the transfer box. Remove the needle bearings 52, thrust washers 53 and shims 54 if fitted.

6 Detach the transfer casing from the main gearbox. Three of the fixing nuts are inside the transfer box casing.

To dismantle the transfer box:

1 Remove the speedometer drive pinion unit (see 79 to 81 in **FIG 7:2**), then remove the speedometer drive housing complete, carefully retaining any shims. Withdraw the worm 69 (see **FIG 7:2**) from the shaft 62.

2 Remove the front output shaft housing (see **FIG 7:14**) complete as illustrated but with the dog clutch selector shaft and selector fork also. These latter two items are not shown in **FIG 7:14**. Refer to **FIG 7:13**, items 1 to 8.

3 Remove the top coverplate from the transfer box, then remove the transfer gear fork 11 and selector shaft 9 (see **FIG 7:13**).

4 Release the circlip (see 66 in **FIG 7:2**), then gently tap the shaft rearwards to release the rear bearing 67.

5 Protect the casing bearing bores with pads of rag to prevent damage during these next operations.

6 Fit the protection cap (Part No. 243241) over the threaded portion of shaft 62 (see **FIG 7:2**) and tap the shaft forwards as far as possible to start the front bearing outer race out of the casing. Slide the shaft back and fit a packing piece as shown in **FIG**

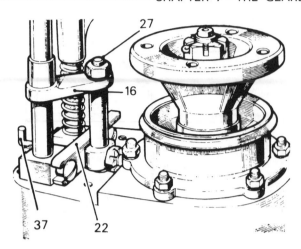

FIG 7:15   Aligning the pivot shaft. For key refer to FIG 7:13

7:9. Tap the shaft forward again to finally release the race.

7   Drive the front bearing inner race from the shaft using a chisel-ended mild steel bar or wedge (see **FIG 7:10**).

8   Remove the circlip 64 and thrust washer 63 (see **FIG 7:2**), then push the shaft 62 out of the casing and remove the gears 60 and 61 through the bottom of the casing.

The box is now dismantled but, if the rear bearing is worn, the inner race must be pulled off the output shaft with an extractor.

To rebuild the transfer box:

Clean and examine all parts as described in the main gearbox section. Renew where necessary, but always use new locking washers, splitpins and joint washers. Proceed as follows:

1   Place the gears 61 and 60 (see **FIG 7:2**) in the transfer casing, gear 61 at the front with its face teeth to the rear and gear 60 at the rear with its selector groove facing rearwards.

2   Insert shaft 62 from the rear and engage its splines in gear 60. Fit gear 61, then thrust washer 63 and a new circlip 64.

3   Fit the inner members of the two bearings 65 and 67 to the shaft; smaller bearing to the front. These must be a light press fit on the shaft.

4   Drive the front bearing outer race into the casing and secure with circlip 66. Drive the rear bearing outer race into the casing. Protect the threaded end of the shaft, then tap the shaft forwards until the front bearing is hard against the circlip. Lightly tap the outer race of the rear bearing until the shaft has no end float.

5   Check that gear 61 has .006 to .008 inch (.15 to .20 mm) end float.

6   Engage the transfer gear selector fork in the groove of gear 60 with the threaded end of the pinch bolt hole to the left. Slide the selector shaft through the casing and fork and secure the fork with the pinch bolt.

7   If necessary, renew the oil seal 68. Fit with the knife edge inwards and smear the outer diameter with jointing cement. Warm the speedometer drive housing before fitting the seal to it.

8   Fit the speedometer pinion 79 to sleeve 82, then fit the sleeve and pinion to the speedometer drive housing, the flat on the sleeve towards the bottom. Replace the oil seal 85.

9   Fit the speedometer housing without any shims. Refer to **FIG 7:12**. Measure the rolling resistance of the output shaft using a nylon cord wrapped around the low speed gear wheel selector groove. Tighten the speedometer housing securing nuts to give a preload such that the reading on the spring balance is 2 to 4 lb with the shaft rotating. Measure the gap between the speedometer and transfer gear housings and fit shims of this thickness between the two housings.

Slide the worm 69 in **FIG 7:2** over the shaft 62 with its conical end inwards, then fit the speedometer housing to the transfer box casing, fitting the correct shims.

10   The intermediate gear end float must now be checked. Position the two thrust washers 53 in the transfer casing, bronze face inwards. Hold them in place with a little grease. Fit the two needle roller bearings 52 in the gear 51, then hold the gear in the casing with the larger wheel to the front. Tap the shaft 55 gently home. The gear 51 must have .004 to .008 inch (.10 to .20 mm) end float; adjust by either grinding the thrust washers or fitting shims 54 between the thrust washers and the casing. When correct, remove the shaft and withdraw the gear, thrust washers and shims.

11   Fit the bolts 72 to the output shaft flange 70, then slide the retaining plate 73 on the flange. Fit the bolts 74 and secure with the circlip 75. Fit the mudshield 71 to the flange.

12   Replace the front output shaft housing assembly (see **Section 7:5**).

13   Fit the transfer box to the main gearbox, using a new joint washer and locating it on the dowels (see **FIG 7:1**, item 6). (Note the three nuts inside the transfer box).

14   Replace the stud, then replace the intermediate gear (see **FIG 7:2**, item 51), in the casing. Renew the O-ring 56 and fit the shaft with plate 57 in the deepest slot. Replace the nut holding the retaining plate on the stud.

15   Replace the mainshaft rear bearing housing.

16   Replace the bottom cover complete with a new joint washer. See that the drain plug is tight. Remove the wooden support block.

17   Fit the transmission brake assembly and shield to the speedometer housing with the expander rod on the righthand side.

18   Fit the front output shaft drive flange.

19   Fit the rear drive flange (see **FIG 7:2**, item 70) and lock with the nut and washer. Fit the transmission brake drum and the propeller shafts.

20   Refill the box with oil.

All helical box:

Certain transfer boxes are of all helical gear construction and the only visible indication is a selector shaft adjuster fitted to the front output shaft housing on this box only. The general overhaul instructions are as given earlier in this section with the following exceptions.

To remove the output shaft, proceed as follows:

1 Remove the front output shaft housing, speedometer housing and the front bearing retaining circlip.
2 Put two $\frac{5}{8}$ inch (16 mm) distance pieces between the rear face of the low gearwheel and the casting.
3 Drive the shaft back until the wheel just touches the distance pieces.
4 Prise the front bearing forwards $\frac{1}{4}$ inch (6 mm).
5 Part the change speed inner member and high gearwheel and find the position of the shaft peg.
6 With a piece of wire, locate the slot in the thrust washer over the shaft peg. Now drive the shaft right out. Do this gently.

Referring to **FIG 7 : 11** to identify parts, assemble parts **A, B, C** and **D** on the shaft. Hold the bush in firm contact with the steel thrust washer and check that the end float of the low gearwheel is .002 to .009 inch (.05 to .22 mm) by using feeler gauges between **B** and **C**. Adjust the end float by rubbing down the rear end of the bush, using fine emerycloth on plate glass. Now assemble the parts **A, B, D, F, G, H** and **J** and check that the high gearwheel end float is .005 to .022 inch (.12 to .55 mm) by using feeler gauges between the front face of the gear **H** and the flange of bush **J**. Adjust by rubbing down the rear end of bush **J**. The bearing preload is the same as described previously for the spur and helical gearbox.

7:5 Front output shaft assembly, 2¼ and 2.6 litre models

This unit provides the drive to the front wheels and is attached to the front of the transfer box casing. It is illustrated in **FIG 7 : 14**.

The assembly can be removed with the gearbox in the vehicle.

1 Drain the transfer box of oil and remove as described in **Section 7 : 4**.
2 Remove the transfer gear selector shaft plunger parts 28, 29 and 30 of **FIG 7 : 13**.
3 Remove the transfer box top cover.
4 Remove the pinch bolt from the transfer selector fork.
5 The housing can now be unbolted from the transfer box.

To dismantle the front output shaft assembly:

Refer to **FIGS 7 : 13** and **7 : 14**.

1 Remove the four wheel drive selector lever 34 and the link 31. Withdraw the selector shaft assemblies, items 1 to 27 of **FIG 7 : 13**.
2 Remove the block 17 from the shaft 9. Slide from the shaft the connector and link assembly, items 16, 21, 22, 23, 24, 25, 26 and 27, spring 15, bush 14 and tube 13. Do not detach items 16 and 21 unnecessarily.
3 Remove the drive flange 16 complete with mudshields 17 (see **FIG 7 : 14**). The shaft 3 will now come out of the housing 1.

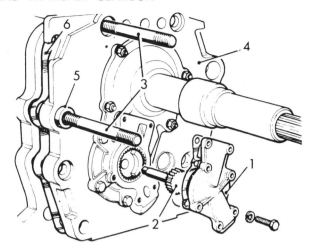

FIG 7 : 16 Bearing plate, front cover and oil pump

Key to Fig 7 : 16   1 Oil pump cover   2 Drive gear
3 Studs   4 Bearing plate   5 Dowel sleeves
6 Joint washer

4 Refer to **FIG 7 : 13**. Remove block 5 and slide the springs 4 and selector fork 2 from the shaft.
5 Refer to **FIG 7 : 14** and undo the nuts holding the oil seal retainer 10, then remove complete with oil seal 9. Drive out the bearing 8.

To rebuild the front output shaft assembly:

Wash and examine all components. Renew all worn parts and obtain new splitpins and joint washers. Renew the bearing if any slack or roughness is noted. The bearing must be a push fit on the shaft and a light drive fit in the housing. Fit a new oil seal in the retainer with its knife edge inwards. Smear the outside diameter with jointing compound and warm the retainer before assembling. Renew the mudshield on the retainer. If the spigot bush 4 (see **FIG 7 : 14**) is removed, press in a new one and ream to .875 inch (22.2 mm). The dog clutch selector springs 4 (see **FIG 7 : 13**) should have a free length of 2.75 inch (69.8 mm) and the transfer selector spring 15, 7.156 inch (181.76 mm).

To assemble the unit, proceed as follows:

1 Replace the oil seal retainer on the front of the housing.
2 Fit the two springs 4 (see **FIG 7 : 13**) and the selector fork 2 to the shaft 1. Replace block 5.
3 If items 16 and 21 have been separated, replace them with the hole for the locking peg vertical and the cut-away underneath item 21. Secure lightly with the nut and washer.
4 Secure item 22 to 21 with the screwed pin 23 and nut 24. Fit a new splitpin 25. The shorter end of the coupling 22 must be towards the transfer selector.
5 Fit the output shaft 3 in the housing 1 (see **FIG 7 : 14**) and secure with the flange 16 and nut, washer and splitpin 18, 19 and 20. Tighten the nut to 85 lb ft (11.75 mkg).
6 Fit the block 17 (**FIG 7 : 13**) to the shaft 9, securing it with the screwed pin 18 and nut 19. Fit a new splitpin.

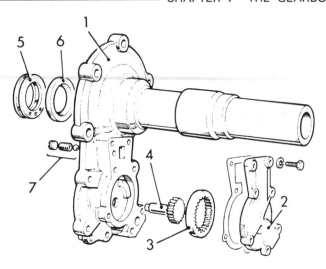

FIG 7:17 Components of front cover and oil pump

Key to Fig 7:17   1 Front cover   2 Pump cover
3 Ring gear   4 Drive gear   5 Oil feed ring   6 Oil seal
7 Relief valve

Ensure that the nut and splitpin are on the same side of the shaft as the plunger grooves.

7 Fit the connector 16 of the pivot shaft over the transfer selector shaft. To ensure that the connector 16 is fitted at the correct angle to the pivot shaft 21, remove the dust cover (24 in **FIG 7:14**) and proceed as follows:

Engage the transfer selector shaft, pivot shaft and dog clutch selector shaft into the front face of the housing, ensuring that the coupling 22 in **FIG 7:13** engages the screwed pins of the transfer and dog clutch shafts as shown in **FIG 7:15**. Locate the pivot shaft in the housing and insert the locking pin 37 in **FIG 7:13**. Tighten the nut 27 securing the connector 16 to the pivot shaft.

8 Remove the locking pin. Withdraw the selector shafts and, keeping them together, engage them in their correct location in the output shaft housing. Fit the spring 15, bush 14 and distance tube 13 to the transfer gear selector shaft.

9 Fit the output shaft housing.

Fit a new joint washer, 21 in **FIG 7:14**, then engage the dog clutch selector fork in the groove of the locking dog 15. Engage the selector shaft in the bush in the transfer box, at the same time sliding the locking dog over the splines of the transfer box output shaft, ensuring that the coupling engages the screw correctly.

Engage the transfer gear selector fork onto the shaft inside the transfer box. Ensure that the threaded half of the pinch bolt hole is to the centre of the transfer box.

10 Select low transfer, through the aperture in the transfer box, place the housing over the shafts and secure to the transfer box casing.

11 Replace the transfer box and refill with oil.

12 Depress the front wheel drive control rod (see **FIG 7:13**, item 41), then screw down the locknut 47 until

the spring 44 is compressed to $2\frac{5}{16}$ inch (58.73 mm). Tighten the knob 46 against the nut 47.

If the transfer box is of the all helical type, adjust the transfer selector shaft stop screw as follows.

Engage four wheel drive low ratio and check that locking pin 37 is an easy slide fit. Adjust the stop bolt if necessary.

7:6 Gearbox servicing, 3.5 litre models

Front output shaft and housing:

1 Remove the front floor.
2 Drain the transfer gearbox oil.
3 Disconnect the front propeller shaft.
4 Note the hose positions, then disconnect them from the differential lock actuator. Remove the fixings and withdraw the unit. Collect the detent ball and spring.
5 Remove the bolts and withdraw the shaft and housing.
6 Lift out the lock-up dog clutch.
7 Remove the nut and washer and withdraw the coupling flange and mudshield.
8 Press out the shaft.
9 Withdraw the oil seal.
10 Remove the circlip and withdraw the output shaft bearing.

Reassembly and refitting are a reversal of these instructions. If only the oil seal requires renewal, it will only be necessary to remove the coupling flange. The oil seal is fitted with the open side towards the bearing. Torque tighten the shaft nut to 85 lb ft (11.75 mkg).

Bellhousing:

1 Remove the gearbox (see **Section 7:2**).
2 Remove the clutch operating mechanism (see **Chapter 6, Section 6:6**).
3 Remove the bellhousing fixings and withdraw the bellhousing.

Refit in the reverse order, using a thin film of Hylomar PL 32M or other suitable jointing compound around the three selector shaft holes in the bellhousing rear face. Do not let the compound enter the holes. Apply a thin film of molybdenum disulphide grease on the front cover extension sleeve.

Bearing plate assembly:

1 Drain the gearbox oil.
2 Remove the gearbox (see **Section 7:2**).
3 Remove the bellhousing as already described.
4 With the front end of the gearbox uppermost, remove the oil pump gears cover 1 (see **FIG 7:16**). Remove the joint washer and the drive gear 2.
5 Temporarily remove the four fixing studs 3 from the gearbox front face.
6 Ease the bearing plate 4 away from the gearbox and remove the two dowel sleeves 5.
7 Withdraw the bearing plate assembly and joint washer 6.
8 Withdraw the layshaft.

The bearing plate and gearbox casing are a mated assembly and, where necessary, must be renewed together.

Reassembly is a reversal of the dismantling operations. When refitting the top two studs, smear the threads securing the studs with Loctite Studlock grade 'CVX.'

Front cover and oil pump:

1 Remove the gearbox (see **Section 7 : 2**).
2 Remove the clutch operating mechanism (see **Chapter 6, Section 6 : 6**).
3 Remove the front cover 1 (see **FIG 7 : 17**) complete with oil pump. Remove the joint washer.
4 Remove the shim washer located between the front cover and the layshaft front bearing.
5 Remove the pump cover 2 and the gasket.
6 Remove the ring gear 3 and drive gear 4.
7 Remove the oil feed ring 5 and oil seal 6.
8 Remove the plug 7 and withdraw the relief valve ball and spring.

Reassemble in the reverse order, pressing in the oil seal, plain face first. Align the centre hole of the three in the oil feed ring with the oil delivery hole in the front cover. The relief valve plug must be flush with, or not more than .01 inch (.25 mm) below, the front cover rear face. Ensure that the pump drive gear engages the square in the layshaft. The primary pinion is aligned with the bellhousing using gauge RO 1005 (see **FIG 7 : 18**). Check that the front cover is concentric about the primary pinion, adjusting the front cover position as necessary.

Gearchange selectors, main gearbox:

1 Remove the gearbox (see **Section 7 : 2**).
2 Remove the bellhousing as already described.
3 Select neutral, remove the reverse light switch 1 (see **FIG 7 : 19**), the top cover 2 and the joint washer.
4 Lift out the detent springs 3 and the balls 4. Use a small magnet or air blast.
5 Slacken the pinch bolt 5.
6 Drive out the four retaining pins 6 to free the shafts and then tap out the shafts 1 (see **FIG 7 : 20**).
7 Withdraw the selector jaws and forks 2.
8 Withdraw the two interlock plungers 3.
9 Remove the lock-wired pivot bolt 4.
10 Lift out the reverse cross-over lever 5.

On reassembly, ensure that all retaining pins are an interference fit and renew as necessary. Proceed as follows.

1 Withdraw the selector jaws retaining pins.
2 Position the reverse cross-over lever in the gearbox.
3 Locate the lever foot in the groove in the reverse idler gear.
4 Fit the pivot bolt and, just before the bolt is fully home, apply Loctite Studlock grade 'CVX' to the remaining threads. Do not allow any Loctite to enter the gearbox.
5 Position the first/second selector fork in the outer member groove with the boss to the rear righthand side (see 1 in **FIG 7 : 21**).
6 Position the third/fourth selector fork in the outer member groove with the retaining pin 2 entry hole at the top righthand side.
7 Fit the third/fourth selector shaft 3 and interlock pin assembly. Secure with a retaining pin.

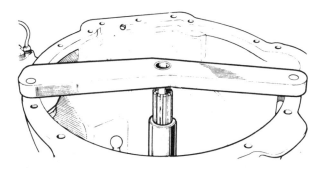

FIG 7 : 18   Centralizing gauge for primary pinion

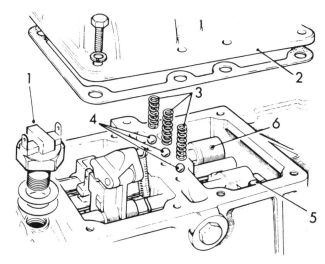

FIG 7 : 19   Main gearbox top cover and selectors

Key to Fig 7 : 19   1 Reverse light switch   2 Top cover
3 Detent springs   4 Balls   5 Pinch bolt
6 Retaining pins

FIG 7 : 20   Main gearbox components

Key to Fig 7 : 20   1 Selector shafts   2 Jaws, forks and
reverse stop hinge   3 Interlock plungers   4 Pivot bolt
5 Reverse cross-over lever

8 Fit the two interlock plungers 4 to engage in the groove each side of the shaft 3.

9 Position the reverse stop hinge plate and selector jaw 5 adjacent to the third/fourth selector jaw.

10 Fit the reverse gear selector shaft 6 and engage the selector jaw and hinge spring.

11 Engage the reverse cross-over lever selector finger 7. Do not tighten the pinch bolt 8 at this time.

12 Fit the reverse gear selector jaw retaining pin 9.

13 Position the first/second selector jaw 10 and push in the shaft 11, engaging the selector jaw and fork. Fit the retaining pins 12, rear pin first.

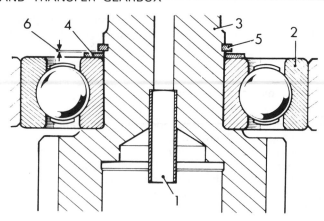

FIG 7:23 Assembly of primary pinion bearing

Key to Fig 7:23   1 Oil tube   2 Bearing   3 Primary pinion
4 Shim washer   5 Circlip   6 Clearance

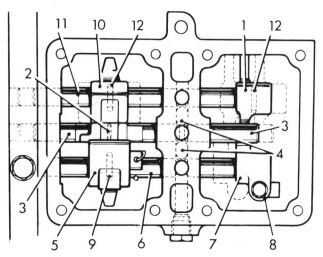

FIG 7:21 Reassembly of gearchange selectors

Key to Fig 7:21   1 First/second gear selector fork
2 Third/fourth gear selector fork   3 Third/fourth gear
selector shaft   4 Interlock plungers   5 Reverse stop hinge
plate and selector jaw   6 Reverse gear selector shaft
7 Reverse cross-over lever selector finger   8 Pinch bolt
9 Retaining pin   10 First/second gear selector jaw
11 First/second gear selector shaft   12 Retaining pins

14 Move the reverse shaft forward until the selector jaw 1 (see **FIG 7:22**) abuts the casing and hold it in this position. Move the reverse selector finger forward on the shaft 2 until it abuts the casing, then move it just clear of the casing.

15 Insert a .010 inch (.25 mm) feeler gauge 3 between the upper edges of the reverse and third/fourth selector jaws as shown in the diagram. Do not insert any further as the jaws taper. Holding the jaws together to hold the feeler gauge, rotate the reverse selector finger until it abuts the selector shaft, then tighten the pinch bolt 4.

16 Check that there is no fouling between the cross-over lever and selector finger. If necessary, increase the .010 inch (.25 mm) setting up to .020 inch (.50 mm).

17 Wire-lock the cross-over lever pivot bolt 4 (see **FIG 7:20**).

18 Fit the hinge spring, large hook first, to the selector shaft, then the small hook to the hinge pin.

The remaining operations are a reversal of the removal procedure.

Reverse idler gear and shaft:

1 Drain the main and transfer gearboxes.

2 Remove the gearbox side and bottom covers.

3 Remove the shaft securing bolt from the casing.

4 Extract the shaft and remove the O-ring.

5 Lift out the gear assembly.

6 Remove the circlip and plain washer, the needle roller bearings and the other plain washer. Withdraw the remaining circlip.

7 Withdraw the shaft support bush if required.

Reassembly is a reversal of the removal procedure. If the support bush was removed, refit using Locquic primer grade 'T' and 'AVV' grade. Align the retaining bolt holes and use gearbox oil on the O-ring. Engage the selector foot in the groove. Treat the threads of the retaining bolt with Locquic primer grade 'T' and allow to dry, then fit the bolt using Loctite Studlock grade.

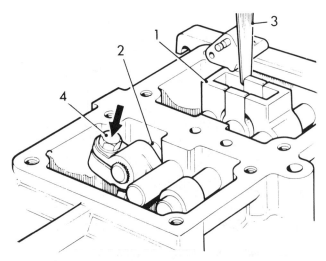

FIG 7:22 Setting the reverse selector finger

Key to Fig 7:22   1 Reverse shaft selector jaw   2 Reverse
selector shaft   3 Feeler gauge   4 Pinch bolt

Primary pinion:

1 Drain and remove the gearbox (see **Section 7:2**).
2 Remove the bellhousing, the front cover and oil pump assembly and the bearing plate assembly all as described earlier.
3 Remove the circlip and shim washer, then press out the pinion.
4 Withdraw the bearing retaining plates and serrated bolts, then press out the bearing.
5 Check that the orifice drilled in the oil tube 1 (see **FIG 7:23**) is clear. Avoid damage to the tube and ensure that it is straight when the primary shaft can be rotated.
6 Using suitable wooden blocks positioned across the bearing housing aperture to act as stops, press in the bearing 2 until flush with the plate.
7 Press in the primary pinion shaft 3 and check that the bearing has not moved.
8 Fit the retaining plates, the shim washer 4 and circlip 5.
9 Measure the clearance 6 between the circlip and shim washer which should be a maximum of .002 inch (.05 mm). Shims are available in .002 inch (.05 mm) stages from .079 to .085 inch (2 to 2.15 mm) if adjustment is necessary.

The remaining operations are a reversal of removal.

Mainshaft assembly:

1 Drain and remove the gearbox, the bellhousing, the front bearing plate and the main gearchange selectors all as described previously.
2 Remove the rear bearing housing and roller bearing.
3 Remove the transfer gearbox bottom cover.
4 Remove the snap ring 1 (see **FIG 7:24**), shim washer 2 and transfer gear 3.
5 Withdraw the transfer gear spacer along the mainshaft, using extractor RO 1004, as far as possible, then tap the mainshaft forward and free the spacer and extractor.
6 Withdraw the mainshaft assembly, leaving the first speed gear behind.
7 Lift out the first speed gear, scalloped thrust washer, thrust needle bearing, stepped thrust washer and mainshaft spacer.
8 Remove the snap ring 1 (see **FIG 7:25**) and shim washer 2 from the front of the shaft.
9 Lift off the third/fourth gears synchromesh assembly complete.
10 Withdraw the third and second speed gears and the associated thrust washers and needle roller bearings.
11 Dismantle both synchromesh units in a similar manner. It is advisable to enclose the units in a cloth to prevent loss of sliding blocks, balls and springs. Mark the parts, as far as possible, for reassembly in the same relative positions. Push down the sliding blocks 3 to free the balls 4 from the retaining groove in the outer member 5 and carefully slide out the inner member 6. Collect the blocks, springs and balls. Do not interchange parts between units.
12 Withdraw the oil seal 7 from the front of the shaft.

When reassembling, do not degrease new thrust washers or roller bearings and lubricate all parts with

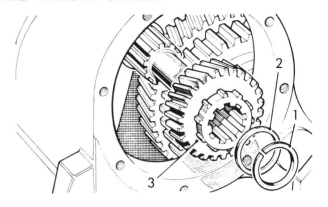

FIG 7:24   Mainshaft transfer gear

Key to Fig 7:24   1 Snap ring   2 Shim washer
3 Transfer gear

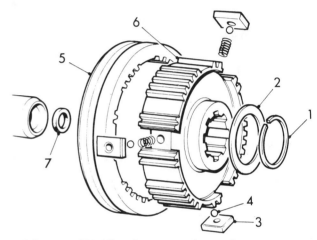

FIG 7:25   Third/fourth gears synchromesh components

Key to Fig 7:25   1 Snap ring   2 Shim washer
3 Sliding blocks   4 Balls   5 Outer member
6 Inner member   7 Oil seal

clean main gearbox oil. Reassemble in the reverse order with attention to the following items.

1 Fit the coned face of the outer member of the first/second synchromesh unit towards the front end of the shaft.
2 The second speed gear is fitted to the front of the shaft in the order shown in **FIG 7:26**.
3 The third speed gear and synchromesh unit are fitted in a similar manner, but the thrust washers are all scalloped.
4 The synchromesh unit is fitted with its coned face to the rear.
5 Take up all end float and fit the snap ring.
6 Measure the distance between the snap ring and the inner synchromesh member and select a shim to reduce this to .001 to .006 inch (.025 to .150 mm) when fitted. Shims are available in steps of .006 inch (.15 mm) from .073 to .096 inch (1.85 to 2.45 mm).
7 Remove the snap ring, fit the selected shim washer and refit the snap ring.

8 Assemble the rear end of the shaft in the order shown in **FIG 7:27**.

9 Place the gearbox on its righthand side and remove the side cover.

10 Move the first speed gear towards the rear and place the mainshaft into the gearbox, manoeuvring the first speed gear past the reverse idler gear and entering the shaft into the main bearing.

11 Engage the synchromesh outer member and the reverse idler gear.

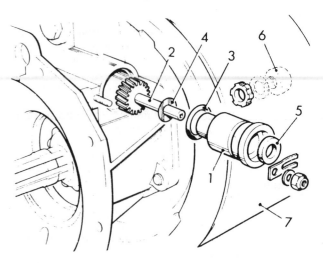

FIG 7:28   Speedometer drive components

Key to Fig 7:28   1 Speedometer spindle housing
2 Driven gear and spindle   3 O-ring   4 Thrust washer
5 Oil seal   6 Output shaft nut   7 Brake drum

12 Locate the spacer on the rear end of the shaft with its larger diameter forward of the transfer gearlever cross-shaft.

13 Reposition the first speed gear and push the mainshaft fully home, ensuring that the thrust washers and bearing are correctly located against the gear.

14 Move the spacer along the shaft into the oil seal until it abuts the main bearing.

15 Fit the transfer gear 3 (see **FIG 7:24**) and the snap ring 1 without a shim washer. Measure the distance between the snap ring and transfer gear with the mainshaft fully to the rear and select a shim washer to reduce this to .002 inch (.050 mm) maximum clearance when fitted. Shims are available in steps of .002 inch (.050 mm) from .071 to .079 inch (1.8 to 2 mm).

16 Remove the snap ring and transfer gear, slide the spacer back as far as possible and apply a thin coating of Loctite 'AVV' grade to the exposed area of the mainshaft, then push home the spacer.

17 Fit the transfer gear, selected shim washer and snap ring.

Reassemble the remaining items in the reverse order.

Rear output shaft oil seal:

1 Disconnect the rear propeller shaft at the transmission brake.

2 Remove the locking nut, washer, felt rubber oil seal if fitted, and withdraw the drum and coupling flange.

3 Remove the oil catcher, prise off the oil shield and withdraw the oil seal.

Reassemble in the reverse order, pressing in the oil seal, open end first, until the plain face just clears the chamfer on the housing bore. Using Bostik compound 771, seal the oil catcher against the brake backplate. On completion, torque tighten the output shaft nut to 85 lb ft (11.75 mkg).

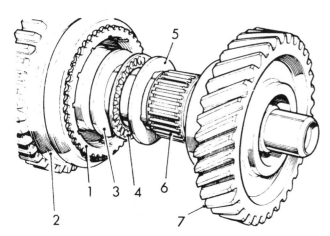

FIG 7:26   Assembling mainshaft front end

Key to Fig 7:26   1 Synchromesh cone   2 First/second gear synchromesh outer member   3 Chamfered thrust washer
4 Thrust needle bearing   5 Scalloped thrust washer
6 Radial needle bearing   7 Second speed gear

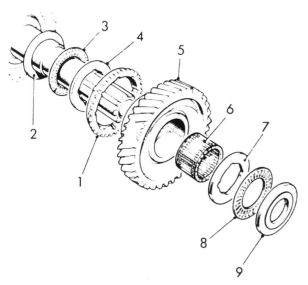

FIG 7:27   Assembling mainshaft rear end

Key to Fig 7:27   1 Synchromesh cone   2 Chamfered thrust washer   3 Thrust needle bearing   4 Scalloped thrust washer   5 First speed gear   6 Radial needle bearing
7 Scalloped thrust washer   8 Thrust needle bearing
9 Stepped thrust washer, stepped face outwards

Speedometer drive housing :

1 Chock the wheels and release the handbrake.
2 Disconnect the rear propeller shaft at the transmission brake.
3 Disconnect the handbrake linkage and the speedometer drive cable.
4 Remove the drive housing fixings and withdraw the housing complete with the transmission brake.
5 Remove the speedometer spindle housing 1 (see **FIG 7:28**).
6 Lift out the driven gear and spindle 2.
7 Take off the O-ring 3.
8 Remove the thrust washer 4.
9 Withdraw the oil seal 5.
10 Remove the output coupling flange to output shaft locking nut 6, washer and felt seal.
11 Withdraw the brake drum and coupling flange 7.
12 Drive out the rear output shaft, using a hide mallet on the threaded end.
13 Slide off the spacer and speedometer worm.
14 Remove the oil catcher and withdraw the oil shield and oil seal.
15 Remove the circlip and tap out the bearing.
16 If a new drive housing, gearbox, differential unit or differential unit bearing is being fitted, proceed as follows.

    (a) Measure the thickness of the new joint washer for the speedometer drive housing.

    (b) Offer the speedometer housing 1 (see **FIG 7:29**), less the joint washer, to the gearbox 2, engaging the differential bearing 3 with the outer race 4.

    (c) Measure the clearance 5 between the drive housing and gearbox joint faces. This must be .002 inch (.05 mm) more than the thickness of the new joint washer.

    (d) To adjust the clearance, drive out the outer race 4 and withdraw the shim washer 6. Select a shim washer of the required thickness to give the necessary clearance 5. Shim washers are available in steps of .002 inch (.05 mm) from .065 to .110 inch (1.65 to 2.80 mm).

Reassemble and refit in the reverse order of dismantling and removal, using the instruction, where necessary, given in 'Rear output shaft oil seal'. Engage the rear output shaft splines in the differential unit and position the flat on the drive housing adjacent to the flat on the intermediate shaft. Torque tighten the output flange nut 6 (see **FIG 7:28**) to 85 lb ft (11.75 mkg), the drive housing fixings to 22 lb ft (3.1 mkg) and the propeller shaft fixings to 35 lb ft (4.8 mkg).

Reverse light switch :

Refer to **Chapter 12, Section 12:14**.

Differential lock actuator switch :

Refer to **Chapter 12, Section 12:14**.

Transfer gearbox gearlever and cross-shaft :

1 Remove the gearbox (see **Section 7:2**).
2 Remove the top cover 1 (see **FIG 7:30**).
3 Slacken the selector finger pinch bolt 2.

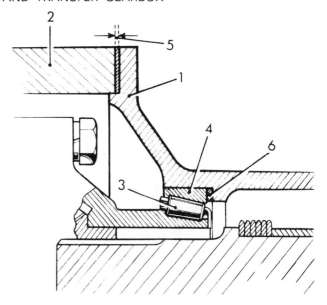

FIG 7:29 Differential bearing preload

Key to Fig 7:29　　　1 Speedometer housing　　2 Gearbox
3 Differential bearing　　4 Outer race　　5 Clearance
6 Shim washer

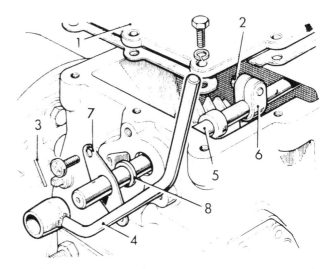

FIG 7:30 Transfer gearbox gearlever and cross-shaft

Key to Fig 7:30　　　1 Top cover　　2 Pinch bolt
3 Retaining pin　　4 Gearlever　　5 Cross-shaft　　6 Selector
finger　　7 Retaining plate　　8 Sealing ring

4 Drive out the retaining pin 3 and withdraw the gearlever 4.
5 Withdraw the cross-shaft 5 and distance collar.
6 Lift out the selector finger 6.
7 Remove the retaining plates 7.
8 Withdraw the sealing rings 8.

Refit in the reverse order, selecting the 'High' transfer range (larger intermediate gear engaged). Slacken the selector pinch bolt and rotate the cross-shaft until the gearlever is inclined 45 deg. rearward of the vertical position, then tighten the pinch bolt.

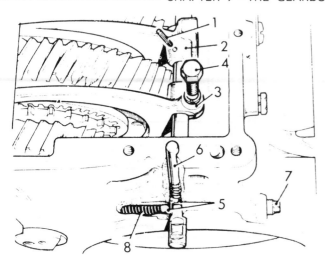

FIG 7:31 Transfer gearbox selectors and shaft

Key to Fig 7:31   1 Retaining pin   2 Front fork
3 Rear fork   4 Pinch bolt   5 Detent balls   6 Spacing rod
7 Plug   8 Spring

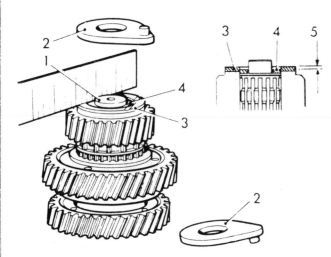

FIG 7:32 Intermediate gears end float

Key to Fig 7:32   1 Slave shaft RO 1003   2 Pear-shaped
thrust washers   3 Thrust bearing washer   4 Inner ring
5 Clearance

Transfer gearbox selectors and shaft:

1 Remove the gearbox tunnel cover and the centre panel from the seat base.
2 Remove the speedometer drive housing as described earlier.
3 Remove the top cover.
4 Select 'Low' range transfer gear.
5 Drive out the retaining pin 1 (see **FIG 7:31**) far enough to free the front fork 2.
6 Ease the differential unit to the rear.
7 Push the fork forward on the shaft and pull the rear selector fork 3 to the rear, moving the shaft out of engagement with the detent balls.

8 Remove the pinch bolt 4, withdrawing the shaft far enough to be able to lift out the forks. Remove the retaining pin 1.
9 Withdraw the shaft carefully, closing the inner shaft housing by hand to prevent the detent balls falling into the casing. Withdraw the detent balls 5.
10 Lift out the spacing rod 6 and spring.
11 Remove the plug 7 and the spring 8 from the cross drilling.

Reassemble in the reverse order with attention to the following points.

1 Push the detent ball against the spring 8 when entering the shaft.
2 Position the rear fork, plain face to the rear.
3 Position the front fork, extended boss to the rear.
4 With the transfer gears in 'neutral', adjust the rear fork position until there is .005 to .010 inch (.12 to .25 mm) clearance between the front face of the rear fork and the rear face of the input gear inner member. Tighten the pinch bolt.

Intermediate gears:

A slave intermediate shaft will be required during this operation. The official tool is RO 1003.

1 Drain the transfer gearbox.
2 Remove the speedometer drive housing as described earlier.
3 Remove the intermediate exhaust pipe if necessary.
4 Remove the gearbox bottom cover.
5 Using the 8 mm threaded hole and a suitable extractor, and supporting the intermediate gear cluster, withdraw the shaft. Insert the slave shaft and withdraw the assembly.
6 Slide the components from the slave shaft and inspect for wear, damage and condition. Renew as necessary.
7 With the slave shaft on a surface plate, extractor thread end uppermost, assemble the components as follows: inner ring, grooved face downwards, thrust bearing washer, groove upwards, a needle roller bearing and the 'high' gear, plain face first, a thrust bearing washer, groove upwards, a spacer, needle roller bearing and the second spacer. Position the first spacer in the thrust bearing washer, the input gear locating a thrust bearing washer, groove upwards, around the top spacer, a needle roller bearing and the 'low' gear, plain side last. Fit the remaining inner ring, grooves upwards, and the thrust washer, groove upwards.
8 Place a straightedge across the thrust bearing washer 3 (see **FIG 7:32**) and check that a clearance exists between the straightedge and the inner ring 4. If no clearance exists, obtain clearance by selective assembly of alternative components or, failing this, it is permissible to reduce the thickness of each spacer up to .005 inch (.13 mm).
9 Fit the pear-shaped washers 2 and enter the assembly into the transfer gearbox. Support the gears and withdraw the slave shaft. Check that the selector forks are properly engaged, lubricate the bearings and fit the intermediate shaft with the flat towards the differential unit.
10 Measure the clearance between the rear pear-shaped washer and the gear casing. This should be

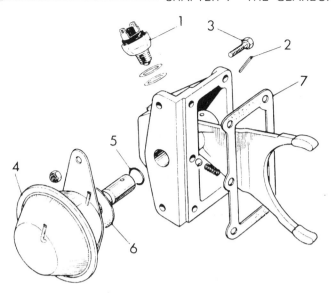

FIG 7 : 33   Differential lock actuator components

Key to Fig 7 : 33   1 Warning switch   2 Retaining pin
3 Securing bolts   4 Actuator and shaft   5 O-ring
6 Joint washer   7 Gasket

between .006 to .009 inch (.15 to .23 mm). To adjust, substitute one or both pear-shaped washers, available in thicknesses of .139 inch (3.55 mm), .143 inch (3.63 mm) or .147 inch (3.74 mm), if necessary.

The remainder of the operations are a reversal of the removal procedures.

Differential unit :

1 Remove the front output shaft and housing as described earlier.
2 Remove the speedometer drive housing as described earlier.
3 Withdraw the differential unit.

Reassembly is a reversal of the removal procedure. If a replacement unit is being fitted, carry out operation 16 of 'Speedometer drive housing.'

Differential lock actuator :

1 Carry out operation 4 of 'Front output shaft and housing.'
2 Remove the warning switch 1 (see **FIG 7 : 33**).
3 Drive out the retaining pin 2.
4 Remove the bolts 3.
5 Withdraw the actuator and shaft 4.
6 Withdraw the O-ring 5 and joint washers 6 and 7.

Refit in the reverse order, applying Hylomar PL 32M jointing compound to both sides of joint washer 6 and to the joint faces and both sides of joint washer 7.

7:7   The main gearchange lever

To overhaul this unit, refer to **FIG 7 : 34** and proceed as follows :

1 Remove the front floor complete, then undo the two bolts and two nuts. Lift the lever out complete.

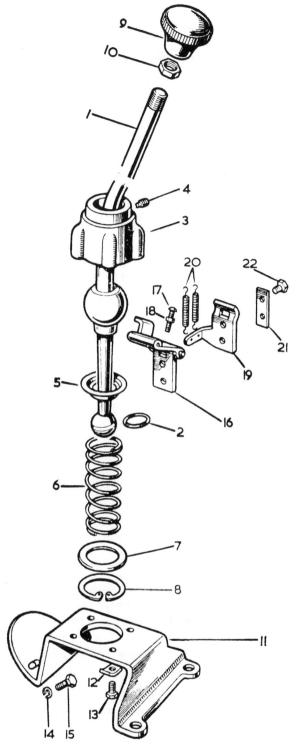

FIG 7 : 34   Main gearchange lever

Key to Fig 7 : 34   1 Gearchange lever   2 O-ring for lever
3 Housing for lever 4 Locating pin for lever ball 5 Spherical seat for gearlever   6 Retaining spring for lever   7 Retaining plate for spring   8 Circlip fixing retaining plate   9 Knob for lever   10 Locknut for knob   11 Mounting plate for gearchange   12, 13 Fixings for housing   14, 15 Fixings for mounting plate   16* Reverse stop hinge complete
17* Adjusting screw (for hinge)   18* Locknut (for hinge)
19* Bracket for reverse stop spring   20* Spring for reverse stop   21, 22* Fixings for hinge and bracket

* 2¼ and 2.6 litre models

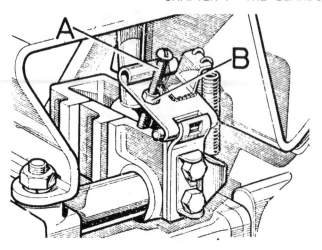

FIG 7:35   Adjusting reverse selector stop

Key to Fig 7:35   **A** Adjusting screw   **B** Locknut

2 Remove the circlip 8 and draw the gearlever out of the housing.

3 Renew any worn components.

Rebuilding the unit is a reversal of the dismantling process.

To adjust the reverse stop, 2¼ and 2.6 litre models (see FIG 7:35):

1 The screw and locknut on the reverse stop hinge should be adjusted so that:

(a) The hinge rides easily up the gearlever when reverse gear is selected.

(b) Appreciable resistance is felt on moving the gearlever to the reverse gear position.

(c) When selecting first gear, reverse gear is not simultaneously engaged.

2 This adjustment should be carried out on any gearbox removed for attention, before the gearbox cover is fitted.

3 It can also be carried out at any time after:

(a) Detaching the inspection cover from the righthand side of the gearbox cover on vehicles so fitted.

(b) Selecting reverse gear and sliding the inspection cover up the front wheel drive control rod.

7:8 *Fault diagnosis*

(a) Gearbox noisy in neutral

1 Primary pinion bearing worn
2 Constant mesh gears worn

3 Layshaft bearing(s) worn
4 Insufficient oil

(b) Gearbox noisy in gear

1 Worn speedometer gears
2 Noise in 1st, 2nd and 3rd; see 2 and 3 at (a)
3 Noise in either 1st, 2nd or 3rd only; renew the pair of gears in question
4 Noise in all gears, worn bearings

(c) Oil leaks

1 Oil level too high
2 Damaged joint washers
3 Damaged or worn oil seals
4 Level plugs missing
5 Cracked casing
6 Breather blocked, if fitted

(d) Difficulty in engaging gears

1 Incorrect adjustment of control levers
2 Clutch sticking
3 Worn primary pinion splines
4 Worn synchromesh units

(e) Difficulty in disengaging gears

1 Incorrect adjustment of control levers
2 Clutch not being released completely
3 Worn or damaged mainshaft splines in gearbox
4 Worn synchromesh units

(f) Difficulty in engaging reverse

1 Bush loose in gear
2 Faulty stop setting on selector fork
3 Faulty clutch operation

(g) Jumping out of high transfer

1 Selector spring weak

(h) Jumping out of low transfer

1 Transfer fork assembled wrongly
2 Excessive end float of intermediate gear
3 Selector spring weak

(j) Noisy transfer box

1 Excessive end float of intermediate gear
2 End float on output shaft
3 Worn bearings

(k) Four wheel drive will not engage

1 Return spring below yellow knob wrongly adjusted
2 Shafts sticking in casing

CHAPTER 8

PROPELLER SHAFT, REAR AXLE, REAR SUSPENSION

8 : 1 *Description*

The Land-Rover is a four wheel drive vehicle. Therefore, the drive must be transmitted to two axles. The two propeller shafts on $2\frac{1}{4}$ litre and 2.6 litre models are basically similar so that overhaul instructions are given which apply to both. The universal joints are identical. The front shaft on 3.5 litre models has a conventional universal joint at the front end and a double Hooke's Cardan universal joint at the rear. Suspension is by leaf spring, damped by hydraulic dampers mounted between the axle and the chassis frame. Differential units are usually of Rover manufacture and are fitted to both front and rear axles.

(Note that some vehicles built to special order may have the ENV differential).

8 : 2 *Servicing the universal joints*

The propeller shafts can be removed by simply undoing the four nuts and bolts at each end flange and withdrawing the shaft from the transfer box and differentials.

If a rear power takeoff drive is fitted, to 107 and 109 models, the shaft to this must be disconnected at the centre bearing assembly first. Then proceed as for the road wheel transmission shafts and disconnect at the rear power takeoff unit or remove the unit first, then disconnect the shaft, depending on the accessibility of the particular vehicle.

To renew conventional universal joints:

Refer to **FIG 8 : 1**. Check that the arrows on the halves of the sliding joint are marked, then unscrew the dust cap and withdraw the shaft from the sleeve. The dust cap is covered by a rubber bellows held at each end by large hose clips to retain the lubricant. Undo the hose clips and slide the bellows up the shaft before undoing the cap.

Proceed to dismantle each joint as follows:
1 Remove the circlips **B** (see **FIG 8 : 2**).
2 Hold the joint in the left hand with one of the yoke lugs uppermost and tap the radius of the yoke lightly with a soft-faced mallet. The top bearing should then emerge from the yoke (see **FIG 8 : 3**).
3 Turn the joint over and remove the bearing downwards so as not to drop the needle rollers (see **FIG 8 : 4**).
4 Repeat for the opposite side bearing. Remove the shaft as shown in **FIG 8 : 5**.
5 Rest the yoke on a short piece of tubing and, with the aid of a brass drift, drive out the remaining two bearings as shown in **FIG 8 : 6**.

Wash all the parts and inspect for wear. The most likely location will be the spider journals and the bearing races. An overhaul kit which consists of a new spider, four races and cork seals will cure this type of wear. If, however, the shaft has been allowed to so deteriorate that the races have hammered the yoke bores oval, then the complete shaft must be renewed.

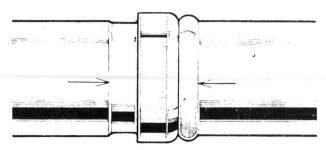

FIG 8:1   Alignment marks

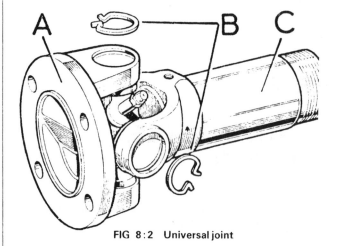

FIG 8:2   Universal joint

Key to Fig 8:2   A Flange yoke **B** Circlips **C** Shaft yoke

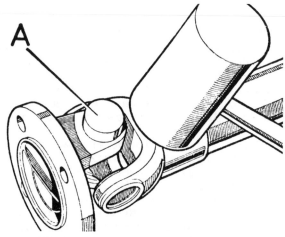

FIG 8:3   Removing a yoke bearing, Stage 1

Key to Fig 8:3   A Bearing emerging

At this stage, when all is clean, check the sliding joint for movement. If more than .004 inch (.1 mm) of circumferential movement is found, then, again, the whole shaft must be renewed.

Assuming that the wear can be eliminated by fitting an overhaul kit, proceed now as follows:

1 Assemble the needle rollers in the bearing races, if necessary using a smear of petroleum jelly to hold them in. About half fill the races with a recommended grease.

2 Assemble the new spider in the flange yoke with its journals in the yoke holes. Gently tap the first bearing upwards from the lower hole into position. Do not forget to assemble the cork oil seal on the journal. Repeat for the other bearing. Fit the shaft over the spider and fit the two bearings in the shaft yoke by the same method.

3 Use a brass drift to tap the bearings home, then fit the circlips, making sure that they seat properly in their grooves.

4 Tap the yokes a few times with a soft-faced mallet to ensure that the bearings seat back against the circlips.

The shaft sliding portion must now have the splines liberally smeared with grease and must then be assembled to the sleeve, making sure that the arrows are in alignment (see **FIG 8:1**). Tighten the dust cap by hand only, slide the rubber bellows back over the shaft and sleeve and tighten the hose clips. (Fit the clips so that their fixings are 180 deg. so as to maintain shaft balance).

Replace the shaft by reversing the dismantling procedure but make sure that the mating faces of the flanges on the shaft, the differential and the transfer box are clean. Ensure that the register engages and the joint faces of the flanges have bedded down all round.

When the shaft flange is bolted to the differential, see that the bolts face the differential, i.e. the nuts are nearest to the differential, behind the differential flange. On Series 3 models, the bolt heads are on the differential side of the flange.

Double Hooke's Cardan universal joint:

On initial assembly, the bearing cups are retained by internally moulded plastic rings which will have to be

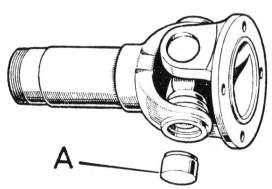

FIG 8:4   Removing a yoke bearing, Stage 2

Key to Fig 8:4   A Bearing withdrawn

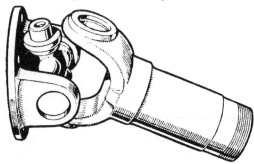

FIG 8:5   Removing the shaft

sheared. The bearing cups and spiders, in this case, cannot be reassembled and must be renewed. Replacement bearing cups are retained with circlips.

Mark one side of each of the three yokes for reassembly in the same relative positions to preserve balance.

1 Press out the bearing cups from the coupling flange 1 (see **FIG 8:7**), using a $1\frac{1}{8}$ inch (30 mm) socket 2, open end uppermost, and a mandrel 3. Repeat on the opposite cup.

2 Disengage the spider from the coupling yoke and pull from the centring ball on the shaft yoke.

3 If necessary, remove the ball socket components (see **FIG 8:8**) by prising out the seal 1 and drifting out the ball seats 3. Fully assembled sockets are obtainable and worn or damaged sockets can be renewed in one operation.

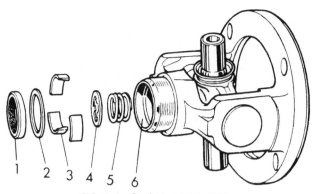

FIG 8:8 Socket components

Key to Fig 8:8   1 Seal   2 Washer   3 Ball seats
4 Tongued washer   5 Spring   6 Socket cavity

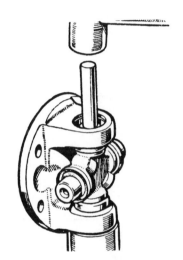

FIG 8:6 Removing the flange yoke

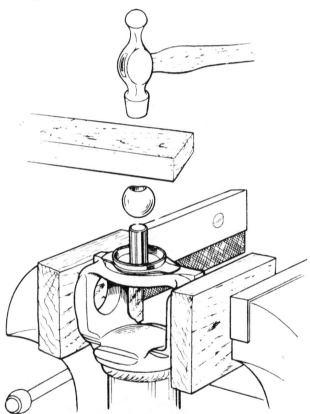

FIG 8:9 Fitting centring ball

4 If necessary, remove the ball from the shaft yoke by removing the complete spider in the manner described earlier. Grind a flat on each side of the ball equally to a minimum of $\frac{1}{2}$ inch (13 mm) across the flats. Do not damage the mounting stud. Grip the flats in a vice and, using a rod through the yoke bearing cup holes, loosen and remove the yoke from the ball.

5 Remove the remaining bearing cups from the flange yoke.

6 Clean out any remnants of plastic from the yoke grooves by using a small pin punch through the injection holes used during initial assembly.

Reassembly is, generally, a reversal of the dismantling procedure with attention to the following points.

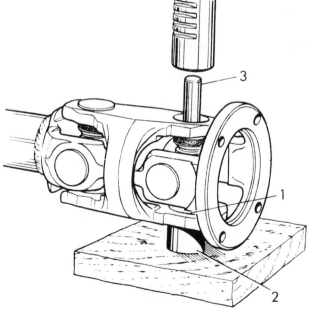

FIG 8:7 Removing bearing cups

Key to Fig 8:7   1 Yoke   2 Socket   3 Mandrel

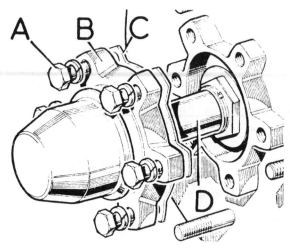

FIG 8:10   Rover axle shaft

Key to Fig 8:10   **A** Bolts   **B** Driving member   **C** Joint washer   **D** Axle shaft

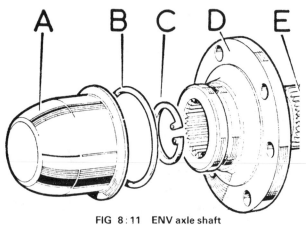

FIG 8:11   ENV axle shaft

Key to Fig 8:11   **A** Hub cap   **B** O-ring   **C** Circlip **D** Driving member   **E** Axle shaft

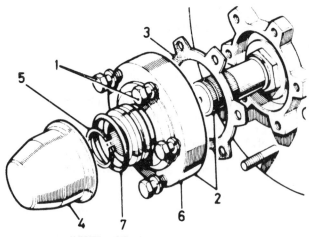

FIG 8:12   Salisbury axle shaft

Key to Fig 8:12   1 Driving bolts   2 Axle shaft   3 Joint washer   4 Hub cap   5 Circlip   6 Driving member 7 O-ring seal

1 If a new ball is being fitted, either support the shaft vertically or use the method shown in **FIG 8:9**, being careful not to damage the yoke. **Do not clamp the tubular section.** The ball must seat firmly against the shoulder on the mounting stud.

2 Reassemble the ball seat as shown in **FIG 8:8**, the three ball seats 3 with the large openings outwards and their joints aligned with the inside tongues of the small washer 4. Apply Hylomar PL 32M to the outer edge of the seal 1 and press the seal into the socket, lip leading, until flush. If assembled sockets are available, renew the complete socket. Fill the socket cavity with grease.

3 During the assembly of bearing cups, press each bearing cup into its yoke until the circlip groove is completely exposed on the **inside** of the yoke and fit the circlips.

4 Fit the coupling yoke to the shaft yoke with the markings aligned.

5 Manoeuvre the coupling yoke and flange yoke together and press the socket over the ball.

6 Move the coupling yoke to its limit to release tension in the socket spring when fitting the bearing cups. Ensure that the spider trunnions remain free. Any resistance may mean a displaced needle roller.

7 Check for freedom of movement of all trunnions. Any tightness can be relieved by a few judicious taps with a hammer on the sides and roots of the yokes.

8 The flange yoke should snap over-centre, up and down or left and right, if the double joint is correctly assembled.

8:3 The rear axle

Three types of differential have been fitted; most vehicles have the Rover unit, but some built to special order and also the One Ton Van have the ENV unit while some Series 3 models have the Salisbury unit. Where the heavier duty ENV and Salisbury units are fitted, this is generally only to the rear axle. Instructions are given in this chapter to cover the removal of the differential from the axle, but overhaul of any unit is best left to a Rover Service Station as it demands special equipment and knowledge. **FIGS 8:15** and **8:16** show the Rover and ENV units respecitvely.

8:4 Servicing axle shafts

On the Rover type axle, the axle shafts (halfshafts) can be removed without removing the road wheel.

Rover differential:

Refer to **FIG 8:10**.

Remove the bolts **A** and withdraw the shaft.

To replace a shaft, first fit a new joint washer **C**, smearing both sides with grease. If the hub is grease lubricated, ensure that the space in the end of the hub and driving member **B** is packed with grease. Fit the shaft, carefully engaging the splines in the differential, then tighten bolts **A** to 28 lb ft (3.9 mkg). If the hub is oil lubricated, top up with $\frac{1}{3}$ pint (.190 litre) of recommended final drive oil. Check and, if necessary, top up the differential with oil.

LRAB2

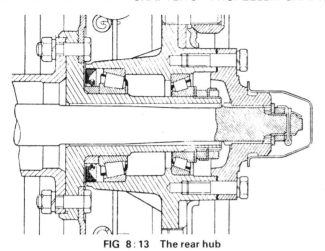

FIG 8:13 The rear hub

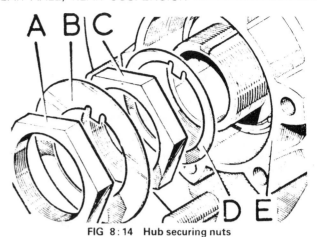

FIG 8:14 Hub securing nuts

Key to Fig 8:14   **A** Locknut   **B** Lockwasher
C Adjuster nut   **D** Key washer   **E** Hub

ENV differential:

Refer to **FIG 8:11**.

To remove the axle shafts, the vehicle must be jacked up and the road wheel taken off.

Remove the brake drum, disconnect the hydraulic pipe and then detach the brake backplate as detailed in **Chapter 11**.

The hub and axle shaft can now be pulled away from the axle. Undo the axle shaft driving member bolts, prise off the hub cap and remove the circlips. The axle shaft will now be free of the hub.

Replacement is a reversal of the removal procedure, but do not forget to bleed the brakes.

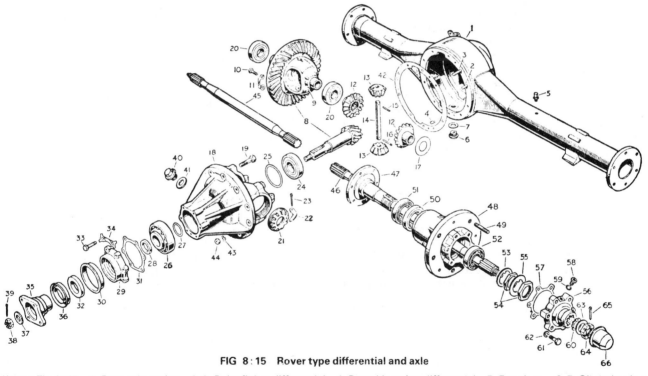

FIG 8:15 Rover type differential and axle

Key to Fig 8:15   1 Rear axle casing   2, 3 Bolts fixing differential   4 Dowel locating differential   5 Breather   6, 7 Oil drain plug   8 Crownwheel and bevel pinion   9 Differential casing   10, 11 Fixings for crownwheel   12 Differential wheel   13 Differential pinion   14 Spindle for pinions   15, 16 Fixings for spindle   17 Thrust washer for differential   18 Bevel pinion housing   19 Bolt fixing bearing cap   20 Roller bearing for differential   21 Serrated nut   22 Lock tab   23 Splitpin   24 Bearing for bevel pinion, pinion end   25 Shims for bearing adjustment, pinion end   26 Bearing for bevel pinion, flange end   27 Shims for bearing adjustment, flange end   28 Washer for bearing   29 Retainer for oil seal   30 Mudshield for retainer   31 Joint washer for retainer   32 Oil seal for pinion   33, 34 Fixings for retainer   35 Driving flange   36 Dust shield for driving flange   37-39 Fixings for driving flange   40, 41 Oil filler plug and washer   42 Joint washer for differential   43, 44 Fixings for differential   45 Axle shaft, righthand   46 Axle shaft, lefthand   47 Rear hub bearing sleeve   48 Rear hub assembly   49 Stud for road wheel   50 Hub bearing, inner   51 Oil seal for inner bearing   52 Hub bearing, outer   53-55 Fixings–for hub bearing   56 Driving member for rear hub   57 Joint washer for driving member   58 Filler plug for hub driving member   59 Joint washer for filler plug   60 Oil seal for rear axle shaft   61, 62 Fixings–driving member to rear hub   63-65 Fixings–axle shaft to driving member   66 Hub cap, rear

Salisbury differential:

Refer to **FIG 8:12**.

Remove the bolts 1 and withdraw the shaft. To free the axle from the driving member, prise off the hub cap and remove the circlip. Renew the O-ring seal 7 if necessary.

To replace a shaft, first fit a new joint washer 3, smearing both sides with grease. Ensure that the space in the end of the hub and driving member 6 is packed with grease. Fit the shaft, carefully engaging the splines in the differential, then tighten the bolts 1 to a torque of 28 lb ft (3.9 mkg).

8:5 *The rear hubs*

Refer to **FIG 8:13** for a cross-sectional view of the hubs.

To remove a hub, first remove the axle shaft on Rover type axles, but on ENV axles prise off the hub cap, remove the circlips from the shaft, then undo the bolts holding the driving member and remove the driving member. The axle shaft can then remain in the axle. Jack the vehicle up and remove the road wheel and brake drum. Undo the hub securing nuts (see **FIG 8:14**), then pull the hub and bearings away from the axle.

Examine and renew the bearings if wear is evident.

Replace the hub by reversing the dismantling process. Adjust the bearings to .002 to .005 inch (.05 to .13 mm) end float, then tighten locknut **A** (see **FIG 8:14**). Always recheck after tightening this nut. Spin the hub to settle the races as adjustment proceeds. If a new single lipped oil seal is fitted, the lipped side must face inwards towards the hub and the seal must not be pressed below the surface of the rear face of the hub. Where a double lipped seal is fitted, smear, not pack, the groove between the lips with Shell Retinax 'A' or equivalent and press in the seal, cavity side leading, so that it is recessed .190 to .210 inch (4.8 to 5.3 mm) from the rear face of the hub.

8:6 *The differential units – Rover and ENV types*

To remove and replace the unit, proceed as follows:
1 Drain the oil from the axle case.
2 Carry out all the relevant operations for removing axle shafts detailed in **Section 8:4**, but withdraw each axle shaft only about six inches (150 mm) from the axle casing.
3 Disconnect the propeller shaft at the differential input flange.
4 Undo the nuts holding the differential unit to the axle casing and lift out the unit.
5 To replace, reverse the above sequence.

On Series 3 models fitted with a Salisbury rear axle a special tool is required to remove the differential from the gearcasing.

8:7 *To remove the rear axle*

1 Jack up and safely support the rear of the vehicle.
2 Remove both road wheels and drain the axle oil.
3 Disconnect the flexible hydraulic brake pipe at the tee-piece on the differential casing. As soon as the pipe is loosened, have an assistant depress the

brake pedal and wedge it down. This will prevent further loss of fluid. Plug the pipe and tee-piece port to prevent dirt entering the system.
4 Disconnect the propeller shaft at the differential flange. Disconnect one end of each check strap.
5 Remove both hydraulic dampers and release the brake pipe from the clips at each end of the axle case.
6 Place a jack under each rear road spring at the hydraulic damper plate position and raise the spring slightly. Remove the U-bolts from the axle.
7 Lower the jacks so that they are only just taking the weight of the springs and axle.
8 Remove the self locking nuts and shackle bolts from the rear ends of the springs, then lower the jacks and springs to the ground. Prevent the axle sliding back suddenly. Lift the axle backwards and away from the vehicle.

Replacing the axle is a reversal of the removal process.

The brakes will require bleeding (see **Chapter 11**). Refill the axle with the correct quantity of SAE.90.EP oil as specified in **Technical Data** of the **Appendix**. See **Section 8:8** for details of the road spring fitting procedure.

8:8 *The rear springs*

It is most important that the rear road springs are not interchanged from one side of the vehicle to the other. The free camber of the driver's side spring is greater to compensate for the extra weight carried on that side of the vehicle. This must be borne in mind when ordering new springs.

To remove a spring:

1 Jack up and safely support the rear of the vehicle.
2 Remove the road wheels.
3 Jack up the spring under the damper plate and remove the damper at the lower fixing, then remove the U-bolt nuts. Lower the damper plate and remove the jack so that the axle is supported by the check strap and the spring is relaxed.
4 Remove the self-locking nut from the shackle pin in each spring eye.
5 Remove the shackle pin from the rear of the spring; note that it is threaded into the inner plate.
6 Remove the shackle pin from the front of the spring and lift the spring away.
7 Remove the shackle pin self-locking nut securing the shackle plates to the chassis frame.

To replace a spring:

1 If necessary, remove the bushes from the spring eyes by the use of a drift. Fit new bushes by the same method. They must be a drive fit.
2 Replace the spring by reversing the removal procedure, being careful to finally tighten the pins and locking nuts after the vehicle has been lowered to the ground and loaded to obtain a dimension between the top of the U-bolts and the chassis frame on 88 inch models of $5\frac{1}{2}$ to $5\frac{3}{4}$ inch (142 to 146 mm) or on 109 inch models of $6\frac{1}{4}$ to $6\frac{1}{2}$ inch (158 to 162 mm). Failure to observe this will result in premature spring failure.

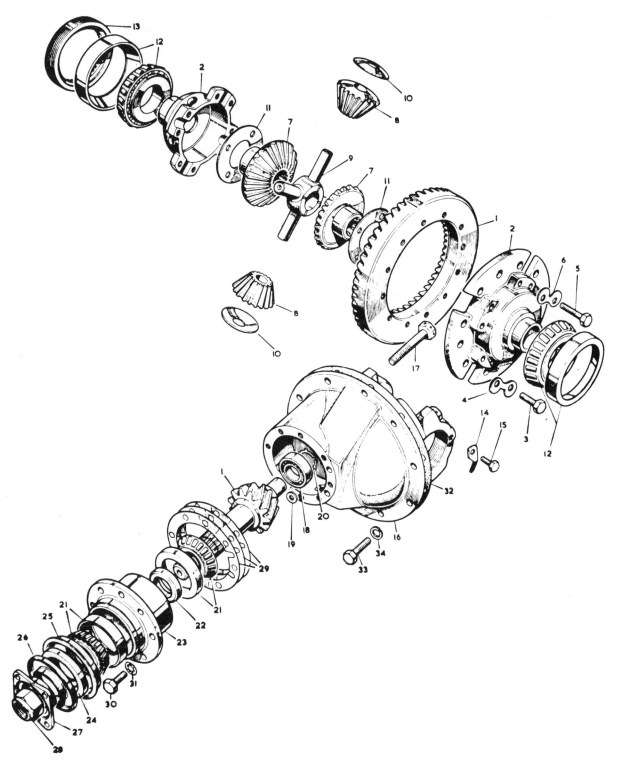

FIG 8:16   ENV differential

Key to Fig 8:16   1 Crownwheel and bevel pinion   2 Differential casing   3 Setbolt ($\frac{7}{16}$ inch UNF x 1 inch long)   4 Locking plate
5 Setbolt ($\frac{7}{16}$ inch UNF x 1$\frac{3}{4}$ inch long)   6 Locking plate   7 Differential wheel   8 Differential pinion   9 Spindle for pinions
10 Spherical washer, differential pinion   11 Washer, differential wheel   12 Taper roller bearing for differential   13 Adjuster,
differential bearings   14 Locking plate   15 Setbolt   16 Nose piece complete with bearing caps   17 Special bolt fixing bearing
cap   18 Bearing for bevel pinion, nose end   19 Retaining washer   20 Circlip   21 Bearing for bevel pinion   22 Spacer for
bearing adjustment   23 Bevel pinion housing   24 Oil seal for pinion   25 Mudshield for bevel pinion housing   26 Mudshield for
driving flange   27 Driving flange for bevel pinion   28 Special nut fixing driving flange   29 Shim, bevel pinion to crownwheel
engagement   30 Setbolt   31 Shakeproof washer   32 Joint washer, differential to axle casing   33 Setbolt   34 Spring washer

To overhaul a spring:

1 Remove the four leaf clips.
2 Drive out the bushes in the spring eyes.
3 Remove the centre bolt and nut to release the leaves.
4 Degrease the leaves and carefully examine for cracks. Only the main and second leaves are supplied as replacements. Failure of the others involves renewal of the whole spring.
5 Grease each leaf with graphite grease and reassemble by fitting the centre bolt and leaf clips. Fit new bushes.

8:9 *The hydraulic dampers*

These cannot be overhauled; in the event of failure, renewal is the only answer.

To check the function of a damper, remove it from the vehicle and mount it vertically in a vice by its lower eye. It should then be extended and compressed when a uniform resistance throughout the stroke should be felt. The resistance when extending the damper should be much greater than when it is being compressed.

When fitting a new damper, always renew any doubtful rubber mounting bushes.

Always tighten the mounting nuts with the spring in its mid-position. This can be estimated by raising or lowering the vehicle on the jack.

On some models the dampers are secured at the lower end by a splitpin and washer. To remove and replace the splitpin, make up a piece of tube with a slot cut at one end. Pressing on the washer with the slot in line with the splitpin or, when refitting, the hole, will facilitate this operation.

8:10 *Fault diagnosis*

(a) Vibrating propeller shaft

1 Arrows on shaft and sleeve not in line
2 Worn splines
3 Unbalanced shaft
4 Loose flange bolts

(b) Universal joints noisy

1 Lack of lubrication
2 Loose flange bolts
3 Worn bearings or splines

CHAPTER 9

FRONT SUSPENSION, DIFFERENTIAL AND HUBS

9:1 Description

This axle combines the functions of a steering and a driving unit. A differential, similar to that fitted to the rear axle, accepts the power input from the propeller shaft connected to the front of the transfer box and transmits it via two universally jointed shafts on 2¼ and 2.6 litre models or constant velocity jointed shafts on 3.5 litre models to the front wheels. Steering and braking functions are accomplished by swivelling stub axles mounted in massive housings. The suspension is by leaf springs controlled by telescopic hydraulic dampers. Reference to **FIG 9:1** will clearly show the axle construction.

9:2 The hubs

To remove a hub, refer to **FIGS 9:1** and **9:2**.

1 Drain the lubricating oil from the swivel pin housing, slacken the road wheel nuts, then jack up and safely support the front of the vehicle. Remove the road wheel.
2 Slacken the brake adjusters and remove the drum.
3 Prise off the hub cap, then undo the axle shaft nut or circlip and shim, as applicable. Remove the driving member from the shaft and hub.
4 Undo the hub locking nut and remove it with its tabwasher. Unscrew the inner adjusting nut and remove this and the inner tabwasher.

5 The hub and bearing assembly will now come away as a unit, leaving the axle shaft in the stub axle.
6 If it is necessary to remove the stub axle, first disconnect the hydraulic brake pipe at the connection to the flexible pipe, then undo the bolts holding the brake backplate, remove the backplate and stub axle.

With the hub away from the axle, examine the bearing races and renew where required. It is advisable to renew the oil seal at the same time. The oil seal on 3.5 litre models is recessed as described for the rear hub in **Chapter 8, Section 8:5**. This can be easily prised out and the new one pressed in. The hub bearings must be a press fit in the hub and a sliding fit on the axle.

Pay particular attention to the stub axle distance piece. This is a press fit on the stub axle and its outer surface provides the seat upon which the oil seal runs. If it is damaged, the seal will fail. The only way to remove it is to grip the stub axle carefully in a vice and shatter the distance piece with a heavy cold chisel. Take care not to damage the stub axle. The new distance piece is pressed on.

Note that the early stub axles are fitted with a bush at the inner end which must be reamed after fitting to 1.250 + .004 inch (31.75 + .10 mm). Later axles are of strengthened design and do not need this bush. Both types are interchangeable.

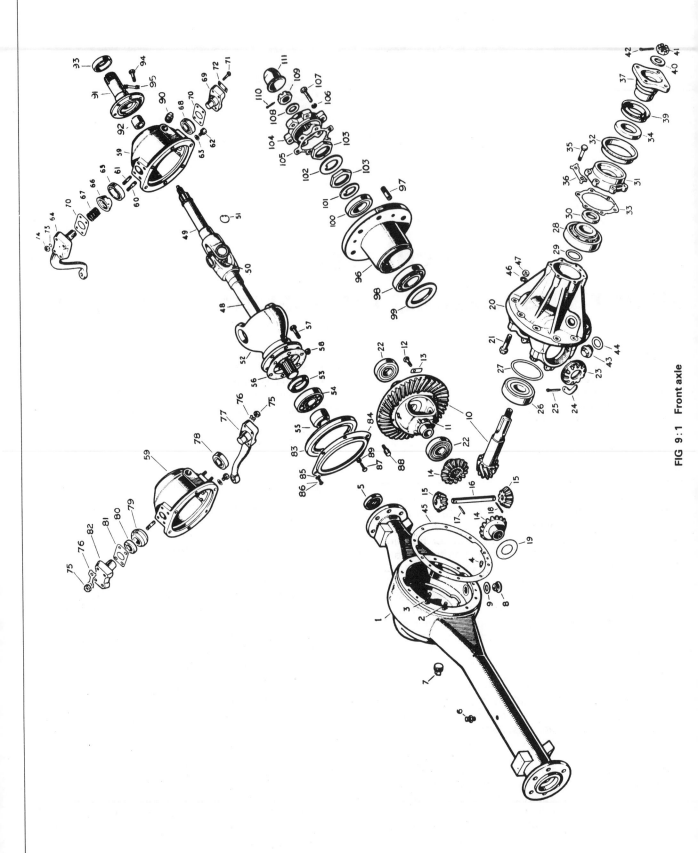

FIG 9:1 Front axle

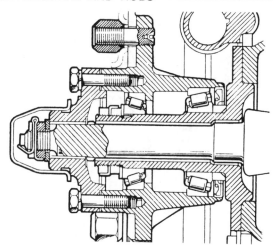

FIG 9:2 Cross-section of front hub

Key to Fig 9:1   1 Axle casing complete   2, 3 Fixings, bevel pinion housing to axle casing   4 Dowel, locating housing   5 Oil seal, in casing   6 Breather   7 Oil filler plug   8, 9 Drain plug and joint washer   10 Crownwheel and bevel pinion   11 Differential casing   12 Setbolt   13 Locker (double type)   14 Differential wheel   15 Differential pinion   16 Spindle for pinion   17 Plain pin   18 Splitpin   19 Thrust washer   20 Bevel pinion housing   21 Special bolt, fixing bearing cap   22 Taper roller bearing for differential   23, 24 Bearing adjustment   25 Splitpin, fixing lock tab   26 Bearing for bevel pinion, pinion end   27 Shim, bearing adjustment, pinion end   28 Bearing for bevel pinion, flange end   29 Shim, bearing adjustment, flange end   30 Washer for pinion bearing   31 Retainer for oil seal   32 Mudshield for pinion   33 Joint washer for oil seal retainer   34 Oil seal for pinion   35, 36 Fixings for oil seal retainer   37 Driving flange   39 Mudshield for driving flange   40-42 Fixings for flange   43, 44 Oil filler plug and joint washer   45 Joint washer, differential to axle casing   46, 47 Fixings, differential to axle casing   48 Halfshaft   49 Stub shaft bearing   50 Journal assembly   51 Circlip for journal   52 Housing for swivel pin bearing   53 Distance piece for bearing   54 Bearing for halfshaft   55 Retaining collar for bearing   56 Joint washer for housing   57, 58 Fixings, housing to front axle casing*   59 Housing assembly for swivel pin*   60 Special stud for steering lever   61 Stud for steering lever*   62, 63 Drain plug and joint washer*   64 Swivel pin and steering lever*   65 Cone seat for swivel pin, top*   66 Cone bearing for swivel pin, top*   67 Spring for cone bearing*   68 Bearing for swivel pin, bottom*   69 Swivel pin and bracket*   70 Shim, for swivel pin bearing*   71-74 Fixings, swivel pin to swivel pin housings*   75, 76 Fixings, swivel pins to swivel pin housing**   77 Swivel pin and steering lever**   78 Bearing for bottom swivel pin**   79 Bush for top swivel pin**   80 Thrust washer for bush**   81 Shim for top swivel pin**   82 Swivel pin and bracket**   83 Oil seal for swivel pin bearing housing   84 Retainer for oil seal   85-89 Fixings, retainer and lock stop plate to swivel pin housing   90 Oil filler plug for swivel pin housing   91 Stub axle assembly   92 Bush for driving shaft, early models only   93 Distance piece for inner bearing.   94, 95 Fixings, stub axle to swivel pin housing   96 Front hub assembly   97 Stud for road wheel   98 Bearing for front hub, inner   99 Oil seal for inner bearing   100 Bearing for front hub   101 Keywasher   102 Locker   103 Special nut   104 Driving member for front hub   105 Joint washer for driving member   106, 107 Fixings, driving member to front hub   108 Plain washer   109 Slotted nut   110 Splitpin   111 Hub cap, front

*Early type   **Latest type

To replace a hub:

1 Smear a new joint washer with grease and place it on the rear face of the stub axle.
2 Fit the stub axle, keyway uppermost, then the brake backplate to the swivel pin housing.
3 Fit new lockplates to the bolts and tighten the bolts. Connect the brake hydraulic pipe.
4 Grease the inner roller bearings but do not pack the hub centre with grease.
5 Slide the hub onto the stub axle and fit the inner tab-washer and the adjusting nut. Adjust the hub end float to between .004 to .006 inch (.10 to .15 mm). Fit the outer tabwasher and locknut. Check the float after tightening the locknut. The end float on Series 3 models should be .002 to .004 inch (.05 to .10 mm).
6 Using a new joint washer and felt oil seal, fit the driving member, ensuring that the oil seal is fitted with the **rubber side facing outwards**. Tighten the driving member bolts on $2\frac{1}{4}$ or 2.6 litre models to 28 lb ft (3.9 mkg) and the axle shaft nut to 10 to 15 lb ft (1.4 to 2.0 mkg). Fit a new splitpin. On 3.5 litre models, tighten the bolts to 30 to 38 lb ft (4.2 to 5.2 mkg), fit the circlip without the shim, draw the axle shaft as far as possible through the hub driving member and measure the clearance between the circlip and the driving member. This should be between .003 and .008 inch (.07 and .20 mm). Shims are available in stages of .006 inch (.15 mm) from .044 to .122 inch (1.12 to 3.10 mm) if adjustment is necessary. Fit the selected shim and circlip.
7 Bleed and adjust the brakes, then refill the hub with oil.
8 Refit the road wheel, then lower the vehicle to the ground. Check the tightness of the road wheel securing nuts.

9:3 The axle shafts

Removing an axle shaft:

1 Drain the oil from the axle and swivel pin housing, jack up and safely support the front of the vehicle, then remove the road wheel.
2 Remove the front hub (see **Section 9:2**), brake anchor plate and stub axle.
3 Gently pull the axle shaft out of the axle case.

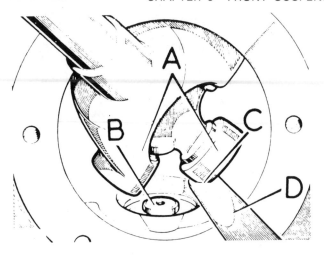

FIG 9:3   Checking axle shaft clearance

Key to Fig 9:3   A Yokes   **B** Swivel pin   **C** Yoke radius
D Feeler gauge .050 inch (1.2 mm) minimum

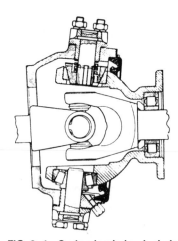

FIG 9:4   Spring-loaded swivel pin

Servicing the axle shaft:

The universal joints are identical to those used on the propeller shafts. Full details of the overhaul of these are given in **Chapter 8**. The halfshafts with CV joints on 3.5 litre models are only serviced as a unit.

Replacing an axle shaft:

1 Be careful not to damage the oil seal in the axle case or swivel housing, as applicable, when inserting the axle shaft.

2 Rotate the axle shaft on 2¼ and 2.6 litre models and check that there is a minimum clearance of .050 inch (1.2 mm) between the universal joint yoke ears and the swivel pin end faces (see **FIG 9:3**). If the clearance is insufficient, grind the chamfer on the yoke ears.

3 Complete the reassembly by reversing the dismantling process.

9:4 *The swivel pin housings*

Design modifications over the years have resulted in two main variations of swivel pin assemblies. The earlier type has a coil spring damper and the later type a 'Railko' bush. Both are shown in **FIG 9:1**. Cross sections of both are also shown in **FIGS 9:4** and **9:5**. In this section servicing instructions are given for both types.

Removing the housing, both types:

To remove a swivel pin housing, first remove the hub and stub axle as described in **Section 9:2**, but, in addition, drain the oil from the axle case. It is sometimes possible to release the brake backplate without disconnecting the hydraulic pipe, thereby avoiding having to bleed the brakes. If so, suspend the backplate without straining the flexible pipe.

Now proceed as follows:

1 Very carefully pull the axle shaft out of the casing to avoid damaging the oil seal.

2 Disconnect the steering ball joints using the special extractor, Rover Part No. 600590 or 601763.

3 Undo the bolts between the housing and the axle case and withdraw the housing complete.

Replacing the housing, both types:

1 Examine and, if necessary, renew the oil seal in the end of the axle case.

2 Smear a new joint washer with grease and fit to the axle case.

3 Fit the swivel pin housing to the axle case and tighten the bolts.

4 Connect the steering ball joints, tightening the nuts to 30 lb ft (4.0 mkg).

5 Continue reassembly by reversing the dismantling procedure. Refill the axle and hub with oil.

6 Check the setting of the lock stops.

Servicing the housing; spring-loaded type:

Refer to **FIG 9:1**.

1 Remove the oil seal retainer 84 and prise the oil seal 83 from the housing 59.

2 Undo the nuts 74 and remove the swivel pin and steering lever 64. Keep the shims 70 together. Remove the cone bearing 66 and spring 67.

3 Now remove the bottom swivel pin bracket 69, again keeping the shims 70 together. The swivel pin bearing housing 52 will now come away from the housing 59.

4 Examine the bearings carefully. Replace either if wear is evinced by roughness or flaking tracks. The roller bearing must be a light press fit in the housing and a light push fit on the pin. The cone seat of the upper bearing must be a light press fit in the housing.

5 If the swivel pins themselves are worn, drill out the grooved pin by means of a ⅛ inch (3.17 mm) drill, then drive the swivel pin out of its bracket. Support the bracket on a solid object and use a brass drift for this operation.

6 A new swivel pin can be pressed into the bottom bracket in any relative position and a new grooved

pin pressed in to retain it. Drill the hole for the grooved pin $\frac{5}{32}$ inch (4 mm) and fit a $\frac{5}{32}$ inch pin in place of the $\frac{1}{2}$ inch pin removed when dismantling.

7 The new swivel pin for the top steering lever assembly must be positioned as shown in **FIG 9:6** to ensure that the cone is seated correctly.

8 To reassemble the unit, press any new race outer members into their seatings and the bottom swivel pin race inner member onto the swivel pin.

9 Smear the cone bearing with oil and locate it in its outer member, being careful to position the vertical oil hole towards the rear of the vehicle (see **FIG 9:7**).

10 Hold the bottom roller cage in its outer race and then put the swivel pin bearing housing inside the swivel pin housing. Smear the faces of the bottom swivel pin bracket and the swivel pin housing with sealing compound. Now fit the bracket, using .040 inch (1.0 mm) thickness of shims removed when dismantling. Push the bracket upwards so that the pin enters the bottom roller race cage. Tighten the bracket nuts securely.

11 Insert the cone spring in the top bearing, then fit the swivel pin and steering bracket. Use sealing compound and shims to the thickness of .040 inch (1.0 mm) exactly as described for the bottom bearings. Tighten the nuts.

12 Grip the swivel pin bearing housing in a vice fitted with soft jaws or temporarily mount it on the axle. Attach a spring balance to the track rod eye of the steering lever and check the resistance to turning of the swivel pin housing. This must lie between 14 to 16 lb (6.3 to 7.3 kg) after overcoming the inertia. Add or subtract shims at the top bearing only until the correct resistance figure is obtained. Check on the tightness of all nuts, then lock them with the lockplates.

13 Pack the housing oil seal with heavy grease and fit the seal and its retainer to the housing, making sure that it wipes the whole surface of the bearing housing. Slacken the retainer and reposition the seal if necessary. Note that the steering lock stop adjustment bolt goes in the forwardmost hole. The unit can now be replaced on the vehicle.

Servicing the housing, Railko bush type:

Refer to **FIG 9:1**.

1 Separate the inner and outer members of the housing in a manner similar to that used for the spring-loaded type of housing, i.e. remove the oil seal and the swivel pin brackets, then pull the housing apart. An additional oil seal is fitted to the inner housing in a separate retainer on 3.5 litre models. Prise out the retainer and oil seal assembly.

2 Clean and examine all the components, replacing any worn or damaged items. Note that the Railko bush and thrust washer, if fitted, must not be cleaned in any type of cleaning fluid as this can spoil their damping characteristics. The bush must be a light push fit on the swivel pin. If not, renew the worn component. Only the early models have a thust washer.

3 To assemble the unit, first press into the housing any new races. Lubricate the inner diameter of the Railko bush with the grade of oil recommended for

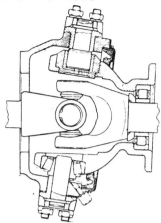

FIG 9:5 Railko bush swivel pin

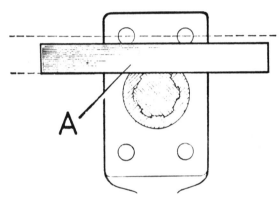

FIG 9:6 Setting the top swivel pin

Key to Fig 9:6 **A** Straightedge

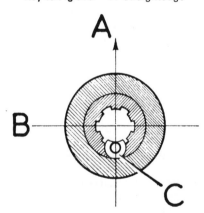

FIG 9:7 Setting the cone bearing

Key to Fig 9:7 **A** Front of vehicle **B** Centre line of axle **C** Vertical oil hole

the swivel pin housing and press it into its seating. If fitted, place the thrust washer in the bush. On 3.5 litre models, fit the inner housing oil seal into the retainer and press the assembly into the housing.

4 Assemble the housing as described for the spring-loaded type, but, in addition, fit a new O-ring to the bottom swivel pin as shown in **FIG 9:8**.

5 Connect the spring balance to the track rod eye and adjust the resistance to movement to 12 to 14 lb

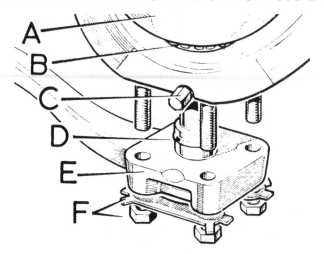

FIG 9:8 Swivel pin assembly, late type

Key to Fig 9:8   A Swivel pin bearing housing   **B** Roller bearing   **C** Drain plug   **D** O-ring   **E** Steering lever **F** Fixing nuts

(5.4 to 6.3 kg), or 8 to 10 lb (3.6 to 4.5 kg) on 3.5 litre models, by adding or removing shims from the top swivel pin bracket.
6 Check all the nuts for tightness, then lock with the lockplates.
7 Refit the oil seal and retainer to the outer housing as described for the spring-loaded swivel pin housing. The unit is ready for replacing on the vehicle.

9:5 *The differential*

It is not an economic proposition for the private owner to attempt to dismantle and re-build this unit due to the special equipment and knowledge needed to make a satisfactory job of it. Instructions are given for removing and replacing the differential so that it may be taken to a Rover Service Station and an exchange unit obtained.

To remove the differential:

1 Drain the oil from the axle, loosen the road wheel nuts, then jack up and safely support the front of the vehicle. Remove the road wheels.
2 Disconnect the flexible hydraulic brake pipes at each side of the vehicle. It is wise to wedge the brake pedal down to prevent fluid loss while these pipes are disconnected.
3 Disconnect the track rod and drag link by using the special ball joint extractor, Rover Part No. 600590 or 601763.
4 Undo the bolts holding each swivel pin housing to the axle case, then remove each housing complete with brake drum, hub and axle shaft.
5 Disconnect the propeller shaft, undo the nuts round the differential housing and lift it away from the axle case.

Replacing the differential:

This is, generally, a reversal of the removal operation, but always use a new joint washer smeared with grease on both sides between the differential and the axle. Use

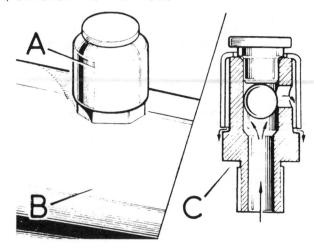

FIG 9:9 Axle breather unit

Key to Fig 9:9   A Breather   **B** Axle   **C** Air-flow path

new washers, similarly smeared with grease, between the swivel pin housings and the axle ends. Be careful to ease the axle shafts gently into the axle case, engaging their splines with the differential as the housing is brought into position.
The steering ball joints are tightened to a torque of 30 lb ft (4.0 mkg).
Refill the axle with oil and bleed the brakes.

9:6 *The axle breather unit*

It is important to regularly check that the axle breathers are operating correctly and also whenever a hub or axle oil seal has been replaced.
Every 12,000 miles (20,000 km) or 12 months, whichever comes sooner, clean the axle case breathers. There is one in each axle case (see **FIG 9:9**).
1 Clean off the axle breathers and the surrounding surfaces of the axle cases, taking care to remove all dirt and grit.
2 Unscrew the axle breathers and soak them in petrol or a suitable cleaning solvent for several minutes, then clean with a soft brush.
3 Shake each breather to ensure the ball valve is free. If it sticks, the breather valve must be renewed.
4 Lubricate the balls lightly with engine oil before replacing the breathers.

9:7 *The suspension*

The front suspension is identical with the rear suspension and the instructions regarding the springs and hydraulic dampers given in **Chapter 8** apply here.
Note that if new or reconditioned springs are fitted, the shackle bolts must not be finally tightened until the vehicle is standing on its own wheels and loaded to obtain a dimension between the top of the U-bolts and the chassis frame on 88 inch models of 4.3 to 4.5 inch (110 to 114 mm) or on 109 inch models of 4.7 to 4.8 inch (118 to 122 mm).

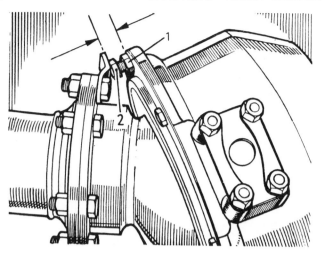

FIG 9:10   Adjusting the lock stops

Key to Fig 9:10   1 Locknut   2 Bolt

9:8 *Suspension geometry*

No adjustment is provided for castor, camber or swivel pin inclination. If the angles are different from those given here, damage has been sustained and immediate steps must be taken to correct the faults.

Castor	3 deg.
Camber	$1\frac{1}{2}$ deg.
Swivel pin inclination	7 deg.

The toe-in on $2\frac{1}{4}$ or 2.6 litre models should lie between $\frac{3}{64}$ to $\frac{3}{32}$ inch (1.2 to 2.4 mm). The toe-out on 3.5 litre models should lie between $\frac{3}{64}$ to $\frac{3}{32}$ inch (1.2 to 2.4 mm). Adjust this by loosening the track rod clamps and turning the track rod. It must be emphasized that this operation is best left to a Rover Service Station equipped with the proper optical gauges as an incorrect setting can dangerously affect the handling of the vehicle as well as causing rapid front tyre wear.

9:9 *Modifications*

It is possible on $2\frac{1}{4}$ or 2.6 litre models to fit the Railko bush type bearing to swivel pin housings having the earlier spring-loaded type. A conversion kit, Rover Part No. 532268, complete with full fitting instructions is available.

The parts supplied can be easily fitted to any Land-Rover from 1954 onwards by removing the existing swivel pin, coil spring, cone and cone seat and fitting, in their place, the new swivel pin and swivel pin bearing housing and bush.

From axles numbered :
  141107339 88 righthand drive
  144104520 88 lefthand drive
  151108875 109 righthand drive
  154103275 109 lefthand drive onwards
the steering levers are fitted to the bottom of the swivel housings with the ball joints above the levers.

Swivel pin and steering levers are not interchangeable as individual items : they can, however, be fitted in pairs provided either the swivel pin housing complete is changed for the latest type, or studs are fitted in the bottom position of the existing swivel pin housing. Studs required are six off 508152, two off 508153. **It is most important that the latest type steering levers are not fitted to an early type housing in the lower position with the existing bolts; the studs detailed above including the special fitting studs 508153 must be fitted. This prevents any tendency for movement between lever and housing which could give rise to premature breakage of the bolts with the possibility of serious damage.**

9:10 *Steering lock stops*

Check the setting of the lock stops and adjust, if necessary, to give .5 inch (12.5 mm) between the bolt head top face and the oil seal retainer face as shown in **FIG 9:10**.

9:11 *Fault diagnosis*

(a) Vehicle pulls to one side

1 Incorrect camber
2 Incorrect castor
3 Uneven tyre pressures
4 Dragging brake
5 Tight swivel pin
6 Incorrect toe-in (toe-out)

(b) Vehicle wanders

1 Incorrect tyre pressures
2 Loose U-bolts
3 Incorrect toe-in (toe-out)
4 Worn front wheel bearings
5 Worn swivel pins
6 Incorrect castor

(c) Wheel wobble

1 Incorrect tyre pressures
2 Eccentric wheels or tyres
3 Loose hub bearings
4 Worn swivel pins
5 Insufficient damping at swivel pins

NOTES

CHAPTER 10

THE STEERING GEAR

10:1 *Description*

The steering gear fitted to Mk 2, 2A and 3 Land-Rovers is of the recirculating ball type. From the steering gearbox, a longitudinal rod carries the movement from the drop arm to a steering relay mounted on the front of the chassis. This relay has two spring-loaded tapered tufnol bushes which damp out road shocks. From the relay, a drag link carries the steering effort to either one or the other swivel housings depending on whether the vehicle is righthand or lefthand drive. Some models, additionally, have a telescopic damper mounted between a chassis bracket and the drag link. A track rod, adjustable for length, connects the two swivel housings. **FIGS 10:1** and **10:2** show the layout of these components in detail. Apart from maintaining the oil level in the steering gearbox, no other maintenance is needed. The ball joints are fitted with rubber 'boots' which retain the lubricant for the life of the vehicle.

10:2 *Removing the steering column*

Refer to **FIG 10:1**.

1 Unscrew the clamp bolt 44 or nut 48 after removing the centre cover 49, 57 or 58 and remove the steering wheel.

2 Unscrew bolt 52 and release the horn pushbutton or flasher switch bracket from the steering column (early models only). Remove the column support clamp and the steering column switch assembly from the steering column.

3 Remove the engine air cleaner (righthand drive models only).

4 Remove the nameplate and withdraw the radiator grille.

5 Refer to **FIG 10:2**. Loosen the bolt 16 and prise the upper relay lever 15 clear of the relay.

6 Turn the steering shaft to bring the longitudinal rod 54 as far forward as possible. Undo clamp 64 and unscrew the longitudinal rod.

7 Remove the bolts holding the steering box to the support bracket and the steering column to the dash. Jack up and safely support the front of the vehicle, then remove the road wheel.

8 The steering cover box can now be removed from under the front wing, followed by the steering column itself.

9 At this stage, the nut 32 (see **FIG 10:1**) and washer 33 can be removed and the drop arm 34 pulled from the shaft 17 by the use of a heavy extractor tool. Mark the shaft and drop arm so that they can be replaced in the same relative position if necessary.

10 Remove the ball joint 55 (see **FIG 10:2**) from the drop arm 34 (see **FIG 10:1**), again using an extractor or tapping the side of the drop arm adjacent to the ball joint.

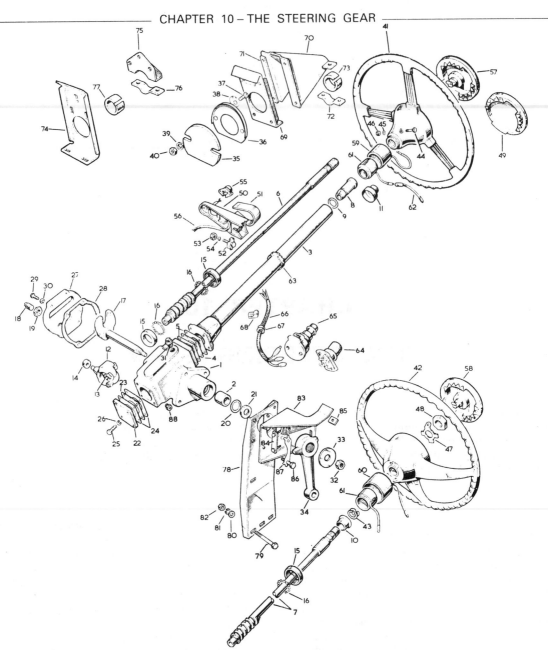

FIG 10:1 Layout of steering column

Key to Fig 10:1   1 Steering box assembly   2 Bush for rocker shaft   3 Outer column   4 Joint washer, steel   5 Joint washer, paper   6 Inner column, early type   7 Inner column, latest type   8 Bush for inner column   9 Spring ring for inner column bush   10 Ballbearing for inner column   11 Dust shield for inner column   12 Main nut assembly   13 Steel ball ($\frac{1}{8}$ inch) for main nut   14 Roller for main nut   15 Adjustable ballrace   16 Steel balls (.280 inch) for adjustable race   17 Rocker shaft   18 Adjuster screw for rocker shaft   19 Locknut for adjuster screw   20 Oil seal for rocker shaft   21 Washer for rocker shaft oil seal   22 End plate   23 Joint washer, steel   24 Joint washer, paper   25 Bolt ($\frac{5}{16}$ inch UNC x $\frac{29}{32}$ inch long)   26 Spring washer   27 Side coverplate   28 Joint washer for side coverplate   29 Bolt ($\frac{5}{16}$ inch UNC x $1\frac{1}{16}$ inch long)   30 Spring washer   31 Oil filler plug   32 Special nut   33 Lockwasher   34 Steering drop arm   35 Rubber seal for steering column   36 Cover for steering column seal   37 Screw (2 BA x $\frac{3}{4}$ inch long)   38 Special washer   39 Spring washer   40 Nut (2 BA)   41 Steering wheel, early type   42 Steering wheel, latest type   43 Special spring washer on inner column for wheel   44 Bolt ($\frac{5}{16}$ inch UNF x 2 inch long)   45 Plain washer   46 Nut ($\frac{5}{16}$ inch UNF)   47 Tag washer   48 Special nut   49 Steering wheel centre cover, early type   50 Horn push bracket   51 Clip for horn push bracket   52 Yoke assembly for horn push bracket   53 Nut ($\frac{1}{4}$ inch BSF)   54 Shakeproof washer   55 Horn push   56 Lead, horn push to junction box   57 Horn push and centre cover for steering wheel, early type   58 Horn push and centre cover for steering wheel, latest type   59 Dust cover and horn contact, early type   60 Dust cover and horn contact, latest type   61 Slip ring complete for horn contact   62 Lead, slip ring to junction box   63 Cable cleat on steering column   64 Dipswitch, early type   65 Dipswitch, latest type   66 Lead, dipswitch to junction box   67 Grommet for lead in toe box floor   68 Clip fixing dipswitch lead to floor   69 Support bracket for steering column   70 Support bracket for steering column   71 Packing piece for steering column support bracket   72 Clip for steering column   73 Rubber strip for clip   74 Support bracket on dash   75 Clamp, upper, for steering column   76 Clamp, lower, for steering column   77 Rubber strip for clamp   78 Support bracket, steering box to chassis   79 Bolt ($\frac{5}{16}$ inch UNF x $3\frac{1}{4}$ inch long)   80 Plain washer, thin   81 Spring washer   82 Nut ($\frac{5}{16}$ inch UNF)   83 Stiffener bracket for steering box   84 Bolt plate   85 Shim washer   86 Setbolt ($\frac{3}{8}$ inch UNC x $\frac{7}{8}$ inch long)   87 Locking plate   88 Self-locking nut ($\frac{5}{16}$ inch UNF)

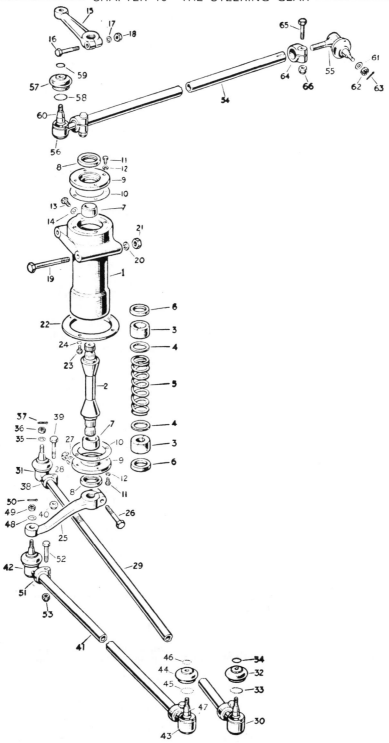

FIG 10:2 Layout of relay unit

Key to Fig 10:2   1 Housing for relay shaft   2 Shaft for steering relay levers   3 Split bush for housing   4 Washer for spring
5 Spring for bushes   6 Thrust washer for shaft   7 Distance piece for shaft   8 Oil seal for shaft   9 Retainer for oil seal
10 Joint washer for retainer   11, 12 Fixings for retainer   13 Plug for oil hole   14 Joint washer for plug   15 Relay lever, upper
16-18 Fixings for lever   19-21 Fixings for housing   22 Flange plate for relay mounting   23, 24 Fixings for flange plate
25 Relay lever, lower   26-28 Fixings for lever   29 Steering track rod assembly   30 Ball joint assembly, righthand thread
31 Ball joint assembly, lefthand thread   32 Rubber cover for ball joint   33 Spring ring, cover to body   34 Spring ring and
retainer, cover to ball   35-37 Fixings for ball joints   38 Clip for ball joint   39, 40 Fixings for ball joint clips   41 Steering drag
link assembly   42 Ball joint assembly, righthand thread   43 Ball joint assembly, lefthand thread   44 Rubber cover for ball joint
45 Spring ring, cover to body   46 Spring ring   47 Retainer   48-50 Fixings for ball joints   51 Clip for ball joint
52, 53 Fixings for ball joint clips   54 Longitudinal steering tube assembly   55 Ball joint assembly, righthand thread
56 Ball joint assembly, lefthand thread   57 Rubber cover for ball joint   58 Spring ring, cover to body   59 Spring ring
60 Retainer   61-63 Fixings for ball joints to levers   64 Clip for ball joint   65, 66 Fixings for ball joint clips

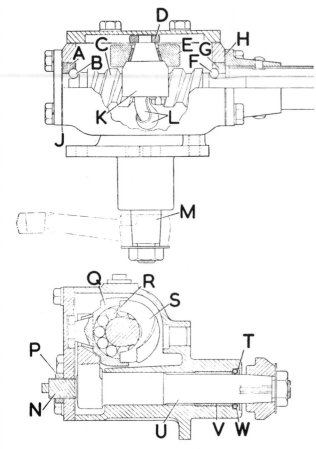

FIG 10:3 Recirculating ball steering box

Key to Fig 10:3   A Lower ballrace   B Balls for lower race   C Inner column worm shaft   D Roller   E Rocker   F Balls for upper race   G Upper ballrace   H Joint washer   J Shims   K Main nut   L Ball transfer tube and retainer   M Rocker shaft and drop arm   N Adjusting screw, rocker shaft   P Locknut   Q Main nut   R Main nut balls   S Transfer tube   T Seal retainer   U Rocker shaft   V Rocker shaft bush   W Rocker shaft seal

10:3 Overhauling the steering gearbox

1 Refer to **FIG 10:3**. Remove the side cover and drain off the oil.
2 Lift off the roller **D** and withdraw the rocker shaft **U**.
3 With the outer column held in a vice, unscrew the bolts holding the steering box and tap the inner column at the steering wheel end with a soft mallet to partially remove the box.
4 Withdraw the box and inner column complete. On early models, the dust cover at the top of the column will be freed by this. Take care not to lose it or any balls from the steering box.
5 Position the main nut **K** midway on the worm **C** and tap the box away from the inner column sufficiently to release the ballrace **G**.
6 Turn the inner column to release the main nut, then remove the inner column and main nut from the box.
7 Remove the end cover with shims **J** and ballrace **A**. The ball transfer tube **L** can be removed from the main nut.

8 If worn, remove the retaining washer **T** and oil seal **W**, then press the rocker shaft bush **V** out of the box.
9 If the tufnol bush at the top of the outer column is worn, tap it out using a long wooden rod (early models; later types have a ballrace).
10 Clean and examine all components for wear. Indentation of the inner column worm at the centre of its length, i.e. steering straightahead, involves renewal. Indentations at the ends of the worm can be ignored. Check that the ballraces and balls are free from any pitting, cracks, flaking or other damage. Renew as necessary.
11 Assemble the steering gear by first pressing a new tufnol bush complete with oil seal into the top of the outer column (early models).
12 Press a new rocker shaft bush into the box; check that the rocker shaft will push through and rotate without binding. Reaming should not be required.
13 Locate the rocker shaft oil seal and retaining washer.
14 Replace the paper washer **H** on the end of the outer column. Grease both sides of the paper washer.
15 Mount the outer column vertically in a vice with the steering box end uppermost.
16 Place ballrace **G** over the inner column, then slide the inner column into the outer column. Make sure it rotates freely in the tufnol bush, if fitted. Lift the inner column a little, grease the race **G** and fit ten balls **F**.
17 Replace the balls in the main nut **K** and retain with grease. Put the main nut in the steering box, then place the box on the end of the inner column, carefully rotating the inner column to screw the worm **C** into the nut. Make sure the box is the right way round, filler plug towards the outer column, and that no balls have been displaced. Apply non-hardening jointing compound to the tapped holes, then bolt the steering box to the outer column.
18 Grease race **A** and load with ten balls **B**. Push the race into the steering box, then fit the shims **J** with a paper washer each side. Apply non-hardening jointing compound to the tapped holes, then bolt the end cover to the steering box. Do this carefully, checking to see that the inner column can be turned by hand, but has no end float. Add or remove shims to achieve this condition.
19 Re-grip the assembly in the vice in a horizontal position. Oil all bearing surfaces, then slide in the rocker shaft **U** and replace roller **D**. Replace the cover complete with a new joint washer, making sure that the roller **D** is correctly located in the slot. Tighten the cover bolts. **FIG 10:4** shows the rocker shaft fitted.
20 With the main nut at mid-position on the worm, tighten the adjusting screw on the cover by hand until resistance is felt as it contacts the rocker shaft. Lock the locknut, ensuring that the adjuster does not move.
21 Refit the dust cover to the top of the inner column (early models).

10:4 Replacing the steering column

Reverse the dismantling operations, but do not fit the drop arm until the column is securely bolted to the vehicle. Turn the inner column lock to lock and find the exact intermediate position. Refit the steering wheel, tightening the centre nut on later models to 40 lb ft (5.4 mkg). Connect the ball joints of the longitudinal side rod to the drop arm and relay lever, tightening the nuts to 30 lb ft (4 mkg). Slide the rod along the side of the vehicle and connect the relay lever to the relay unit, tightening the pinch bolt to 55 lb ft (7.6 mkg). Adjust the length of the side rod until the drop arm will fit on the tapered splines of the rocker shaft exactly. Have the road wheels straightahead while doing this. Fit the drop arm and washer, then the nut. Tighten the nut to 60 to 80 lb ft (8.5 to 11 mkg) and engage the lockwasher. Tighten the clamps on the side rod.

Check that the steering will turn freely from lock to lock, then refill the steering box with oil and securely replace the filler plug.

10 : 5 The relay unit and damper

To remove the unit (refer to **FIG 10 : 2**) :

1 Remove the nameplate and withdraw the radiator grille.
2 Remove the pinch bolts from the upper and lower relay levers, then prise the levers clear of the unit.
3 Remove the fixings between the relay housing and the chassis top face.
4 Remove the relay mounting flange plate from the underside of the chassis (see **FIG 10 : 5**).
5 Undo the bolts and remove the unit upwards, tapping gently with a soft mallet if necessary.

To service the unit :

1 Drain off as much oil as possible by removing the oil filler and bleed plugs.
2 Undo bolts 11 and remove the oil seal retainer 9 and oil seal 8.
3 Secure a strong sack over the bottom half of the relay and then mount the unit in the vice with the bottom pointing downwards into the sack. Carefully tap out shaft 2 complete with spring 5, rings 4 and tufnol bushes 3 into the sack. The spring will be released with great force into the sack since it is compressed to over 100 lb (45 kg) when in position.
4 Remove the top oil seal retainer 9 and oil seal 8.
5 Examine all components for wear and renew as necessary. Pay particular attention to the outer surfaces of the two distance pieces 7 on which the oil seals 8 seat. Any roughness must involve renewal. The oil seal should be renewed as a matter of course. On later models, the distance pieces 7 are integral with the shaft ; therefore, if these are damaged, the whole shaft must be renewed.
6 Check that the free length of the spring 5 is $7\frac{1}{4}$ inches (184 mm). Renew if appreciably shorter.
7 Fit the oil seals to their retainers, making sure that the lipped side is facing inwards. Use jointing cement on the outside diameter.
8 Locate the split bush 3 on the top cone of the shaft 2. Insert into the housing from the bottom, then grip in a vice as shown in **FIG 10 : 6**.
9 Insert the washer 4, then fit two oil seal retaining bolts 11 diametrically opposite each other. Insert the spring followed by the other washer 4.

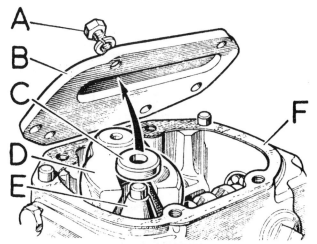

FIG 10 : 4   View of rocker shaft fitted

Key to Fig 10 : 4   **A** Fixings for side cover   **B** Side cover   **C** Roller for main nut   **D** Rocker shaft   **E** Main nut   **F** Joint washer

FIG 10 : 5   Relay mounting flange plate

Key to Fig 10 : 5   **A** Chassis   **B** Flange plate   **C** Bolts

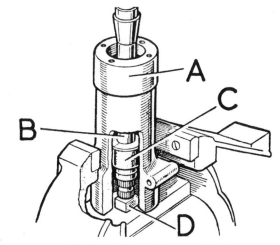

FIG 10 : 6   Relay shaft assembled

Key to Fig 10 : 6   **A** Housing   **B** Shaft   **C** Split bush halves   **D** $\frac{3}{4}$ inch (19 mm) block

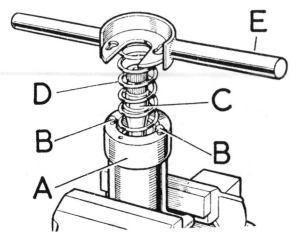

FIG 10:7   Method of compressing spring

Key to Fig 10:7   **A** Housing   **B** Bolts for oil seal retainer
C Shaft   **D** Spring   **E** Special tool

10 Refer to **FIG 10:7** and, by the use of special tool, Rover Part No. 600536, compress the spring and lock the tool under the bolt heads 11 (see **FIG 10:2**).

11 Locate the other split bush 3 on the exposed cone of the shaft and secure with a 2 inch (50 mm) hose clip (see **FIG 10:8**).

12 Carefully remove the special tool and the two bolts 11 (see **FIG 10:2**).

13 Remove the assembly from the vice and tap the shaft into position until the split bush 3 is halfway into the housing. Slacken the hose clip and tap the shaft fully home.

14 Fit new joint washers 10, smearing each side with grease.

15 Fit the thrust washer 6 and oil seal retainer 9 to the bottom of the housing.

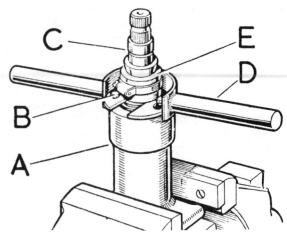

FIG 10:8   Spring fully compressed

Key to Fig 10:8   **A** Housing   **B** Bolts for oil seal retainer
C Shaft   **D** Special tool   **E** Split bush secured with hose clip

16 Using one of the top oil seal retainer bolt holes, completely fill the housing with oil, then fit the top thrust washer and oil seal retainer. Note that all threads in the housing should have non-hardening jointing compound applied.

17 Hold the unit in the vice, temporarily attach the upper relay lever and, by using a spring balance, check that the resistance to movement lies between 12 and 16 lb (5.4 and 7.3 kg). If the resistance is less than 12 lb (5.4 kg), fit a new spring. If the resistance is greater than 16 lb (7.3 kg), remove the oil seal retainers and thrust washers, then, using a suitable piece of tubing, push each split bush in turn until it is clear of its cone and inject some oil. Reassemble and recheck.

To refit the unit:

Reverse the removal procedure, but ensure that the filler plug boss faces the driver's side of the vehicle.

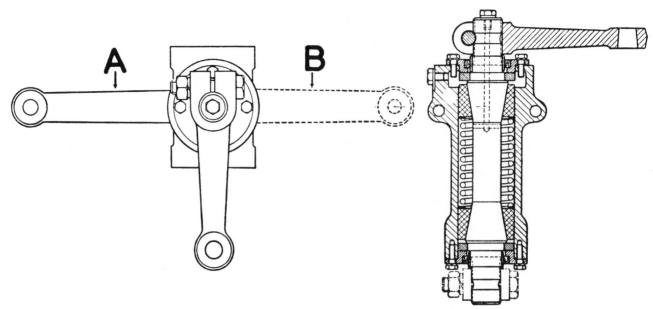

FIG 10:9   Relay unit showing righthand or lefthand drive

Key to Fig 10:9   **A** Lower relay lever, lefthand steering   **B** Lower relay lever, righthand steering

Refer to **FIG 10 : 9**. The lower relay lever must be fitted at either **A** or **B** positions depending on whether the vehicle is righthand or lefthand drive.

Telescopic damper:

The telescopic steering damper fitted to some models is illustrated in **FIG 10 : 10**. To remove the damper, release the locknut and nut from the chassis bracket. Remove the outer rubber mounting complete with inner and outer seating washers. Repeat this operation at the drag link end. Withdraw the damper and the inner rubber mountings. To refit, reverse the procedure, ensuring that the outer sleeve end of the damper is nearest the chassis bracket.

10 : 6 *The ball joints*

These should be examined periodically to see that the rubber covers are undamaged. The ball joints themselves are not adjustable and wear must involve renewal. The rubber covers and their spring rings are separately obtainable and can be fitted once the ball joints are removed from the vehicle. To remove a ball joint, pull out the splitpin and undo the nut. Either use a proper extractor or else release the tapers by holding a heavy hammer against one side of the lever and tapping the other side sharply with a light hammer. Release the tube clamp and unscrew the ball joint from the tube. Screw the nut on to the first few threads of the taper pin, then compress the ball joint in a vice by gripping it between the nut and the bottom of the joint. Clean round the inside of the joint as much as possible and squirt heavy oil or thin grease into it. Release the vice. Pack a new rubber cover with grease and fit to the joint with new spring rings. Wipe the taper clean and dry before fitting to the vehicle. Refit by reversing the dismantling procedure.

10 : 7 *Wheel alignment*

See **Chapter 9**.

10 : 8 *Steering lock stops*

See **Chapter 9**.

10 : 9 *Steering column lock*

Removal:

1 Disconnect the battery earth lead.
2 Disconnect the choke control or, on diesel engines, the engine stop control, in the engine compartment.
3 Remove the steering column shroud.

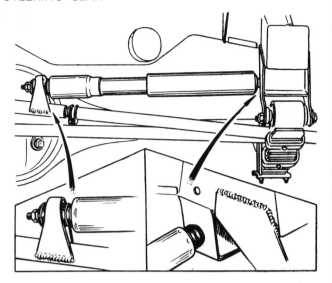

FIG 10 : 10 Telescopic steering damper installation

4 The steering lock assembly is fitted using shearhead bolts. These are bolts designed so that their heads shear off when tightened to a specific torque. To remove these bolts, centre punch and drill centrally into the bolts and use an Easy-out extractor.
5 Withdraw the steering lock assembly.
6 The ignition switch can be removed from the rear of the steering lock housing after removing the fixing screws which go through the housing.

To refit the steering lock housing, use new shearhead bolts. Do not shear off the bolt heads before checking that the lock operates correctly.

10 : 10 *Fault diagnosis*

(a) Backlash in steering

1 Worn or badly adjusted rocker shaft
2 Worn or loose linkage
3 Worn swivel hub assembly
4 Worn or loose front wheel bearings
5 Steering box loose on chassis

(b) Tight steering

1 Low or unequal tyre pressures
2 Steering box oil level low
3 Rocker shaft adjusted too lightly
4 Inner column binding
5 Seized ball joint
6 Relay unit damaged or oil level low

(c) Rattle in steering column

1 Rocker shaft worn or badly adjusted

NOTES

CHAPTER 11

THE BRAKING SYSTEM

11:1 Description

The Land-Rover braking system is unusual in that although the foot pedal operates the road wheel brakes, the hand lever operates a transmission brake. Two types of master cylinder have been fitted, the C.V. (centre valve) and C.B. (compression barrel). **FIG 11:1** shows how to identify either one. In addition, some vehicles are fitted with servo assistance and, again, two types exist. One type operates directly on the master cylinder and the other is installed remotely from the master cylinder and generates pressure in the hydraulic line. On diesel engined vehicles, an exhauster pump is fitted to produce the vacuum and on Series 3 vehicles a vacuum reservoir tank is fitted under the lefthand seat, access to which is gained by removing the seat cushion and the cover panel. This reservoir is kept at low pressure for servo operation by means of the butterfly valve and one-way valve arrangement described in **Chapter 3B, Section 3B:9** so that an exhauster pump is not required.

A dual braking system is employed on later cars so that adequate braking is still available even after a complete failure in the hydraulic circuit to either the front or the rear wheel units.

11:2 Routine maintenance and adjustments

Occasionally, apply a little heavy oil to all the wearing parts of the handbrake linkage, clevis pins, bearing bushes, etc., being careful to keep oil away from the brake itself.

Regularly, inspect the level of fluid in the hydraulic system supply tank and top up with Castrol Girling Crimson Brake Fluid (all models) if necessary. This should be an infrequent requirement; if the level drops at short intervals, immediately inspect all the fluid lines, wheel cylinders and master cylinder until the leak is found, then rectify at once.

To adjust the brake shoes, jack up the vehicle and safely support on substantial packing so that the road wheel is clear of the ground. At the rear of the brake backplate will be seen one hexagonal adjuster on 10 inch front and rear brakes, two hexagonal adjusters on the front wheels of 11 inch brakes and one square-ended adjuster at the rear brakes. Spin the wheel and turn each adjuster until the shoes just contact the drum, then slacken back one notch in the case of all front wheel brakes and two 'clicks' in the case of all rear wheel brakes. The adjuster at the rear may not give a definite 'click' but differences in effort needed to turn the adjuster will be noticeable. Lower the wheel to the ground and repeat for the other three wheels. The transmission brake (handbrake) is of similar contruction to the 11 inch rear wheel brakes and is adjusted by the same method.

11:3 The master cylinder

To remove, type C.B. (compression barrel):

1 Remove the fluid reservoir, then disconnect the pipes from the master cylinder.
2 Disconnect the pedal return spring, then undo the bolts holding the pedal bracket to the bulkhead.

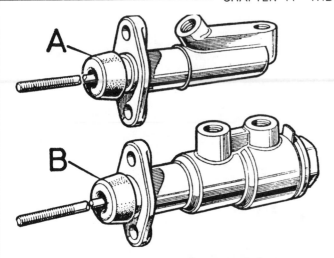

FIG 11:1   Identification of master cylinders

Key to Fig 11:1   **A** C.V. type   **B** C.B. type

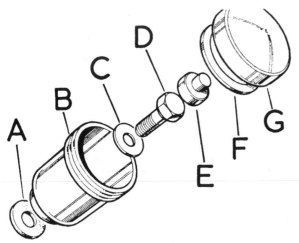

FIG 11:2   Fluid reservoir, C.V. cylinder

Key to Fig 11:2   **A** Seal   **B** Body   **C** Washer   **D** Bolt
E Plastic cover   **F** Gasket   **G** Cap

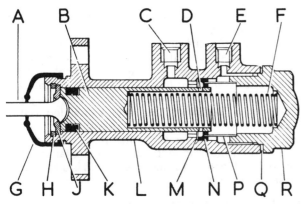

FIG 11:3   Master cylinder, type C.B.

Key to Fig 11:3   **A** Pushrod   **B** Piston
C Inlet from reservoir   **D** Inlet ports   **E** Outlet to
wheel cylinders   **F** Piston spring   **G** Dust cover
H Circlip   **J** Retaining washer   **K** End seal
L Cylinder   **M** Shim   **N** Recuperating seal
P Seal support   **Q** Gasket   **R** End cap

Manoeuvre the pedal through the bulkhead and withdraw the complete assembly from the engine compartment.

3 Remove the cover from the pedal bracket, release the pushrod, then undo the bolts holding the master cylinder to the bracket.

To remove, type C.V. (centre valve):

1 Proceed as for the C.B. type, but do not remove the pedal bracket. The coverplate can be taken away with the bracket still bolted to the bulkhead, thus exposing the pushrod nuts and the bolts holding the master cylinder. Undo these and the unit can be lifted away.

2 This type of master cylinder is the one to which the mechanical servo unit is usually fitted. To remove the master cylinder, simply remove the pipes, then unbolt the master cylinder from the face of the servo unit.

3 If this master cylinder is fitted to a servo unit, it will have the fluid reservoir attached to the inlet port. To remove the reservoir, drain off the fluid, withdraw the plastic cover at the bottom of the reservoir **E** (see **FIG 11:2**), then undo the bolt thus exposed. When the reservoir is parted from the master cylinder, do not attempt to remove the distance piece from the base of the reservoir.

To service the master cylinder:
Type C.B. Refer to FIG 11:3:

1 Wipe the outside of the unit as clean as possible, using a rag soaked in methylated spirit. Do not let petrol or paraffin come near it at any stage of the operation. Exercise extreme measures to ensure cleanliness; use clean newspaper on the work bench and clean, lint-free rag.

2 Grip the unit carefully in a vice and remove the cover **R** and copper washer **Q**.

3 Withdraw spring **F**.

4 If the pushrod **A** has the locking nut or trunnion nut still attached, remove it.

5 Remove the pushrod rubber boot **G**, the circlip **H** and pull the pushrod **A** and retaining washer **J** away.

6 Push out the piston **B**, seal **K** and seal support **P**.

7 Remove the recuperating seal **N** and shim **M**.

8 Carefully wash the body in Girling Cleaning Fluid, Girling Crimson Brake Fluid or, in emergency, methylated spirit. Examine the bore carefully; any scores, discoloration or damage involves renewal of the whole unit.

9 Obtain an overhaul kit. This will contain all new rubber components, a piston and a new copper washer.

10 Lubricate the bore freely with Girling Crimson Brake Fluid. Dip the piston seal **K** in fluid and assemble to the piston **B**. The large diameter of the seal **K** must face forwards away from the pushrod **A**. Gently insert the piston and piston seal into the body, making sure both are well wetted with brake fluid.

11 Insert the pushrod **A** and retaining washer **J**, then fit a new circlip **H**.

12 Smear the inside of the new rubber boot **G** with Girling rubber grease and assemble to the body.

13 Insert the shim **M** into the body followed by the recuperating seal **N**. This seal also has the recess facing forwards (see **FIG 11 : 4**). Latest type cylinders have a plastic washer in place of the shim.

14 Put the seal support **P** in position. If it is plastic, locate it in the seal ; if metal, locate it in the end cap **R**.

15 Fit spring **F**, then replace and securely tighten the end cover **R** on a new copper washer **Q**.

Type C.V. Refer to Chapter 6 :

The procedure detailed in **Chapter 6** for the clutch master cylinder applies to this brake cylinder since they are identical. Reference to **FIGS 6 : 7** and **6 : 10** will clearly show the method of assembly. Be careful to fit the seals as shown and lubricate the rubber boot with rubber grease.

To replace the master cylinder :

Type C.B. :

1 Reverse the removal procedure.
2 Refill the supply tank (reservoir) with Girling Crimson Brake Fluid and bleed the brakes (see **Section 11 : 6**).
3 Check for leaks.
4 Ensure the pushrod has $\frac{1}{16}$ inch (1.6 mm) free play.

Type C.V. :

1 Reverse the removal procedure.
2 Refill the reservoir and bleed the brakes (see **Section 11 : 6**).
3 Check for leaks.
4 Adjust the pushrod to give $\frac{1}{16}$ inch (1.6 mm) free play by slackening the nuts and moving the rod in the trunnion. Tighten the nuts.

11 : 4 Servicing the brakes

10 inch brakes, 86 and 88 models :

These models use the same single leading shoe assembly both front and rear. Refer to **FIG 11 : 5** for an exploded view and **FIG 11 : 6** for an assembled view.

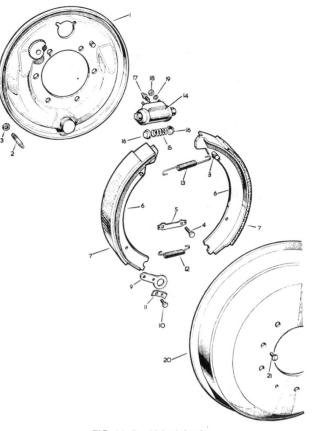

FIG 11 : 5   10 inch brake

Key to Fig 11 : 5   1 Brake anchor plate assembly
2 Shoe steady post   3 Locknut for steady post
4 Setbolt ($\frac{3}{8}$ inch x 1 inch long)   5 Locker   6 Brake shoe assembly, front and rear   7 Linings complete with rivets for brake shoe   8 Spring post for brake shoe
9 Anchor for brake shoe   10 Special setscrew, fixing anchor
11 Locking plate for bolt   12 Pull-off spring for brake shoe
13 Pull-off spring for leading shoe   14 Wheel cylinder assembly   15 Spring for piston, front   16 Washer for spring, front   17 Bleed screw   18 Special nut   19 Spring washer   20 Brake drum   21 Setscrew, fixing brake drum

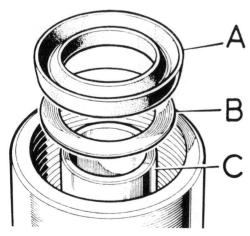

FIG 11 : 4   Fitting recuperating seal and shim

Key to Fig 11 : 4   **A** Seal   **B** Shim   **C** Piston

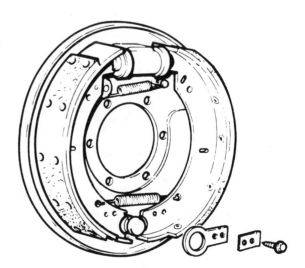

FIG 11 : 6   10 inch brake assembly

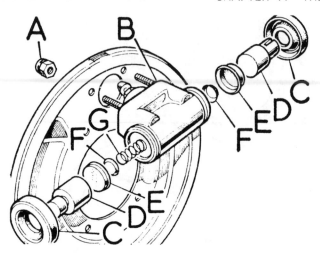

FIG 11:7   10 inch brake wheel cylinder

Key to Fig 11:7   A Nut   **B** Cylinder   **C** Dust cover
D Piston   **E** Seal   **F** Seal support   **G** Spring

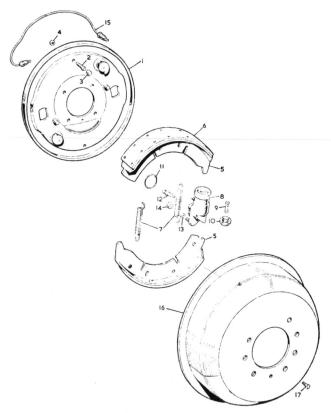

FIG 11:8   11 inch brake, 2¼ litre models

Key to Fig 11:8   1 Brake anchor plate   2 Steady post for
brake shoe   3 Bush for steady post   4 Special nut, fixing
steady post   5 Brake shoe assembly   6 Lining complete
with rivets for brake shoe   7 Pull-off spring for brake shoe
8 Wheel cylinder assembly   9 Spring (⅜ inch diameter)
10 Air excluder   11 Sealing ring for cylinder
12 Bleed screw   13 Spring washer   14 Special nut
15 Connecting pipe for wheel cylinder   16 Brake drum
17 Setscrew, fixing brake drum

To remove the brake assembly:

1 Loosen the road wheel nuts, then jack up and safely
support the vehicle. Remove the road wheel, undo
the setscrew retaining the brake drum and pull the
drum off the wheel studs.

2 Turn back the adjuster to release the tension of the
leading shoe pull-off spring 13 (see **FIG 11:5**), then
remove the spring.

3 Remove the two setbolts 10, locking plate 11 and
trailing shoe anchor plate 9. Take a careful note of
the positions of the return springs. There are several alternative arrangements on different models
and incorrect refitting can seriously affect braking.

4 Take off the brake shoes by pulling them apart at the
pivot pin, then part them by removing spring 12. If
the wheel cylinder is not being removed, wind a
piece of soft wire or put a heavy rubber band over
the two pistons to prevent them coming out of the
cylinder. If the brake shoes are not being relined, be
very careful not to touch the friction surface with
oily or greasy hands. This applies, of course, to
relined or new shoes also. Never allow oil, grease,
paint or any foreign matter to come into contact
with the friction material.

5 If the hydraulic cylinder is to be dismantled, the
front brakes must be disconnected from the flexible
hose by the method described in **Section 11:5**. This
is important to avoid twisting and thereby damaging the hose. The rear brake cylinder can be
removed by simply undoing the union nut on the
hydraulic pipe. At this stage, depress the footbrake
pedal to its fullest extent and wedge it down. This
will prevent undue loss of fluid. Support the front
wheel brakes flexible hoses as high as possible; this
will also help to minimize fluid loss from the
pipelines.

6 Remove the wheel cylinder by undoing the nuts 18
(see **FIG 11:5**). Detach the rubber dust covers **C** (see
FIG 11:7), pistons **D**, piston seals **E** and the piston
spring **G** with its supports **F**. Take off the bleed
nipple cap, then unscrew the bleed nipple and
remove the steel ball.

To reline the brake shoes:

If it is necessary to reline the shoes, make sure that
the correct linings are obtained and always reline both
shoes on each wheel of the axle being dealt with. Never
mix makes and grades of lining. Cut off the old rivets
with the shoes gripped in a vice, then punch out the
rivet shanks and strip off the old lining. Clean the shoes
and run a file lightly over the seating face to remove any
burrs. With clean hands, position a new lining on the
shoe, insert a rivet in one of the centre pairs of holes
and, holding the shoe, lining and rivet against a steel
dolly rod gripped in the vice, securely clinch the end of
the rivet over in the shoe by using a centre punch in the
hollow shank. Repeat with another rivet in the other
hole of the pair, then continue riveting, working outwards equally towards the end of the linings. With a
fairly coarse file, chamfer the ends of the linings to
prevent brake snatch.

Most brake shoes today are fitted with bonded
linings. When these become worn, replacement brake
shoes should be fitted in complete sets; that is four
shoes to an axle.

To reassemble the brake (see FIG 11:5):

1 If removed, clean and replace the backplate 1 and the hub components. Screw the steady post 2 into the backplate, but do not tighten the nut 3 at this stage. Make sure the steady post will be well clear of the shoe.

2 Clean all the wheel cylinder components, using Girling Crimson Brake Fluid and renew as necessary. Any scores on the pistons or in the cylinder bore must mean renewal. Renew all the rubber components from the maker's overhaul kit supplied for this purpose.

3 Reassemble the wheel cylinder components, ensuring that the cylinder bore, pistons and piston seals are copiously smeared with brake fluid. Refit the dust covers, bleed nipple ball, nipple and cover. Retain the pistons by the method described earlier. Attach the cylinder to the backplate.

4 Connect the spring 12 to the shoes, then apply them to the brake by first positioning them against the hydraulic pistons. Pull the other ends apart and fit to the pivot (anchor) pin.

5 Reconnect the pull-off spring 13.

6 Replace the anchor plate 9, renew the locking plate 11 and fit the setbolts 10. Tighten up and then bend up the ends of the locking plate 11 (see **FIG 11:6**).

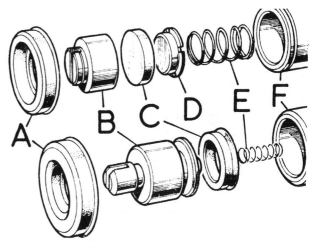

FIG 11:10   11 inch brake, wheel cylinder components

Key to Fig 11:10   A Dust cover   **B** Piston   **C** Seal
D Seal support   **E** Spring   **F** Cylinder

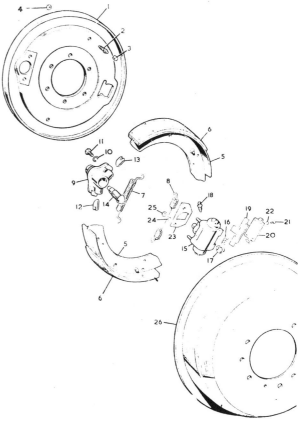

FIG 11:11   Rear brake, Series 2

Key to Fig 11:11   1 Brake anchor plate   **2** Steady post for brake shoe   **3** Bush for steady post   **4** Special nut for steady post   **5** Brake shoe assembly   **6** Lining complete with rivets for brake shoe   **7** Spring, adjuster end **8** Spring, wheel cylinder end   **9** Adjuster housing **10** Spring washer   **11** Special setbolt   **12** Plunger, lefthand **13** Plunger, righthand   **14** Cone for adjuster   **15** Wheel cylinder assembly   **16** Spring   **17** Air excluder **18** Bleed screw   **19** Brake shoe abutment plate **20** Retainer for brake shoe abutment plate   **21** Screw **22** Shakeproof washer   **23** Dust coverplate for brake wheel cylinder   **24** Spring washer   **25** Self-locking nut **26** Brake drum   **27** Setscrew, fixing brake drum

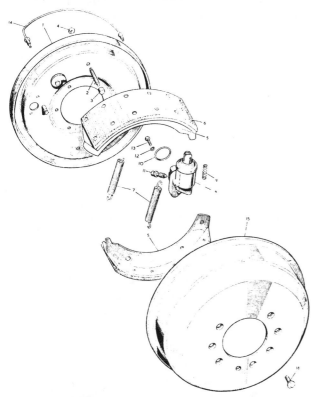

FIG 11:9   11 inch brake, 2.6 litre models

Key to Fig 11:9   1 Brake anchor plate, lefthand front **2** Steady post for brake shoe   **3** Bush for steady post **4** Special nut, fixing steady post   **5** Brake shoe assembly **6** Lining complete with rivets   **7** Pull-off spring for brake shoe   **8** Wheel cylinder assembly   **9** Spring **10** Sealing ring for cylinder   **11** Bleed screw   **12** Spring washer   **13** Special setbolt   **14** Connecting pipe for wheel cylinder   **15** Brake drum   **16** Setscrew, fixing brake drum

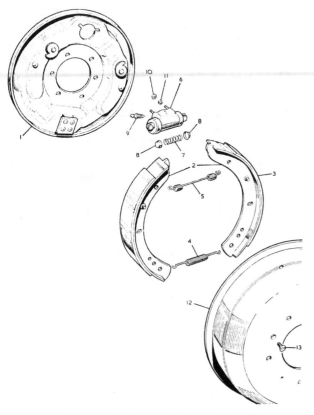

FIG 11:12 Rear brake, Series 2A and 3

Key to Fig 11:12   1 Brake anchor plate   2 Brake shoe
assembly   3 Lining complete with rivets for brake shoe
4 Spring, abutment end   5 Spring, wheel cylinder end
6 Wheel cylinder assembly   7 Spring for piston
8 Washer for spring   9 Bleed screw   10 Special nut
11 Spring washer   12 Brake drum   13 Setscrew,
fixing brake drum

7 Reconnect the hydraulic pipe and release the footbrake pedal.

8 Examine the brake drum for scoring or ovality. If
necessary, the drum can be skimmed oversize by
not more than .03 inch (.75 mm). Replace the brake
drum and fit the retaining screw.

9 Set the leading shoe adjuster so that the shoe just
contacts the drum.

10 If necessary, bleed the brakes as described in
Section 11:6.

11 To set the steady post, apply the brakes lightly and
turn the drum by hand to centralize the shoes. Apply
the brakes hard, then screw the steady post in until
it just contacts the shoe web and tighten the locknut.

12 Replace the road wheel, lower the vehicle to the
ground and tighten the road wheel nuts.

11 inch brakes:
Front wheels. Refer to FIGS 11:8 and 11:9:

These brakes differ considerably from the 10 inch
brake previously described. Two hydraulic cylinders
are fitted, each one operating against the leading end of
a shoe. This is known as a 'two leading shoe' brake and
has twice the self-servo action of the single leading
shoe design.

The method of removing the road wheel and brake
drum is the same as for the 10 inch brake, but the shoes
are removed separately. Slacken the adjusters, then
lever the trailing end of each shoe away from the back
of the hydraulic cylinder and disconnect the spring.
Reline the shoes as described earlier.

If the wheel cylinders are not being removed, retain
the pistons by winding soft wire round or by attaching a
strong rubber band to the cylinder unit.

If it is intended to remove the cylinders, release the
bleed nipple, depress the footbrake pedal and wedge it
down to prevent undue fluid loss. Disconnect the pipe
connecting the two cylinders and then the flexible hose
(see **Section 11:5**). This should be done before the
shoes are removed so that the pistons do not come
away inadvertently.

Remove the cylinders by undoing the retaining bolts
and service them exactly as described for the 10 inch
brake cylinder, observing the most scrupulous cleanliness throughout the operation. Refer to **FIG 11:10** for
details of the two types of cylinder components which
may be encountered.

Rebuild the brake by reversing the dismantling operation. The steady posts are adjusted by the same
method as described for the 10 inch brake. If the wheel
cylinders have been disturbed, bleed the hydraulic system as described in **Section 11:6**. Adjust each shoe by
rotating the drum by hand and turning the adjuster until
the shoe just contacts the drum, then slacken back two
serrations. The drum can be skimmed .03 inch (.75 mm)
oversize if scored or distorted.

11 inch brakes:
Rear wheels. Refer to FIGS 11:11 and 11:12:

These brakes are of single leading shoe design and
are similar in principle. Only the adjuster mechanism
varies. The Series 2 has the cone type adjuster, whereas
the Series 2A and 3 have a pair of snail cams. The latter
construction is self-explanatory but the cone type is
described in more detail.

Dismantle the brake assembly generally as described
for the 10 inch brake, but, before removing the drum,
slacken the adjusters right off. Reline the shoes and

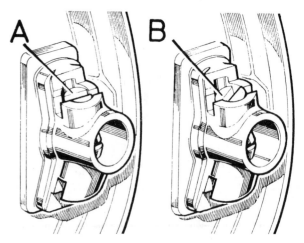

FIG 11:13 Plunger locations

Key to Fig 11:13   **A** Correct   **B** Incorrect

service the cylinder as already described. The cone adjuster assembly, Series 2, should be stripped by pulling the two plungers out of their bores and then screwing the adjuster cone right through the housing. Clean thoroughly and apply a little Girling Brake grease or any good high melting point grease to the adjuster thread, cone and the two plungers. Reassemble and check that, when the plungers are pressed down onto the flats of the adjuster cone, the slot for the brake shoe web is in line with the slot in the housing. If the plungers have been inadvertently reversed, this will not be the case. Refer to **FIG 11:13** for illustrations of correct and incorrect assembly.

Reassemble the brake and bleed the system as described for the other types of brake. An important point to note, if the wheel cylinder has been removed, is that, when replaced, it must not be tight on the brake backplate. See that a good spring washer is fitted under each nut and then tighten the nuts moderately hard. Slacken back one turn and check that the cylinder is just free to float on the backplate. If this is not done, the shoes may not centralize properly. The brake drum can be skimmed .03 inch (.75 mm) oversize if scored or distorted.

11:5 Removing a brake flexible hose

Refer to **FIG 11:14**.

It is essential that the following procedure is adopted whenever a flexible hose is removed or replaced. Otherwise, the hose can be twisted and ruined.
1 Unscrew the metal pipe union nut **A**.
2 Hold the nut **D** with a spanner and remove nut **B** and shakeproof washer **C**.
3 Withdraw the hose from the bracket, then disconnect at the wheel cylinder end.
4 Replace by reversing this procedure, always making sure that dirt does not become trapped in the system or between the mating faces of the hose, wheel cylinder or metal pipe.

11:6 Bleeding the brakes, single system

If the level of the fluid in the supply tank has been allowed to fall too low or if any section of the system

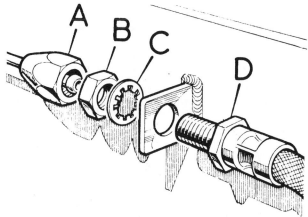

FIG 11:14 Flexible hose connections

Key to Fig 11:14 **A** Metal pipe **B** Locknut
C Shakeproof washer **D** Flexible pipe

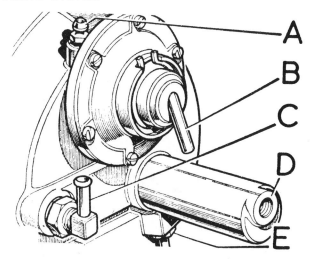

FIG 11:15 Servo unit connections

Key to Fig 11:15 **A** Bleed nipple **B** Atmospheric inlet
C Vacuum connection **D** Fluid outlet **E** Fluid inlet
from master cylinder

has been disconnected, the pedal will feel 'spongy' due to the presence of air trapped in the pipes or cylinders. This air must be removed by the process of bleeding. During this operation, exercise the most scrupulous cleanliness and **never allow any petrol, paraffin or any type of mineral oil near the system as this contamination can spread rapidly, leading to dangerous deterioration of the rubber seals**. Proceed as follows:
1 Check the level of fluid in the reservoir and top up if necessary. Note that if a C.B. type master cylinder has been drained, the system must be refilled under a pressure of 14 lb/sq inch (1 kg/sq cm) since the angled position of the cylinder leads to air becoming trapped at the cap end. Even so, it may be necessary to raise the vehicle until the cylinder is horizontal and also to slacken off the outlet pipe while filling.
2 If the system incorporates a servo unit of the hydraulic type, refer to **FIG 11:15** and bleed this unit first as follows:
   (a) Make sure no vacuum exists by applying the brakes at least six times.
   (b) Release the pipe nut at **D** one turn. Now operate the brake pedal slowly, using only half to three quarters of the stroke. Continue until no more air bubbles appear round the nut and then tighten the nut during a down stroke of the pedal.
   (c) Loosen the nipple **A** and attach a length of tubing with the other end submerged in a little clean fluid in a glass jar. Operate the pedal as at (b). When no more air bubbles appear, tighten the nipple on a down stroke of the pedal.
3 For all brake systems continue as follows:
   (a) Slacken all brake shoe adjusters right off.
   (b) Commence at the wheel **nearest** the master cylinder and finish at the one **furthest** from the master cylinder.
   (c) Fit a bleed tube to the wheel cylinder bleed nipple and submerge the other end in a little clean fluid in a glass jar. Slacken the nipple and operate

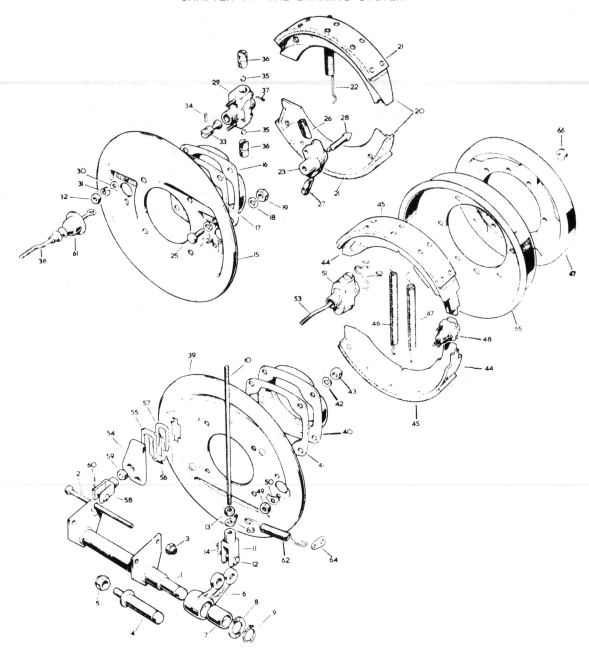

FIG 11:16 Transmission brake

Key to Fig 11:16   1 Shaft for handbrake relay lever*   2 Bolt (⅜ inch UNF x 4 inch long)*   3 Self-locking nut (⅜ inch UNF)*
4 Shaft for handbrake relay lever   5 Self-locking nut (⅜ inch UNF) fixing shaft to chassis frame   6 Relay lever assembly for
handbrake   7 Bush for relay lever   8 Plain washer   9 Circlip   10 Brake rod, relay to handbrake lever   11 Clevis fork end
12 Clevis pin complete   13 Locknut (⅝ inch UNF)   14 Splitpin   15 Anchor plate, transmission brake**   16 Oil catcher for
transmission brake**   17 Joint washer for oil catcher**   18 Spring washer**   19 Nut (⅜ inch UNF)**   20 Brake shoe
assembly, boxed pair**   21 Lining complete with rivets for shoe**   22 Pull-off spring for brake shoe**   23 Adjuster housing**
24 Spring washer**   25 Setbolt**   26 Plunger, righthand**   27 Plunger, lefthand**   28 Adjuster cone**
29 Expander housing**   30 Special washer**   31 Spring washer**   32 Simmonds nut**   33 Expander cone**
34 Pin, fixing cone to brake rod**   35 Roller for expander**   36 Plunger for expander**   37 Splitpin, fixing plunger**
38 Brake rod, expander to relay lever**   39 Anchor plate, transmission brake***   40 Oil catcher for transmission brake***
41 Joint washer for oil catcher***   42 Spring washer***   43 Nut (⅜ inch BSF)***   44 Brake shoe assembly, boxed pair***
45 Lining complete for shoe, boxed pair***   46 Pull-off spring, expander end***   47 Return spring, adjuster end***
48 Adjuster unit assembly***   49 Nut (¼ inch UNF)***   50 Tabwasher***   51 Expander unit assembly***
52 Clip retaining tappets***   53 Brake rod, expander to relay lever***   54 Dust cover for expander unit***
55 Packing plate***   56 Locking plate***   57 Retaining spring***   58 Clevis complete   59 Locknut (⅝ inch BSF)
60 Splitpin   61 Dust cover for brake rod   62 Return spring for brake rod   63 Anchor for spring   64 Anchor for spring,
on transfer box   65 Brake drum   66 Self-locking nut (⅜ inch BSF) fixing brake drum and damper   67 Transmission damper
at rear end of gearbox
* Up to vehicle suffix 'C' inclusive   ** Up to gearboxes numbered : 146000565 156000430 151005187
*** From gearboxes numbered : 146000566 156000431 151005188 onwards

the brake pedal, see (d) and (e), until no more air bubbles appear. Tighten the nipple at the beginning of a pedal stroke downwards.

(d) If a C.V. type master cylinder, push the pedal down through the full stroke, give three short strokes, then let the pedal fly back quickly. Repeat until all air is expelled. Refer to (c).

(e) If a C.B. type master cylinder, push the pedal down through the whole stroke slowly, return slowly, wait three or four seconds, then repeat until all air is expelled. Refer to (c).

(f) Rebleed the servo unit as at 2(c) when all wheel cylinders have been bled.

4 During all these operations, keep the fluid level up in the supply tank so that air cannot enter and cause the whole process to be repeated. Never top up the supply tank with fluid just bled from the system since air may be held in suspension.

11:7 *The handbrake (transmission brake)*

Refer to **FIG 11 : 16** for details of this brake layout.

To service the transmission brake unit :

If access is only required to the brake shoes, e.g. for relining, the propeller shaft may be left in position. It is

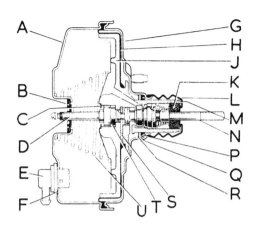

FIG 11 : 17   Girling mechanical servo

Key to Fig 11 : 17   **A** Front shell   **B** Seal and plate assembly   **C** Retainer sprag washer   **D** Hydraulic pushrod   **E** Non-return valve   **F** O-ring   **G** Rear shell   **H** Diaphragm   **J** Diaphragm plate   **K** Filter   **L** Dust cover   **M** End cap   **N** Valve operating rod assembly   **P** Seal   **Q** Bearing   **R** Retainer   **S** Valve retaining plate   **T** Reaction disc   **U** Diaphragm return spring

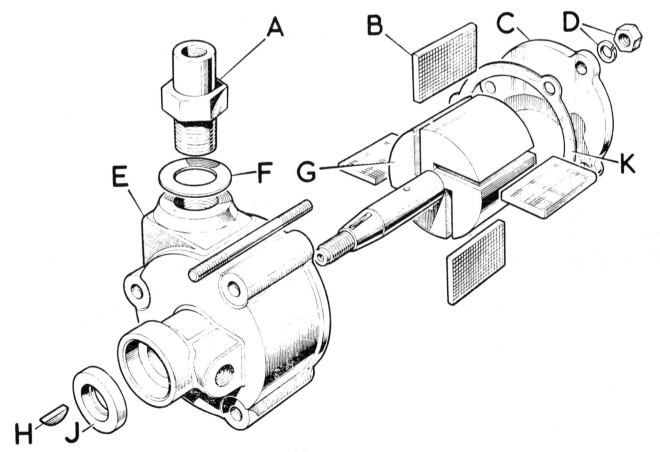

FIG 11 : 18   Rotary exhauster

Key to Fig 11 : 18   **A** Inlet union   **B** Vane for rotor   **C** Cover for housing   **D** Fixings for cover   **E** Rotor housing   **F** Washer for union   **G** Rotor   **H** Woodruff key   **J** Oil seal   **K** Joint washer for cover

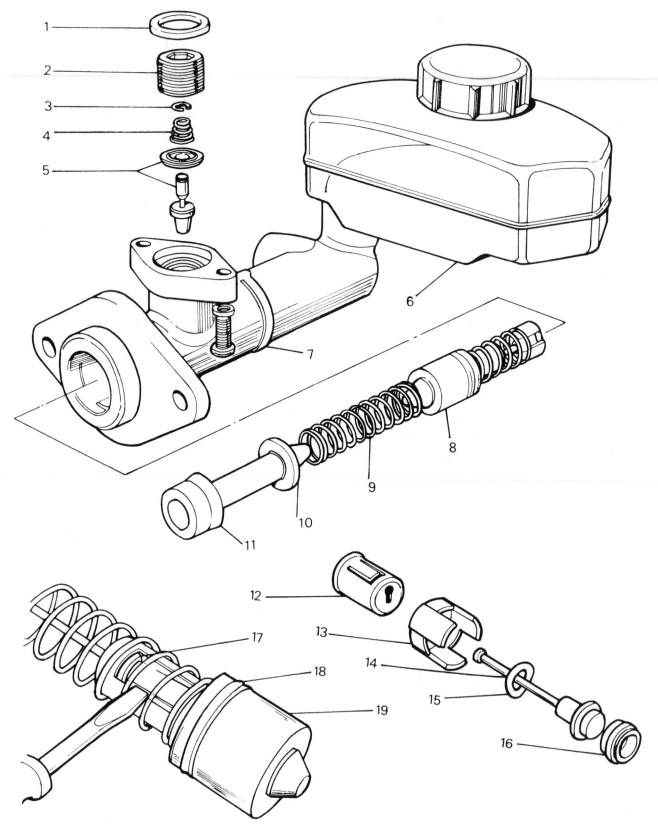

FIG 11:19   Tandem master cylinder

Key to Fig 11:19   1 Seal ring   2 Tipping valve assembly retainer   3 Circlip   4 Spring   5 Tipping valve and plate   6 Reservoir   7 Screw   8 Secondary piston   9 Piston spring   10 Primary piston   11 Seal   12 Valve retainer   13 Valve spacer   14 Valve stem   15 Wave washer   16 Seal   17 Locking prong   18 Seal   19 Secondary piston and valve assembly

only necessary to detach the brake drum and push it back over the shaft.

1 Remove the brake shoes complete with springs by levering them apart and pulling off the expander plungers and adjuster plungers. Remove the springs and separate the shoes.

2 Release the rod 38 or 53 if the expander is to be removed, then release the nuts (early type) or clips (later type) and the expander will come away. Remove the adjuster housing by releasing the bolts or nuts.

3 Remove the two splitpins 37 or clip 52 and lift out the plungers, being careful not to lose the rollers.

4 Push out pin 34 and separate rod 38 and expander cone 33.

5 Clean all the parts and examine for wear or damage. Reline the shoes as described in **Section 11:4** if necessary.

6 Reassembly is a reversal of the dismantling procedure, but, on early type brakes, make sure that the adjuster plungers are replaced in the correct bores. These plungers are handed, righthand and lefthand. Therefore, assemble the adjuster housing to the anchor plate, but leave the bolts finger tight. Screw the adjuster cone right home, then try the plungers in their bores. When pushed hard down against the flats of the adjuster cone, the slots in their outer ends must be in line with the plane of the brake shoe webs. Smear a little high melting point grease on all the bearing surfaces and, finally, assemble the plungers with the adjuster cone right back as far as it will go. Later type plungers are not handed and can be fitted either side.

7 Refit the expander cone to the brake rod and dust cover, lightly greasing the expander cone. Refit the housing to the anchor plate, but leave the retaining nuts one turn slack at this stage. Grease the expander plungers and stick the rollers to them. Insert the expander cone, then replace the two plungers and rollers. Fit two new splitpins or spring 52 to retain the assembly.

8 Replace the shoes and their return springs. The half round cut-out in the ends of the shoe webs goes to the adjuster plungers (early type).

9 To adjust the brake, first tighten the adjuster cone until the shoes are hard against the drum. Now tighten the bolts holding the adjuster housing to the anchor plate. Slacken the adjuster cone two clicks, then apply the handbrake lever hard and immediately release it. This should centralize the shoes and the drum will be free to rotate. Again hold the handbrake on and just nip up the nuts holding the expander housing (early type only). Release them slightly and then release the handbrake. This will ensure that the expander housing is free to float on the anchor plate. Adjust the handbrake linkage at the vertical rod 10 so that the brake comes on after moving the hand lever one or two clicks (three clicks with cable).

10 It is unlikely that this brake drum will be scored but, in the event that it is damaged, it can be skimmed oversize by .03 inch (.75 mm) in the same way as the road wheel brake drums.

11:8 Servo units

(a) Girling mechanical servo:

The private owner is not recommended to attempt to service this unit. In the event of failure, denoted by greatly increased pedal pressures, the unit should be removed and an exchange component obtained. To remove the unit, first remove the brake master cylinder as described in **Section 11:3**, disconnect the brake switch leads and the vacuum pipe. Undo the bolts holding the pedal bracket to the bulkhead and remove the pedal bracket and pedal by manoeuvring the pedal through the bulkhead. Remove the pivot pin coupling the pedal to the servo, undo the bolts and part the servo and bracket. Replacement is a reversal of the removal procedure. Bleed the brakes as described in **Section 11:6**.

FIG 11:17 shows the unit in section and it will be seen that, in the event of failure of vacuum, braking effort is not lost as the rods **N** and **D** work as one and operate the hydraulic cylinder directly.

(b) Clayton Dewandre hydraulic servo:

It is not advisable to attempt to service this unit and, in the event of failure, an exchange unit should be obtained. To remove it, disconnect both hydraulic pipes, wedge the brake pedal down to prevent fluid leakage, then undo the vacuum hose. Release the bolts and lift the unit clear. Replacement is a reversal of this procedure, but the brakes will need bleeding.

(c) Series 3 servo removal:

A different mounting is used on these vehicles and, therefore, a different procedure is required.

First, remove the master cylinder from the forward face of the unit, then disconnect the vacuum hose and remove the switch plate from the top of the pedal mounting bracket.

Remove the rubber plugs at each side of the pedal box and pull out the splitpin to free the clevis pin securing the servo rod to the brake pedal.

Remove the four securing nuts and lift away the servo unit.

Refitting is the reverse of the removal procedure.

For diesel engined models, refer also to **Chapter 3B, Section 3B:9**, 'Setting the throttle controls.'

11:9 The exhauster

Refer to **FIG 11:18**. This unit is fitted to diesel engined vehicles to provide the vacuum for the servo. The illustration makes clear the method of dismantling and reassembly. When the exhauster is serviced, always replace the rotor vanes, oil seal and the joint washers. These are all included in the overhaul kit. Adjust the rotor end float by means of different thicknesses of joint washer **K**. The rotor must turn freely without excessive end float. Note that the radiused edges of the vanes are fitted pointing outwards.

11:10 Dual braking system

On certain later cars, a dual braking system is available in which a tandem master cylinder is used, having

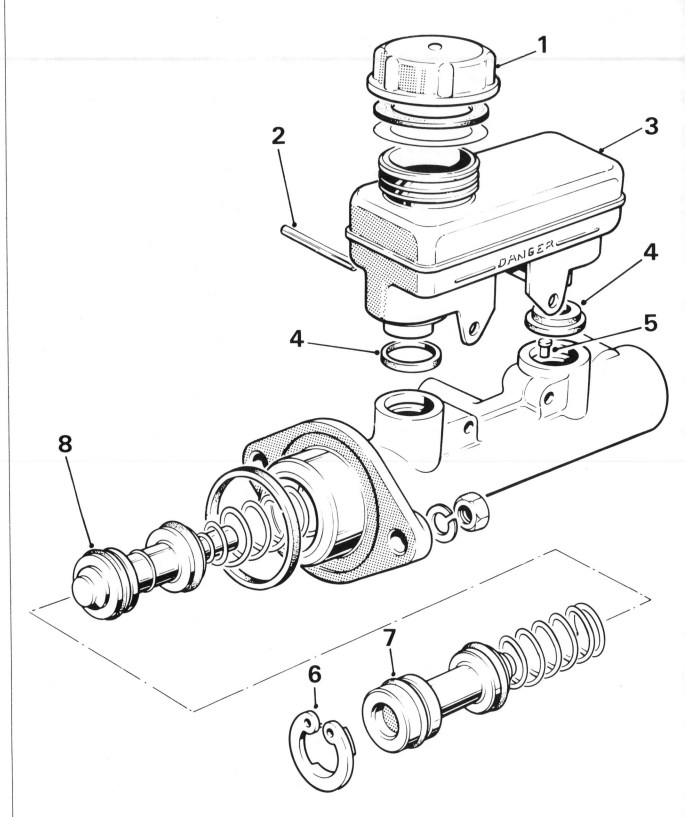

FIG 11:20 Tandem master cylinder

Key to Fig 11:20   1 Filler cap and washers   2 Retaining pins   3 Reservoir   4 Seals   5 Stop pin   6 Circlip
7 Primary piston assembly   8 Secondary piston assembly

LRAB2

two individual piston/cylinder assemblies in order to serve two separate braking circuits, one for the front and the other for the rear brakes.

This type of system also includes a brake failure switch whose purpose is to warn the driver of a breakdown in either of the two circuits.

Master cylinder, 2¼ and 2.6 litre models:

This is shown in the exploded diagram of **FIG 11:19** to which reference should be made when dismantling. It also shows how, in the event of a complete failure in one circuit, full braking is still available on the other.

Removal is effected by disconnecting the two brake pipes and unscrewing the two flange nuts.

Remove the two reservoir fixing screws and then pivot the reservoir as shown. Do not attempt to remove it completely as it is retained by an internal fixing at the rear inlet bore.

Withdraw the oil seal ring and unscrew the tipping valve assembly retainer. Lift out the tipping valve assembly, remove the circlip and withdraw the spring and the tipping valve.

Withdraw the primary piston, remove and discard the oil seal. Withdraw the piston spring.

Withdraw the secondary piston and valve assembly. Prise the spring retainer locking prong clear of the piston shoulder and withdraw the piston and spring. Remove and discard the seal.

Align the valve stem with the enlarged hole in the retainer and pull out. Separate the remaining pieces as shown.

Clean all the components in brake fluid and examine them for wear or corrosion. Replace as necessary including all seals. These will be included in the master cylinder overhaul kit.

Before assembly, dip all the pieces in clean brake fluid, then :

Fit the valve seal, flat side first, to the end of the valve stem. Fit the wave washer, domed side towards the valve head. Fit the valve spacer legs first and then the valve retainer. Locate the spring over the retainer and seat squarely on the spacer.

Insert the secondary piston into the spring and engage the locking prong on the retainer in the piston groove. Fit the piston seal, then insert the piston and valve assembly into the cylinder.

The remaining items are assembled in the reverse order to dismantling. Torque figures are : tipping valve retainer, 35 to 45 lb ft (4.7 to 6 mkg) ; reservoir screws, 2 to 3 lb ft (0.3 to 0.4 mkg).

Master cylinder, 3.5 litre models:

Unscrew the filler cap 1 (see **FIG 11:20**) and remove the washers. Remove the clips and withdraw the retaining pins 2. Lift off the reservoir 3 and empty the fluid. Note their fitted positions and extract the two seals 4 from the body. Carefully mount the master cylinder in a vice, press the piston assemblies into the bore and withdraw the secondary piston stop pin 5. Remove the circlip 6 and withdraw the primary piston assembly 7 and secondary piston assembly 8 from the bore. Tap the cylinder on a soft or wooden surface or use compressed air at the secondary outlet if necessary. Note the difference in the springs : the secondary spring is

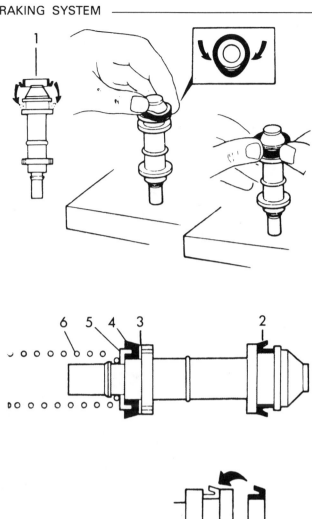

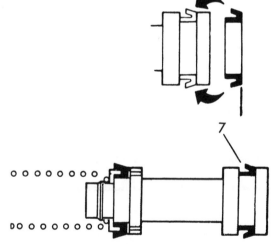

FIG 11:21 Method of fitting new seals

Key to Fig 11:21
1 Method of fitting seals
2 Secondary piston seal   3 Washer   4 Recuperating seal
5 Retainer   6 Spring   7 Primary piston seal

necked down where it fits on the spindle. If new seals are being fitted, refer to **FIG 11:21**.

Clean all parts in Girling cleaning fluid and allow to dry. Check the bore of the cylinder for any scoring, pitting or excessive wear and renew the complete unit if these faults are present. Dip all the parts in clean fluid and assemble them wet.

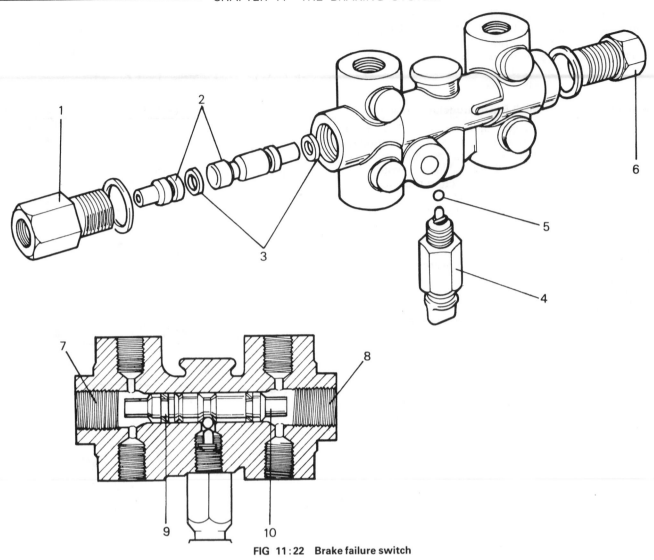

FIG 11:22 Brake failure switch

Key to Fig 11:22   1 Union nut   2 Shuttle valve   3 Seals   4 Switch unit   5 Plunger ball   6 End plug   7 End plug
8 Union   9 Short section   10 Long section

Reassembly is a reversal of the dismantling procedure. Take care not to damage the lips of the piston seals when inserting them into the bore.

Brake failure switch:

This, as will be seen from the section view in **FIG 11:22**, is in the form of an 'H' in which the two arms are inserted in the two braking circuits and the cross bar carries a shuttle type piston. Under normal conditions, the pressure in each arm will be equal and the piston will remain in its central position. In the event of a failure in either hydraulic circuit, pressure will be decreased on that side of the unit and the piston will move in that direction and, in so doing, will actuate the plunger type switch and illuminate the warning lamp on the instrument panel.

No maintenance is required and the illustration should enable the unit to be dismantled and reassembled if this should be necessary.

Bleeding the dual system:

This will be a similar procedure to that described in **Section 11:6**, but do not use full pedal travel as this may decentralize the shuttle valve in the brake failure switch.

If the plunger should operate the switch, causing the warning light to come on, the bleed screw must be closed and a bleed screw at the other end of the car opened.

Apply a steady pressure to the pedal until the light goes out, then release the pedal immediately and close the bleed screw, otherwise the piston will move too far in the opposite direction and require resetting again.

11:11 *Fault diagnosis*

(a) Spongy pedal action
1 Air in system
2 Swollen rubber components (use of incorrect fluid)
3 Incorrect brake shoe adjustment

(b) Loss of pedal pressure

1 Leak in hydraulic system

(c) Hard brake pedal

1 Incorrect grade of lining
2 Restriction in master cylinder
3 Incorrect shoe adjustment

(d) Poor brakes

1 Water-soaked linings
2 Incorrect or glazed linings
3 Incorrect shoe adjustment
4 Incorrect master cylinder adjustment

(e) Grabbing brakes

1 Grease, oil or fluid-soaked linings
2 Scored or cracked drum
3 Incorrect shoe adjustment

(f) Squealing brakes

1 Incorrect linings
2 Distorted brake drum
3 Bent anchor plate
4 Damaged brake shoe
5 Dust in drums
6 Shoes binding on the steady posts
7 Loose wheel cylinder

(g) Brakes drag

1 Incorrect shoe adjustment
2 Distorted rubber boots
3 Seized shoes
4 Weak pull-off springs
5 Loose wheel bearings
6 Restriction in brake pipe
7 Distorted drum

NOTES

CHAPTER 12

THE ELECTRICAL EQUIPMENT

12:1 *Description of system*

Over the years, important changes have been made to the system, particularly the charging circuits and generators. The polarity has been changed from positive earth to negative earth; therefore, make very sure which system is used when carrying out any work on the electrical components. Transistorized equipment will be ruined if connected wrongly. All 2¼ litre petrol and diesel vehicles up to suffix chassis C, inclusive, are **positive** earth. 2¼ litre petrol and diesel vehicles from suffix chassis D, and all 2.6 and 3.5 litre petrol models are equipped with **negative earth systems**.

Three dynamo types have been fitted, each with its own particular control box. It is important to check that the correct dynamo and control box are mated. Incorrect control box types will burn out the dynamo. Only one dynamo type is illustrated and described as all are basically similar. Some vehicles are fitted with an alternator and as this needs a different technique for servicing, full details of its construction and testing are given.

12:2 *Batteries*

Keep the top of the battery and surrounding parts dry and clean. Clean off any corrosion from the metal parts of the battery mounting with diluted ammonia and paint with anti-sulphuric paint. If the terminal posts are corroded, remove the cables and clean with diluted ammonia. Before refitting the cables, smear the terminal posts with petroleum jelly.

If the electrolyte level of the cells is below the plate separators, top up with distilled water; never add neat acid. If it is ever necessary to make up new electrolyte due to loss by spillage, add the sulphuric acid to the distilled water. **It is highly dangerous to add water to acid.**

The hydrometer readings of a battery in good condition should be as follows:

For climates below 80°F (26.5°C)

Cell fully charged	1.270 to 1.290
Cell three-quarters charged	1.230 to 1.250
Cell half-charged	1.190 to 1.210

For climates above 80°F (26.5°C)

Cell fully charged	1.210 to 1.230
Cell three-quarters charged	1.170 to 1.190
Cell half-charged	1.130 to 1.150

When bench charging a battery, take out the vent plugs and charge at 4 amps until it gasses freely. Never put a naked light near the vents when the battery is gassing as an explosion is possible.

The drive screws securing the battery leads are made from a special non-corrosive metal and must never be replaced with ordinary drive screws.

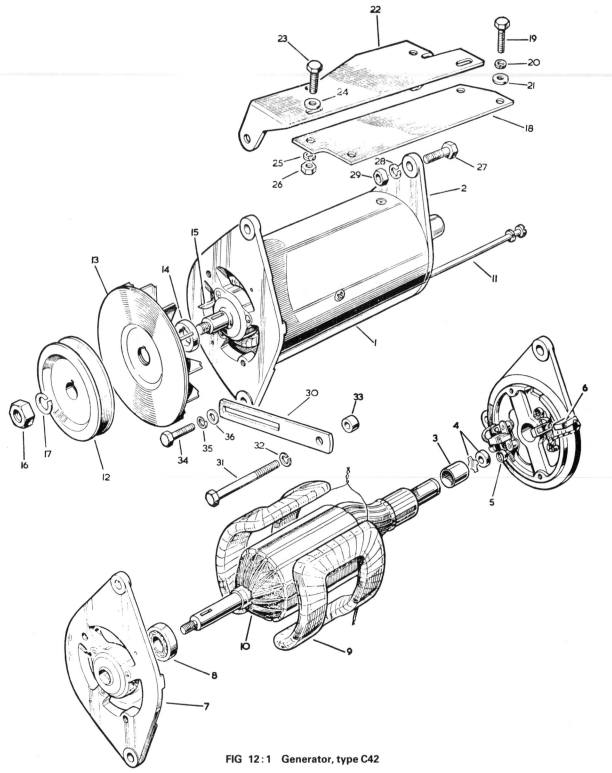

FIG 12:1 Generator, type C42

Key to Fig 12:1   1 Yoke   2 Bracket, commutator end   3 Bush for armature, commutator end   4 Oiler for dynamo
5 Springs, set, for brush tension   6 Brushes, set, for dynamo   7 Bracket, drive end   8 Ballbearing, drive end
9 Field coil for dynamo   10 Armature for dynamo   11 Bolt for bracket   12 Pulley for dynamo   13 Fan for dynamo
14 Distance washer for fan   15 Woodruff key   16 Special nut   17 Spring washer   18 Mounting plate for dynamo
19 Setbolt ($\frac{5}{16}$ inch UNF x $\frac{3}{4}$ inch long)   20 Spring washer   21 Plain washer   22 Anchor bracket for dynamo
23 Bolt ($\frac{5}{16}$ inch UNF x 1 inch long)   24 Plain washer   25 Spring washer   26 Nut ($\frac{5}{16}$ inch UNF)
27 Bolt ($\frac{5}{16}$ inch UNF x 1 inch long)   28 Spring washer   29 Nut ($\frac{5}{16}$ inch UNF)   30 Adjusting link for dynamo
31 Setbolt ($\frac{5}{16}$ inch UNF x $2\frac{1}{4}$ inch long)   32 Spring washer   33 Distance piece   34 Setbolt ($\frac{5}{16}$ inch UNC x $\frac{7}{8}$ inch long)
35 Spring washer   36 Plain washer

When removing one battery from a diesel vehicle, always remove the connecting battery lead from both batteries.

12:3 The generator (dynamo)

Although detail differences exist between the three types, all the generators conform to the general configuration of **FIG 12:1**.

To test the generator in situ:

If the generator fails to charge, first check and, if necessary, adjust the driving belt tension. Petrol models should have $\frac{1}{2}$ to $\frac{3}{4}$ inch (12 to 19 mm) and diesel models $\frac{3}{16}$ to $\frac{1}{4}$ inch (4 to 6 mm) deflection of the belt at the mid point between the crankshaft and generator pulleys. Should this fail to correct the trouble, proceed as follows:

1 Disconnect the two cables from the generator, then link the terminals together with a short lead.
2 Start the engine and allow to run at idling speed. Clip one lead of a good quality moving coil voltmeter, calibrated 0 to 20 volts, to the linked terminals of the generator. Clip the other lead from the voltmeter to a good earthing point on the body (yoke) of the generator.
3 Gradually increase the engine speed; the voltmeter reading should rise rapidly without fluctuations. Do not allow the voltmeter reading to reach 20 volts and do not race the engine in an attempt to obtain a reading. An engine speed of 1000 rev/min should not be exceeded.
4 No reading points to brush gear failure, a reading of $\frac{1}{2}$ to 1 volt is a possible fault in the field winding and 4 to 5 volts, a faulty armature.
5 If the generator is found to be serviceable, remove the link connecting the terminals and reconnect the cables to the control box.

To service the generator:

If the armature or field coil is faulty, the wisest plan is to exchange the whole generator for a factory rebuilt unit. However, it may be that attention to the brush gear and commutator will effect a cure.

Refer to **FIG 12:1**.

1 Unscrew the two through-bolts 11 and withdraw them.
2 Pull off the commutator end bracket, 2, complete with the brush gear attached.
3 Pull off the drive end bracket 7, complete with the armature. A thin steel or fibre thrust washer may be fitted to the spindle at the commutator end; do not lose this.
4 If the ball race 8 is slack or roughness can be felt when the bracket is rotated, the race can be renewed (refer to **FIGS 12:3** and **12:4**).
5 With the armature free of its bearings, examine the commutator. Early types are fabricated, later ones are moulded. If it is only discoloured, it can be cleaned up by rotating the armature in a lathe and holding a piece of glasspaper to the surface. If it is pitted or burnt, mount the armature in the lathe between centres and, using a sharp tool, fine feed and medium speed, remove the minimum amount of metal to just clean up the surface. A moulded commutator must not be reduced beyond 1.450 inch (36.83 mm) diameter.

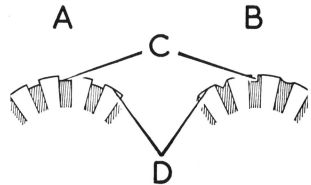

FIG 12:2 Undercutting the commutator

Key to Fig 12:2   **A** Correct   **B** Incorrect
C Insulators   **D** Segments

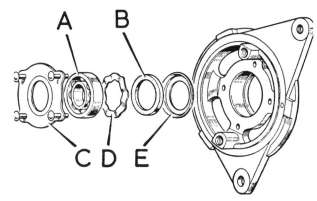

FIG 12:3 Bearing location, early type

Key to Fig 12:3   **A** Bearing   **B** Felt washer
C Retaining plate   **D** Corrugated washer
E Retaining washer

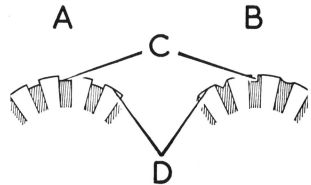

FIG 12:4 Bearing location, latest type

Key to Fig 12:4   **A** Circlip   **B** Bearing   **C** Felt ring
retaining plate   **D** Circlip extractor notch   **E** Bearing
retaining plate   **F** Pressure ring   **G** Felt ring   **H** End plate

After this, the insulation between the copper segments of the early type fabricated commutator must be undercut as shown in **FIG 12:2** to a depth of $\frac{1}{32}$ inch (.7 mm). A hacksaw blade ground to the width of the insulation is the best tool for this operation. **A moulded commutator cannot be undercut.**

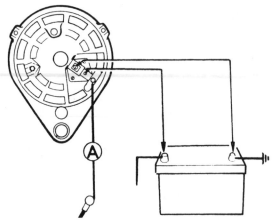

FIG 12:5   Alternator output test

Key to Fig 12:5   A Ammeter

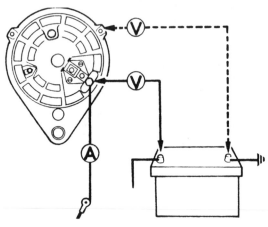

FIG 12:6   Charging circuit, voltage drop test

Key to Fig 12:6   A Ammeter   **V** Voltmeter

6 Press the drive end bracket on to the armature spindle, refit the Woodruff key and the pulley.

7 Clean up the brush gear and brushes using a petrol moistened cloth. Hold the armature in the commutator end bracket and position the brushes against the commutator. If they are well down in the brush boxes, renew them. Make sure all the brushes move freely ; ease any high spots with a fine file if necessary. If only one brush is worn or damaged all the brushes must be renewed.

8 Reassemble the generator by first inserting the armature and drive end bracket into the yoke (body). Place the brushes in their boxes with the springs against the side of each brush. Replace the commutator end bracket until the brushes are just over the commutator, then with a thin screwdriver press the brushes down and position the brush springs behind the brushes. Complete the insertion of the armature.

9 Replace and tighten the through-bolts.

10 Inject a few drops of SAE.30 oil into the oil hole at the end of the commutator bearing housing.

12:4 *The 11 ACR alternator*

Warning: If a fast charger is used to boost the battery or start the engine, withdraw the three-way connector from the 4TR control box. Do not reconnect until the charger is withdrawn and the engine speed is reduced to idling. Disconnect the battery completely when any work is being done on the alternator or its control gear.

Testing the system :

1 Check the alternator driving belt for correct tension.

2 Disconnect the battery negative terminal and the 35 amp alternator output lead. Connect a good quality moving coil ammeter between the output terminal and the alternator output lead.

3 Disconnect the leads from the alternator field terminals and connect them to the battery terminals with extension leads. Polarity is not important (see **FIG 12:5**).

4 Reconnect the battery negative terminal. Start the engine and speed up until the alternator is running at about 4000 rev/min. The ammeter should read 40 amps if the alternator and output cable are in order.

5 If a zero or low reading is obtained, check the output circuit and wiring by connecting a voltmeter between the alternator output terminal and the battery positive terminal and noting the reading (see **FIG 12:6**), then transfer the voltmeter to the alternator frame and the battery negative terminal, noting the reading. If either reading exceeds .5-volt, there is high resistance in the circuit that must be corrected.

6 If the test at paragraph 5 does not reveal high resistance and the alternator output is low, examine the brush gear. If no fault can be found here, the alternator must either be overhauled or renewed.

7 If the alternator output is in order, disconnect the battery negative terminal, remove the ammeter and connect the alternator output cable to its terminal. Remove the extension leads from the alternator field cables.

8 Connect the battery negative terminal. Switch on the ignition and check that battery voltage is applied to the cable normally attached to the alternator field terminals by connecting a voltmeter across them. A reading of battery voltage proves that the field isolating relay circuit and wiring is in order. Conversely, a low or zero reading indicates a fault in the field isolating relay or the isolating contacts in the ignition switch (as applicable) associated wiring or the alternator control unit. To test the field isolating relay, refer to **FIG 12:7** and connect terminals **C1** and **C2** in series with a 1.5 watt bulb and a 12-volt battery. Connect terminals **W1** and **W2** to the

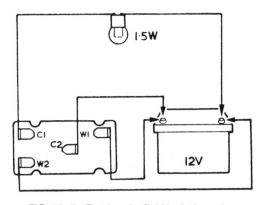

FIG 12:7   Testing the field isolating relay

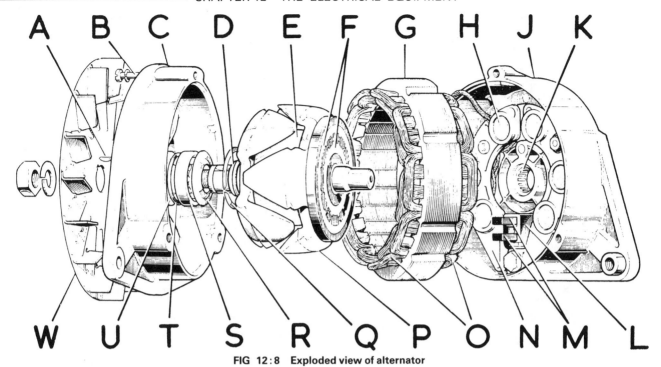

FIG 12:8 Exploded view of alternator

Key to Fig 12:8   **A** Woodruff key   **B** Through-bolt (3)   **C** Drive end bracket   **D** Jump ring shroud   **E** Rotor (field) winding
F Slip rings   **G** Stator laminations   **H** Silicon diodes (6)   **J** Slip ring end bracket   **K** Needle roller bearing   **L** Brush box
M Brushes (2)   **N** Diode heat sink (2)   **O** Stator winding   **P** Rotor   **Q** Circlip   **R** Bearing retainer plate
S Ballbearing, drive end   **T** O-ring   **U** O-ring retaining washer   **W** Fan

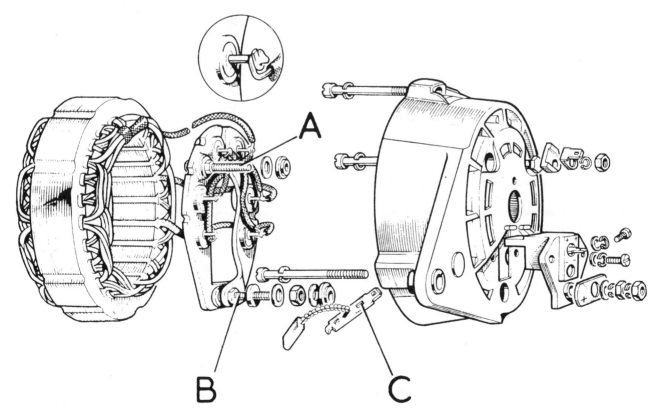

FIG 12:9 Slip ring end showing heat sinks

Key to Fig 12:9   **A** Warning light terminal 'AL'   **B** Output terminal   **C** Terminal block retaining tongue

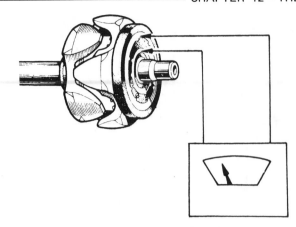

FIG 12:10   Testing rotor with an ohmmeter

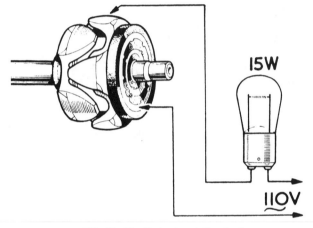

FIG 12:11   Rotor insulation test

battery terminals. The bulb should light when the relay winding between **W1** and **W2** is energized. If the bulb does not light, the relay winding or contacts are faulty and the relay must be renewed.

Servicing the alternator:

In this section, refer to **FIG 12:8**.
To strip the unit, proceed as follows:

1 Remove the nut and spring washer from the rotor shaft and withdraw the pulley and fan.
2 Scribe a line from the drive end bracket **C** across the laminations **G** and on to the slip ring end bracket **J**. This is to enable them to be reassembled in the right angular relationship with one another.
3 Remove the three through-bolts **B** and withdraw the drive end bracket and rotor as one assembly from the stator.
4 Remove the Woodruff key and bearing collar, then press out the rotor shaft from the drive end bracket.
5 Remove the circlip **Q** and the retaining plate **R**, then press out the ballbearing **S**. Remove the O-ring **T** and its retaining washer **U**.
6 Remove the plastic cover from the brush box **L**. Undo the nut and remove the 35 amp Lucar blade and plastic strip from the output terminal. Remove the locknut and washer. Undo the two securing screws and washers and withdraw the brush box **L**.

7 Withdraw the brush-spring-terminal assemblies **M** from the brush box **L**.
8 Remove the nut and washer from the warning light 'AL' terminal. Lift off the 17½ amp Lucar blade and the insulating bush.
9 Remove the bolt and washer securing the slip ring end to the heat sinks. Withdraw the stator end heat sinks from the end bracket as shown in **FIG 12:9**, noting the insulating and plain washers at the 'AL' and output terminal posts.
10 Note the connections to the diodes and unsolder them, using a pair of long-nosed pliers as a thermal shunt. Great care must be taken to do this operation quickly to avoid overheating the diodes. Be careful not to bend their pins. Remove the nut holding the heat sinks together, then separate them, noting the insulation washers. The alternator is now dismantled.

Inspection and testing of alternator:

1 Measure the brush spring length. A new brush is $\frac{5}{8}$ inch long (15.9 mm) and must be replaced at $\frac{5}{32}$ inch long (4mm). Check that the brushes move freely in their holders. If not, clean with petrol moistened cloth and lightly polish the brush sides with a smooth file if necessary. Note that the brush which bears on the inner slip ring is the positive brush.

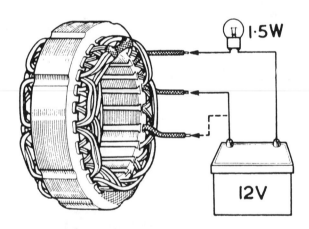

FIG 12:12   Stator winding continuity test

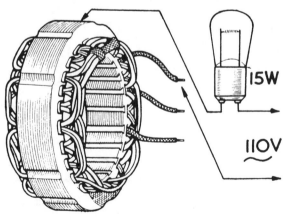

FIG 12:13   Stator winding insulation test

2 The surfaces of the slip rings must be smooth and clean. Wipe the surfaces with a petrol moistened cloth, or, if there are signs of burning, with smooth glasspaper. No attempt should be made to machine the rings.

3 Test the rotor windings by connecting an ohmmeter between the slip rings (see **FIG 12 : 10**). The reading should be 3.8 ohms at 68°F (20°C.)

Test the slip ring/rotor winding insulation by using a 110-volt AC mains supply with a test lamp in series with a slip ring and rotor pole (see **FIG 12 : 11**). If the lamp lights, the insulation has broken down and the rotor must be renewed.

4 Check the continuity of the stator windings with the stator cables separated from the heat sinks. Connect any two of the three cables in series with a 1.5 watt test lamp and a 12-volt battery (see **FIG 12 : 12**). Repeat, replacing one of the two cables with the third cable. If the lamp fails to light, part of the winding is open circuit and the stator must be renewed.

Test the insulation between the coils and laminations with a 110-volt AC supply and 15 watt bulb in series with any one of the three cable ends and the lamination (see **FIG 12 : 13**). If the bulb lights, the stator coils are earthing and the stator must be renewed.

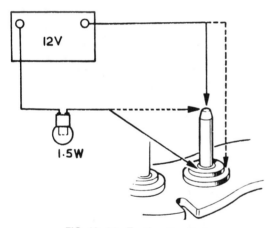

FIG 12 : 14   Testing the diodes

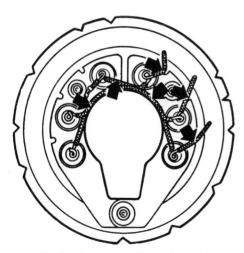

FIG 12 : 15   Layout of heat sink cables

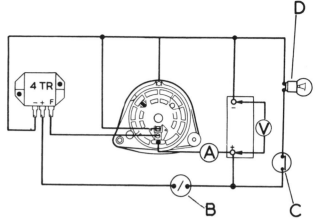

FIG 12 : 16   Control unit test circuit

Key to Fig 12 : 16   **A** Ammeter   **B** Field isolating relay
C Side and tail lamp switch   **D** Side and tail lamps
V Voltmeter

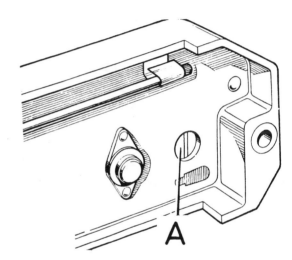

FIG 12 : 17   Control unit rear view

Key to FIG 12 : 17   A Potentiometer adjuster

5 There are two heat sink assemblies, one positive and the other negative. Each carries three diodes which are not separately replaceable. If one is defective the whole heat sink must be replaced.

For service purposes, the diodes can be tested as shown in **FIG 12 : 14**. Disconnect the stator leads from the diodes as described earlier if this has not already been done. Connect a 12-volt battery and 1.5 watt bulb in series with each diode and reverse the connections. The bulb should light up in one direction only. If it lights with the connections made in either direction or fails to light at all, the diode is defective and the heat sink must be renewed.

Warning : Never use the type of ohmmeter which incorporates a hand driven generator for checking diodes.

6 Check the ballbearing for roughness or slack. Any doubt must involve renewal. In the unlikely event of the needle roller bearing becoming defective, the whole slip ring end bracket must be renewed.

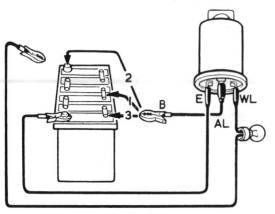

FIG 12:18 **Warning light control test**

Key to Fig 12:18   Connect battery clip **B** in sequence 1, 2 and 3

Reassembly of the alternator:

1 Resolder the stator wires to the diodes using M grade 45/55 tin/lead solder. Observe the same precautions against overheating or bending the pins as described for dismantling.

2 After soldering, tack the connections down with 3M.EC.1022 adhesive so that the layout appears as shown in **FIG 12:15** and gives adequate clearance for the rotor.

3 The rest of the assembly procedure is the reverse of dismantling, but particularly note these points:

(a) The insulation washers between the heat sinks are in the order of: thick plain washer, thin plain washer, then small plain washer.

(b) Refit the plain and insulating washers to the 'AL' and output terminal posts before fitting the stator to the slip ring end bracket.

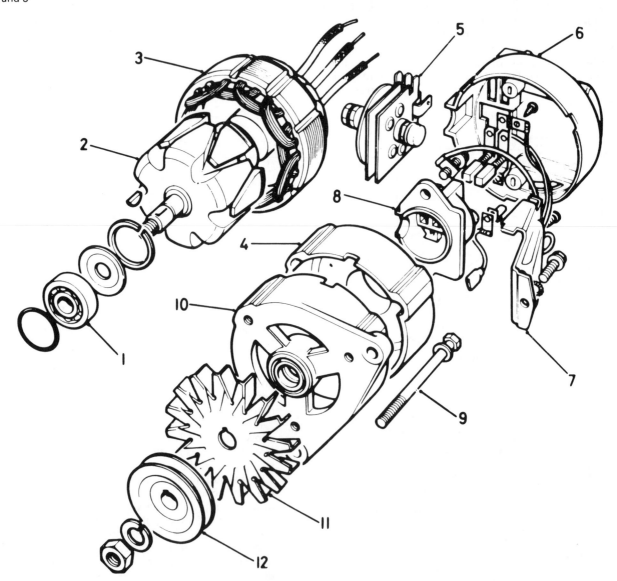

FIG 12:19 **The 16 ACR alternator**

Key to Fig 12:19   1 Drive end bearing   2 Rotor and slip ring   3 Stator   4 Slip ring end bracket   5 Rectifier
6 End cover   7 Regulator   8 Brush box   9 Through-bolt   10 Drive end bracket   11 Fan   12 Pulley

(c) Fit the two small insulating washers under the brush box.

(d) To ensure the Lucar terminals of the brushes are properly retained, the tongue should be levered up to make an angle of 30 deg. with the terminal blade.

(e) Support the inner journal of the drive end bearing when pressing in the rotor shaft. Do not use the bracket as support for the bearing while fitting the rotor shaft.

(f) Align the drive end bracket, laminations and slip ring bracket with the line previously scribed along these three components and tighten the three bolts evenly. Check that the rotor spins freely.

The control unit, test and adjust :

Testing the unit :

1 Refer to **FIG 12 : 16**. Disconnect the alternator main output lead and connect a 50 amp range ammeter in series with the lead and the alternator. Connect a voltmeter of at least one per cent accuracy between the battery terminals and note the reading with all the electrical equipment switched off.

2 Switch on the side and tail lamps to give a load of approximately 2 amps.

3 Start the engine and run the alternator at 3000 rev/min for at least 8 minutes to stabilize the system. If the charging current is then still above 10 amps, continue to run until this figure has been reached. The voltmeter should then read 13.9 to 14.3 volts.

4 If the reading on the voltmeter is stable but outside these limits, adjustment is possible. If the reading remains unchanged at open circuit battery voltage or increases in an uncontrollable manner, the control unit must be renewed.

Adjusting the unit :

1 Stop the engine and remove the control unit securing screws, invert the unit and carefully scrape away the compound that covers the potentiometer adjuster (see **FIG 12 : 17)**.

2 Start the engine and run the alternator at about 3000 rev/min with the voltmeter firmly connected to the battery. Turn the adjuster clockwise to increase the voltage or anticlockwise to decrease it. A small movement makes an appreciable difference to the voltage reading.

3 Check the setting by stopping the engine, then restarting and running up to 3000 rev/min again when the correct voltage should be shown.

The alternator warning light control :

The warning light control is a thermally operated relay for controlling the switching on and off of an instrument panel warning light. It is connected to the centre point of one pair of the alternator diodes through terminal 'AL' on the alternator, and to earth. The indication given by the warning light is similar to that provided by the ignition ('No charge') warning light used with dynamo charging systems.

Warning : Due to the external similarity of the alternator warning light control model 3AW to flasher unit model FL5, a distinctive green label is applied to the aluminium case of model 3AW.

FIG 12 : 20   Unsoldering the stator connections

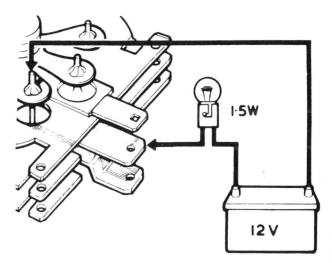

FIG 12 : 21   Testing the diodes

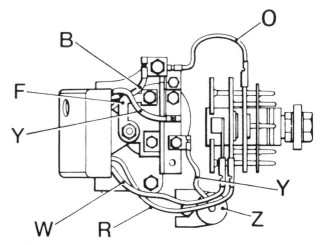

FIG 12 : 22   Regulator, brush box and rectifier leads, 16ACR

Key to Fig 12 : 22	**B** Black	**F** Metal link	**O** Orange
R Red	**W** White	**Y** Yellow	**Z** Surge protection

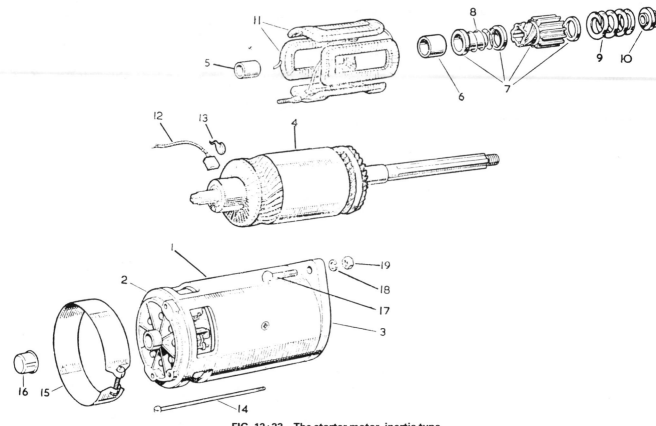

FIG 12:23 The starter motor, inertia type

Key to Fig 12:23 1 Yoke 2 Bracket for starter, commutator end 3 Bracket, drive end 4 Armature 5 Brush, commutator end 6 Bush, pinion end 7 Pinion and sleeve 8 Spring for pinion 9 Main spring for pinion 10 Nut for pinion 11 Field coil for starter 12 Brushes for starter motor, set 13 Spring set for brushes 14 Bolt for bracket 15 Coverband 16 Grease cap 17 Bolt ($\frac{3}{8}$ inch BSF x $1\frac{1}{2}$ inch long) 18 Spring washer 19 Nut ($\frac{3}{8}$ inch BSF)

Care must be taken to avoid connecting either of these units into a circuit designed for the other.

Warning light control, to test (see FIG 12:18) :

1 Connect terminal **E** of the warning light control to the battery negative terminal.
2 Connect the 2.2 watt bulb in series with the terminal **WL** of the warning light control and the positive battery terminal. The bulb should light up immediately. If the bulb does not light up, the warning light control is faulty and must be replaced.
3 With the terminals connected as in 1 and 2 above, connect terminal **AL** of the warning light control to the 6-volt tapping of the battery. The bulb should go out within five seconds.
4 Transfer the battery connection of terminal **AL** to the positive battery terminal for ten seconds only. Then quickly transfer it to the battery 2-volt tapping. The bulb should light up within five seconds.
5 If the performance in items 3 and 4 differs appreciably from the test requirements, the unit is faulty and must be replaced.

12:5 *The 16 or 18 ACR alternator*

Testing the system :

1 Check that the fan belt tension is correct and that all charging circuit connections are secure. The ignition warning light is connected in series with the alternator field circuit. Bulb failure will prevent the alternator charging except at very high engine speeds.
2 Run the engine at the fast-idle speed until the engine is at its normal operating temperature. Stop the engine.
3 Withdraw the connector from the alternator and remove the end cover. Link the terminals marked 'F' and '–'.
4 Connect a 0-75 ammeter between the alternator and the battery. Connect a 0-30 voltmeter across the battery terminals. Connect a 15 ohm 35 amp variable resistor across the battery terminals. Do not connect for longer than is necessary to conduct the tests as it will become hot.
5 Start the engine and run it at 750 rev/min. The warning light should go out. Increase the engine speed to 3000 rev/min and adjust the variable resistance until the voltmeter reads 14 volts. The ammeter should then read 34 or 45 amps. If appreciable deviation is found, as applicable, dismantle and service the alternator. If the test is satisfactory, proceed with the regulator test.

Regulator test :

6 Disconnect the variable resistor and remove the link joining the terminals marked 'F' and '–'.

7 With the remainder of the circuit unaltered, run the engine at 3000 rev/min until the ammeter shows an output current of less than 10 amps.

8 The voltmeter reading should then be between 13.6 and 14.4 volts. Any appreciable deviation from the test figures stated indicates that a new regulator is required.

Dismantling the alternator:

1 Refer to the exploded diagram of the components in **FIG 12:19**; the 18 ACR is similar. Remove the rear cover.

2 Unsolder the stator connections from the rectifier pack, noting the position of the connections. The diodes will be damaged unless pliers are used as a heat sink as shown in **FIG 12:20**.

3 Unscrew the brush moulding securing screws and, if necessary, the lower regulator pack securing screw. Slacken the rectifier pack retaining nuts and withdraw both brush moulding, with or without regulator pack, and rectifier pack.

4 Remove the three through-bolts.

5 Fit a tube over the slip ring moulding so that it registers against the outer track of the slip ring end bearing and carefully drive out the bearing from its housing.

6 Remove the pulley and fan, taking care to collect the shaft key. Press the rotor from the drive end bracket if required.

7 Remove the circlip securing the drive end bearing and remove the bearing.

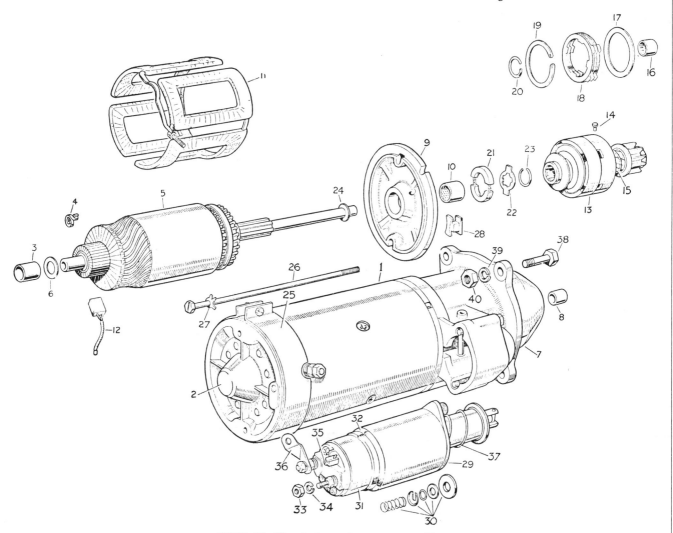

FIG 12:24 The starter motor, pre-engaged type

Key to Fig 12:24 1 Yoke 2 Bracket, commutator end 3 Bush, commutator end 4 Spring set for brushes 5 Armature 6 Thrust washer, commutator end 7 Bracket for starter, drive end 8 Bush for bracket 9 Bracket for brake 10 Bush for brake bracket 11 Field coil for starter 12 Brushes for starter motor, set 13 Drive assembly for starter motor 14 Rivet for pinion retaining ring 15 Return spring for starter pinion 16 Bush, pinion end 17 Clutch adjusting shim 18 Clutch plates 19 Circlip retaining clutch assembly 20 Lockring retaining clutch plates 21 Brake shoe complete with springs 22 Driving washer for brake shoe 23 Lockring retaining brake 24 Lockring 25 Coverband for starter 26 Bolt for starter motor 27 Lockwasher for bolt 28 Rubber grommet in drive end bracket 29 Solenoid for starter motor 30 Contact plate for solenoid 31 Base for solenoid 32 Gasket for starter solenoid base 33 Terminal nut for starter solenoid 34 Terminal washer for starter solenoid 35 Terminal screw for solenoid 36 Terminal connector for starter motor 37 Plunger spring for solenoid 38 Bolt ($\frac{7}{16}$ inch UNC x $1\frac{1}{4}$ inch long) Setbolt ($\frac{7}{16}$ UNF x 2 inch long) 39 Spring washer 40 Nut ($\frac{7}{16}$ inch UNF)

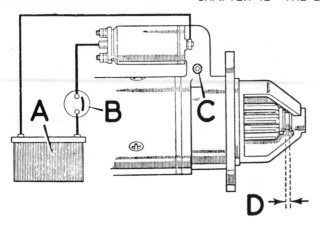

FIG 12:25 Adjusting pinion clearance

Key to Fig 12:25   A Battery   **B** Switch   **C** Eccentric pin
D Clearance .005 to .015 inch (.12 to .40 mm)

8 To remove the slip ring end bearing, the field connections to the slip ring assembly must first be unsoldered.

Inspection and testing of alternator:

The brushes should be replaced if less than .2 inch (5 mm) for 16 ACR or .3 inch (8 mm) for 18 ACR protrudes from the brush box moulding. Check that the brushes move freely in their holders, cleaning their sides with a petrol moistened cloth or very fine file if necessary. The spring pressure should be 9 to 13 oz when the face of the brush is pushed back flush with the housing.

Test the stator as for the 11 ACR alternator, but note that a 15 watt lamp should be used in place of the 1.5 watt lamp used for the 11 ACR.

To check the diodes in the rectifier pack, refer to **FIG 12:21**. Connect the 12 volt battery and 1.5 watt test lamp to each of the nine diode pins and corresponding heat sinks in turn. Reverse the connections. The lamp must light when connected one way but not the other. If this is not so, renew the rectifier pack.

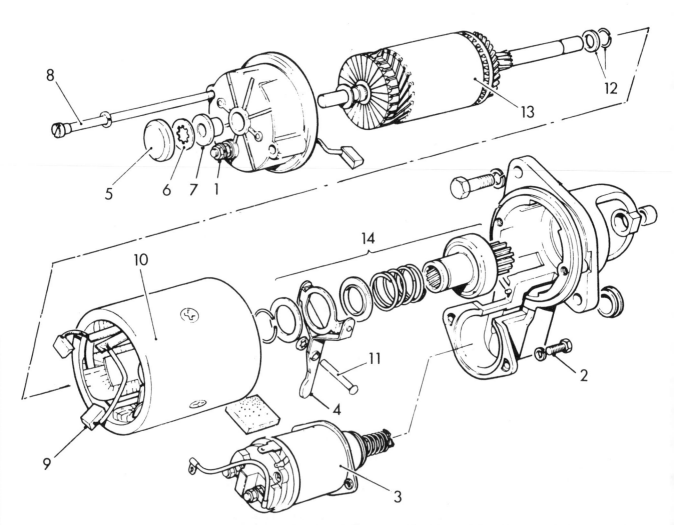

FIG 12:26 Lucas 3M100PE starter motor

Key to Fig 12:26   1 Nut   2 Bolts   3 Solenoid   4 Lever   5 End cap seal   6 Spire ring   7 Bush   8 Bolts
9 Field brushes   10 Yoke   11 Pivot pin   12 Thrust collar and jump ring   13 Armature   14 Roller clutch lever and drive

Reassembly:

Reverse the dismantling procedure. Lubricate the bearings with Shell Alvania 'RA'. Use Fry's H.T.3 solder on the slip ring field connections.

When refitting the rotor to the drive end bracket, ensure that the inner track of the bearing is supported.

Reconnect the leads between the regulator, brush box and rectifier as shown in **FIG 12:22** for the 16 ACR or as noted on the 18 ACR.

12:6 *The starter motors*

(a) Inertia type:

Servicing the starter, refer to FIG 12:23:

1 Remove the coverband 15, hold back the brush springs and release the brushes 12.
2 Pull out the splitpin and unscrew the nut holding the starter drive pinion, early models; on later models, compress the spring and remove the circlip. Remove the drive pinion assembly.
3 Unscrew the two long through-bolts 14, then pull off the brackets from each end of the yoke. Remove the armature.
4 Clean all the components with a petrol moistened cloth, then service the brushes and brush gear as described in **Section 12:3** for the generator. If new brushes are to be fitted, the flexible connectors must be soldered to the terminal tags. Two are connected to the brush boxes and two to the free ends of the field coil.
5 Clean up or machine the commutator in exactly the same way as described for the generator, see **Section 12:3, but do not undercut the insulation.**
6 Reassemble the starter by reversing the dismantling process, fitting the brushes by holding them in place with the springs at their sides and then moving the springs over to bear on their rear faces when the unit has been assembled. Refit the coverband.
7 The starter drive components must be cleaned thoroughly before reassembly. Do not use grease or oil to lubricate the parts as this will collect dirt and cause the drive to jam. The best lubricant is flake graphite rubbed on the bearing surfaces.

Servicing the starter:

(b) Pre-engaged type, refer to FIG 12:24:

1 Remove the coverband 25, then disconnect the copper link between the lower solenoid terminal and the starter casing.
2 Remove the solenoid securing bolts and withdraw it from the drive end bracket, ensuring that the plunger is free from the fork in the engagement lever.
3 Remove the two through-bolts, then pull off the commutator end bracket and brush gear 2.
4 Remove the rubber seal from the drive end bracket 7.
5 Remove the eccentric pin on which the engagement lever pivots.
6 Split the yoke 1, intermediate bracket 9 and drive end bracket 7.
7 Slide the drive assembly 13 and engagement lever off the shaft, first removing the lockring 24 from the end of the armature shaft extension.

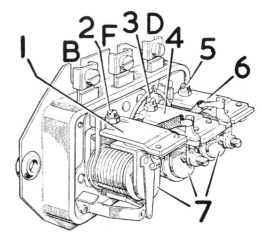

FIG 12:27 Current voltage regulator, RB106

Key to Fig 12:27　1 Cut-out　2 Cut-out adjusting screw
3 Current adjusting screw　　　4 Current regulator
5 Voltage adjusting screw　　　6 Voltage regulator
7 Armature　**B** Terminal　**F** Terminal　**D** Terminal

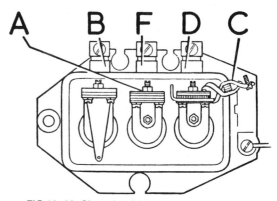

FIG 12:28 Shortcircuiting the voltage regulator

Key to Fig 12:28　　**A** Current regulator adjusting screw
B Terminal　　**C** Clip, shortcircuiting　　**D** Terminal
F Terminal

8 Slide the intermediate bracket 9 and brake assembly 21 off the shaft.
9 Clean all components thoroughly with a petrol moistened cloth.
10 Service the brushes and commutator exactly as described for the petrol engine starter.

To rebuild the starter, reverse the dismantling process. When fitting the starter drive clutch unit, make sure it moves freely on the armature shaft, then smear the shaft with general purpose grease.

The engagement of the pinion movement must now be set. Proceed as follows, referring to **FIG 12:25** for clarity.

1 Connect a 12 volt supply to the small centre terminal and a solenoid as shown.
2 Close the switch **B**, thus throwing the drive into engagement.
3 Keep light pressure against the pinion to take up any slack, then turn the eccentric pivot pin **C**, until the dimension **D** is .005 to .015 inch (.12 to .40 mm). After setting, lock the nut.

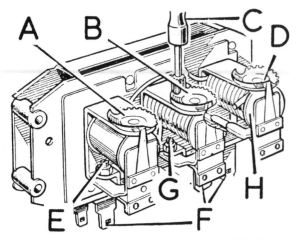

FIG 12:29   Current voltage regulator, RB340

Key to Fig 12:29   A Adjustment cam of voltage regulator
B Adjustment cam of current regulator   **C** Special setting tool
D Adjustment cam of cut-out relay   **E** Adjustable contact
of voltage regulator   **F** Lucar connection terminals
G Adjustable contact of current regulator   **H** Core face of
cut-out relay

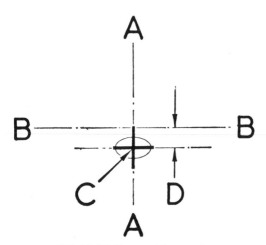

FIG 12:30   Beam setting marks

Key to Fig 12:30   AA Vertical centreline of headlamp
BB Horizontal centreline of headlamp measured from level floor
C Centre of concentrated area of light   **D** 2 inch ± 1 inch
(50 mm ± 25 mm)

(c) Pre-engaged type, 3.5 litre, refer to FIG 12:26 :

Remove the nut 1 and the washers securing the starter to the solenoid link, then remove the two bolts 2 securing the solenoid to the bracket. Lift the terminal end of the solenoid clear of the connecting link and remove the solenoid.

Remove the piston by pushing against the spring and detaching the drive engagement lever 4.

Remove the end cap seal 5. Remove the spire retaining ring by using a chisel to cut off some of its claws. Remove the bush 7.

Remove the two through-bolts 8 and the commutator end cover, disengaging the two field coil brushes 9 from the brush box. Withdraw the yoke and field coil assembly 10.

The mounting bracket is removed from the roller clutch and lever assembly by removing the spire ring and pivot pin 11 from the drive engagement lever. Remove the clutch drive and lever assembly by driving the thrust collar 12 from the jump ring with a tubular drift.

The starter motor is reassembled in the reverse order, noting that new spire rings must be fitted, the ring on the armature shaft being driven on to give a maximum clearance of .010 inch (.25 mm) between the retaining ring and the bearing bush shoulder.

12:7 The control box, DC generator (dynamo)

When cleaning current or voltage regulator contacts, use a fine carborundum stone or silicone carbide paper followed by washing with methylated spirit. When cleaning the cut-out contacts, use fine glasspaper; never carborundum stone or emerycloth.

Checking the voltage regulator, type RB106 (see FIG 12:27) :

Place a piece of paper between the cut-out contacts 1, connect a 0 to 20 moving coil voltmeter to the **D** terminal on the regulator and to a good earth (not the one on the box). Start the engine and increase the rev/min until the voltage remains constant. This should occur between 15.8 and 16.4 volts. If it does, transfer the earth lead of the voltmeter to the **E** terminal on the box. If the reading is now lower, the fault lies in a bad connection between the box and earth. If the reading was incorrect in the first instance, reset the voltage regulator as follows :

1 Disconnect control box terminal **B**. Connect a good moving coil 0 to 20 voltmeter between terminal **D** and earth.
2 Start the engine and increase speed until the voltmeter needle flicks and steadies. This should occur at between 14.2 and 14.8 volts. If it does not, stop the engine and remove the control box cover. Slacken the adjusting screw locknut 5 and turn the screw clockwise to raise the voltage setting, anticlockwise to lower it. Turn the screw a fraction at a time and retighten the locknut. Start the engine and check the reading. Repeat until the correct reading is obtained. Reconnect terminal **B** to its cable.

When the generator is run at high speed on open circuit it builds up a high voltage. When carrying out this adjustment, do not run the engine up to more than half throttle or a false reading will be obtained. Try to keep the periods of running below 30 seconds, otherwise heating of the regulator winding can also cause a false reading to be given.

Checking the current regulator :

1 Refer to **FIG 12:28** and shortcircuit the voltage regulator with a large crocodile clip as shown.
2 Disconnect the two cables from terminal **B** and connect a good 0 to 40 amp ammeter between the cables and the terminal. Do not leave any cables attached to terminal **B** except the ammeter cable.
3 Switch on all lamps and accessories to load the circuit. Check that the ammeter is correctly wired to show a discharge.

4 Start the engine and speed up until the generator is running at approximately 3000 rev/min. The ammeter should be steady and show a current of 19 amps (C39 dynamo). If not, slacken the locknut on the adjusting screw **A** and turn as described for setting the voltage regulator. Remake the terminal **B** connection.

To set the cut-out:

1 Connect a good moving coil 0 to 20 voltmeter between terminal **D** and earth.
2 Switch on the headlamps, start the engine and slowly speed up. A slight drop in the meter reading should occur between 12.7 and 13.3 volts to indicate closure of the contacts. If this does not occur, adjust screw 2 (see **FIG 12:27**) until it does. Stop the engine.
3 Disconnect the cable from terminal **B** and connect the voltmeter between the terminal and earth. Start the engine, run up to a good charging speed, then slowly decelerate. Note the point at which the reading suddenly drops to zero. This should be between 9.5 and 10.5 volts. If not, carefully bow the legs of the fixed contact post until the armature releases at the proper voltage. Reconnect the cable to terminal **B**.

To set the air gaps, current and voltage regulators:

1 Slacken the two screws so that the armature is loosely attached to the frame.

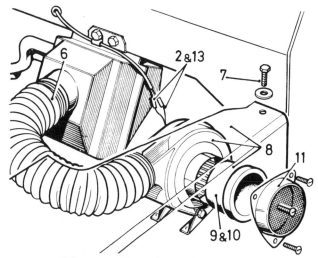

FIG 12:31 **Removing the heater motor**

Ket to Fig 12:31 2 Electrical connection 6 Air hose 7 Wing panel bolt 9 and 10 Air inlet and seal 11 Air intake grille 13 Electrical connection

2 Unscrew the fixed contact adjustment screw until it is well clear of the armature contact.
3 Unscrew the adjustment screw, 3 or 5 (see **FIG 12:27**), well clear of the tension spring.
4 Insert a .015 inch (.381 mm) feeler gauge between the armature and the copper disc. Take care not to damage the copper disc.

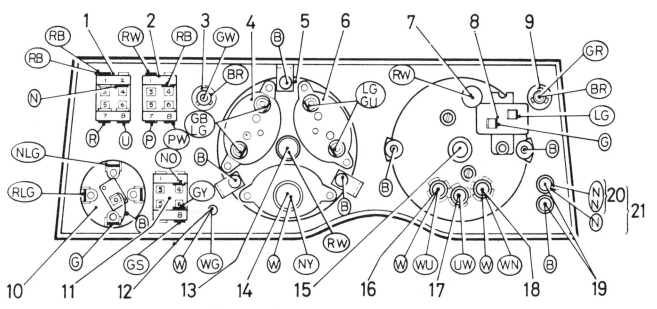

FIG 12:32 **Instrument panel (Series 3) from the rear**

Key to Fig 12:32 1 Lighting switch 2 Panel light switch, also interior light switch on Station Wagon models 3 RH turn indicator warning light 4 Fuel contents gauge 5 Grouped instruments 6 Coolant temperature gauge 7 Panel illumination light 8 Instruments voltage stabilizer 9 LH turn indicator warning light 10 Wiper/wash switch 11 Heater switch (where fitted) 12 Fuel level warning light (diesel models) 13 Panel illumination light 14 Battery charge warning light 15 Speedometer drive head 16 Cold start warning light 17 Headlamp main beam warning light 18 Oil pressure warning light 19 Inspection lamp sockets 20 Leads for petrol models 21 Leads for diesel models

Key to electrical cable colours: Where cables have two colour code letters, the first denotes the main colour and the latter denotes the tracer colour
B Black **G** Green **R** Red **U** Blue **O** Orange **S** Slate **N** Brown **P** Purple **W** White **Y** Yellow **D** Dark **L** Light

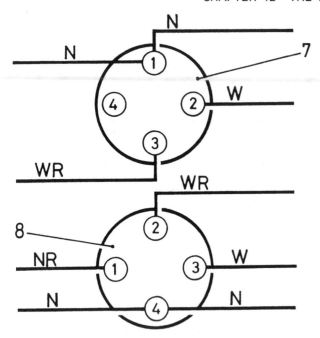

FIG 12:33   Ignition starter switch connection

Key to Fig 12:33   7 Petrol engines   8 Diesel engines
N Brown   **W** White   **R** Red

5 Press the armature firmly against the gauge and tighten the screws.
6 Hold the gauge in position and screw in the fixed contact adjustment screw until it just touches the armature, then tighten the locknut.
7 Carry out the electrical settings as previously described.

To set the air gap (cut-out relay):

1 Slacken the two screws so that the armature is loosely attached to the frame.
2 Unscrew adjustment screw 2 (see **FIG 12:27**) well clear of the spring.
3 Press the armature down squarely on to the core face and tighten the two screws.
4 Hold the armature down and adjust the backstop so that there is a gap of .018 inch (.45 mm) between it and the armature moving contact blade.
5 Insert a .01 inch (.25 mm) feeler gauge between the armature and core. The gauge should be inserted from the side of the core nearest to the fixed contact post. The leading edge of the gauge should not be inserted beyond the centreline of the core face. Press the armature down and, if necessary, bow the fixed contact post legs until the contacts are just touching.
6 Carry out the electrical settings as described previously.

Current voltage regulators, type RB.310 and RB.340 (see FIG 12:29):

Setting of these control boxes is carried out in a similar manner to the RB.106 except that a special tool is needed to set the geared cams on the RB.340. This is Lucas Part No. 54381742.

Checking the voltage regulator:

1 Disconnect all cables from terminal **B** and then connect them together without touching any part of the vehicle.
2 Connect a 0 to 20 voltmeter between terminal **D** and earth.
3 Speed the generator up to 3000 rev/min. The reading should rise to a maximum value, then flick back and remain steady. This steady reading should lie within the following limits.

Ambient temperature	Voltage setting RB.310	RB.340
10°C (50°F)	15.1 to 15.7	14.9 to 15.5
20°C (68°F)	14.9 to 15.5	14.7 to 15.3
30°C (86°F)	14.7 to 15.3	14.5 to 15.1
40°C (104°F)	14.5 to 15.1	14.3 to 14.9

4 If the reading lies outside these limits, adjust the voltage regulator by turning the adjusting screw or cam exactly as described for the RB.106.

Checking the current regulator:

Proceed as for the type RB.106, but run the generator at 4500 rev/min. Adjust the current screw or cam until the meter reads 22 amps for a type C40 generator or 30 amps for a type C42.

To set the cut-out:

Proceed as for the RB.106. The drop in the meter reading should occur at the same value (12.7 to 13.3 volts). If not, adjust the cut-out with the engine idling and speed up to recheck. Repeat as necessary.

The drop off voltage (when the meter reading suddenly drops to zero) should occur between 9.5 and 11 volts.

To set the air gaps, current and voltage regulators:

RB.310   Set as for the RB.106.
RB.340   Proceed as follows:
1 Disconnect the battery, then turn the adjustment cam fully anticlockwise.
2 Screw the adjustable contact right back.
3 Insert a .045 inch (1.00 mm) gauge between the armature and the core, pushing it back as far as the two rivet heads on the underside of the armature (on the latest units, use a .052 inch (1.30 mm) gauge).
4 Screw in the contact until the gauge is just trapped. Tighten the locknut.
5 Check that the narrowest gap between the armature back face and the frame on both sides of the armature is between .030 to .040 inch (.76 to 1.00 mm) with a maximum of .010 inch (.25 mm) taper for current regulators.
6 Carry out the electrical setting of the voltage regulator, leaving the current regulator until the cut-out has been set mechanically and electrically.

To set the air gap, cut-out relay:

RB.310   Set as for the RB.106.
RB.340   Proceed as follows:
1 Turn the cam fully clockwise.
2 Press the armature down against the copper on the core face. Check that the narrowest part of the back gap, between the armature back face and the frame, is between .030 and .040 inch (.76 and 1.00 mm).

3 Insert a .015 inch (.38 mm) gauge between the head of the core and the armature. Press the armature down and bend the fixed contact bracket until the contacts just touch. Now adjust the armature backstop until it just touches the armature.

4 Check that the top gap, controlled by the backstop and using the nearest rivet as a datum, is from .035 to .045 inch (.8 to 1.0 mm).

5 Set the cut-out electrically as previously described.

12:8 Headlamp beam setting

Refer to **FIG 12:30**.

Draw the mark **C** on a vertical surface in two places the centre distance of the headlamps apart. Position the vehicle, unladen, 25 feet (7.6 metres) away on a level floor. Adjust the headlamps so that on main beam the concentrated area of light corresponds with mark **C**.

12:9 The heater plugs, diesel models

The heater plugs require no maintenance, but if, when they are in use, the warning lamp glows brightly, a shortcircuit is indicated. No light shows an open circuit.

If either of these conditions occur, first examine the fuse in the fuse box and replace if blown. Check the warning bulb and replace if necessary, although failure here will not affect the heater circuit.

For further tests, proceed as follows:

Connect one lead of a 12 volt test lamp to the earth lead terminal on No. 1 heater plug and the other lead to the battery positive terminal on negative earth vehicles or vice versa, whereon the bulb should light. If the bulb remains unlit, a faulty earth lead is indicated.

Move the test lamp lead from the earth terminal on No. 1 heater plug to the terminal, also on No. 1 plug, to which the interconnecting lead is attached. If the plug is serviceable the bulb will light, but a broken heater plug filament will be indicated by the lamp remaining unlit.

Check the remaining plugs in the same manner until the fault is located.

If the heater plugs are found serviceable, check each terminal of the resistance unit in the same way.

If the heater plugs are to be removed, proceed as follows, taking the greatest care not to distort or damage the element.

1 Disconnect the leads from the plugs, using two spanners at each terminal to prevent the central rod or insulating tube from twisting. Unscrew the plug from the cylinder.

2 Remove carbon from base of heater plug to avoid possible shortcircuiting of the element. Do not sandblast.

3 Examine the element for signs of fracture or severe heat attack and the seating for scores. Plugs with fractured elements must be replaced. Where scoring of the seating is sufficient to allow gas leakage or erosion of the element such that a fracture is likely to occur, then a replacement plug must be fitted.

4 Test the plug internal circuit for continuity by connecting it and a 12 volt sidelamp bulb in circuit to a 12 volt battery. **The inclusion of a bulb in circuit is essential.**

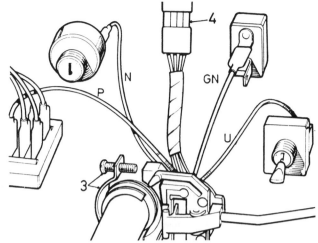

FIG 12:34 Combined flasher, headlamp and horn switch

Key to Fig 12:34   3 Clamp   4 Connector plug
G Green   **N** Brown   **P** Purple   **U** Blue

5 Ensure that the terminal nuts and threads are clean and that the thread at the base of the plug is free of carbon, then refit the plugs and tighten to 25 lb ft (3.4 mkg).

Note: Make sure the shakeproof washers are fitted under the terminals in order to maintain good electrical contact.

Replace the leads in accordance with the wiring diagram and tighten the terminals, using two spanners to each terminal.

12:10 The heater

The procedure for removing the blower motor is as follows:

See **FIG 12:31**. Disconnect the battery earth lead and the two leads to the blower, noting the colour connections.

From inside the cab, remove the trim board rail and withdraw the trim board from the clip. Remove the five screws securing the blower motor.

Disconnect the air hose at the inlet to the matrix.

Remove the wing panel rear top fixing bolt and manoeuvre the motor assembly clear, lifting the wing panel sufficiently to allow passage. Withdraw the air inlet seal.

Refitting:

Fit the blower motor, but omit the air inlet seal at this stage. Remove the air intake grille, then fit the air inlet seal and replace the grille.

Reverse the removal procedure for the rest of the operation.

12:11 The instrument panel, Series 3

It is necessary to remove the instrument panel to gain access to many instruments, switches and lamps as shown in the view from the rear given in **FIG 12:32**.

Disconnect the battery earth lead. Remove the two securing screws (one at each end of the panel) and pull the panel forward clear of the dash. It may be of assistance if the steering wheel is removed.

Press in the spring clip and pull out the cable assembly from the speedometer, then pull the panel out sufficiently to gain access to the wiring connections. Remove the inspection lamp socket leads and withdraw all warning and illumination lamp leads and bulbs complete with holders.

Disconnect the earth lead terminals at the knurled nuts on the combination instrument. Disconnect all Lucar connectors, then lift off the instrument panel and instruments complete.

Fitting is the reverse of the above.

12 : 12 *Ignition starter switch*

This is removed as follows:
Disconnect the battery earth lead, then remove the upper half of the switch shroud from the steering column. Disconnect the electrical leads from the switch.

On cars with a steering column lock there are two small screws locating the switch in the housing which must be removed to free the switch.

On cars without a steering column lock there is a locking ring which must be unscrewed.

Refitting is the reverse of the above, but refer to **FIG 12 : 33** for the correct wiring connections.

12 : 13 *Combined flasher, headlights and horn switch*

This is removed as follows:
Disconnect the battery earth lead, then remove the upper half of the switch shroud from the steering column.

Unscrew the securing screw in the clamp to free the switch, then pull it out sufficiently to disconnect the main harness at the plug connector.

Withdraw the instrument panel clear of the dash as detailed in **Section 12 : 11** and disconnect the switch leads from the flasher unit, lighting switch, fuse box and ignition switch. Withdraw the combined switch.

Reverse the above procedure to refit. See **FIG 12 : 34** for details of the wiring and connections.

12 : 14 *Setting switches*

Reverse light switch:

Engage reverse gear, with the switch connected, and switch the ignition on. Screw in the switch until the contacts are made and then a further half turn. Measure the clearance between the lower face of the switch and the gearbox, then select shim washers to suit the clearance. Shims are available in thicknesses of .020 inch (.5 mm) and .005 inch (.127 mm).

Fit the selected shim washers, screw in the switch and tighten to 15 to 20 lb ft (1.4 to 2 mkg).

Differential lock actuator switch:

Start the engine and move the vacuum control valve to the 'up' position, then proceed in exactly the same manner as for the reverse light switch just described.

12 : 15 *Fault diagnosis*

(a) Battery discharged

1 Battery unserviceable
2 Corroded battery terminals
3 Control box faulty
4 Generator faulty
5 Break in charging circuit

(b) Generator not charging

1 Slack driving belt
2 Generator loose
3 Break in circuit
4 Worn brushes
5 Commutator burnt (dynamo only)
6 Control box faulty

(c) Starter failure, petrol engine

1 Tight engine
2 Battery discharged
3 Break in starter circuit
4 Commutator burnt
5 Worn or sticking brushes
6 Pinion jammed in mesh

(d) Starter failure, diesel engine

1 Check 1 to 5 in (c)
2 Starter/heater switch unserviceable
3 Solenoid circuit broken
4 Solenoid defective

CHAPTER 13

THE BODYWORK

13:1 Description
13:2 Panel beating 'Birmabright' alloy
13:3 Gas welding 'Birmabright'
13:4 Riveting 'Birmabright'
13:5 Painting 'Birmabright'

13:6 General construction
13:7 Fitting seat belts
13:8 Removing the radiator grille panel
13:9 The heater water valve

13:1 Description

The Land-Rover bodywork is practical and rugged as befits the type of vehicle and the many duties it can undertake. With the exception of the steel radiator grille, dash panel door and tailboard frames, all the rest of the body is made from 'Birmabright' alloy. This is a magnesium-aluminium alloy which will not rust or corrode under any normal circumstances. It is work hardening and so becomes brittle when hammered, but is easily annealed. It has the property of forming a hard oxide skin when exposed to the air and so care and special preparation are necessary when painting is undertaken. Some hints on the working of this alloy are given in the following sections.

13:2 Panel beating 'Birmabright' alloy

This alloy can be beaten out after accidental damage in the same way as sheet steel, but protracted hammering will harden the material and cracking is likely. The affected area must be annealed by the application of heat, but, as the melting point of the alloy is low, this must be applied carefully. Check the temperature by applying oil or a smear of soap to the cleaned surface to

be annealed, then play the flame of a welding torch over the opposite side of the panel. Hold the torch well away from the surface and keep it moving steadily over the whole area. When the oil or soap clears and leaves the panel bright and clean, remove the heat and allow the panel to cool slowly in air. The clearing of the oil or soap takes place quite quickly. Do not quench the panel in oil or water. Repeat the operation as soon as the panel shows signs of re-hardening under the panel beating hammer or dolly.

13:3 Gas welding 'Birmabright'

Use a jet one or two sizes less than would be used for a comparable thickness of steel sheet. For instance, use a No. 2 nozzle for welding 18 S.W.G. (.048 inch) and a No. 3 for 16 S.W.G. (.064 inch) sheet. The flame should be neutral or slightly reducing (see **FIG 13:1**). Use only 5% magnesium-aluminium welding rod such as 'Sifalumin' No. 27 (MG5 alloy) or a strip of metal cut from a scrap 'Birmabright' panel. 'Sifbronze' Special Flux must be used with the 'Sifalumin' rod.

Clean off all grease and paint, dry thoroughly, then clean the edges and half an inch each side with a stiff wire brush or wire wool. Clean the rod or filler strip with

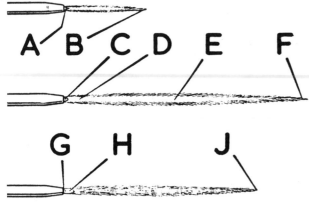

FIG 13:1   Welding jet, Oxidizing, Neutral and Reducing

the wire wool. Cleanliness is absolutely essential for successful welding.

Use special acid flux, either 'Hari-Kari' from the Midland Welding Supply Co. Ltd., 105 Lakey Lane, Birmingham 28, England, or 'Sifbronze' Special Flux from the Suffolk Iron Foundry (1920) Ltd., Sifbronze Works, Stowmarket, England. The 'Hari-Kari' flux is made into a paste with water and the paste applied to both surfaces to be welded and also to the rod. Use the 'Sifbronze' flux in a powder as directed on the tin.

Key to Fig 13:1   **A** Short pointed inner cone bluish white   **B** Bluish envelope   **C** Brilliant inner cone well defined rounded end   **D** Hottest point of flame   **E** Blue to orange envelope   **F** Nearly colourless   **G** Brilliant inner cone   **H** Feathery white plume   **J** Blue to orange envelope

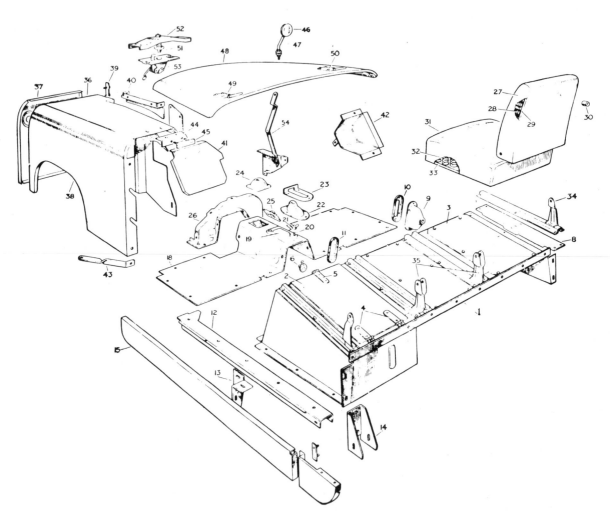

FIG 13:2   Layout of seats, floor and bonnet

Key to Fig 13:2   1 Seat base and floor assembly   2 Tool locker lid   3 Fuel tank cover panel   4 Lid hinge   5 Locker lid hasp   6 Locker lid turnbuckle   7 Centre cover panel   8 Extension panel, at seat base ends   9 Handbrake rubber cover   10 Retainer for rubber cover   11 Handbrake slot coverplate   12 Sill channel lefthand front   13 Sill channel securing bracket   14 Sill channel mounting bracket, to rear body   15 Front sill panel   16 Rear sill panel   17 Fixing plate for sill panels   18 Front floor complete   19 Inspection cover, for front floor   20 Stud plate for inspection cover wingnut   21 Wingnut, fixing inspection cover   22 Transfer gearlever seal   23 Transfer lever seal retainer   24 Gearlever rubber seal   25 Operating rod coverplate   26 Gearbox cover complete   27 Seat squab   28 Squab spring case   29 Squab frame   30 Buffer for seat backrest on bracket   31 Seat cushion   32 Cushion spring case   33 Cushion frame   34 Cushion support, outer   35 Seat support, centre   36 Front wing   37 Front panel and registration plate   38 Front wing outer panel   39 Fixing plate, wings to grille panel   40 Wing valance bottom panel   41 Mudshield, front wing   42 Steering unit cover box   43 Front wing stay   44 Bracket, for rear of wing   45 Fixing plate, brackets to dash   46 Mirror   47 Arm for mirror   48 Bonnet top panel   49, 50 Bonnet hinges   51 Bonnet catch striker pin   52 Bonnet striker bracket   53 Bonnet control   54 Bonnet prop rod

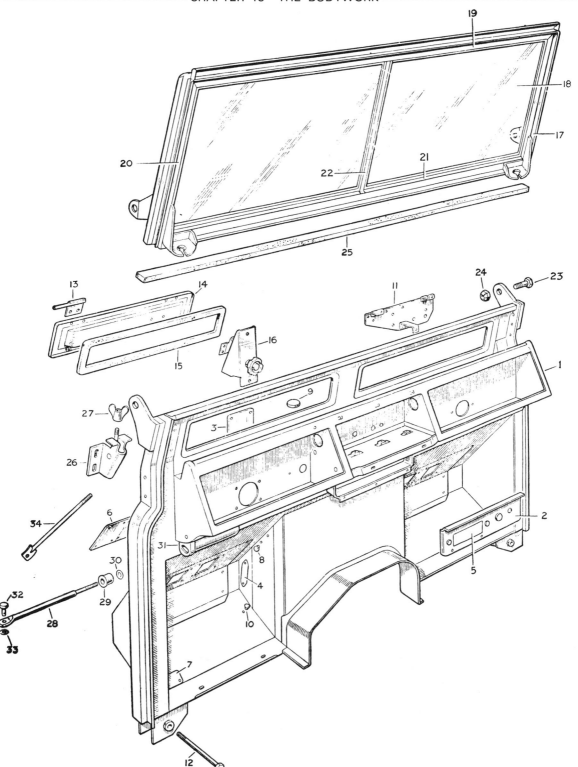

FIG 13:3 Layout of dash and windscreen, Series 2 and 2A

Key to Fig 13:3   1 Dash complete   2 Panel for controls   3 Cover panel for steering cut-out   4 Coverplate for accelerator pedal hole   5 Cover panel for governor cut-out in dash (petrol models)   6 Coverplate for pedal holes   7 Coverplate for dipswitch hole   8 Rubber plug, redundant accelerator holes   9 Rubber grommet for demister holes   10 Rubber plug, redundant accelerator stop holes   11 Mounting plate for pump   12 Tie bolt   13 Ventilator hinge   14 Ventilator lid for dash   15 Sealing rubber for ventilator lids   16 Ventilator control mechanism complete   17 Windscreen complete assembly   18 Glass for windscreen   19 Retainer for windscreen glass, top   20 Retainer for windscreen glass, side   21 Retainer for windscreen glass, bottom   22 Cover for centre strip   23, 24 Fixings for windscreen to dash   25 Rubber sealing strip for windscreen   26 Fastener for windscreen, righthand   27 Wingnut for fastener   28 Check strap rod   29 Check strap buffer   30 Fixings, buffer to rod   31 Check strap mounting bracket   32, 33 Fixings, check strap rod to front door   34 Tie rod

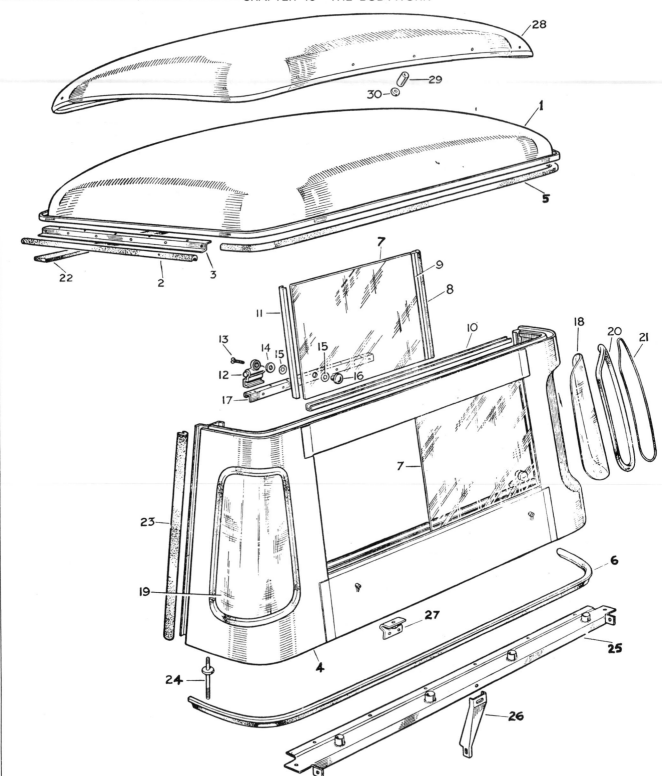

FIG 13:4 Cab unit

Key to Fig 13:4   1 Cab roof   2 Sealing rubber, door top   3 Retainer for seal   4 Cab rear panel assembly   5 Rubber seal, roof to back panel, top   6 Rubber seal, back panel to rear body   7 Sliding backlight   8 Sealing rubber for backlight   9 Channel for rubber   10 Channel, top and bottom   11 Channel, sides   12 Backlight catch   13-16 Fixings for catches   17 Runner for sliding backlight catch   18 Cab quarterlight, righthand   19 Cab quarterlight, lefthand   20 Weatherstrip   21 Sealing strip   22 Sealing rubber, windscreen to roof   23 Sealing rubber, door side   24 Mounting stud   25 Mounting rail for cab   26 Mounting rail support bracket   27 Cab mounting distance piece   28 Cab tropical roof panel   29 Distance piece   30 Rubber

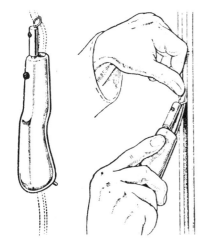

FIG 13:5   Fitting filler strip

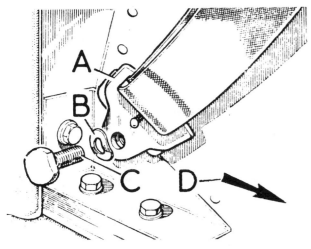

FIG 13:6   Diagonal safety belt fitted to sill

Key to Fig 13:6   A Adjusting buckle   **B** Wave washer
C Screw   **D** Front of vehicle

To judge the point when the metal reaches welding temperature, sprinkle a little sawdust over the work; this will sparkle and char as the right temperature is approached.

When the weld is completed, wash the surfaces very thoroughly with hot soapy water, using a wire brush or wire wool. This is essential due to the acid flux used.

If the welded area is judged to be too soft due to the annealing caused by the heat of the welding torch, hammer the part with many light blows from a medium hammer, using a dolly behind the panel to support it.

13:4 Riveting 'Birmabright'

If riveting is undertaken, use solid aluminium rivets if both sides are accessible or 'pop' rivets if only one side can be worked on. These latter rivets are inserted and closed by special pliers.

13:5 Painting 'Birmabright'

Owing to the hard oxide skin which forms on the surface when exposed to air, it is necessary to etch a repaired panel before painting to make sure that the paint will adhere properly. Wipe the area with thinners, dry thoroughly, then apply 'Deoxidine 125' acid etch supplied by I.C.I. Paints Division. Wash off thoroughly with hot water, then dry absolutely clean and moisture free. Slightly roughen the surface with 100 grade emerypaper and apply a thin coat of 'Glasso' primer or similar suitable primer. Apply three coats of filler and finish with the appropriate colour. It is essential that the initial etching is properly carried out, otherwise all the subsequent time and trouble will be wasted.

13:6 General construction

The general construction of the body is by panels riveted or bolted together and inspection of the vehicle will reveal how any particular item is attached. **FIGS 13:2, 13:3** and **13:4** show typical examples of the front

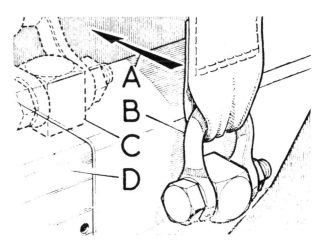

FIG 13:7   Tongue strap fixing

Key to Fig 13:7   A Gusset bracket   **B** Shackle fixing bolt
C Front of vehicle

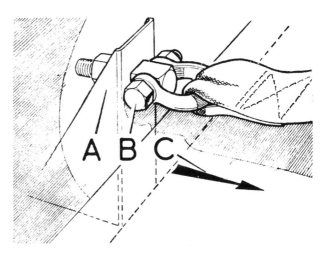

FIG 13:8   Diagonal strap fitted to bulkhead panel

Key to Fig 13:8   A Front of vehicle
B Shackle position (early models)   **C** Shackle position
(late models, in dotted line)   **D** Seat panel capping

FIG 13:9   Diagonal strap fitted to BC post

Key to Fig 13:9   A Shackle fixing bolt   **B** Mounting bracket
C Front of vehicle

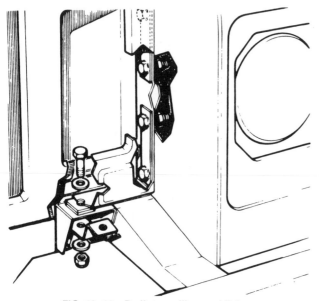

FIG 13:10   Radiator grille panel fixings

seats, floor and bonnet, the dash and windscreen and a cab unit.

Windscreen glass can be easily replaced without special tools. Undo the drive screws securing the glass retainers, prise the retainers free and remove the glass. Fit sealing strip $\frac{1}{2}$ inch (12 mm) wide round the outside on both faces of the new glass and refit by reversing the removal procedure.

Some models have quarterlights held by a rubber weatherstrip and filler strip. To remove these, prise the filler strip out, then push the weatherstrip and glass out of the aperture.

To fit new rubbers and glass, first square off one end of the rubber weatherstrip, start at the bottom centre and fit the narrow groove of the strip to the panel aperture edges. The filler strip groove goes to the outside. Push the strip into the aperture all round, then cut off with about 1 inch (25 mm) overlap. Now compress the

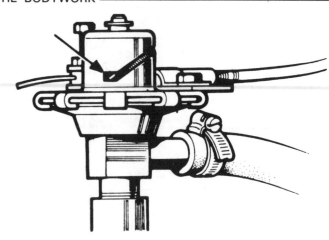

FIG 13:11   Heater water valve closed

strip until the ends butt. Fit the glass and then force the filler strip into the groove in the weatherstrip, using special tool Rover Part No. 262771 (see **FIG 13:5**). Allow $\frac{1}{4}$ inch (6 mm) overlap, cut off and force the filler strip into the groove so that it is compressed and the ends butt in the groove.

13:7 *Fitting seat belts*

If the vehicle does not have built-in attachment points, it is advisable to consult a Rover agent regarding the correct fittings. If the vehicle has built-in attachment points, fit the adjusting buckle strap to the sill bracket (see **FIG 13:6**), the short tongue strap to the lower bulkhead panel (see **FIG 13:7**) and the diagonal strap to the upper bulkhead panel (see **FIG 13:8**) or, in the case of the 109 Station Wagon, to the BC post (see **FIG 13:9**). Make very sure that all fixings are sound and securely attached to the vehicle.

13:8 *Removing the radiator grille panel*

1 Remove the bonnet. Disconnect the battery and, on 2.6 litre models, remove the air cleaner.
2 Remove the front apron panel secured by four screws. Remove the nameplate and radiator grille.
3 Drain the coolant. Remove the shroud from the radiator fan cowl. Remove the coolant hoses. Detach the fan and rest it on the lower part of the fan cowl.
4 Disconnect the leads to the front lamps.
5 Remove the grille panel fixings in the wheelarches and on the chassis crossmember (see **FIG 13:10**).

13:9 *The heater water valve*

Before removing the valve, partially drain the coolant. After removing the control cable, the water valve can be unscrewed.

When refitting the water valve, set the cable as follows.

Refer to **FIG 13:11** and set the water valve in the closed position as shown. With the heater control on the dash fully in the cold position, take up the slack in the inner cable and tighten the cable fixings at the water valve.

CHAPTER 14

OPTIONAL EQUIPMENT

14:1 Centre power takeoff

The same unit is applicable to all models, but the latest types have a modified selector lever. This is shown in **FIG 14:4** and involves a different cutting pattern for access to the control knob through the seat panels. Both patterns with all dimensions necessary are shown in this section.

It is essential that the centre power takeoff is only used in conjunction with an engine speed governor. See **Section 14:5** for instructions for fitting and servicing the governor.

Reference to **FIG 14:2** will show that two types of housing 1 and 2 and drive shaft 4 and 5 are illustrated. Two bearings 11 and 12 and two flanges 19 and 20 are also included. The upper assembly in **FIG 14:2** is used to drive the welding generator, compressor, etc.; where it is an advantage to reverse the pulley to bring it over the housing, thus putting the load from the Vee-belts directly over the heavier bearing 12.

To fit the centre power takeoff:

1 Remove the centre inspection panel from the seat box and mark out and cut the holes as shown in **FIG 14:5** (early type selector). Rivet the cover retaining clip to the panel, placing the plain washer between the clip and the panel. Engage the tongues of the cover in the slots **C**. If the late type selector is being fitted, do not cut this panel. Remove the seat retaining bollard and then drill a hole in the heel board as shown in **FIG 14:6**. Fit a grommet to the hole, then replace the bollard.

2 Remove the top coverplate from the transfer casing.

3 Remove the mainshaft rear bearing housing assembly from the transfer casing.

4 Fit the power takeoff assembly with a new joint washer to the rear of the transfer casing. See that the oil drain hole in the assembly is to the bottom.

5 Fit the selector assembly with a new joint washer to the top of the casing. Ensure that the selector fork engages with the sliding dog clutch (see **FIG 14:2**, item 27). Tighten all the bolts evenly.

6 Operations 4 and 5 refer to units with the early type selector lever (see **FIG 14:1**). If a unit with the late type selector lever (see **FIG 14:4**) is being installed, the following additional operations are necessary:

(a) Remove the bearing housing fixing stud from the lefthand top corner on the transfer casing and replace it with the new stud supplied with the unit.

(b) Fit the selector rod to the lever, using a clevis pin, spring and splitpin. Pass the rod through the hole previously cut in the heel board, screw the

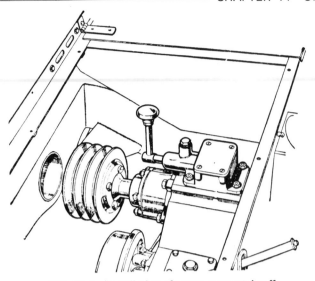

FIG 14:1   Installation of centre power takeoff

knob on and secure with a locknut. Attach the lever to the selector shaft and to the new stud on the transfer casing. Use a locknut on the stud and check that the link moves freely without excessive slack.

7 Replace the centre inspection panel after fitting the pulley or, if a rear power takeoff is to be added, the drive shaft.

Servicing the centre power takeoff:

Refer to **FIGS 14:2** and **14:3**.

Remove the selector assembly and power takeoff unit by reversing the preceding fitting instructions.

The selector assembly is easily dismantled by removing the brass plug, releasing the detent spring and ball, then undoing the bolts holding the coverplate and loosening the selector fork clamp bolt. The shaft and fork will now come out of the housing. Replace any worn parts and reassemble by reversing the dismantling procedure.

The drive unit is dismantled as follows:

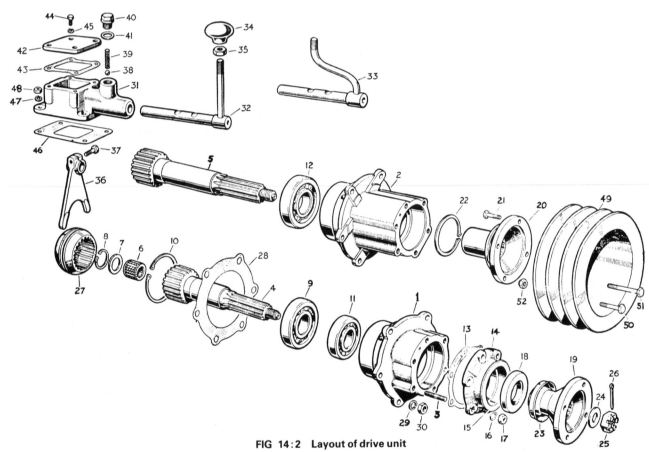

FIG 14:2   Layout of drive unit

Key to Fig 14:2   1 Housing assembly for drive bearing   2 Housing assembly for drive bearing (with welder, compressor, etc.)
3 Stud for oil seal housing   4 Shaft for power takeoff drive   5 Shaft for power takeoff drive (with welder, compressor, etc.)
6 Bearing for gearbox mainshaft   7 Retaining plate for bearing   8 Circlip fixing retaining plate   9 Bearing for drive shaft, front
10 Circlip, bearing to housing   11 Bearing for drive shaft, rear   12 Bearing for drive shaft, rear (with welder, compressor, etc.)
13 Shim for bearing   14 Housing for oil seal   15 Mudshield for housing   16, 17 Fixings for oil seal housing   18 Oil seal for
drive shaft   19 Flange for power takeoff drive shaft   20 Flange for power takeoff drive shaft (with welder, compressor, etc.)
21 Bolt for flange (with welder, compressor, etc.)   22 Circlip retaining bolts (with welder, compressor, etc.)   23 Mudshield for flange
24-26 Fixings for flange   27 Dog clutch for power takeoff shaft   28 Joint washer for housing   29, 30 Fixings for housing
31 Housing for power takeoff selector   32 Selector shaft and rod for power takeoff   33 Selector shaft for rod and power takeoff
(with welder, compressor, etc.)   34 Knob for rod   35 Locknut for knob   36 Fork for selector shaft   37 Setbolt fixing fork to shaft
38 Steel ball (for selector shaft)   39 Spring (for selector shaft)   40 Plug for spring   41 Joint washer for plug
42 Coverplate for housing   43 Joint washer for plate   44, 45 Fixings for plate   46 Joint washer for housing
47, 48 Fixings for housing   49 Pulley for centre power takeoff   50-52 Fixings for pulley

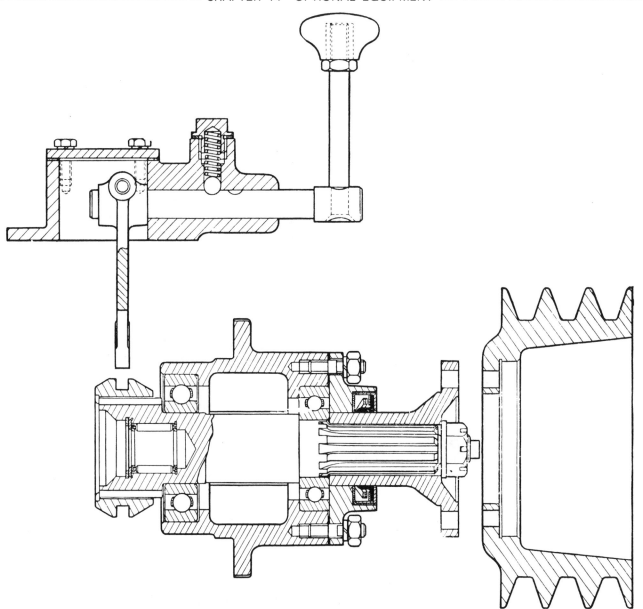

FIG 14:3   Cross-section of unit

1 Remove the pulley, if fitted.
2 Slide the dog clutch off and grip the shaft in a vice
   with soft jaws. Undo the flange retaining nut and
   pull the flange from the shaft.
3 Remove the oil seal housing 14 (see **FIG 14:2**), and
   drift out the oil seal 18. If any shims 13 are fitted, preserve them for reassembly.
4 Remove the front bearing retaining circlip 10, then
   protect the threaded end of the shaft and drive the
   shaft and front bearing out of the housing.
5 Remove the circlip 8 and washer 7, then release the
   needle roller bearing 6 from the bore of the shaft.
6 Drift the rear bearing 11 out of the housing and
   extract the front bearing from the shaft.
7 Wash all parts in paraffin and dry throughly. Spin
   the bearings and take note of any slack or roughness which will indicate flaking tracks or broken
   balls. Renew any other worn components.

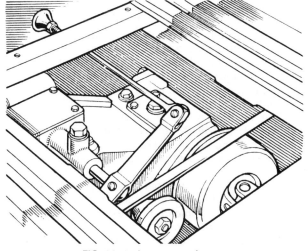

FIG 14:4   Late type selector

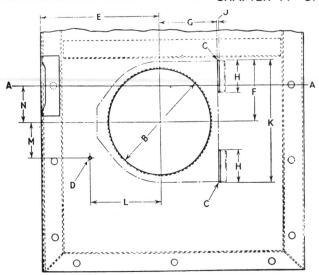

FIG 14:5   Cutting dimensions for centre panel

Key to Fig 14:5

B 7 inch (177.8 mm)	**AA** Centreline of body
D One hole .204 inch (5.18 mm)	**C** Two slots as shown
F 4$\frac{1}{32}$ inch (103.94 mm)	**E** 7$\frac{15}{16}$ inch (201.6 mm)
H 2$\frac{1}{16}$ inch (52.38 mm)	**G** 4 inch (101.56 mm)
K 8$\frac{1}{16}$ inch (204.77 mm)	**J** $\frac{1}{8}$ inch (3.17 mm)
M 2$\frac{1}{4}$ inch (57.12 mm)	**L** 4$\frac{3}{4}$ inch (120.60 mm)
	N 2$\frac{1}{2}$ inch (63.46 mm)

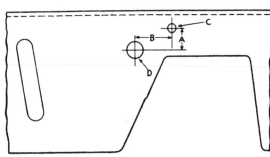

FIG 14:6   Drilling the heel board

Key to Fig 14:6   **A** 1.187 inch (30 mm)
B 1.968 inch (50 mm)   **C** Hole for seat strap retaining bolt
D $\frac{3}{4}$ inch (19 mm) diameter hole

To reassemble, reverse the dismantling procedure, but take particular note of the following points:

1 The front (large) bearing must be a light drive fit both on the shaft and in the housing.

2 The rear bearing must also be a light drive fit on the shaft and in the housing.

3 The oil seal must be fitted with its knife edge inwards. **FIG 14:3** shows the right location.

4 When fitting the oil seal retainer to the housing, line up its oil drain slot with the oil drain hole in the housing.

5 Adjust the shaft end float to nil by fitting shims between the oil seal retainer and the housing. These shims are available in thicknesses of .003 and .005 inch (.076 and .12 mm).

6 The dog clutch must be fitted with its recessed end towards the gearbox.

14:2 *Rear power takeoff*

This unit takes its power from, and is controlled by, the centre power takeoff. Therefore, if the centre power takeoff is not already installed, it must now be fitted in accordance with **Section 14:1**.

Note that short wheel base vehicles have the drive shaft coupled directly between the centre and rear power takeoff units, but on long wheel base models a centre bearing assembly is interposed.

Instructions are given for installing the drive shaft or shafts to either the long or short wheel base vehicles.

To install the rear power takeoff:

Short wheel base (86 and 88) models:

1 Secure the drive shaft to the input flange of the unit with the shaft sliding joint towards the front. Pass the shaft forwards through the holes in the vehicle chassis until the unit can be bolted to the rear chassis crossmember.

2 Bolt the front flange of the shaft to the drive flange of the centre power takeoff unit. It is possible to leave the centre power takeoff Vee drive pulley in place if longer bolts (1$\frac{23}{32}$ inch – 43.7 mm long) are used to secure the shaft to the flange.

Long wheel base models:

1 Secure the crossmember intermediate bearing support to the chassis sidemembers.

2 Pass the universal joint end of the front propeller shaft forwards through the chassis and secure the front end to the centre power takeoff drive flange.

3 Fit the centre bearing housing to the crossmember intermediate bearing support.

4 Secure the rear end of the rear propeller shaft to the input flange of the rear power takeoff unit. Have the shaft sliding joint to the front.

5 Pass the rear shaft forwards through the chassis until the rear power takeoff unit can be bolted to the rear chassis crossmember.

6 Bolt the front and rear shafts together at the intermediate bearing.

All models:

Fill the unit with 1 pint (.5 litre) of oil.

To service the rear power takeoff unit:

Refer to **FIGS 14:7** and **14:8**.

Remove the unit by reversing the installation procedure.

1 Remove plug 62 and drain off the oil, then grip the unit in the vice by the input flange. Remove guard 68.

2 Remove coverplate 56 and washer 57. Remove the breather 60.

3 Undo nut 30 and pull the inner bearing race 22 out of the housing 25. Preserve any shims 23.

4 Undo the nuts 28 and pull the housing 25 from the main housing 11. If necessary, remove circlip 24 and drift the outer race of the bearing 22 from the housing.

5 Pull gearwheel 21 from the input shaft 14.

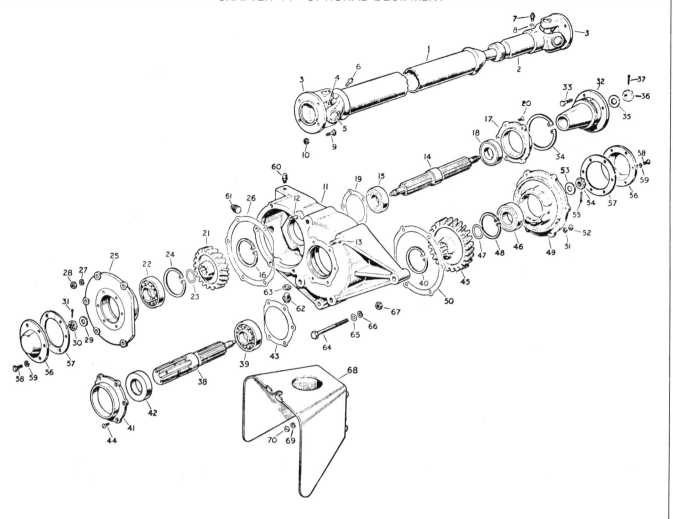

FIG 14:7   Rear power takeoff unit

Key to Fig 14:7   1 Propeller shaft, power takeoff drive   2 Splined end (for propeller shaft)   3 Flange (for propeller shaft)
4 Journal complete for propeller shaft   5 Circlip for journal   6 Grease nipple for journal   7 Grease nipple for propeller shaft,
.250 inch (6.35 mm) diameter   8 Washer for nipple   9, 10 Fixings for propeller shaft   11 Housing assembly for power takeoff
12 Stud for bearing housing   13 Stud for pulley housing or guard   14 Input shaft for power takeoff   15 Bearing for
input shaft, front   16 Circlip, bearing to housing   17 Retainer for oil seal (for input shaft)   18 Oil seal (for input shaft)
19 Joint washer for retainer   20 Screw fixing retainer   21 Gearwheel, 20 teeth   22 Bearing for input shaft, rear
23 Shim for rear input shaft bearing   24 Circlip, bearing to housing   25 Housing for rear input shaft bearing   26 Joint washer for
rear bearing housing   27, 28 Fixings for bearing housing   29-31 Fixings for rear bearing   32 Flange for power takeoff input shaft
33 Special bolts for propeller shaft   34 Circlip retaining bolts to flange   35-37 Fixings for flange   38 Output shaft for
power takeoff, 6-spline   39 Bearing for output shaft, rear   40 Circlip for bearing   41 Retainer for oil seal (for output shaft)
42 Oil seal (for output shaft)   43 Joint washer for retainer   44 Screw fixing retainer   45 Gearwheel, 24 teeth   46 Bearing for
output shaft, front   47 Shim, for front output shaft bearing   48 Circlip, bearing to housing   49 Housing for output shaft front
bearing   50 Joint washer for bearing housing   51, 52 Fixings for bearing housing   53-55 Fixings for front bearing
56 Coverplate for bearings   57 Joint washer for coverplate   58, 59 Fixings for cover   60 Breather for casing   61 Filler plug
62 Drain plug for casing   63 Fibre washer for plug   64-67 Fixings for power takeoff assembly   68 Guard for power takeoff spline
69, 70 Fixings for guard

6 Remove circlip 34, then detach the input flange bolts 33.

7 Undo the nut 36 and pull flange 32 from the shaft 14. The unit must be relocated in the vice for this.

8 Unscrew the screws holding the oil seal retainer 17 and slide the retainer and seal carefully off the shaft. The shaft 14, complete with the inner race of bearing 15, will now slide out of the unit. If necessary, remove circlip 16 and drift out the outer race of bearing 15 from the unit. (See later operation 17; it may be possible to combine these).

9 Drift the oil seal 18 from the retainer 17 if necessary.

10 Remove the cover 56 and washer 57 from the front of the output shaft. Grip the unit in a soft jawed vice by the splined end of the output shaft.

11 Remove nut 54 and washer 53 from the output shaft, then pull the inner race of bearing 46 from the shaft. Preserve shims 47 if fitted.

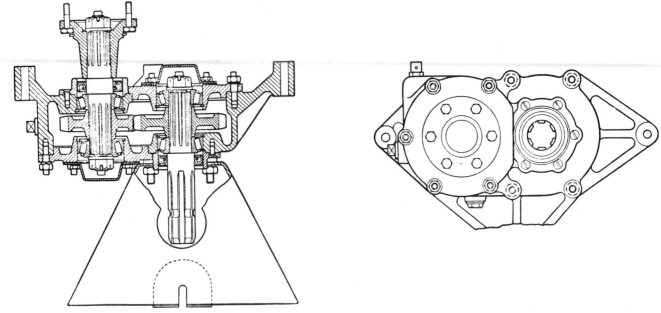

FIG 14:8   Cross-section of rear power takeoff unit

12 Remove housing 49, then, if necessary, remove circlip 48 and drift out the outer race of bearing 46.

13 Pull the gearwheel 45 from the shaft.

14 Relocate the unit in the vice, gripping it across a fixing bolt boss.

15 Undo screws 44 and slide the oil seal retainer 41 carefully off the shaft. Drift the oil seal 42 from the retainer if necessary.

16 Pull out the output shaft 38 from the housing 11 and then extract the inner race of bearing 39 from the shaft.

17 Remove the circlip 40 and drift the outer race of bearing 39 from the housing. The housing must be removed from the vice and supported on the bench for this operation. (See previous operation 8.) It is also advisable to heat the housing in hot water before starting to drift the bearing races out.

18 Wash all components thoroughly in paraffin and dry carefully. Check and, if necessary, renew the bearings if any damage or discoloration shows on their rollers or tracks. Renew all joint washers and

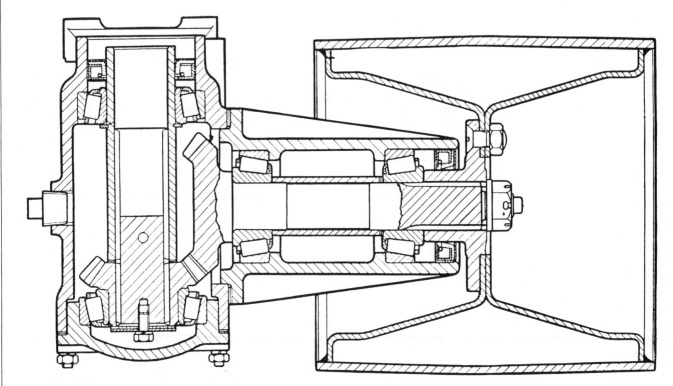

FIG 14:9   Cross-section of rear drive pulley

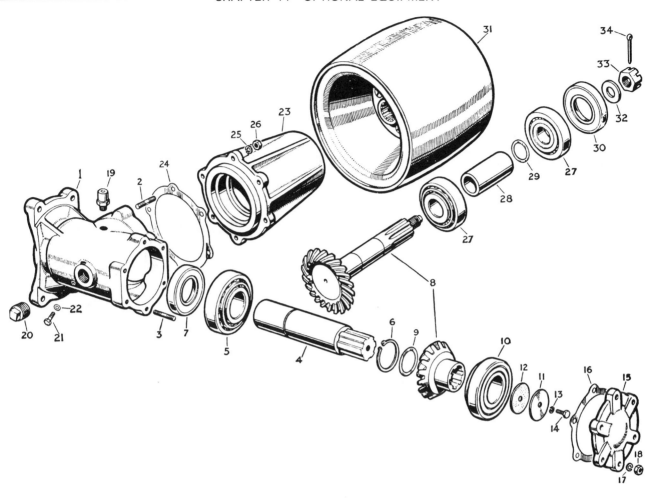

FIG 14:10   Rear pulley unit

Key to Fig 14:10   1 Housing assembly for power takeoff pinion   2 Stud for pulley drive housing   3 Stud for end plate   4 Pinion driving sleeve, 6-spline   5 Bearing for sleeve   6 Circlip, bearing to sleeve   7 Oil seal for driving sleeve   8 Spiral bevel wheel and pinion   9 Shim   10 Bearing for bevel wheel   11 Retaining plate for bevel wheel   12 Cork washer for retaining plate   13, 14 Fixings for plate   15 End plate for bevel wheel bearing   16 Shim for bevel wheel end plate   17, 18 Fixings for bearing end plate   19 Breather for housing   20 Filler plug for housing   21 Plug for oil level   22 Washer for plug   23 Housing for pulley drive pinion   24 Shim for pulley drive pinion housing   25, 26 Fixings for pulley drive   27 Bearings for pinion   28 Distance tube for bearings   29 Shim for bevel pinion bearings   30 Oil seal for bevel pinion bearings   31 Pulley   32-34 Fixings for pulley

splitpins. If the unit has leaked oil from the shafts, then the oil seals must be renewed. Press the new ones into their retainers with their lips facing inwards. The plain face must be pressed $\frac{5}{16}$ inch (8 mm) below the outer face of the retainer. When replacing the seals in the unit, wrap a piece of stiff paper or a strip of aluminium cooking foil over the splines, then slide the seal gently over this. The spline edges can cut and ruin the seal if this precaution is omitted. Check the gears for wear and damage. These can only be renewed as a pair. Examine the housings for cracks or excessive wear in any bearing bore and, if these are present, scrap the housing.

19 Reassemble the unit by reversing the dismantling process, but note the following points:

   (a) Warm the main housing before fitting the two outer bearing races. These must only be a tap fit.

   (b) The other two outer bearing races in hous-

ings 25 and 49 must be a light drive fit, cold.

   (c) The bearing inner races must be a light tap fit on the shafts.

   (d) The backlash between the gears must lie between .008 to .012 inch (.2 to .3 mm).

   (e) The recess in the splined bore in each gear must be fitted adjacent to the centre flange on each shaft. The input shaft gear 21 must be fitted on the longer end of the shaft 14.

20 Adjust the bearings by tightening the nuts on the ends of the shafts, then tapping both ends of each shaft to settle the bearings. Each shaft must turn freely with no end float. Add or take away shims 47 and 23 until this condition is achieved. These shims are available in thicknesses of .005, .01 and .02 inch (.12, .25 and .5 mm).

21 Replace the spline guard and refit the unit to the vehicle. Refill with oil.

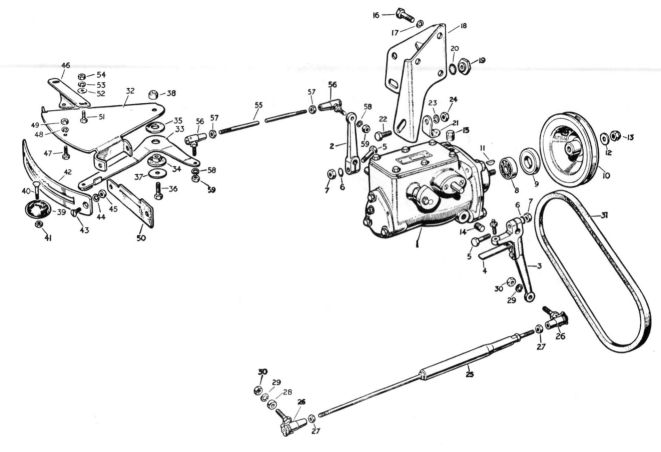

FIG 14 : 11 Layout of engine governor

Key to Fig 14 : 11   1 Engine governor complete   2 Lever, governor to quadrant   3 Lever, grommet to bellcrank
4 Spring blade for bellcrank 5-7 Fixings for levers 8 Bearing, large (for engine governors) – bearing, small (for engine governor)
9 Oil seal for pulley end 10 Pulley for governor 11 Woodruff key for pulley 12, 13 Fixings for pulley 14 Level plug for governor
15 Filler plug for governor   16, 17 Fixings for governor   18 Bracket for governor   19, 20 Fixings for bracket   21 Support
for bracket   22-24 Fixings for support   25 Control rod, governor to bellcrank   26 Ball joint complete for rod   27 Locknut for
ball joint   28 Distance piece, bellcrank lever end   29, 30 Fixings for rod   31 Belt for governor drive   32 Housing for governor
control quadrant   33 Lever for control   34 Bush for lever   35 Washer for lever   36-38 Fixings for control lever to housing
39 Knob for lever   40, 41 Fixings for knob   42 Quadrant plate   43-45 Fixings for quadrant plate   46 Support for governor
control   47-49 Fixings for support   50 Rubber draught excluder   51-54 Fixings for control   55 Operating rod, quadrant
to governor   56 Ball joint for rod   57 Locknut for ball joint on rod   58, 59 Fixings for operating rod

14 : 3 *To transpose the power takeoff gears*

If it is desired to alter the speed of the power output shaft at the rear power takeoff in relation to the engine or vehicle speed, the gears in the rear unit may be transposed. To carry out this operation, proceed as follows :

1 Remove the rear drive pulley if fitted, then drain the oil from the power takeoff unit.
2 Remove the unit from the chassis frame (see **Section 14 : 2**).
3 Remove the input shaft coverplate; take out the splitpin and unscrew the castle nut from the shaft.
4 Remove the input shaft bearing housing and bearing.
5 Remove the 20 tooth gear, carefully preserving any shims fitted to the shaft.
6 Repeat the process for the output shaft and withdraw the 24 tooth gear.

7 Transpose the gears, replacing any shims on the shaft from which they were removed. **This is important.**
8 Reassemble the unit, using new splitpins to lock the castle nuts.
9 Replace it on the vehicle and refill with 1 pint (.5 litre) of oil.

14 : 4 *Rear drive pulley*

In this section, refer to **FIGS 14 : 9** and **14 : 10**.

To fit the rear drive pulley :

1 Remove the output shaft guard from the rear power takeoff.
2 Slide the pulley unit over the output shaft and secure it to the rear power takeoff casing in place of the output shaft guard.

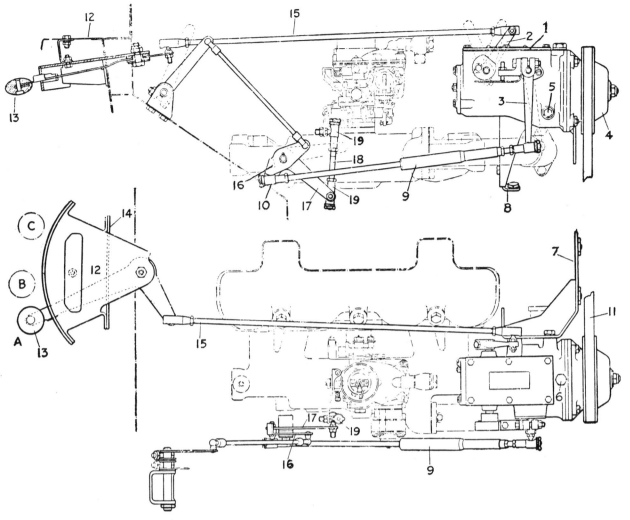

FIG 14:12 Governor control linkage

Key to Fig 14:12   **A** Inoperative position   **B** 1500 rev/min   **C** 3000 rev/min   1 Engine governor   2 Loading lever
3 Throttle control lever   4 Governor pulley   5 Oil level plug   6 Oil filler plug   7 Bracket for governor   8 Support for bracket
9 Collapsible control rod   10 Adjustable ball joint for rod   11 Drive belt   12 Control quadrant   13 Operating lever
14 Draught excluder   15 Governor operating rod   16 Relay lever   17 Carburetter bellcrank   18 Rod, bellcrank to carburetter
19 Adjustable ball joint for rod

3 Fill the unit with oil, $\frac{3}{4}$ pint (.4 litre).

4 When the belt is connected to the driven machine, the tension is correct if the handbrake will hold the vehicle and the two sides of the belt cannot be made to touch when compressed by hand midway between the vehicle and the driven machine.

To service the pulley unit:

1 Remove the pulley from the shaft, then remove the whole unit from the vehicle by reversing the installation procedure. Drain off the oil.

2 Refer to **FIG 14:10** and undo the six nuts 26 and pull the pinion housing 23 from the housing 1. Retain any shims 24.

3 Tap out the pinion shaft 8, inner element of race 27, tube 28 and shims 29 out of the pinion housing.

4 Warm the pinion housing, drift out the oil seal 30,

remove the inner element of race 27, then drift out both of the race outer elements.

5 Remove end plate 15 and shims 16. The race 10 will come away with the end plate and can be released if the plate is heated.

6 Pull shaft 4 complete with the bevel wheel 8 from the housing, then remove the setbolt 14. Dismantle the bevel wheel and races from the shaft. Preserve any shims 9.

7 Heat the housing and drive the outer element of race 5 from the bore with the oil seal 7.

8 Wash all the components carefully in paraffin and dry thoroughly. Inspect the races, shafts and gears for damage and renew as required. The gears must be renewed as a pair. New oil seals must be fitted.

9 Assemble the unit by reversing the dismantling process, noting that the outer elements of the races must be a tap fit in warm housings, the inner elements

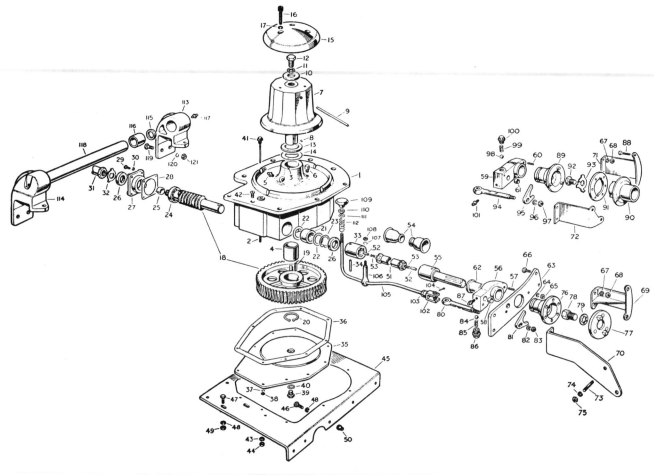

FIG 14 : 13   Layout of front winch

Key to Fig 14 : 13   1 Casing assembly for front winch   2 Stud for bottom cover   3 Dowel for thrust washer   4 Bush for bollard shaft   5 Grease point for shaft   6 Breather cup for housing   7 Bollard and shaft assembly   8 Dowel for shaft   9 Pin for bollard   10-12 Fixings for bollard   13 Thrust washer (for bollard)   14 Shim (for bollard)   15 Cap for bollard   16, 17 Fixings for cap   18 Worm wheel and worm complete   19 Special key to worm wheel   20 Circlip fixing worm wheel   21 Roller bearing for worm   22 Washer for bearing   23 Circlip fixing bearing to casing   24 Ballbearing for worm shaft   25 Distance piece for worm shaft   26 Oil seal for worm shaft   27 Retainer for oil seal   28 Joint washer for oil seal retainer   29, 30 Fixings for oil seal retainer   31 Starting dog   32 Lockwasher for starting dog   33 Universal joint sleeve   34 Special pin fixing sleeve to worm   35 Bottom cover for winch casing   36 Joint washer for bottom cover   37, 38 Fixings for bottom cover   39 Drain plug for front winch   40 Joint washer for drain plug   41 Filler plug and dipstick   42-44 Fixings for front winch   45 Support plate for front winch   46-49 Fixings for support plate   50 Rivnut   51 Propeller shaft for front winch   52 Plunger (for propeller shaft)   53 Plunger spring (for propeller shaft)   54 Dust cover (for propeller shaft)   55 Driving shaft for front winch   56 Winch shaft housing assembly (2¼ litre petrol/diesel models)   57 Stud for support plate (2¼ litre petrol/diesel models)   58 Bush for control shaft (2¼ litre petrol/diesel models)   59 Winch shaft housing assembly (2 litre petrol models)   60 Stud for support plate (2 litre petrol models)   61 Bush for control shaft (2 litre petrol models)   62 Bush for winch driving shaft   63 Support plate for winch shaft   64, 65 Fixings for housing   66-68 Fixings for support   69 Bracket for winch shaft support plate, righthand (2¼ litre petrol/diesel models)   70 Bracket for winch shaft support plate, lefthand (2¼ litre petrol/diesel models)   71 Bracket for winch shaft support plate, righthand (2 litre petrol models)   72 Bracket for winch shaft support plate, lefthand (2 litre petrol models)

2¼ litre petrol/diesel models :
73-75 Fixings (bracket to front cover)   76 Driving flange for front winch   77 Winch driving plate   78, 79 Fixings for driving plate   80 Control shaft for driving flange   81 Selector fork for control shaft   82, 83 Fixings for fork   84 Steel ball (for control shaft)   85 Spring (for control shaft)   86 Plug for spring (for control shaft)   87 Grease point for control shaft

2 litre petrol models :
88 Setbolt fixing bracket to front cover   89 Driving flange for front winch   90 Driving flange for fan pulley   91 Winch driving plate   92, 93 Fixings for driving flange and plate   94 Control shaft for driving flange   95 Selector fork for control shaft   96, 97 Fixings for fork   98 Steel ball (for control shaft)   99 Spring (for control shaft)   100 Plug for spring (for control shaft)   101 Grease point for control shaft   102-104 Clevis, locknut and splitpin   105 Control rod for winch   106 Eyebolt for winch control rod   107, 108 Fixings for eyebolt   109 Knob for control rod   110 Locknut for knob   111 Plain washer for spring   112 Spring for control rod   113 Rope guide bracket assembly, righthand   114 Rope guide bracket assembly, lefthand   115 Thrust washer   116 Bush for guide bar   117 Grease point for bush   118 Guide bar for winch rope   119-121 Fixings for rope guide

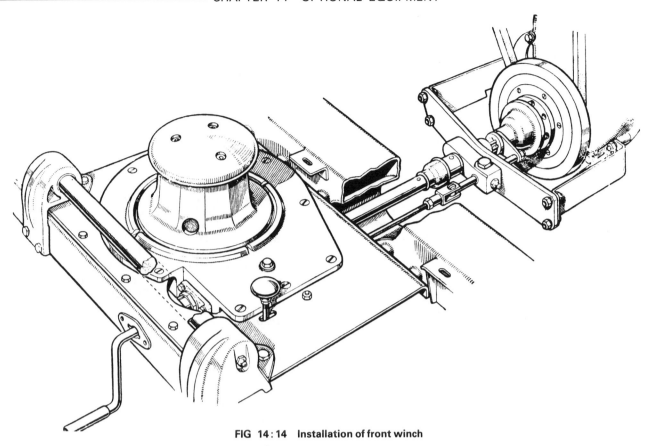

FIG 14:14   Installation of front winch

of the drive shaft races must be a light drive fit and those on the pinion shaft an easy tap fit.

10 The shims 9 provide adjustment for the bevel wheel and are available in .005, .01 and .02 inch (.12, .25 and .5 mm) thickness. The bevel wheel must align with the pinion face as shown in **FIG 14:9**.

11 The drive shaft and pinion shaft oil seals must be fitted with their lips inwards.

12 Adjust the drive shaft to a condition of free movement without end float by means of shims 16. These are also available in the same range of sizes as those for the bevel wheel.

13 The pinion shaft 8 is adjusted to the same condition as the drive shaft by means of shims 29. These are also available in the same three thicknesses as shims 9 and 16.

14 Add or remove shims 24 until there is definite backlash between the bevel wheel and pinion throughout a complete revolution. This backlash must not exceed .004 inch (.1 mm) at any point.

14:5   *The engine governor. Petrol models*

In this section, refer to **FIGS 14:11** and **14:12**.

To install the governor:

1 Remove the bonnet for easy access to the engine.

2 Refer to **FIG 14:11**. Fit bracket 21 on top of the existing generator support bracket, turn it to the rear and leave the bolt slack. Fit the governor to bracket 18.

3 Slacken the fan belt, remove the original fan pulley and distance piece and fit the new double groove pulley and distance piece. Readjust the belt tension.

4 Replace the bolts holding the thermostat housing with three studs, fit the governor driving belt, then attach the governor bracket to the thermostat housing, but leave the nuts on the studs slack. Connect bracket 21 to bracket 18, but leave the nut and bolt slack. See that the distributor vacuum pipe clears the bracket.

5 Hold the governor out to tension the belt so that it can be depressed $\frac{1}{2}$ inch (12.5 mm) midway between the pulleys by thumb pressure. Tighten all the supporting bracket nuts and bolts.

6 Check the oil level in the governor and replenish as necessary until the level reaches the bottom of the level plug hole.

Refer to **FIG 14:12** and install the linkage as follows:

7 Discard the throttle spring between the bellcrank lever and the petrol filter bracket.

8 Remove the coverplate on the dash below the instrument panel.

9 Insert the control quadrant in the hole thus uncovered in the dash using the fixings originally holding the coverplate. Fit the rubber draught excluder between the quadrant housing and the dash. Leave all the fixings slack at this stage.

10 Remove the instrument panel complete without disconnecting the instruments, then secure the quadrant bracket to the bottom of the instrument box. Tighten the nuts securing the quadrant to the

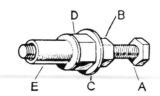

FIG 14:15   Rivnut fitting, stage 1

Key to Fig 14:15   **A** Setbolt   **B** $\frac{5}{16}$ inch UNF nut
C Plain washer   **D** Distance piece   **E** Rivnut

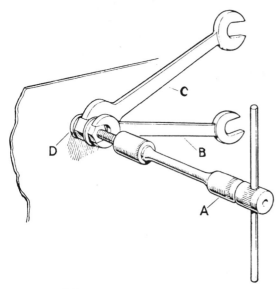

FIG 14:16   Rivnut fitting, stage 2

Key to Fig 14:16   **A** $\frac{5}{16}$ inch UNF spanner
B $\frac{5}{16}$ inch UNF spanner   **C** $\frac{3}{8}$ inch UNF spanner   **D** Rivnut

dash and then the nuts fixing the bracket to the box. Replace the instrument panel.

11 Fit the operating rod 15 to the control quadrant lever 13. Loosen the lever 3 on the governor, put the control lever 13 in the inoperative (extreme righthand) notch, then push lever 2 forward until a marked resistance is felt. Hold in this position and adjust the length of rod 15 until it can be fitted to lever 2. Tighten the ball joint locknuts.

12 Fit rod 9 between the relay lever 16 and the governor lever 3. A distance piece must be fitted between the ball joint 10 and the relay lever 16 to allow the rod to clear the end of the shaft.

13 Adjust the throttle linkage to ensure that the carburetter butterfly is fully open when the accelerator is fully depressed.

Set the control linkage as follows :

1 Place the quadrant lever in the extreme lefthand notch.

2 Hold the throttle wide open and tighten lever 3 on its shaft. Return the quadrant lever to the righthand notch.

3 Start the engine and warm up. Move the control lever to the first operating notch (1500 rev/min) and check the anti-surge stop clearance. This should be .02 to .025 inch (.5 to .65 mm) measured between the spring leaf attached to lever 3 and the cam on

the shaft which carries lever 2. Adjust by the screw in the bracket attached to lever 3.

4 Return the quadrant lever to the extreme righthand position. The linkage is now correctly set to control the engine speed between 1500 and 3000 rev/min.

5 The engine speed can be checked with a revolution counter applied to the rear power takeoff. The relationship between the power takeoff and engine speeds is given in the following tables.

(a) Rear power takeoff pulley :

Governor position	Engine speed	Pulley speed	
		5:6 Power takeoff ratio	6:5 Power takeoff ratio
1	1500	1070	1540
4	1950	1390	2000
8	2550	1820	2630
11	3000	2145	3100

(b) Rear power takeoff drive shaft :

Governor position	Engine speed	Drive shaft speed	
		5:6 Power takeoff ratio	6:5 Power takeoff ratio
1	1500	1250	1800
4	1950	1625	2350
8	2550	2125	3050
11	3000	2500	3600

Rectifying governor surging :

1 Ensure that backlash in the linkage does not exceed .01 inch (.25 mm) and that there are no tight spots in the linkage operation.

2 See that the carburetter jets are clean and that the governor and fan belts are correctly tensioned.

3 Fit a new spring to the accelerator pump rod.

4 If the governor still surges, insert 2 BA washers behind the spring on the accelerator pump actuating rod. Initially, add washers to make $\frac{1}{8}$ inch thickness and then add one at a time until the surging stops. Fit the washers as follows :

(a) Remove the pump lever from the throttle spindle and then unscrew it from the actuating rod, counting the number of turns to unscrew.

(b) Remove the splitpin holding the spring abutment washer and thread the new washers onto the rod. Replace the lever on the rod, screwing it on the same number of turns as were made to unscrew it, then reassemble it to the carburetter.

Note : On no account remove the splitpin from the end of the pump rod and only insert just enough washers to cure the surging as their addition preloads the linkage. Do not add further washers after the point when the spring is compressed to $\frac{1}{2}$ inch (12.5 mm) with the throttle wide open.

To remove the governor, disconnect the operating rod and control rod at the governor end, then undo the nuts and remove the governor and bracket complete.

14:6   *The front capstan winch, mechanical*

In this section, refer to **FIGS 14:13** and **14:14**. Note, particularly, that there are minor component differences between the kit for installation on petrol and diesel vehicles and these are listed in **FIG 14:13**.

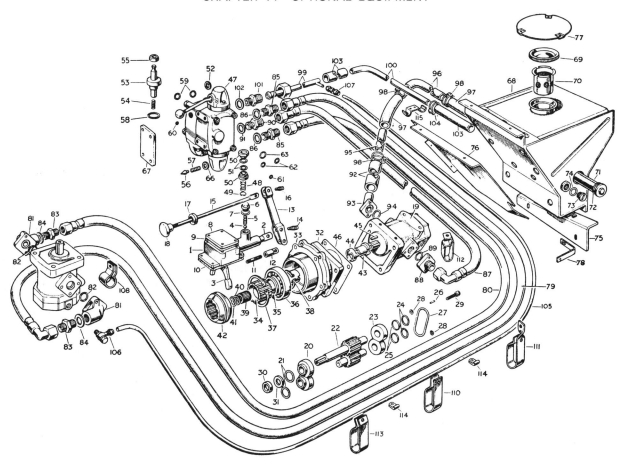

FIG 14:17   Hydraulic system layout

Key to Fig 14:17   1 Selector housing   2 Selector shaft   3 Selector fork   4 Ball (for selector control mechanism) 5 Spring (for selector control mechanism)   6 Plug for spring (for selector control mechanism)   7 Joint washer (for selector control mechanism)   8 Coverplate for selector housing   9 Joint washer, top coverplate   10 Joint washer   11 Stud for selector pivot 12 Pivot for selector lever 13 Operating lever for shaft 14 Clevis complete (fixing lever and pivot to selector shaft) 15 Rod for operating lever   16 Clevis complete (fixing rod to operating lever)   17 Grommet for rod   18 Knob 19 Hydraulic pump for power takeoff unit   20 Bush 'A' for gearshafts   21 O-ring for 'A' bushes   22 Gears and shafts 23 Bush 'C' for gearshafts 24 Sealing ring for 'C' bushes 25 Support ring for 'C' bushes 26 Special dowel for body and bush 27 O-ring for housing 28 O-ring, body ports 29 Special screw fixing body cover to body 30 Oil seal for shaft 31 Baffle for oil seal   32 Adaptor for hydraulic pump 33 Joint washer (for power takeoff unit) 34 Drive shaft (for power takeoff unit) 35 Distance piece (for power takeoff unit)   36 Ballbearing (for power takeoff unit)   37 Circlip (for power takeoff unit) 38 Circlip (for power takeoff unit)   39 Roller bearing (for power takeoff unit)   40 Retaining ring (fixing roller bearing to shaft) 41 Circlip (fixing roller bearing to shaft)   42 Dog clutch   43 Coupling sleeve (connecting hydraulic pump to drive shaft) 44 Coupling dog (connecting hydraulic pump to drive shaft) 45 Key (connecting hydraulic pump to drive shaft) 46 Joint washer, hydraulic motor   47 Control valve assembly   48 Piston return spring   49 Retaining ring for piston   50 Gland washer for piston   51 O-ring for piston   52 Washer for selector lever   53 Unloader piston   54 Spring for unloader piston 55 Valve seat for unloader piston   56 Relief valve   57 Spring, relief valve   58 O-ring, relief valve housing to unloader housing   59, 60, 61 O-ring, body face   62, 63 O-ring, lefthand coverplate   64, 65 O-ring, lefthand unloader   66 Special seal 67 Mounting plate (fixing control valve to heel board)   68 Oil tank   69 Filler cap   70 Filter gauze   71 Oil filter 72 Joint washer, oil filter   73 Drain plug   74 Joint washer, drain plug   75 Brackets for oil tank   76 Protection panel 77 Coverplate   78 Rear wing stay   79 Flexible pipe, control valve to motor, 113 inch long   80 Flexible pipe, control valve to motor, 101½ inch long   81 Elbow for flexible pipe   82 O-ring   83 Adaptor   84 Special seal   85 Adaptor (fixing flexible pipe to control valve)   86 Special seal (fixing flexible pipe to control valve)   87 Flexible pipe, pump to control valve, 26 inch long   88 Connection for pipe, pump to control valve   89 O-ring (connection to pump)   90 Adaptor (for pipe, pump to control valve, on control valve)   91 Special seal (for pipe, pump to control valve, on control valve) 92 Flexible pipe, pump to tank, pump end   93 Elbow on pump for flexible pipe   94 O-ring (fixing elbow to pump) 95 Pipe, steel, front (pump to tank)   96 Pipe, steel, rear (pump to tank)   97 Rubber connection, front to rear pipe and rear pipe to tank   98 Hose clip   99 Pipe, steel, front (control valve to tank)   100 Pipe, steel, rear (control valve to tank) 101 Adaptor on control valve for tank pipe   102 Joint washer for adaptor   103 Rubber connection, front to rear pipe and rear pipe to tank   104 Hose clip 105 Oil exhaust pipe for motor 106 Banjo complete 107 Union for exhaust pipe at rear 108-115 Clip (fixing oil pipes)

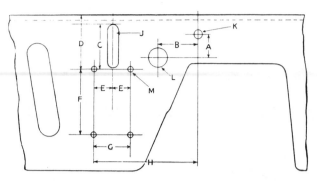

FIG 14:18   Drilling the heel board

Key to Fig 14:18
B 1.968 inch (50 mm)
D 2.750 inch (69 mm)   **E** Equal
G 1.500 inch (38 mm)
J Slot ½ inch (12.5 mm) wide
retaining bolt
M Four holes, ⅜ inch (9.5 mm) diameter

A 1.187 inch (30 mm)
C 2.250 inch (57 mm)
F 3 inch (76 mm)
H 4.968 inch (126 mm)
K Hole for seat strap
L ¾ inch (19 mm) diameter hole

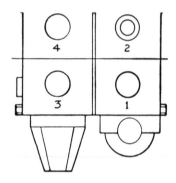

FIG 14:19   Position of control box connections

Key to Fig 14:19
2 Brass union and washer
4 Steel adaptor and seal

1 Steel adaptor and seal
3 Steel adaptor and seal

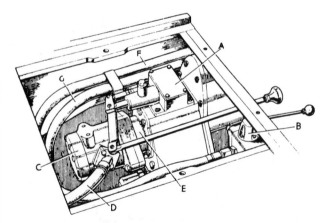

FIG 14:20   Hydraulic pump mounted in position

Key to Fig 14:20   **A** Power takeoff   **B** Control valve
C Pump   **D** Suction pipe to tank   **E** Pump adaptor
F Hose, winch motor to control valve, lefthand side
G Hose, winch motor to control valve, righthand side

A hand throttle (see **Section 14:8**) must be used in conjunction with the winch on petrol engined vehicles. New heavy duty front springs should also be fitted to these vehicles.

To fit the winch:

1 Remove the grille and radiator, then slacken the belt and withdraw the fan.

2 Drill a $\frac{27}{64}$ inch (10.318 mm) hole in the front face of the second chassis crossmember (the bumper is the first), midway between the sidemembers and $3\frac{9}{32}$ inch (83.3 mm) from the top face.

3 Fit a nut and plain washer to a $\frac{5}{16}$ inch UNF bolt screwed 1½ inches long. Drill the thread out of a $\frac{3}{8}$ inch UNF nut, slide it on the bolt, then screw on a Rivnut. Have $\frac{1}{8}$ inch (3.2 mm) of the bolt protruding, then lock the $\frac{5}{16}$ inch nut onto the distance piece ($\frac{3}{8}$ inch nut) and Rivnut (see **FIG 14:15**). Insert the assembly into the drilled hole, then, keeping the bolt and $\frac{3}{8}$ inch nut stationary, turn the $\frac{5}{16}$ inch nut clockwise 2½ turns. Remove bolt, nut, plain washer and distance piece. **FIG 14:16** shows the method of inserting and locking the Rivnut in the chassis.

4 Assemble the winch support plate (see **FIG 14:13**, item 45) to the chassis crossmember, securing it with a bolt in the Rivnut. Using the support plate as a template, mark off the other four holes for Rivnuts in the second chassis crossmember and the five $\frac{5}{16}$ inch (8 mm) clearance holes in the front bumper. Remove the support plate and bumper; drill all the holes and fit the four Rivnuts.

5 Remove the starting dog.

6 Remove the crankshaft pulley, strip it and fit the new driving plate, making sure the correct one for the engine, either petrol or diesel, is fitted.

7 Secure the shaft support brackets to the engine front cover, using the longer bolts or studs supplied. These brackets are items 69 and 70 or 71 and 72 (see **FIG 14:13**).

8 Replace the crankshaft pulley and the fan belt.

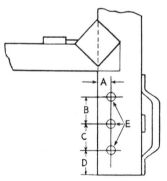

FIG 14:21   Mounting holes in rear crossmember, 88 models

Key to Fig 14:21
B 2⅝ inch (67 mm)
D 2½ inch (63.5 mm)

A 1¼ inch (32 mm)
C 2⅝ inch (67 mm)
E Three holes $\frac{11}{32}$ inch (9 mm) diameter

9 Secure the shaft housing 56 or 59 to plate 63, grease the shaft 55 and insert in the housing 56 or 59, sliding the driving flange 76 or 89 onto the splines. Insert the control shaft 80 or 94 into the housing 56 or 59 and secure the selector fork 81 or 95 to it with the fork in the groove of the driving flange. Fit the detent ball, spring and plug. Fit the grease nipple in the shaft housing. Bolt the shaft housing and support plate to the engine brackets.

10 Slide the two dust covers 54 onto shaft 51, then fit a spring 53 and plunger 52 into each end of shaft 51. Insert shaft 51 into shaft 55 and push one dust cover 54 over the joint.

11 Bolt the winch support plate 45 to the front bumper, then bolt the winch to the support plate. Offer the winch, plate and bumper up to position, engage shaft 51 with sleeve 33. Bolt the winch, bumper and support plate firmly in position. Slide the second dust cover 54 over the shaft to sleeve joint. Note that $\frac{1}{8}$ inch (3.2 mm) plain washers must be fitted between the plate and the Rivnuts on 86 and 107 models.

12 Slide the eyebolt 106 onto the rod 105, then fit the clevis 102 to the end of the rod. Fit the rod through the crossmember and bolt the eyebolt to the support plate. Fit the control knob 109. Fit the clevis 102 to the control shaft 80 or 94, adjusting the clevis so that when the knob is moved to the drive and free positions, the detent ball is engaged in the slot in the control shaft.

13 Drill holes in the bumper and mount the rope guide brackets 113 and the rope guide 118. Make sure the rope guide turns freely.

14 Fill the unit with SAE.40 oil and grease all other moving parts, not forgetting nipple 5 for the bollard shaft.

15 Replace the fan blade, grille panel and radiator.

To service the unit:

Remove the winch from the vehicle by reversing the fitting procedure, then proceed as follows:

1 Drain off the oil.

2 Drive out pin 34 and remove sleeve 33, then unscrew dog 31. Remove the oil seal retainer 27, then turn the worm shaft 18 while tapping it forwards out of the casing. Pull the ballbearing 24 from the shaft.

3 Remove cover 35, turn the unit over and remove screws 16 and cap 15. Undo bolt 12, drift out pin 9 and lift the bollard 7 from the shaft. Preserve the thrust washer 13 and any shims 14, then withdraw the shaft and worm wheel 18 from the casing.

4 Remove circlip 20 and press the shaft from the wheel.

5 If necessary, press out the bollard shaft bushes, the worm shaft oil seals and remove the roller bearing 21.

6 Thoroughly wash and inspect all parts for wear or damage. Renew any worn components, noting that the worm shaft and wheel and the bollard and shaft are only supplied as pairs.

7 Assemble the unit by reversing the dismantling procedure, but note the following points:

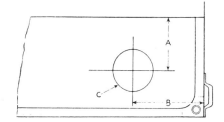

FIG 14:22   Hole in rear wheel arch, 88 models

Key to Fig 14:22   **A** 7 inch (178 mm)
B 9 inch (229 mm)   **C** 6 inch (152 mm) diameter

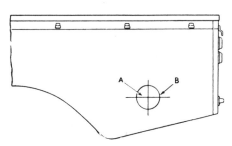

FIG 14:23   Hole in lefthand body side, 88 models

Key to Fig 14:23   **A** 4 inch (102 mm) hole central to oil filter plug   **B** Rubber grommet

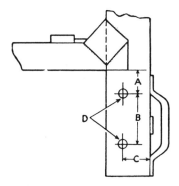

FIG 14:24   Mounting holes in rear crossmember, 109 models

Key to Fig 14:24   **A** $4\frac{3}{4}$ inch (121 mm)
B $7\frac{1}{2}$ inch (191 mm)   **C** $2\frac{1}{2}$ inch (64 mm)
D Two holes $\frac{17}{64}$ inch (7 mm) diameter

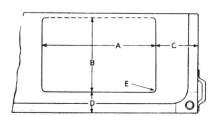

FIG 14:25   Aperture in lefthand side wheel arch, 109 models

Key to Fig 14:25   **A** 15 inch (381 mm)
B 12 inch (304 mm)   **C** $3\frac{1}{2}$ inch (89 mm)
D $1\frac{1}{2}$ inch (38 mm)   **E** $\frac{1}{4}$ inch (6 mm) radius

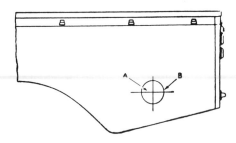

FIG 14:26 Hole in lefthand side panel, 109 models

Key to Fig 14:26   **A** 4 inch (102 mm) hole central to oil filter plug   **B** Grommet

(a) The roller bearing must be a push fit on the shaft and in the casing. The ballbearing must be a light press fit on the shaft and in the casing.

(b) The bollard shaft bushes must be a press fit in the casing and a sliding fit on the shaft. Ream to 1.312 inch (33.4 mm) after fitting. The upper bearing must stand $\frac{1}{8}$ inch (3.17 mm) proud of the casing.

(c) The oil seal lips must face inwards and the worm shaft must turn freely with no end float.

(d) Adjust the shims on the bollard shaft to give .003 to .005 inch (.075 to .125 mm) end float.

(e) The drive shaft bush 62 must be a press fit in the housing and must be reamed to .75 inch (19.05 mm) after fitting.

8 Refill the unit with oil and grease all moving parts.

14:7 *The hydraulic front winch*

To fit the winch:

1 Ensure that the bumper is level and undamaged. Remove and discard the front valance. Remove the radiator grille.

2 Fit the hydraulic pipe elbows to the motor as shown in **FIG 14:17**.

3 Install the winch between the front bumper and the chassis crossmember, using the winch mounting bracket holes as drilling templates. For fitting the necessary Rivnuts, refer to **Section 14:6**. It will be necessary to remove and replace the front bumper during this operation. Replace the radiator grille.

4 Drill the heel board as shown in **FIG14:18**, then fit the hydraulic control valve to it. Before fitting the control valve, install the adaptors and brass union in the positions shown at **FIG 14:19**.

5 Fit the power takeoff unit with the hydraulic pump and selector to the transfer casing in a similar manner to that adopted for the centre power takeoff described in **Section 14:1**. Pass the selector control rod through the hole in the heel board. **FIG 14:20** shows the layout. The port marked 'inlet' must be to the righthand side.

6 The oil reservoir must now be installed. Slightly different fittings are needed for the 88 and 109 models. Therefore, the 88 will be described first.

(a) Drill three holes in the underside of the rear crossmember as shown in **FIG 14:21**.

(b) Cut the hole in the lefthand wheel arch box to the dimensions given in **FIG 14:22**.

(c) Using the coverplate as a template, drill the wheel arch box and fit the three spire nuts.

(d) Jack up the vehicle and remove the lefthand road wheel and wing stay.

(e) Bolt the tank mounting bracket to the chassis, then mount the tank. Drill all other holes for fixing bolts, fit the bolts and tighten all nuts.

(f) Cut a 3 inch hole in the lefthand side rear wing as shown in **FIG 14:23**.

7 To fit the oil reservoir, 109 models:

(a) Drill the holes in the rear crossmember as shown in **FIG 14:24**, then cut the aperture in the lefthand side wheel arch shown in **FIG 14:25**.

(b) Attach the tank and its brackets, using the brackets to drill the remaining holes. Tighten all bolts and nuts securely.

(c) Cut the hole in the lefthand side body panel shown in **FIG 14:26**.

8 Connect the hydraulic pipes as shown in **FIG 14:27**. This shows the 109 model layout, but the 88 model is generally similar. Fit the pipes to the control valve as shown in **FIG 14:28**.

9 Fill the hydraulic reservoir and winch gearbox with the correct grade of oil as shown in the table below.

To service the winch:

Refer to **FIG 14:29**. Dismantling is straightforward provided the following points are noted:

1 Remove the screw plugs 51 and withdraw the springs and pads first of all.

2 Drain off the oil, then remove the support bracket and selector lever from the winch drum end of the unit. Pull off the winch drum.

3 Withdraw the hydraulic motor complete.

4 Remove the end plate 13, support the worm wheel and gently drive the shaft 39 out.

5 Slacken the brake band, then remove items 20 to 30 and drive out the worm shaft 19. Note which way round the distance piece 24 is fitted.

Components

	Hydraulic winch supply tank	*Hydraulic winch gearbox*	*Lubrication nipples*
Capacities	4$\frac{1}{2}$ gallons (20 litres)	2 pints (1 litre)	–
SAE	–	90 EP	–
BP	–	Energol EP SAE.90	Energrease L.2
Duckhams	–	Duckhams Hypoid 90	Duckhams L.B.10 Grease
Esso	Terresso 43 or Essolube HD 10/W	Esso Gear Oil G.P.90	Esso Multi-purpose Grease H
Mobil	D.T.E. Light	Mobilube G.X.90	Mobilgrease M.P.
Shell	Tellus 27	Spirax 90 EP	Retinax A
Wakefield	Hyspin 70 or Castrolite	Castrol Hypoy	Castrolease L.M.

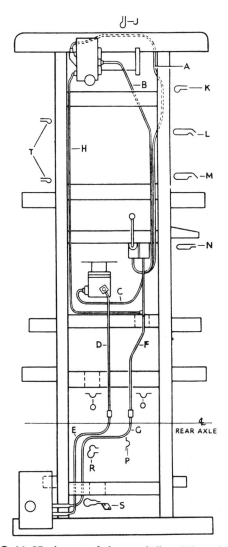

FIG 14:27 Layout of pipes and clips, 109 models

Key to Fig 14:27   **A** Pipe, upper, on control valve
B Pipe, lower, on control valve   **C** Pipe, lower, on control valve   **D** Pipe, suction   **E** Pipe, suction   **F** Pipe, upper, on control valve   **G** Pipe, return reservoir
H Pipe, exhaust   **J** Clip, front bumper (single)
K Clip, righthand chassis sidemember (single)   **L** Clip, righthand chassis sidemember (double)   **M** Clip, righthand chassis sidemember (double)   **N** Clip, righthand, rear engine mounting (double)   **O** Clip, chassis crossmember
P Clip, return pipe to body   **R** Clip, suction and return pipes together   **S** Clip, suction return pipe to rear crossmember   **T** Clip, motor exhaust pipe to chassis frame

6 Clean all the components and renew where needed. The worm shaft and wheel must be renewed as a pair if damaged.
7 First fit the worm shaft and its bearings. Make sure the bearings are fitted the correct way round as they are thrust bearings. Adjust the end float to .002 inch (.05 mm) by shims 21. Fit the brake components.
8 Fit the oil seal 44 and bearing 41 to the casing.
9 Check that shaft 39, key 40 and wheel 19 can be assembled to a smooth sliding fit. Place the wheel in the casing in mesh with the worm shaft. Fit shaft 39

without the key 40. Fit the distance ring 43 and then measure with feeler gauges the gap between this ring and the wheel. Remove the shaft and wheel and place shims 42 to this value between the wheel and bearing 41. Reassemble the shaft wheel and key.
10 Complete the assembly by reversing the dismantling procedure.

The hydraulic motor:

Refer to **FIG 14:30**. This unit should not be dismantled unless conditions of absolute cleanliness can be provided. If this is possible, proceed as follows:
1 Remove all dirt from the exterior, then withdraw the end cover screws and the end cover. Lift out the seals **H, J, K** and **G**.
2 Slide out the shafts **D** and **E** and then jar out the seals **F, L** and **M**.
3 Renew the shaft seal **N** if necessary.
4 Renew any damaged components or worn seals.
5 Reassemble by reversing the dismantling operation but, when fitting the drive shaft, put a thimble with a tapered nose over the keyway end so that the shaft seal is not cut by forcing over the larger diameter. A smear of Silicone MS.4 grease will hold the seals **J, K, L** and **M** in position while fitting.
6 When the motor is completely assembled, pour a small quantity of hydraulic oil in the ports and see that the shaft rotates easily by hand. If new seals have been fitted, the motor must be carefully run in for at least thirty minutes.
7 Refit to the winch, using a new joint washer.

The hydraulic pump:

Refer to **FIG 14:31**. This unit is almost identical to the hydraulic motor and similar procedures are necessary to strip and recondition it. The necessity for running in

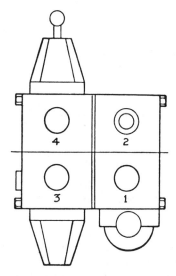

FIG 14:28 Pipe fitting sequence, control valve

Key to Fig 14:28   **1** Flexible pipe from pump, to be fitted first   **2** Return pipe to tank, to be fitted second   **3** Flexible pipe from front winch, righthand side connection, fitted third   **4** Flexible pipe from front winch, lefthand side connection, fitted last

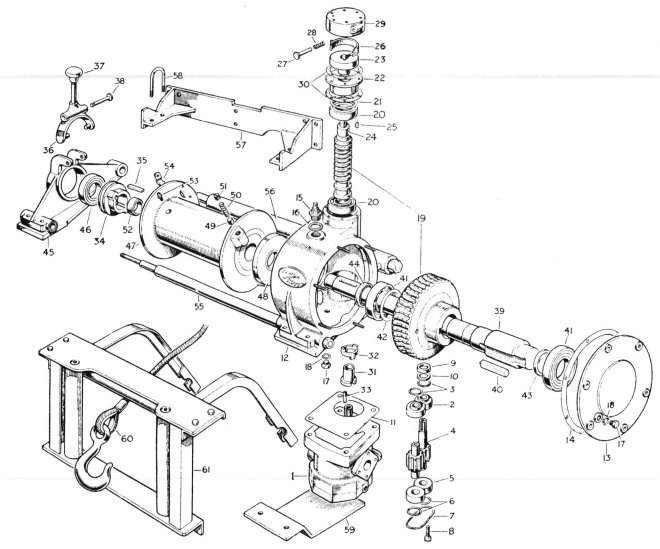

FIG 14:29   Layout of hydraulic winch

Key to Fig 14:29   1 Hydraulic motor   2 Bushes, 'B' for gearshaft   3 O-rings   4 Gears and shaft   5 Bush, 'A' for gearshafts
6 Sealing ring for 'A' bushes   7 O-ring for housing   8 Special screw fixing body cover and body   9 Shaft oil seal
10 Oil seal baffle   11 Joint washer   12 Gearbox casing   13 End plate for casing   14 Joint washer   15 Oil filler plug
16 Joint washer   17 Oil level and drain plug   18 Joint washer   19 Worm wheel, worm shaft and distance pieces
20 Bearing for worm shaft   21 Shims   22 Retaining cap   23 Brake drum   24 Distance piece (for brake drum)
25 Key (for brake drum)   26 Brake band   27 Plunger   28 Spring   29 Brake drum cover   30 Joint washer   31 Coupling
sleeve (connecting motor unit to worm shaft)   32 Coupling dog (connecting motor unit to worm shaft)   33 Key (connecting
motor unit to worm shaft)   34 Dog clutch   35 Key   36 Selector lever   37 Knob   38 Retaining pin   39 Worm and drum shaft
40 Key fixing worm to shaft   41 Bearing for shaft, worm end   42 Shims   43 Distance ring for shaft, worm end
44 Oil seal for shaft, worm end   45 Support bracket for worm and drum shaft   46 Bearing for worm and drum shaft
47 Cable drum   48 Friction disc   49 Pad (for friction disc)   50 Spring (for friction disc)   51 Retaining plug (for friction disc)
52 Thrust ring   53 Grease point   54 Cleat   55 Connecting tube, front   56 Connecting tube, rear   57 Rear mounting bracket
58 U-bolt   59 Protection shield   60 Winch cable   61 Guide frame for cable

also applies if new seals have been fitted. **FIG 14:17**
shows the attachment of the pump to the power takeoff
unit. Removal and replacement is effected by releasing
the nuts holding the pump flange to the power takeoff
unit.

14:8   *The hand speed control. Petrol models*

Refer to **FIG 14:32**. To fit the control, proceed as
follows:

1 Disconnect the throttle linkage, then remove the
existing spindle, bellcrank and relay levers and
replace them with the new spindle 5, hand control
lever 11, bellcrank 8 and relay lever 9. Reconnect the
linkage.
2 Secure bracket 13 to the tapped hole in the top rear
face of the inlet manifold.
3 Drill a suitable hole in the dash control panel and fit
the hand control 1. Connect the outer cable to the
bracket 13 with the clip 17 and the inner cable to the

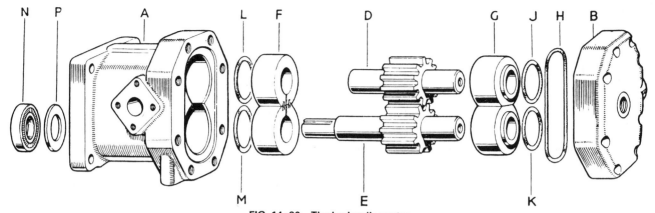

FIG 14:30   The hydraulic motor

Key to Fig 14:30   **A** Body   **B** Coverplate   **D** Drive shaft and gear (matched pair)   **E** Driven gear (matched pair)
F Bushes 'A'   **G** Bushes 'C'   **H** O-ring   **J** Support ring   **K** Support ring   **L** O-ring   **M** O-ring   **N** Shaft seal
P Baffle washer

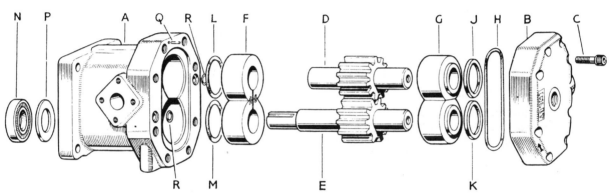

FIG 14:31   The hydraulic pump

Key to Fig 14:31   **A** Body   **B** Coverplate   **C** Special bolts   **D** Drive shaft and gear (matched pair)
E Driven gear (matched pair)   **F** Bushes 'A'   **G** Bushes 'C'   **H** O-ring   **J** Support ring   **K** Support ring   **L** O-ring
M O-ring   **N** Shaft seal   **P** Baffle washer   **Q** Dowel   **R** O-ring

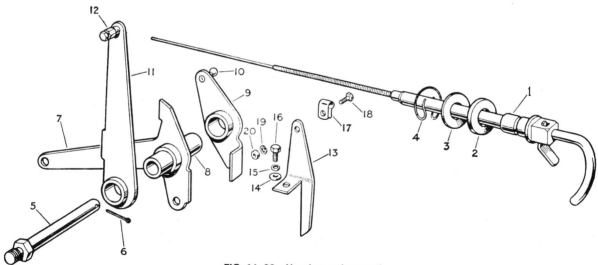

FIG 14:32   Hand speed control

Key to Fig 14:32   1-4 Hand throttle control   5, 6 Spindle for bellcrank   7, 8 Bellcrank lever   9, 10 Relay lever
11, 12 Hand throttle lever   13 Abutment bracket for hand throttle   14 Plain washer (fixing abutment bracket)
15 Spring washer (fixing abutment bracket)   16 Setbolt (fixing abutment bracket)   17 Cable clip (fixing hand throttle cable to
abutment bracket)   18 Screw (fixing hand throttle cable to abutment bracket)   19 Spring washer (fixing hand throttle cable
to abutment bracket)   20 Nut (fixing hand throttle cable to abutment bracket)

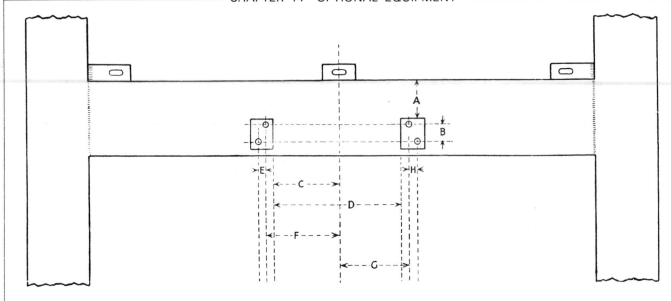

FIG 14:33   Location of tapping plate

Key to Fig 14:33   **A** $1\frac{15}{16}$ inch (49.2 mm)   **B** $1\frac{1}{4}$ inch (31.7 mm)   **C** $4\frac{7}{8}$ inch (123.8 mm)   **D** $8\frac{1}{4}$ inch (209.5 mm)
E $\frac{1}{2}$ inch (12.7 mm)   **F** $5\frac{7}{8}$ inch (149.2 mm)   **G** $4\frac{3}{8}$ inch (111 mm)   **H** $\frac{1}{2}$ inch (12.7 mm)

lever 11. See that the cable is not kinked or taken round sharp corners. Adjust until there is $\frac{1}{16}$ inch (1.58 mm) play between lever 11 and the bellcrank 8 and the same between the bellcrank and the relay lever 9.

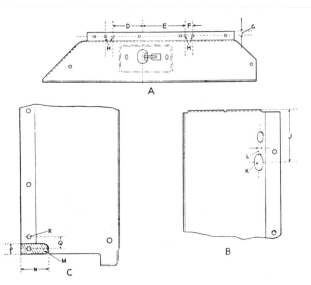

FIG 14:34   Drilling the grille panels

Key to Fig 14:34   **A** Top panel   **B** Lefthand side panel
C Righthand side panel   **D** $3\frac{15}{16}$ inch (100 mm)
E $5\frac{7}{16}$ inch (138 mm)   **F** $\frac{15}{16}$ inch (23.8 mm)
G $\frac{9}{16}$ inch (14.3 mm)   **H** Four new holes $\frac{9}{32}$ inch (7.1 mm)
diameter   **J** $3\frac{1}{4}$ inch (82.5 mm)   **K** One new hole $1\frac{1}{8}$ inch
(28.6 mm) diameter   **L** $\frac{1}{8}$ inch (3.2 mm)   **M** Shaded area
represents section to be cut away   **N** $1\frac{3}{4}$ inch (44.4 mm)
P $\frac{5}{8}$ inch (15.8 mm)   **Q** $\frac{1}{2}$ inch (12.7 mm)
R One new hole $\frac{9}{32}$ inch (7.1 mm) diameter

14:9 *The oil cooler. All models*

This is essential equipment whenever the vehicle is used as a stationary power unit or operates in high ambient temperatures for any appreciable time.

To fit the oil cooler:

1 Drain the engine oil and remove the sump.
2 Diesel models: remove the oil relief plug from the pump, fit the new plug and replace the sump.
   Petrol models: discard the existing pressure relief valve screw and spring and withdraw the oil pump. Fit the new pump gears, cover, bolts and splitpins. Replace the pump and fit the new pressure relief valve screw and spring. Replace the sump.
3 Attach the flexible oil pipe to the sump by the banjo and two joint washers.
4 Remove the air cleaner, the battery (or batteries), drain and remove the radiator and grille panel.
5 Discard the fan and, on petrol models, the distance piece.
6 Drive screw the two tapping plates to the chassis, then tap them $\frac{1}{4}$ inch UNF as shown in **FIG 14:33**.
7 Fit the oil relief valve to the top union of the cooler.
8 Discard the inner lefthand nut and bolt securing the grille panel assembly to the top of the radiator, detach the earth clip and retighten the top panel bolt.
9 Drill the grille panels as shown in **FIG 14:34**.
10 Petrol models: fit the new fan cowl and radiator cap.
11 Diesel models: fit the new crankshaft double pulley assembly and the generator double pulley.
12 Both models: fit the new fan and driving belts and replace the radiator and grille panel assembly.
13 Fit the oil cooler and connect the pipes as shown in **FIGS 14:35** or **14:36**.

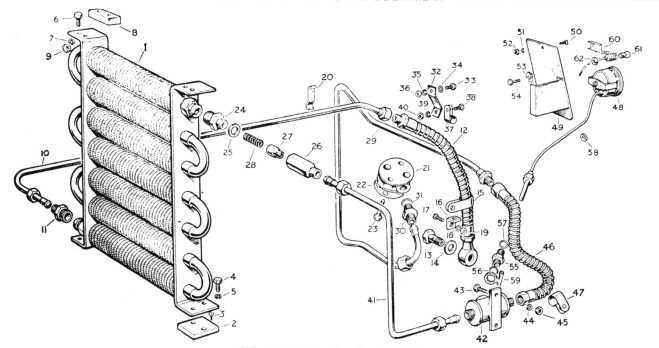

FIG 14:35 Oil cooler, diesel models

Key to Fig 14:35   1 Oil cooler   2 Tapping plate   3 Drive screw, plate to frame   4, 5 Fixings (cooler to chassis frame)
6-9 Fixings (cooler to radiator and grille panel)   10 Oil return pipe   11 Union for return pipe   12 Flexible oil pipe, return to sump
13, 14 Fixings (flexible pipe to sump)   15 Clip, for flexible oil pipe   16 Bracket for clip   17-19 Fixings (return pipe clip to bracket)
20 Clip for oil return pipe   21 Adaptor for engine oil filter   22 Joint washer for adaptor   23 Bolt, fixing adaptor
24, 25 Oil union and joint washer   26 Body   27 Plunger   28 Spring for plunger   29 Oil pipe, union to flexible pipe
30 Union for oil pipe   31 Joint washer for union   32 Bracket for clip   33-36 Fixings (bracket to front engine lifting bracket)
37 Clip for union to flexible oil pipe   38-40 Fixings (clip to bracket)   41 Oil pipe to relief valve   42 Thermometer
pocket complete   43-45 Fixings (thermometer pocket to valance)   46 Flexible oil pipe, pump to pocket   47 Clip fixing
flexible pipe to lefthand battery support

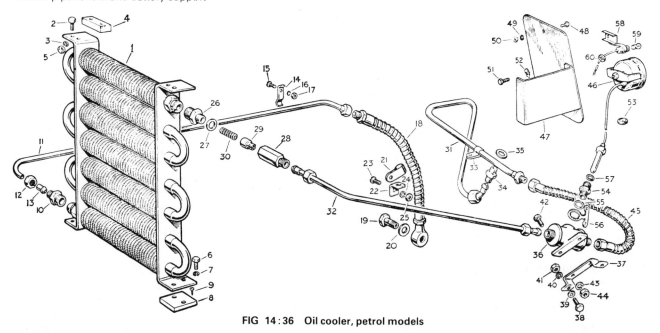

FIG 14:36 Oil cooler, petrol models

Key to Fig 14:36   1 Oil cooler   2-5 Fixings (oil cooler to radiator)   6, 7 Fixings (oil cooler to frame)   8 Tapping plate for oil cooler
9 Drive screw fixing plate to frame   10 Oil return pipe union   11 Oil return pipe   12, 13 Union fixings (for return pipe)
14 Oil return pipe clip   15-17 Fixings (for clip)   18 Flexible oil pipe, return to sump   19, 20 Fixings (flexible pipe to sump)
21 Flexible pipe clip   22 Clip bracket   23-25 Fixings (for clip)   26 Oil union (oil release valve)   27 Joint washer for union
(oil release valve)   28 Body (oil release valve)   29 Plunger (oil release valve)   30 Spring for plunger (oil release valve)
31 Oil pipe, union to flexible pipe   32 Oil pipe to relief valve   33 Clip for pipe (union to flexible pipe)   34 Union for oil pipe
(on oil filter adaptor)   35 Joint washer for union (on oil filter adaptor)   36 Thermometer pocket complete   37-41 Not required
42-44 Fixings (pocket to wing valance)   45 Flexible pipe (pump to pocket)   46 Oil temperature gauge
47 Mounting bracket for gauge   48-52 Fixings (mounting bracket to dash)   53 Grommet for pipe in dash

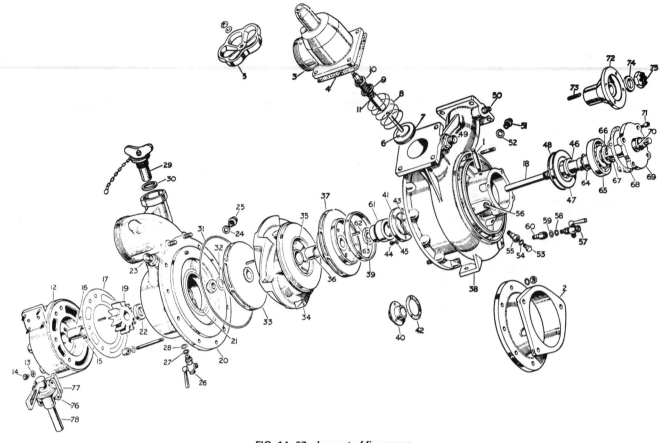

FIG 14:37 Layout of fire pump

Key to Fig 14:37   1 Oil filler tube   2 Mounting ring   3 Delivery valve   4 Joint washer for valve   5 Control wheel
6 Spindle and seal assembly   7 Rubber seal   8 Spring   9 Circlip   10 Seal   11 Spindle body   12 Priming casing
13 Washer (for priming casing)   14 Plug (for priming casing)   15 Grubscrew, securing bush   16 Bush for shaft
17 Gasket for priming casing   18 Shaft with washer and keys   19 Priming impeller   20 Suction casing   21 Wearing ring
22 Seal (in suction casing) for shaft   23 Suction pipe union, first aid   24 Washer (for suction casing)   25 Plug (for suction casing)
26 Drain cock   27 Fibre washer   28 Copper washer   29 Cap and filter assembly   30 Washer for cap   31 Rubber O-ring
32 Locking washer 33 Suction impeller 34 Diffuser ring 35 Wearing ring 36 Distance piece 37 Suction and pressure impeller
38 Main casing (main casing)   39 Wearing ring   40 Stationary sealing ring   41 Stationary sealing ring   42 Joint washer
43 Sealing ring   44 Screw (for sealing ring)   45 Washer (for sealing ring)   46 Seal   47 Cover for rear seal   48 Sealing ring
49 Union for delivery pipe, first aid   50 Union for pressure gauge pipe   51 Plug   52 Washer for plug   53 Plug, oil drain
54 Joint washer   55 Extension tube   56 Grease nipple   57 Drain cock   58 Fibre washer (for drain cock)
59 Copper washer (for drain cock)   60 Extension for drain cock   61 Mechanical seal   62 Fibre washer   63 Rubber O-ring
64 Circlip   65 Ballbearing 67 Circlip 68 Joint washer 69 Bearing cover 70 Seal 71 Screw for cover   72 Driving flange
73 Key for flange   74 Washer for flange   75 Nut for flange   76 Priming cock   77 Joint washer for cock   78 Exhaust pipe

14 Cut a 1 inch (25.4 mm) hole in the lefthand glove box, 3 inches (75 mm) from the base and 2 inches (50.8 mm) from the righthand side.

15 Pass the oil temperature gauge capillary tube through and attach the gauge to the dash with the bracket supplied. Fit the bulb end of the tube in the thermometer pocket. See **FIG 14:35**, item 42, **FIG 14:36**, item 36.

16 Refill the radiator and replace the air cleaner, batteries, etc. Refill the sump with oil.

17 Petrol models : fit a slave oil pressure gauge to the warning light tapping and adjust the oil pressure relief valve to give 75 to 80 lb/sq inch (5.3 to 5.6 kg/sq cm) at 2500 rev/min at normal temperature. Stop the engine, remove the gauge and reconnect the warning light switch.

14 : 10 *Fire fighting equipment*

Land-Rover Fire Tenders are basically the same as standard models and the maintenance procedure, generally, is unchanged.

The pump, mounted at the rear of the vehicle, is a two-stage, self-priming, high-pressure impeller type. A single shaft, supported on a plain bearing at the rearmost end and a ballbearing at the driving end, carries three impellers. The first impeller, furthest from the driving end of the pump, withdraws air from the suction pipe, causing the necessary depression to induce a flow of water to the pump. The two main impellers maintain and pressurize the water flow.

An engine speed governor and oil cooler are used in conjunction with the pump ; drive is taken from the rear of the gearbox transfer casing by propeller shaft.

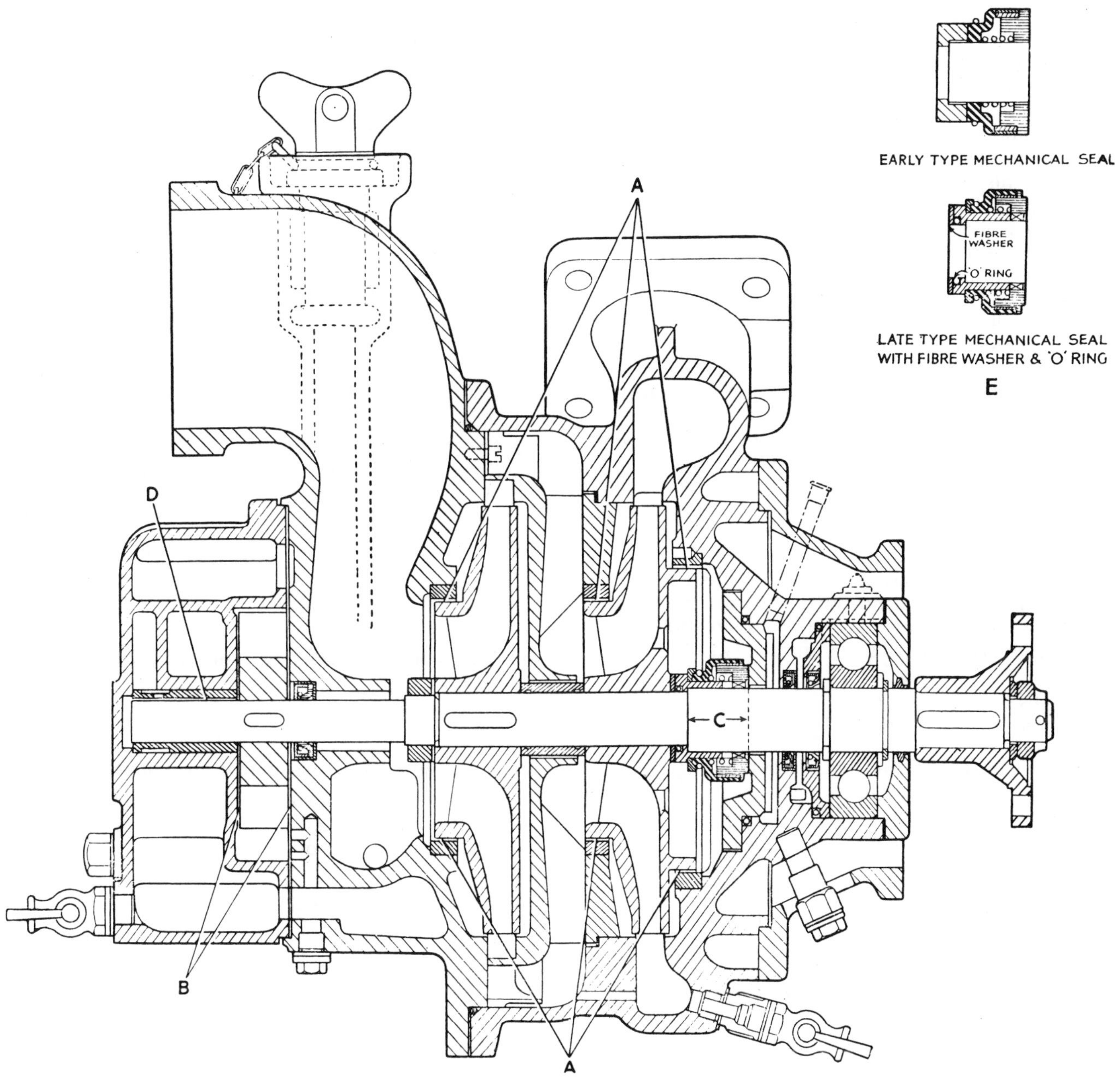

EARLY TYPE MECHANICAL SEAL

LATE TYPE MECHANICAL SEAL
WITH FIBRE WASHER & 'O' RING

E

FIG 14:38 Sectional view of pump

Key to Fig 14:38 **A** Wearing ring clearance .01 inch (.25 mm) **B** Impeller total end float .008 inch (.2 mm)
C 1.102 ± .012 inch (28 ± .3 mm)

The pump:

To remove:

1 Drain the pump and remove the rearmost drain plug or tap. Disconnect the first aid pipes and pressure gauge pipe.

2 Release the driving shaft at the rear of the gearbox.

3 Support the pump on a lifting tackle, then remove the mounting bolts. Either draw the pump and shaft backwards or move the vehicle forwards.

4 Lower the unit to the ground, remove the foremost drain tap and disconnect the propeller shaft.

To dismantle the pump:

In this section, refer to **FIG 14:37**.

1 Unscrew pipe 1, plug 53 and extension 55. The oil will drain off.

2 Remove mounting ring 2.

3 Withdraw the valve assemblies 3 and dismantle the valve.

4 Undo the nuts and gently tap the priming pump cover 12 away from the pump. Remove screw 15 and extract bush 16.

5 Slide the impeller 19 from the shaft and take out the key.

6 Undo the nuts and withdraw casing 20.

7 Unscrew the nut and withdraw the suction impeller 33.

8 Draw the diffuser 34 from the shaft, then remove distance piece 36, pressure impeller 37 and its key.

9 Remove the nut (lefthand thread) securing the driving flange 72, then withdraw the flange and key. Hold the shaft in soft jaws in a vertical position while doing this, otherwise it can easily be bent.

10 Unscrew the Allen bolts, then tap the shaft on the impeller side of the main casing to remove the shaft, bearing 65 and cover 69. All the seals may now be removed from the bearing cover and main casing.

11 Check all components for wear which will reduce the efficiency of the pump. Renew the bush 16 and see that the end float of the priming pump impeller 19 does not exceed .008 inch (.2 mm). Renew the seal 22.

12 See that the clearance between the impellers and wearing rings does not exceed .01 inch (.25 mm). If this increases beyond .02 inch (.5 mm), the impeller shoulders must be reground and have undersize rings fitted (see **FIG 14:38**).

13 Early pumps should have the late type mechanical seal with fibre washer and O-ring fitted (see **FIG 14:38**). Ensure that the dimension from the friction face of the stationary seal to the shaft shoulder is 1.102 ± .012 inch (28 ± .3 mm) (see **FIG 14:38**, item **C**).

14 If a new stationary seal (see **FIG 14:37**, item 41) is fitted, it must be accurately turned and lapped in position.

15 Renew the ballbearing if at all doubtful.

To assemble the pump:

1 Reverse the dismantling procedure, but note that the mechanical seal must be fitted with its splines correlated. When it is against the shaft shoulder the end of the shaft keyway for the pressure impeller will be .196 inch (4 mm) from its face.

2 Use grease throughout the assembly and top up with oil when completed.

3 Refit the pump to the vehicle.

14:11 *Fault diagnosis (fire pump)*

(a) No delivery. High vacuum, valves closed but no pressure build up

1 Suction pipe blocked

(b) No delivery. Low vacuum and air escaping from exhaust pipe

1 Leaking hose
2 Leaking delivery valve
3 Leaking mechanical seal

(c) Gauge shows pressure but no delivery

1 Suction hose blocked
2 Foreign matter in pump
3 Pressure gauge failed
4 Water level at supply failing

(d) Vacuum falls after prolonged running with closed valve

1 Water in priming pump overheated

(e) No vacuum, air escaping from exhaust pipe

1 Delivery valve open
2 Drain cock open

(f) No vacuum, no air escaping from exhaust pipe

1 No water in priming pump
2 Filler strainer choked
3 Priming lever in 'Working' position

(g) Water leak from oil filler

1 Worn mechanical seal or scored stationary seal

APPENDIX

CONVERSION TABLE

TECHNICAL DATA

WIRING DIAGRAMS

HINTS ON MAINTENANCE AND OVERHAUL

GLOSSARY OF TERMS

INDEX

Inches	Decimals	Milli-metres	Inches to Millimetres Inches	Inches to Millimetres mm	Millimetres to Inches mm	Millimetres to Inches Inches
1/64	.015625	.3969	.001	.0254	.01	.00039
1/32	.03125	.7937	.002	.0508	.02	.00079
3/64	.046875	1.1906	.003	.0762	.03	.00118
1/16	.0625	1.5875	.004	.1016	.04	.00157
5/64	.078125	1.9844	.005	.1270	.05	.00197
3/32	.09375	2.3812	.006	.1524	.06	.00236
7/64	.109375	2.7781	.007	.1778	.07	.00276
1/8	.125	3.1750	.008	.2032	.08	.00315
9/64	.140625	3.5719	.009	.2286	.09	.00354
5/32	.15625	3.9687	.01	.254	.1	.00394
11/64	.171875	4.3656	.02	.508	.2	.00787
3/16	.1875	4.7625	.03	.762	.3	.01181
13/64	.203125	5.1594	.04	1.016	.4	.01575
7/32	.21875	5.5562	.05	1.270	.5	.01969
15/64	.234375	5.9531	.06	1.524	.6	.02362
1/4	.25	6.3500	.07	1.778	.7	.02756
17/64	.265625	6.7469	.08	2.032	.8	.03150
9/32	.28125	7.1437	.09	2.286	.9	.03543
19/64	.296875	7.5406	.1	2.54	1	.03937
5/16	.3125	7.9375	.2	5.08	2	.07874
21/64	.328125	8.3344	.3	7.62	3	.11811
11/32	.34375	8.7312	.4	10.16	4	.15748
23/64	.359375	9.1281	.5	12.70	5	.19685
3/8	.375	9.5250	.6	15.24	6	.23622
25/64	.390625	9.9219	.7	17.78	7	.27559
13/32	.40625	10.3187	.8	20.32	8	.31496
27/64	.421875	10.7156	.9	22.86	9	.35433
7/16	.4375	11.1125	1	25.4	10	.39370
29/64	.453125	11.5094	2	50.8	11	.43307
15/32	.46875	11.9062	3	76.2	12	.47244
31/64	.484375	12.3031	4	101.6	13	.51181
1/2	.5	12.7000	5	127.0	14	.55118
33/64	.515625	13.0969	6	152.4	15	.59055
17/32	.53125	13.4937	7	177.8	16	.62992
35/64	.546875	13.8906	8	203.2	17	.66929
9/16	.5625	14.2875	9	228.6	18	.70866
37/64	.578125	14.6844	10	254.0	19	.74803
19/32	.59375	15.0812	11	279.4	20	.78740
39/64	.609375	15.4781	12	304.8	21	.82677
5/8	.625	15.8750	13	330.2	22	.86614
41/64	.640625	16.2719	14	355.6	23	.90551
21/32	.65625	16.6687	15	381.0	24	.94488
43/64	.671875	17.0656	16	406.4	25	.98425
11/16	.6875	17.4625	17	431.8	26	1.02362
45/64	.703125	17.8594	18	457.2	27	1.06299
23/32	.71875	18.2562	19	482.6	28	1.10236
47/64	.734375	18.6531	20	508.0	29	1.14173
3/4	.75	19.0500	21	533.4	30	1.18110
49/64	.765625	19.4469	22	558.8	31	1.22047
25/32	.78125	19.8437	23	584.2	32	1.25984
51/64	.796875	20.2406	24	609.6	33	1.29921
13/16	.8125	20.6375	25	635.0	34	1.33858
53/64	.828125	21.0344	26	660.4	35	1.37795
27/32	.84375	21.4312	27	685.8	36	1.41732
55/64	.859375	21.8281	28	711.2	37	1.4567
7/8	.875	22.2250	29	736.6	38	1.4961
57/64	.890625	22.6219	30	762.0	39	1.5354
29/32	.90625	23.0187	31	787.4	40	1.5748
59/64	.921875	23.4156	32	812.8	41	1.6142
15/16	.9375	23.8125	33	838.2	42	1.6535
61/64	.953125	24.2094	34	863.6	43	1.6929
31/32	.96875	24.6062	35	889.0	44	1.7323
63/64	.984375	25.0031	36	914.4	45	1.7717

UNITS	Pints to Litres	Gallons to Litres	Litres to Pints	Litres to Gallons	Miles to Kilometres	Kilometres to Miles	Lbs. per sq. In. to Kg. per sq. Cm.	Kg. per sq. Cm. to Lbs. per sq. In.
1	.57	4.55	1.76	.22	1.61	.62	.07	14.22
2	1.14	9.09	3.52	.44	3.22	1.24	.14	28.50
3	1.70	13.64	5.28	.66	4.83	1.86	.21	42.67
4	2.27	18.18	7.04	.88	6.44	2.49	.28	56.89
5	2.84	22.73	8.80	1.10	8.05	3.11	.35	71.12
6	3.41	27.28	10.56	1.32	9.66	3.73	.42	85.34
7	3.98	31.82	12.32	1.54	11.27	4.35	.49	99.56
8	4.55	36.37	14.08	1.76	12.88	4.97	.56	113.79
9		40.91	15.84	1.98	14.48	5.59	.63	128.00
10		45.46	17.60	2.20	16.09	6.21	.70	142.23
20				4.40	32.19	12.43	1.41	284.47
30				6.60	48.28	18.64	2.11	426.70
40				8.80	64.37	24.85		
50					80.47	31.07		
60					96.56	37.28		
70					112.65	43.50		
80					128.75	49.71		
90					144.84	55.92		
100					160.93	62.14		

UNITS	Lb ft to kgm	Kgm to lb ft	UNITS	Lb ft to kgm	Kgm to lb ft
1	.138	7.233	7	.967	50.631
2	.276	14.466	8	1.106	57.864
3	.414	21.699	9	1.244	65.097
4	.553	28.932	10	1.382	72.330
5	.691	36.165	20	2.765	144.660
6	.829	43.398	30	4.147	216.990

LRAB2

TECHNICAL DATA

Dimensions are in inches unless otherwise stated

PETROL ENGINES

	2¼ litre	2.6 litre
Bore and stroke	90.47 x 88.9 mm	77.8 x 92.075 mm
Capacity	2286 cc	2625 cc
Compression ratio	7 : 1 or 8 : 1	7 : 1 or 7.8 : 1
Crankshaft:		
Main journal diameter	2.4995 to 2.50	2.6240 to 2.6245
Main bearing clearance	.0008 to .00285	.0006 to .002
Main journal minimum regrind diameter	2.460	2.584
End float	.002 to .006	.002 to .006
Crankpin diameter	Early models 2.126	All models 1.875 + .00075
	Late models 2.312	
Crankpin minimum regrind diameter	2.272	1.835
	(Early models may not be ground)	
Connecting rods:		
Bearing fit on crankpin	.00075 to .0027	.00075 to .0025
End float at big-end	.007 to .012	.006 to .015
Gudgeon pin bush, fit in rod, interference	.001 to .003	.001 to .003
Gudgeon pin bush internal diameter	1.000 + .0003	.8755 − .0005
Gudgeon pin fit in bush, clearance	.0003 to .0005	.0002 to .0006
Pistons:		
Clearance, top of skirt	.003 to .004	.003 to .0035
Clearance, bottom of skirt: Series 2, 2A	.0019 to .0023	.002 to .0025
Series 3	.0019 to .0024	.0019 to .0024
Compression rings:		
Type	Taper periphery, both engines	
Gap	.015 to .020 both engines	
Clearance in groove	.0018 to .0038 both engines	
Oil control ring:		
Type	Slotted, square edge	Duaflex 61
Gap	.015 to .020	.015 to .033
Clearance in groove	.0015 to .0035	.002 to .004
Fit of gudgeon pin in piston, interference	0 to .0002	Push fit at 60°F
Camshaft:		
Journal diameter	1.842 − .001	.999
End float	.0025 to .0055	.0045 to .0065
Clearance in bearings	.001 to .002	.001 to .0025
Tappet clearance:		
Inlet	.010 hot or cold	.006 hot
Exhaust	.010 hot or cold	.010 hot or cold
Valves:		
Seat angle, inlet	30 deg.	30 deg.
Seat angle, exhaust	45 deg.	45 deg.
Stem diameter, inlet	.3107 to .3112	.3420 to .3425
Stem diameter, exhaust	.3410 to .3415	.3410 to .3415
Valve springs:		
Inner inlet:		
Free length	1.68	1.703
Length under 17.7 lb load	1.462	
Length under 21.5 lb load		1.437

Outer inlet:
    Free length 1.822   1.960
    Length under 46 lb load 1.587
    Length under 69.5 lb load 1.625

Exhaust valve springs on 2¼ litre models are the same as the inlet

Inner exhaust:
    Free length 1.703
    Length under 16.4 lb load 1.500
Outer exhaust:
    Free length 1.861
    Length under 41.8 lb load 1.625

Valve timing:

Inlet opens	6 deg. BTDC	12 deg. BTDC
Inlet closes	52 deg. ABDC	46 deg. ABDC
Exhaust opens	34 deg. BBDC	47 deg. BBDC
Exhaust closes	24 deg. ATDC	17 deg. ATDC

Oil pump:

Type	Skew gear	Spur gear
Gear end float:		
Steel gear	.002 to .005	.002 to .005
Aluminium gear	.003 to .006	.003 to .006
Radial clearance of gears	.001 to .004	.001 to .004
Backlash	.006 to .012	.006 to .012
Oil pressure, engine warm, 2000 rev/min	35 to 65 lb/sq in	40 to 50 lb/sq in
Relief valve spring free length	2.67	3.425

3.5 litre

Bore and stroke .. ..   88.90 x 71.12 mm
Capacity .. ..   3528 cc
Compression ratio .. ..   8.13 : 1
Firing order .. ..   1 – 8 – 4 – 3 – 6 – 5 – 7 – 2
Cylinder numbering system, front to rear:
    Left bank .. ..   1 – 3 – 5 – 7
    Right bank .. ..   2 – 4 – 6 – 8
Compression pressure (minimum) .. .. ..   135 lb/sq in

Crankshaft:
    Main journal diameter .. ..   2.2992 to 2.2997
    Minimum regrind diameter .. ..   2.2592 to 2.2597
    Crankpin journal diameter .. ..   2.0000 to 2.0005
    Minimum regrind diameter .. ..   1.9600 to 1.9605
    Crankshaft end thrust .. ..   Taken on thrust faces of centre main
                  bearing
    Crankshaft end float .. ..   .004 to .008

Main bearings:
    Diametrical clearance .. ..   .0009 to .0025
    Undersizes .. ..   .010, .020

Connecting rods:
    Length between centres .. ..   5.658 to 5.662

Big-end bearings:
    Clearance on crankshaft .. ..   .0006 to .0022
    End float on crankshaft .. ..   .006 to .014
    Undersizes .. ..   .010, .020

Gudgeon pins:
    Fit in connecting rod .. ..   Press fit
    Clearance in piston .. ..   .0001 to .0003

Pistons:

Clearance in bore measured at bottom of skirt at
rightangles to gudgeon pin .. .. .0007 to .0013

Piston rings:

No. 1 compression ring .. .. Chrome parallel faced
No. 2 compression ring .. .. Stepped to 'L' shape and marked
'T' or 'TOP'
Width of compression rings .. .. .0615 to .0625
Compression ring gap .. .. .017 to .022
Oil ring type .. .. Perfect circle, type 98-6
Oil ring width .. .. .1894 max.
Oil ring gap .. .. .015 to .055

Camshaft:

Bearings .. .. Non-serviceable
Timing chain .. .. 9.52mm pitch x 54 pitches

Valves:

Inlet:
  Overall length .. .. 4.59 to 4.62
  Angle of face .. .. 45 deg.
  Stem diameter .. .. .3402 to .3412 at head and increasing
  to .3407 to .3417

  Stem to guide clearance:
    Top .. .. .001 to .003
    Bottom .. .. .0005 to .0025
Exhaust:
  Overall length .. .. 4.59 to 4.62
  Angle of face .. .. 45 deg.
  Stem diameter .. .. .3397 to .3407 at head and increasing
  to .3402 to .3412

  Stem to guide clearance:
    Top .. .. .0015 to .0035
    Bottom .. .. .002 to .004
Valve spring length .. .. 1.577 at pressure of 66.5 to 73.5 lb

Valve timing:

Inlet opens .. .. 30 deg. BTDC
Inlet closes .. .. 75 deg. ABDC
Exhaust opens .. .. 68 deg. BBDC
Exhaust closes .. .. 37 deg. ATDC

Lubrication:

System pressure, engine warm at 2400 rev/min .. 30 to 40 lb/sq inch
Pressure relief valve spring free length 3.2
Oil filter bypass valve spring free length 1.48

DIESEL ENGINE

Bore and stroke .. .. 90.47 x 88.9 mm
Capacity .. .. 2286 cc
Compression ratio .. .. 23 : 1

Crankshaft:

Main journal diameter .. .. 2.4995 to 2.50
Main bearing clearance .. .. .0008 to .0025
Regrinding not permitted
End float .. .. .002 to .006
Crankpin diameter .. .. 2.312 + .00075
Regrinding not permitted

Connecting rods:
Bearing fit on crankpin	.00075 to .0027
End float at big-end	.007 to .012
Gudgeon pin bush fit in rod	.002 to .004 interference
Gudgeon pin bush internal diameter	1.1875 + .0005
Gudgeon pin fit in bush, clearance:	
Series 2, 2A	.0002 to .0008
Series 3	.0003 to .0006
Gudgeon pin fit in piston	Push fit by hand

Pistons:
Type	Light alloy
Clearance, bottom of skirt	.0044 to .0053
Rings:	
Compression No. 1:	
Type	Square, friction edge, chromium-plated
Gap	.014 to .019
Clearance in groove	.0025 to .0045
Compression Nos. 2 and 3:	
Type	Bevelled, friction edge, marked 'T' on upper side
Gap	.010 to .015
Clearance in groove	.0025 to .0045
Scraper No. 4:	
Early type	Slotted, square edge
Gap	.010 to .015
Clearance in groove	.0025 to .0045
Scraper No. 4:	
Later type	Expander and rails
Gap	.015 to .045
Clearance in groove	.0015 to .0025

Camshaft:
Journal diameter	1.841 to 1.842
End float	.0025 to .0055
Clearance in bearings	.001 to .002

Tappet clearance, all .. ..   .010 hot or cold

Valves:
Face angle, both	45 deg.
Inlet valve stem diameter	.3107 to .3112
Exhaust valve stem diameter	.3410 to .3415
Valve springs	Details as 2¼ litre petrol engine

Valve guides:
Inlet stem fit in guide, clearance	.0013 to .0019
Exhaust stem fit in guide, clearance	.0023 to .0029

Valve timing:
Inlet opens	16 deg. BTDC
Inlet closes	42 deg. ABDC
Exhaust opens	51 deg. BBDC
Exhaust closes	13 deg. ATDC

Oil pump .. ..   Details as 2¼ litre petrol engine
  Oil pressure, engine warm, 2000 rev/min .. ..   35 to 65 lb/sq in

COOLING SYSTEM

Thermostat:
Bellows type	Opens at 161°F to 168°F
	Fully open 185°F

Wax filled type :

2.6 litre engines	Opens at 161°F to 170°F
2.6 litre Series 3 engines	Opens at 167°F to 176°F
2¼ litre engines	Opens at 159°F to 167°F
3.5 litre engines	Opens at 173°F to 182°F
2.6 litre engines	Fully open at 190°F
2¼ litre engines	Fully open at 185°F

FUEL SYSTEM
PETROL ENGINES

	2¼ litre	2.6 litre
Carburetter type, Series 2 and 2A	*Solex*	*Stromberg*
	PA.10-5 and 6	175.CD.2S
	Zenith	*SU*
	36.IV	HD.6
	Solex	*Zenith*
Choke size	28 mm	27 mm
Main jet	125	125
Correction jet	185	—
Enrichment jet	—	150
Pilot jet	50	—
Slow-running jet	—	60
	Stromberg	*SU*
Needle	B18362.Z/41	SS
Air valve return spring	B18277.Z	—
Jet	—	.100
Needle valve	B18353	—
Piston spring	—	Yellow (8 oz)
Carburetter type, Series 3	*Zenith 36.IV*	*Stromberg 175CD.SE*
Choke	27 mm	1.625
Main jet	125	—
Compensating jet	150	—
Pump jet	65	—
Needle	—	B18362.Z/4J
Float height	—	.629 to .669
Fast-idle setting	—	1.1 mm at edge of throttle
Fuel pump	AC mechanical	SU electric

Carburetter type, 3.5 litre	*Two Zenith Stromberg*
European, Australian	CDSE
Other markets	CDS3
Needle :	
Australian	BIDW
Other markets	BIEW
Idle speed (hot) :	
Australian	800 ± 50 rev/min
Other markets	725 ± 25 rev/min
Fast-idle (cold)	1100 to 1300 rev/min
CO at idle :	
Australian	6 ± 1 per cent
Other markets	4.5 per cent
Air cleaner :	
European	AC Delco
Other markets	AC Delco cyclone type
Fuel pump	Facet electrical

FUEL SYSTEM
DIESEL ENGINE

Injection pump	CAV
Injection nozzle	CAV Pintaux
Nozzle size	BDNO/SPC6209
Opening pressure of nozzle valve	135 atm
Fuel lift pump	AC mechanical

IGNITION SYSTEM

Ignition timing:

	Fuel octane rating	Timing point
$2\frac{1}{4}$ litre engines	74 to 76	TDC
	80 to 85	3° BTDC
	90 to 96	6° BTDC
2.6 litre engines (7 : 1 CR)	78	2° ATDC
	80	TDC
	83	2° BTDC
(7.8 : 1 CR)	90	2° ATDC
	95	6° BTDC
$2\frac{1}{4}$ litre Series 3 (7 : 1 CR)	75 to 82	TDC
	83 to 89	3° BTDC
	90	6° BTDC
(8 : 1 CR)	90	TDC
2.6 litre Series 3 (7 : 1 CR)	78	2° ATDC
	80 to 85	2° BTDC
(7.8 : 1 CR)	80 to 85	6° ATDC
	90	2° ATDC
3.5 litre (8.13 : 1 CR)	91 to 93	
Dynamic, emission control		1° BTDC
Dynamic, non-emission		6° BTDC
Static		TDC
Dwell angle, 600 ± 50 rev/min		26° to 28°
$2\frac{1}{4}$ litre, Ducellier distributor:		
Dwell angle idling		57°
Dwell variation		± 2.5°
Vacuum advance starts		4 inch Hg
Vacuum advance maximum		12° at 18 inch Hg
Contact points gap (preliminary setting only) ..	0.017	

Sparking plug:

	Compression ratio	Champion
Series 3	8.0 : 1	UN 12Y
Series 3	7.0 : 1	N 8
Series 3, 2.6 litre	7.8 : 1 and 7.0 : 1	N 5
Series 3, 3.5 litre	8.13 : 1	N 12Y or Unipart GSP 131
Sparking plug gap	.029 to .032 (.025 pre Series 3)	

CLUTCH

Coil spring type	Borg and Beck A6
Springs	9
Free length, petrol	2.680
Free length, diesel	2.688
Colour identification	Early $2\frac{1}{4}$ litre petrol, yellow and light green
	Early $2\frac{1}{4}$ litre diesel, yellow and dark green
	All late models, black

Pressure plate regrind limit	.010 undersize
Operating levers	Set at 1.655 from flywheel face using $\frac{3}{8}$ distance piece in place of driven plate

Driven plate:

Thickness, new	.330
Maximum permissible wear	.120
Diaphragm spring type clutch	Borg and Beck DS
$2\frac{1}{4}$ and 2.6 litre	Other data as coil spring type

3.5 litre:

Driven plate diameter	10.5
Damper spring colour	Light grey/green
Hydraulic master cylinder	Girling CV
Hydraulic slave cylinder	Girling $\frac{7}{8}$ bore

TRANSMISSION

Gearbox:

Ratios, Series 2, 2A:

	Up to gearbox B	Gearbox C on
Top	1:1	1:1
Third	1.377:1	1.50:1
Second	2.043:1	2.22:1
First	2.996:1	2.60:1
Reverse	2.547:1	3.02:1

Ratios, Series 3:

Top	1:1
Third	1.50:1
Second	2.22:1
First	3.68:1
Reverse	3.88:1 or 4.02:1

Ratios, 3.5 litre:

Top	1:1
Third	1.505:1
Second	2.448:1
First	4.069:1
Reverse	3.664:1

Transfer box, helical and spur gear type:

Overall ratios, Series 2, 2A:

	High ratio	Low ratio
Top	5.396:1	13.578:1
Third	7.435:1	18.707:1
Second	11.026:1	27.742:1
First	16.171:1	40.688:1
Reverse	13.745:1	34.585:1

Overall ratios, Series 3:

	High ratio	Low ratio
Top	5.40:1	11.10:1
Third	8.05:1	16.50:1
Second	12.00:1	24.60:1
First	19.88:1	40.70:1
Reverse	20.47:1 or 21.66:1	42.87:1 or 44.30:1

Transfer box, all helical gear type:

Overall ratios, Series 2, 2A:

	High ratio	Low ratio
Top	7.19:1	15.40:1
Third	10.80:1	23.10:1
Second	15.96:1	34.10:1
First	25.90:1	55.30:1
Reverse	21.70:1	46.40:1

Overall ratios, Series 3:

Top	7.19 : 1	15.40 : 1
Third	10.81 : 1	23.10 : 1
Second	15.96 : 1	34.10 : 1
First	26.46 : 1	56.56 : 1
Reverse	27.87 : 1 or 28.91 : 1	56.76 : 1 or 61.78 : 1

Overall ratios, 3.5 litre:

Top	4.73 : 1	11.76 : 1
Third	7.12 : 1	17.69 : 1
Second	11.58 : 1	28.78 : 1
First	19.24 : 1	47.81 : 1
Reverse	17.33 : 1	43.05 : 1

Main gearbox, $2\frac{1}{4}$ and 2.6 litre, fitting dimensions:

Reverse gear bush bore	.812 + .001
Mainshaft bush fit in gears	.0025 to .0035
Main bush fit on shaft	Zero to .001
Main bush end float	.001 to .008
2nd and 3rd speed gears:	
End float on sleeve	.004 to .007
2nd gear stop	.002 clearance
Reverse gear stop	.002 clearance

Main gearbox, 3.5 litre, fitting dimensions:

Primary pinion end float	.002 maximum
Gears end float	.002 maximum

Transfer box, $2\frac{1}{4}$ and 2.6 litre, fitting dimensions:

Dog clutch selector shaft bush	1.148 + .001
Output shaft bearings:	
End float	Zero
Preload	2 to 4 lb
High speed gear—end float	.004 to .008
Intermediate gear—end float	.004 to .008

Transfer box, 3.5 litre, fitting dimensions:

Transfer gear end float	.002 maximum
Intermediate gears end float	.006 to .009
Selector clearance	.005 to .010

Differentials, $2\frac{1}{4}$ and 2.6 litre, front and rear:

Ratio	4.7 : 1	
	Rover type	*ENV type*
Crownwheel backlash	.008 to .010	.006 to .009
Crownwheel bearing preload	.005	.002 to .004
Crownwheel maximum runout	.004	.003
Bevel pinion bearing preload	7 to 12 lb	$4\frac{1}{4}$ to 9 lb

Differentials, 3.5 litre, front and rear:

Ratio	3.54 : 1

STEERING

Type	Recirculating ball
Steering wheel turns, lock to lock	3.3
Steering angles:	
Camber	$1\frac{1}{2}$ deg.
Castor	3 deg.
Swivel pin inclination	7 deg.
Toe-in, $2\frac{1}{4}$ and 2.6 litre, toe-out 3.5 litre	$\frac{3}{64}$ to $\frac{3}{32}$

LRAB2

SUSPENSION

Type	Leaf spring
Dampers	Telescopic hydraulic
Front hub end float:	
Series 2 and 2A	.004 to .006
Series 3, $2\frac{1}{4}$ and 2.6 litre	.002 to .004
Series 3, 3.5 litre	.002 to .005
Swivel pin setting, coil spring	14 to 16 lb resistance
Swivel pin setting, Railko bush	12 to 14 lb resistance
Front drive shaft end float, 3.5 litre ..	.003 to .008
Rear hub end float, 3.5 litre	.002 to .005

BRAKES

	$2\frac{1}{4}$ litre	2.6 and 3.5 litre
Type:		
Wheel brakes	Girling Hydraulic	
Transmission (hand) brake	Girling Mechanical	
10" Brakes, lining:		
Length	$8\frac{1}{2}$	
Width	$2\frac{1}{4}$	
Thickness	$\frac{3}{16}$	
11" Brakes, lining, front:	**$2\frac{1}{4}$ litre**	**2.6 and 3.5 litre**
Length	$10\frac{7}{16}$	$10\frac{7}{16}$
Width	$2\frac{1}{4}$	3
Thickness	$\frac{3}{16}$	$\frac{3}{16}$
11" Brakes, lining, rear:	**All**	
Length	$8\frac{9}{16}$	
Width	$2\frac{1}{4}$	
Thickness	$\frac{3}{16}$	
Transmission brake, lining, all models:		
Length	$8\frac{5}{8}$	
Width	$1\frac{3}{4}$	
Thickness	$\frac{3}{16}$	
Master cylinder – 88 models	Type Girling CV	
Master cylinder – 109 models	Type Girling CB	
Servo unit, hydraulic	Clayton Dewandre	
Servo unit, mechanical	Girling Supervac type 38	

ELECTRICAL EQUIPMENT

Battery, petrol models	Single 12-volt 58 or 60 AH	
Battery, diesel models	Two 6-volt, in series, 120 AH	
Battery, Series 3 diesel models	Single 12-volt, 95 AH	
Polarity:		
$2\frac{1}{4}$ litre petrol and diesel models up to vehicle suffix 'C' inclusive	Positive earth	
As above from suffix 'D' onwards and all 2.6 and 3.5 litre models	Negative earth	

Generators and control boxes:	**Generator**	**Control box**
Series 2, $2\frac{1}{4}$ litre petrol	C39	RB106/37182
Series 2A, $2\frac{1}{4}$ litre petrol	C40	RB106/37290
Series 2A, 2.6 litre petrol	C42	RB340/37517
Series 2 and 2A, $2\frac{1}{4}$ litre diesel up to vehicle suffix 'C' inclusive	C40	RB310/37472
As above from vehicle suffix 'D' onwards	C40	RB340/37387

Alternator:

Type	Lucas 11 AC
Output	43 amps
Field coil resistance at 68°F (20°C)	3.8 ohms
Maximum speed	12,500 rev/min
Stator phases	3
Stator connections	Star
Slip ring brushes:	
Length new	$\frac{5}{8}$
Replace at	$\frac{5}{32}$
Field isolating relay cut-in voltage	6.0 to 7.5
Drop off voltage	4.0
Type (Series 3)	Lucas 16 ACR
Output	35 amps
Minimum brush length	$\frac{3}{16}$
Type (Series 3)	Lucas 18 ACR
Output	45 amps
Minimum brush length	$\frac{5}{16}$
Fuses	Four, on steering column shroud

CAPACITIES

Engine sump 2$\frac{1}{4}$ litre	11 pints + 1$\frac{1}{2}$ pints for filter
Engine sump 2.6 litre	12 pints + 1 pint for filter
Engine sump 3.5 litre	9$\frac{1}{2}$ pints + 1 pint for filter
Air cleaner oil 2$\frac{1}{4}$ litre	1$\frac{1}{2}$ pints
Air cleaner oil 2.6 litre	1 pint
Main gearbox oil, 2$\frac{1}{4}$ and 2.6 litre	2$\frac{1}{2}$ pints
Main gearbox oil, 3.5 litre	4$\frac{3}{4}$ pints
Transfer box oil, 2$\frac{1}{4}$ and 2.6 litre	4$\frac{1}{2}$ pints
Transfer box oil, 3.5 litre	5$\frac{1}{2}$ pints
Rear differential, Rover	3 pints
Rear differential, ENV	2$\frac{5}{8}$ pints
Rear differential, Salisbury	4$\frac{1}{2}$ pints
Front differential, Rover	3 pints
Front differential, ENV	2$\frac{1}{8}$ pints
Swivel pin housing oil	1 pint each
Cooling system 2$\frac{1}{4}$ litre, petrol	18 pints
Cooling system 2$\frac{1}{4}$ litre, diesel	17$\frac{1}{2}$ pints
Cooling system Series 3, 2$\frac{1}{4}$ litre petrol	14$\frac{1}{4}$ pints
Cooling system Series 3, 2$\frac{1}{4}$ litre diesel	13$\frac{3}{4}$ pints
Cooling system 2.6 litre, long model	20 pints
Cooling system, 3.5 litre	17 pints

LUBRICANTS

Refer to garage charts for vehicle concerned or, alternatively, the Owners Handbook.

TORQUE WRENCH SETTINGS

2$\frac{1}{4}$ litre petrol engine:

Inlet to exhaust manifold	17 lb ft
Rocker shaft $\frac{1}{2}$ inch bolts	65 lb ft
Rocker shaft $\frac{5}{16}$ inch bolts	18 lb ft
Cylinder head $\frac{1}{2}$ inch bolts	65 lb ft
Cylinder head $\frac{5}{16}$ inch bolts	18 lb ft
Starter dog	150 lb ft
Flywheel to crankshaft bolts	65 lb ft
Main bearing bolts	85 lb ft
Big-end bolts, machined threads	35 lb ft

Big-end bolts, rolled threads .. .. 25 lb ft
Oil filter bolts:
   Canister to housing .. .. 12 lb ft
   Housing to block .. .. 25 lb ft
Sump bolts .. .. 12 lb ft

2¼ litre diesel engine:
Injector clamps .. .. 8 lb ft
Rocker shaft and cylinder head ½ inch bolts .. .. 90 lb ft
Rocker shaft and cylinder head $\frac{5}{16}$ inch bolts .. .. 18 lb ft
Starter dog .. .. 200 lb ft
Flywheel to crankshaft bolts .. .. 65 lb ft
Clutch to flywheel bolts .. .. 25 lb ft
Main bearing bolts .. .. 100 lb ft
Big-end bolts .. .. 25 lb ft
Oil filter bolts:
   Canister to housing .. .. 12 lb ft
   Housing to block .. .. 25 lb ft
Sump bolts .. .. 12 lb ft
Heater plugs .. .. 25 lb ft

2.6 litre petrol engine:
Cylinder head bolts 'A' .. .. 50 lb ft
Cylinder head bolts 'B' .. .. 30 lb ft
Starter dog .. .. 200 lb ft
Flywheel to crankshaft bolts .. .. 65 lb ft
Clutch to flywheel bolts .. .. 25 lb ft
Main bearing bolts .. .. 75 lb ft
Big-end bolts .. .. 20 lb ft
Sump bolts .. .. 12 lb ft

3.5 litre engine:
Big-end cap nuts .. .. 30 to 35 lb ft
Main bearing cap bolts:
   Nos. 1 to 4 .. .. 50 to 55 lb ft
   Rear .. .. 65 to 70 lb ft
Cylinder head bolts (see **Chapter 1, FIG 1 : 12**)
   Nos. 1 to 10 .. .. 65 to 70 lb ft
   Nos. 11 to 14 .. .. 40 to 45 lb ft
Rocker shaft bolts .. .. 25 to 30 lb ft
Flywheel bolts .. .. 50 to 60 lb ft
Oil pump cover bolts .. .. 10 to 15 lb ft
Oil pressure relief valve .. .. 30 to 35 lb ft
Timing chain cover bolts .. .. 20 to 25 lb ft
Crankshaft starter dog .. .. 140 to 160 lb ft
Distributor drive gear to camshaft bolt .. .. .. 40 to 45 lb ft
Engine mounting rubbers .. .. 13 to 16 lb ft
Water pump bolts:
   ¼ inch .. .. 7 to 10 lb ft
   $\frac{5}{16}$ inch .. .. 16 to 20 lb ft
   $\frac{7}{16}$ inch AF .. .. 6 to 8 lb ft
   ½ inch AF .. .. 20 to 25 lb ft
Induction manifold bolts .. .. 25 to 30 lb ft
Induction manifold gasket clamp bolts .. .. .. 10 to 15 lb ft
Exhaust manifold bolts .. .. 10 to 15 lb ft
Clutch cover bolts .. .. 35 to 38 lb ft
Slave cylinder bolts .. .. 20 lb ft

Gearbox, 2¼ and 2.6 litre:
Output flange nut .. .. 85 lb ft
Layshaft nut .. .. 75 lb ft
Layshaft bolt (Series 3) .. .. 50 lb ft

Gearbox, 3.5 litre:

Bellhousing to engine	25 lb ft
Main gearlever retainer bolts	11 lb ft
Front and rear output flange nut	85 lb ft
Transmission brake shoe pivot bolts	43 lb ft
Transmission brake backplate bolts	25 lb ft
Gearbox casing to bellhousing studs/bolts:	
Larger diameter	120 lb ft
Smaller diameter	70 lb ft

Propeller shafts, 3.5 litre:

Coupling flange bolts	30 to 38 lb ft

Rear axle:

Halfshaft bolts	28 lb ft
Halfshaft nut	15 lb ft
Differential drive flange nut, Rover	85 lb ft
Differential drive flange nut, ENV	120 lb ft
Hub driving flange bolts, 3.5 litre	30 to 38 lb ft
Stub axle bolts, 3.5 litre	30 to 38 lb ft

Front axle:

Halfshaft bolts	28 lb ft
Halfshaft nuts	15 to 20 lb ft
Hub driving flange bolts, 3.5 litre	30 to 38 lb ft
Upper swivel pin bolts, 3.5 litre	50 to 65 lb ft
Lower swivel pin nuts, 3.5 litre	50 to 65 lb ft
Swivel seal retaining ring bolts, 3.5 litre	7 to 9 lb ft
Stub axle bolts, 3.5 litre	30 to 38 lb ft

Steering:

Ball joint nuts	30 lb ft
Drop arm nut	80 lb ft
Relay lever pinch bolt	55 lb ft
Steering wheel nut	40 lb ft
Road wheel nuts	75 to 85 lb ft

Suspension:

Road spring 'U' bolts, $2\frac{1}{4}$ and 2.6 litre	58 lb ft
Road spring 'U' bolts, 3.5 litre	70 to 80 lb ft
Shackle nuts and bolts	60 to 70 lb ft

Brakes:

Wheel cylinder bleed nipple	4 to 6 lb ft
Master cylinder to servo nuts	16 to 19 lb ft
Brake failure switch end pipe union	16 lb ft
Brake failure switch unit to housing	16 lb ft
Fluid reservoir to master cylinder bolt, single line servo	20 to 25 lb ft
Fluid reservoir to master cylinder screws, dual line servo	2 to 3 lb ft
Servo assembly securing nuts	9 lb ft
Brake anchor plate bolts, 3.5 litre	30 to 38 lb ft

Electrical:

Alternator shaft nut	25 to 30 lb ft
Starter motor to engine bolts, 3.5 litre	30 to 35 lb ft
Starter motor:	
Through bolts	8 lb ft
Solenoid fixing stud nut, 3.5 litre	$4\frac{1}{2}$ lb ft
Solenoid upper terminal nut, 3.5 litre	3 lb ft
Reverse light switch, 3.5 litre	15 to 20 lb ft
Wiper blade drive adaptor bolts	$2\frac{1}{2}$ lb ft

SPECIAL TOOLS

Special tools can only be obtained direct from the manufacturers:

Messrs V. L. Churchill & Co. Ltd.,
P.O. Box No. 3,
London Road,
Daventry,
Northants, NN11 4NF,
England.

NOTES

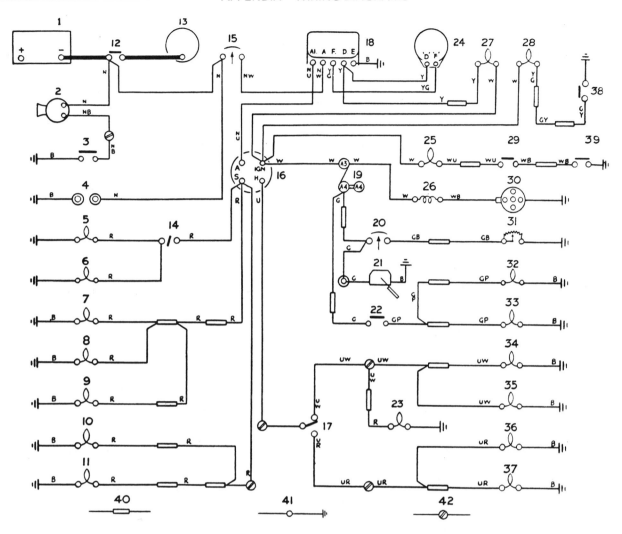

FIG 15:1   2¼ litre petrol models, Series 2, positive earth

Key to Fig 15:1   1 12-volt battery   2 Horn   3 Horn push button   4 Inspection light sockets   5 Panel illumination
6 Panel illumination   7 Tail light   8 Number plate illumination   9 Tail light   10 Sidelight   11 Sidelight
12 Starter switch   13 Starter   14 Panel light switch   15 Ammeter   16 Ignition and lighting switch   17 Headlight dipswitch
18 Voltage control box   19 Fuse box   20 Fuel gauge   21 Screen wiper, plug and socket   22 Stoplight switch
23 Main beam warning light   24 Dynamo   25 Mixture warning light   26 Ignition coil   27 Charging warning light
28 Oil pressure warning light   29 Mixture switch   30 Distributor   31 Fuel gauge, petrol tank   32 Stoplight   33 Stoplight
34 Headlamp, main   35 Headlamp, main   36 Headlamp, dip   37 Headlamp, dip   38 Oil pressure switch   39 Thermostat
40 Snap connectors   41 Earth connections via terminals and fixing bolts   42 Junction box terminals

Key to cable colour code   **B** Black   **G** Green   **N** Brown   **P** Purple   **R** Red   **U** Blue   **W** White   **Y** Yellow
RN Red with Brown, and so on

When cables have two colour code letters, the first denotes the main and the latter the tracer.

On vehicles to the North American specification, the connections at the lighting switch are such that the sidelamps are extinguished when the headlamps are in use.

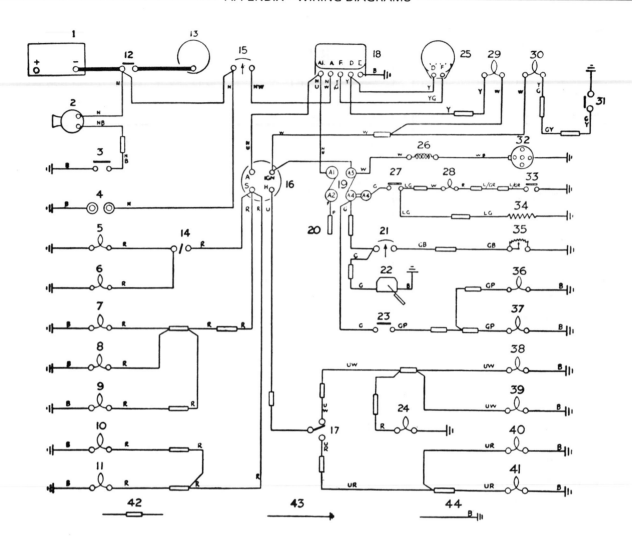

FIG 15:2   2¼ litre petrol models, Series 2A, positive earth

Key to Fig 15:2   1 12-volt battery   2 Horn   3 Horn push button   4 Inspection light sockets   5 Panel illumination
6 Panel illumination   7 Tail light   8 Number plate illumination   9 Tail light   10 Sidelight   11 Sidelight   12 Starter switch
13 Starter   14 Panel light switch   15 Ammeter   16 Ignition and lighting switch   17 Headlamp dipswitch
18 Voltage control box   19 Fuse box   20 To interior lights   21 Fuel gauge   22 Screen wiper, plug and socket
23 Stoplight switch   24 Main beam warning light   25 Dynamo   26 Ignition coil   27 Mixture switch
28 Mixture warning light   29 Charging warning light   30 Oil pressure warning light   31 Oil pressure switch   32 Distributor
33 Mixture thermostat switch   34 Carburetter heater element, optional equipment   35 Gauge, fuel tank   36 Stoplight
37 Stoplight   38 Headlamp, main   39 Headlamp, main   40 Headlamp,dip   41 Headlamp, dip   42 Snap connectors
43 Earth connections via terminals and fixing bolts   44 Earth connections via cables

Key to cable colour code   **B** Black   **G** Green   **N** Brown   **P** Purple   **R** Red   **U** Blue   **W** White   **Y** Yellow
RN Red with Brown, and so on

When cables have two colour code letters, the first denotes the main and the latter the tracer.

On vehicles to the North American specification, the connections at the lighting switch are such that the sidelamps are extinguished when the headlamps are in use.

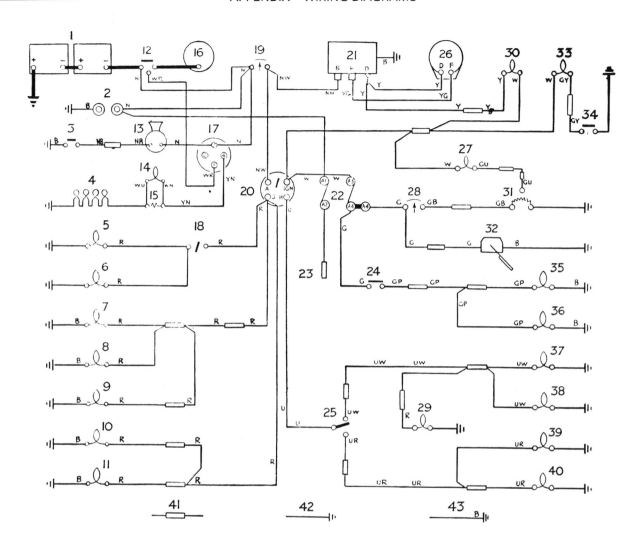

FIG 15:3 2¼ litre diesel models, Series 2A, positive earth

Key to Fig 15:3   1 Two 6-volt positive earth batteries   2 Inspection socket   3 Horn push button   4 Heater plugs
5 Panel illumination   6 Panel illumination   7 Tail lamp   8 Number plate illumination   9 Tail lamp   10 Sidelamp
11 Sidelamp   12 Starter switch   13 Horn   14 Heater plug warning light   15 Resistor for heater plug   16 Starter motor
17 Heater plug switch   18 Panel light switch   19 Ammeter   20 Switch, electrical services and lighting
21 Current/voltage regulator   22 Fuse box   23 To interior lights   24 Stoplight switch   25 Headlamp dipswitch
26 Dynamo   27 Fuel level warning light   28 Fuel gauge   29 Headlamp main beam warning light   30 Charging warning light
31 Fuel tank gauge unit   32 Wiper motor   33 Oil pressure warning light   34 Oil pressure warning light switch   35 Stop lamp
36 Stop lamp   37 Main beam headlamp   38 Main beam headlamp   39 Dip beam headlamp   40 Dip beam headlamp
41 Snap connectors   42 Earth connections via terminals or fixing bolts   43 Earth connections via cables

Key to cable colour code   **B** Black   **G** Green   **L** Light   **N** Brown   **O** Orange   **P** Purple   **R** Red   **S** Slate   **U** Blue
W White   **Y** Yellow   **RN** Red with Brown, and so on

When cables have two colour code letters, the first denotes the main and the latter the tracer.

On vehicles to the North American specification, the connections at the lighting switch are such that the sidelamps are extinguished when the headlamps are in use.

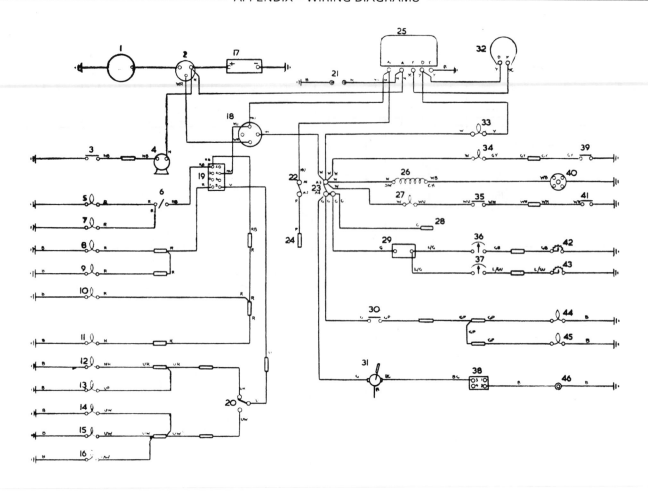

FIG 15:4 2¼ litre petrol models, negative earth

Key to Fig 15:4   1 Starter motor   2 Starter motor solenoid   3 Horn push button   4 Horn   5 Speedometer panel light
6 Panel light switch   7 Instrument panel lights   8 Righthand sidelamp   9 Lefthand sidelamp   10 Righthand tail lamp
11 Lefthand tail lamp   12 Righthand dipped beam headlamp   13 Lefthand dipped beam headlamp   14 Lefthand main
beam headlamp   15 Righthand main beam headlamp   16 Headlamp main beam warning light   17 12-volt battery
18 Ignition and starter switch   19 Lights switch   20 Headlamp dipswitch   21 Inspection sockets   22 A1-A2 (35-amp) fuse
23 A3-A4 (35-amp) fuse   24 Interior light feed   25 Regulator box   26 Ignition coil   27 Choke warning light
28 Flasher lights feed   29 Fuel and temperature gauge voltage stabilizer   30 Stoplamp switch   31 Wiper motor
32 Dynamo   33 Ignition warning light   34 Oil pressure warning light   35 Cold start on control switch   36 Fuel gauge
37 Temperature gauge   38 Wiper switch   39 Oil pressure switch   40 Distributor   41 Cold start in cylinder head switch
42 Fuel tank unit   43 Temperature transmitter unit   44 Righthand stoplamp   45 Lefthand stoplamp   46 Wiper lead

Snap and Lucar connections —⊏⊐—
Earth connections —‖‖‖

Key to cable colour code   **B** Black   **P** Purple   **W** White   **R** Red   **N** Brown   **Y** Yellow   **U** Blue   **G** Green   **L** Light

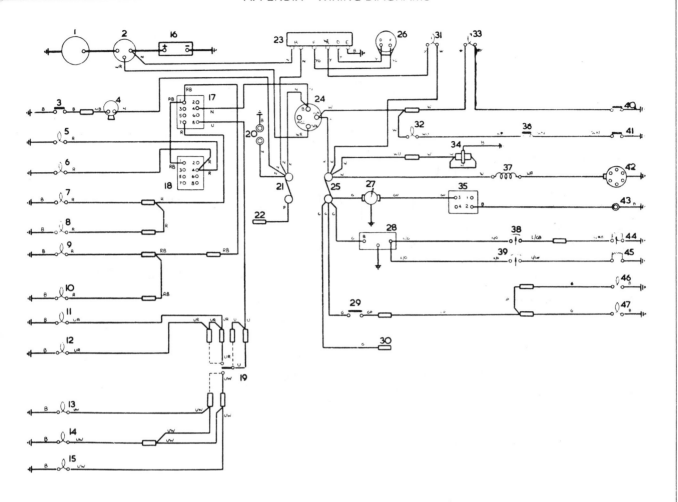

FIG 15:5   2.6 litre petrol models, negative earth

Key to Fig 15:5   1 Starter motor   2 Starter motor solenoid   3 Horn push button   4 Horn   5 Panel illumination
6 Panel Illumination   7 Righthand sidelamp   8 Lefthand sidelamp   9 Righthand tail lamp   10 Lefthand tail lamp
11 Righthand dipped beam headlamp   12 Lefthand dipped beam headlamp   13 Lefthand main beam headlamp
14 Main beam warning light   15 Righthand main beam headlamp   16 Battery   17 Lights switch   18 Panel lights switch
19 Headlamp dipswitch   20 Inspection lamp sockets   21 A1-A2 fuse   22 Interior light feed, where fitted
23 Regulator box   24 Ignition and starter switch   25 A3-A4 fuse   26 Dynamo   27 Wiper motor   28 Fuel and
temperature gauge voltage stabilizer   29 Stoplamp switch   30 Flasher lights feed, where fitted   31 Ignition warning light
32 Cold start warning light   33 Oil pressure warning light   34 Dual fuel pump   35 Wiper switch   36 Cold start switch,
on control   37 Ignition coil   38 Fuel gauge   39 Water temperature indicator   40 Oil pressure switch
41 Cold start switch, in cylinder head   42 Distributor   43 Wiper lead socket   44 Fuel tank unit   45 Water temperature
transmitter   46 Lefthand stoplamp   47 Righthand stoplamp

Snap and Lucar connections —▭—
Earth connections via terminals or fixing bolts —|||||||
Earth connections via cables —B|||||

Key to cable colour code   **B** Black   **P** Purple   **W** White   **R** Red   **N** Brown   **Y** Yellow   **U** Blue   **G** Green   **O** Orange
S Slate   **L** Light

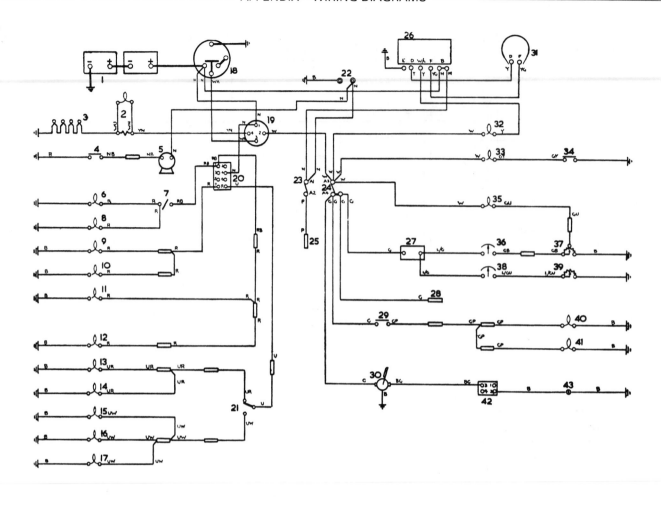

FIG 15:6 2¼ litre diesel models, Series 2A, negative earth

Key to Fig 15:6 1 Two 6-volt batteries 2 Heater plugs warning light and resistor 3 Heater plugs 4 Horn push button
5 Horn 6 Speedometer panel light 7 Panel light switch 8 Instrument panel light 9 Righthand sidelamp
10 Lefthand sidelamp 11 Righthand tail lamp 12 Lefthand tail lamp 13 Righthand dipped beam headlamp
14 Lefthand dipped beam headlamp 15 Lefthand main beam headlamp 16 Righthand main beam headlamp
17 Headlamp main beam warning light 18 Starter motor 19 Starter/heater plugs switch 20 Lights switch
21 Headlamp dipswitch 22 Inspection sockets 23 A1-A2 (35-amp) fuse 24 A3-A4 (35-amp) fuse 25 Interior light feed
26 Regulator box 27 Fuel gauge and water temperature gauge voltage stabilizer 28 Flasher lights feed 29 Stoplamp switch
30 Wiper motor 31 Dynamo 32 Dynamo warning light 33 Oil pressure warning light 34 Oil pressure switch
35 Fuel level warning light 36 Fuel gauge 37 Fuel tank unit 38 Temperature gauge 39 Temperature transmitter unit
40 Righthand stoplamp 41 Lefthand stoplamp 42 Wiper motor switch 43 Wiper lead socket

Snap and Lucar connections —▭—
Earth connections —|||||

Key to cable colour code B Black P Purple W White R Red N Brown Y Yellow U Blue G Green L Light

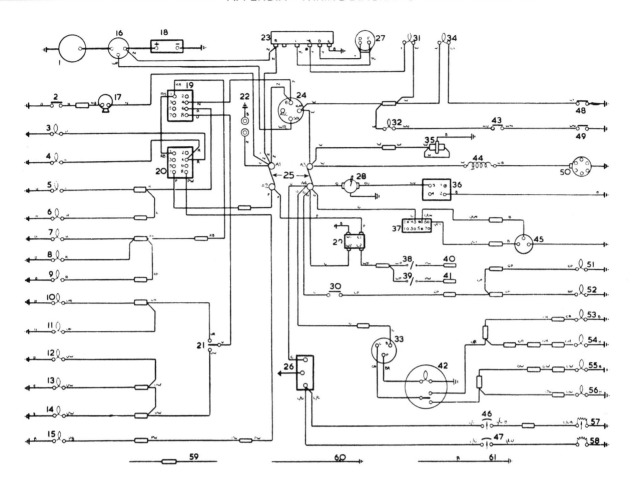

FIG 15:7   2.6 litre, 109 Station wagon, negative earth

Key to Fig 15:7   1 Starter motor   2 Horn push   3 Panel illumination   4 Panel illumination   5 Righthand sidelamp
6 Lefthand sidelamp   7 Righthand tail lamp   8 Number plate illumination   9 Lefthand tail lamp   10 Righthand dip
headlamp   11 Lefthand dip headlamp   12 Righthand headlamp main beam   13 Lefthand headlamp main beam
14 Headlamp main beam warning light   15 Interior light   16 Starter solenoid   17 Horn   18 Battery   19 Lighting switch
20 Panel and interior light switch   21 Foot dipper switch   22 Inspection lamp socket   23 Voltage regulator
24 Ignition/starter switch   25 Fuses   26 10-volt stabilizer   27 Dynamo   28 Windscreen wiper motor   29 Relay for
heated windscreen   30 Stoplight switch   31 Ignition warning light   32 Choke warning light   33 Direction indicator unit
34 Oil pressure warning light   35 Dual petrol pump   36 Windscreen wiper switch   37 Heater switch
38 Switch for heated windscreen, screen No. 1   39 Switch for heated windscreen, screen No. 2   40 Heated windscreen,
screen No. 1   41 Heated windscreen, screen No. 2   42 Direction indicator switch   43 Choke switch   44 Coil
45 Two-speed heater unit   46 Fuel gauge   47 Water temperature gauge   48 Oil pressure switch   49 Choke thermostat
50 Distributor   51 Lefthand stoplamp   52 Righthand stoplamp   53 Lefthand front indicator lamp   54 Lefthand rear
indicator lamp   55 Righthand rear indicator lamp   56 Righthand front indicator lamp   57 Fuel tank unit
58 Water temperature transmitter   59 Snap connector   60 Earth connections via terminals or fixing bolts
61 Earth connections made via cables

Key to cable colour code   **B** Black   **P** Purple   **W** White   **R** Red   **N** Brown   **Y** Yellow   **U** Blue   **G** Green   **L** Light

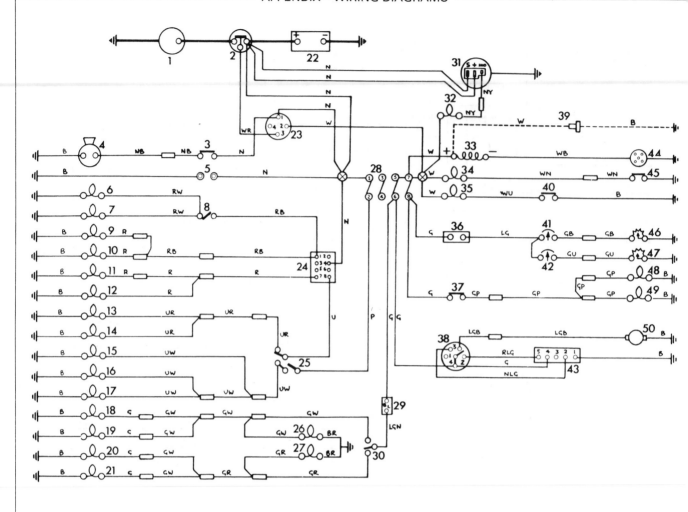

FIG 15:8 2¼ litre and 2.6 litre petrol models, Series 3

Key to Fig 15:8 1 Starter motor 2 Solenoid, starter motor 3 Switch for horns 4 Horn 5 Inspection sockets 6 Instrument panel illumination 7 Instrument panel illumination 8 Switch, panel lights 9 Lefthand tail lamp 10 Righthand tail lamp 11 Lefthand sidelamp 12 Righthand sidelamp 13 Lefthand dipped beam headlamp 14 Righthand dipped beam headlamp 15 Warning light, headlamp main beam 16 Lefthand main beam headlamp 17 Righthand main beam headlamp 18 Righthand rear direction indicator lamp 19 Righthand front direction indicator lamp 20 Lefthand front direction indicator lamp 21 Lefthand rear direction indicator lamp 22 Battery 23 Switch, ignition and starter 24 Switch, lights 25 Switch, headlamp flash and dip 26 Righthand indicator warning light 27 Lefthand indicator warning light 28 Fuses, 1 to 8, 35-amp 29 Indicator unit, flasher 30 Switch, direction indicators 31 Alternator, Lucas 16 ACR 32 Warning light, ignition 33 Ignition coil 34 Warning light, oil pressure 35 Warning light, choke 36 Voltage stabilizer, fuel gauge and water temperature gauge 37 Switch, stoplamp 38 Switch, windscreen wiper 39 Dual fuel pump, 6-cylinder models only 40 Switch, cold start warning light 41 Fuel gauge 42 Water temperature gauge 43 Screenwiper motor 44 Distributor 45 Switch, oil pressure 46 Fuel tank unit 47 Water temperature transmitter unit 48 Lefthand stoplamp 49 Righthand stoplamp 50 Screenwasher motor (when fitted)

Key to cable colour code **B** Black **G** Green **L** Light **N** Brown **P** Purple **R** Red **U** Blue **W** White **Y** Yellow

When cables have two colour code letters, the first denotes the main and the latter the tracer.

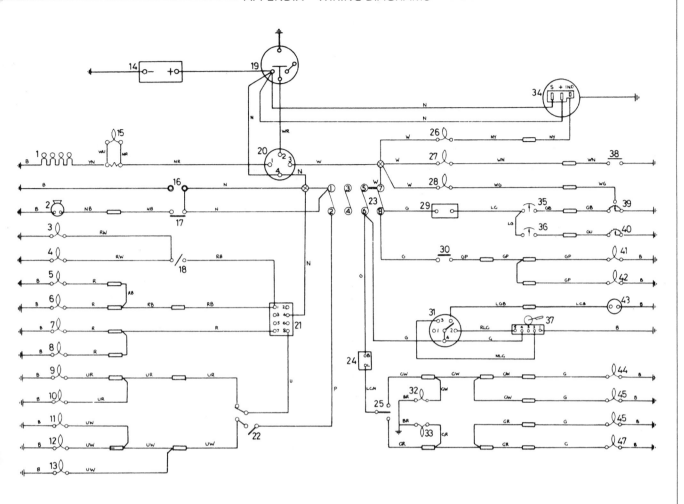

FIG 15:9 2¼ litre diesel models, Series 3

Key to Fig 15:9   1 Heater plugs   2 Horn   3 Instrument panel illumination   4 Instrument panel illumination   5 Lefthand tail lamp   6 Righthand tail lamp   7 Righthand sidelamp   8 Lefthand sidelamp   9 Righthand dipped beam headlamp
10 Lefthand dipped beam headlamp   11 Lefthand main beam headlamp   12 Righthand main beam headlamp
13 Headlamp main beam warning light   14 Battery   15 Warning light and resistor, heater plugs   16 Inspection sockets
17 Switch, horn   18 Switch, panel light   19 Solenoid, starter motor   20 Switch, starter-heater plugs   21 Switch, lights
22 Switch, headlamp dip and flash   23 Fuses, 1 to 8, 35-amp   24 Indicator unit, flasher   25 Switch, indicators
26 Warning light, charge   27 Warning light, oil pressure   28 Warning light, low fuel level   29 Voltage stabilizer unit, fuel gauge and water temperature gauge   30 Switch, stoplamps   31 Switch, windscreen wiper   32 Warning light, righthand indicator   33 Warning light, lefthand indicator   34 Alternator, 16 ACR   35 Fuel gauge   36 Water temperature gauge
37 Wiper motor   38 Switch, oil pressure   39 Fuel tank unit   40 Transmitter, water temperature   41 Lefthand stoplamp
42 Righthand stoplamp   43 Windscreen washer motor (when fitted)   44 Righthand front indicator   45 Righthand rear indicator   46 Lefthand rear indicator   47 Lefthand front Indicator

Key to cable colour code   **B** Black   **G** Green   **L** Light   **N** Brown   **P** Purple   **R** Red   **U** Blue   **W** White   **Y** Yellow

When cables have two colour code letters, the first denotes the main and the latter the tracer.

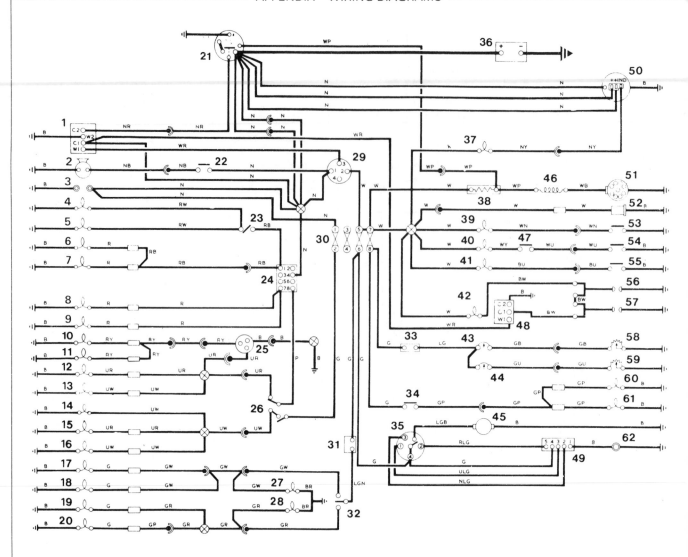

FIG 15 : 10   3.5 litre model, righthand and lefthand steering, with rear foglamps, negative earth

Key to Fig 15 : 10   1 Starter relay   2 Horn   3 Inspection sockets   4 Speedometer panel illumination
5 Grouped instrument panel illumination   6 Lefthand tail lamp   7 Righthand tail lamp   8 Lefthand sidelamp
9 Righthand sidelamp   10 Righthand rear foglamp   11 Lefthand rear foglamp, when fitted   12 Lefthand headlamp
dipped beam   13 Lefthand headlamp main beam   14 Main beam warning light   15 Righthand headlamp dipped beam
16 Righthand headlamp main beam   17 Righthand rear indicator   18 Righthand front indicator   19 Lefthand front indicator
20 Lefthand rear indicator   21 Starter motor (type 3M100)   22 Horn-push   23 Panel light switch   24 Lighting switch
25 Rear foglamp switch and warning light   26 Headlamp flash and dip switch   27 Righthand indicator warning light
28 Lefthand indicator warning light   29 Ignition switch   30 Fuse unit   31 Indicator unit   32 Indicator switch
33 Voltage stabilizer unit   34 Stoplamp switch   35 Two-speed wiper/wash switch   36 Battery   37 Ignition warning light
38 Ballast resistor   39 Oil pressure warning light   40 Choke warning light   41 Differential lock warning light
42 Warning light and test button switch   43 Fuel gauge   44 Water temperature gauge   45 Screen wash motor   46 Coil
47 Choke switch   48 Electric fuel pump   49 Screen wiper motor   50 Alternator   51 Distributor   52 Electric fuel pump
53 Oil pressure switch   54 Choke thermostatic switch   55 Differential lock warning light switch   56 Switch, brake
fluid pressure   57 Brake servo vacuum loss switch   58 Fuel tank unit   59 Water temperature unit   60 Lefthand stoplamp
61 Righthand stoplamp   62 Inhibitor socket

Key to cable colour code   B Black   **G** Green   **L** Light   **N** Brown   **P** Purple   **R** Red   **U** Blue   **W** White   **Y** Yellow

When cables have two colour code letters, the first denotes the main and the latter the tracer.

HINTS ON MAINTENANCE AND OVERHAUL

There are few things more rewarding than the restoration of a vehicle's original peak of efficiency and smooth performance.

The following notes are intended to help the owner to reach that state of perfection. Providing that he possesses the basic manual skills he should have no difficulty in performing most of the operations detailed in this manual. It must be stressed, however, that where recommended in the manual, highly-skilled operations ought to be entrusted to experts, who have the necessary equipment, to carry out the work satisfactorily.

Quality of workmanship :

The hazardous driving conditions on the roads to-day demand that vehicles should be as nearly perfect, mechanically, as possible. It is therefore most important that amateur work be carried out with care, bearing in mind the often inadequate working conditions, and also the inferior tools which may have to be used. It is easy to counsel perfection in all things, and we recognise that it may be setting an impossibly high standard. We do, however, suggest that every care should be taken to ensure that a vehicle is as safe to take on the road as it is humanly possible to make it.

Safe working conditions :

Even though a vehicle may be stationary, it is still potentially dangerous if certain sensible precautions are not taken when working on it while it is supported on jacks or blocks. It is indeed preferable not to use jacks alone, but to supplement them with carefully placed blocks, so that there will be plenty of support if the vehicle rolls off the jacks during a strenuous manoeuvre. Axle stands are an excellent way of providing a rigid base which is not readily disturbed. Piles of bricks are a dangerous substitute. Be careful not to get under heavy loads on lifting tackle, the load could fall. It is preferable not to work alone when lifting an engine, or when working underneath a vehicle which is supported well off the ground. To be trapped, particularly under the vehicle, may have unpleasant results if help is not quickly forthcoming. Make some provision, however humble, to deal with fires. Always disconnect a battery if there is a likelihood of electrical shorts. These may start a fire if there is leaking fuel about. This applies particularly to leads which can carry a heavy current, like those in the starter circuit. While on the subject of electricity, we must also stress the danger of using equipment which is run off the mains and which has no earth or has faulty wiring or connections. So many workshops have damp floors, and electrical shocks are of such a nature that it is sometimes impossible to let go of a live lead or piece of equipment due to the muscular spasms which take place.

Work demanding special care :

This involves the servicing of braking, steering and suspension systems. On the road, failure of the braking system may be disastrous. Make quite sure that there can be no possibility of failure through the bursting of rusty brake pipes or rotten hoses, nor to a sudden loss of pressure due to defective seals or valves.

Problems :

The chief problems which may face an operator are :
1 External dirt.
2 Difficulty in undoing tight fixings.
3 Dismantling unfamiliar mechanisms.
4 Deciding in what respect parts are defective.
5 Confusion about the correct order for reassembly.
6 Adjusting running clearance.
7 Road testing.
8 Final tuning.

Practical suggestions to solve the problems :

1 Preliminary cleaning of large parts – engines, transmissions, steering, suspensions, etc, – should be carried out before removal from the vehicle. Where road dirt and mud alone are present, wash clean with a high-pressure water jet, brushing to remove stubborn adhesions, and allow to drain and dry. Where oil or grease is also present, wash down with a proprietary compound (Gunk, Teepol etc,) applying with a stiff brush – an old paint brush is suitable – into all crevices. Cover the distributor and ignition coils with a polythene bag and then apply a strong water jet to clear the loosened deposits. Allow to drain and dry. The assemblies will then be sufficiently clean to remove and transfer to the bench for the next stage.

On the bench, further cleaning can be carried out, first wiping the parts as free as possible from grease with old newspaper. Avoid using rag or cotton waste which can leave clogging fibres behind. Any remaining grease can be removed with a brush dipped in paraffin. Avoid using paraffin or petrol in large quantities for cleaning in enclosed areas, such as garages, on account of the high fire risk.

When all exteriors have been cleaned, and not before, dismantling can be commenced. This ensures that dirt will not enter into interiors and orifices revealed by dismantling. In the next phases, where components have to be cleaned, use a special solvent or petrol and keep the containers covered except when in use. After the components have been cleaned, plug small holes with tapered hard wood plugs cut to size and blank off larger orifices with greaseproof paper and masking tape. Do not use soft wood plugs or matchsticks as they may break.

2 It is not advisable to hammer on the end of a screw thread, but if it must be done, first screw on a nut to protect the thread, and use a lead hammer. This applies particularly to the removal of tapered cotters. Nuts and bolts seem to 'grow' together, especially in exhaust systems. If penetrating oil does not work, try the judicious application of heat, but be careful of starting a fire. Asbestos sheet or cloth is useful to isolate heat.

Tight bushes or pieces of tail-pipe rusted into a silencer can be removed by splitting them with an open-ended hacksaw. Tight screws can sometimes be started by a tap from a hammer on the end of a suitable screwdriver. Many tight fittings will yield to the judicious use of a hammer, but it must be a soft-faced hammer if damage is to be avoided. Use a heavy block on the opposite side to absorb shock. Any parts of the steering system which have been damaged should be renewed, as attempts to repair them may lead to cracking and subsequent failure, and steering ball joints should be disconnected using a recommended tool to prevent damage.

3 It often happens that an owner is baffled when trying to dismantle an unfamiliar piece of equipment. So many modern devices are pressed together or assembled by spinning-over flanges, that they must be sawn apart. The intention is that the whole assembly must be renewed. However, parts which appear to be in one piece to the naked eye may reveal close-fitting joint lines when inspected with a magnifying glass, and this may provide the necessary clue to dismantling. Lefthanded screw threads are used where rotational forces would tend to unscrew a righthand screw thread.

Be very careful when dismantling mechanisms which may come apart suddenly. Work in an enclosed space where the parts will be contained, and drape a piece of cloth over the device if springs are likely to fly in all directions. Mark everything which might be reassembled in the wrong position, scratched symbols may be used on unstressed parts, or a sequence of tiny dots from a centre punch can be useful. Stressed parts should never be scratched or centre-popped as this may lead to cracking under working conditions. Store parts which look alike in the correct order for reassembly. Never rely upon memory to assist in the assembly of complicated mechanisms, especially when they will be dismantled for a long time, but make notes and drawings to supplement the diagrams in the manual, and put labels on detached wires. Rust stains may indicate unlubricated wear. This can sometimes be seen round the outside edge of a bearing cup in a universal joint. Look for bright rubbing marks on parts which normally should not make heavy contact. These might prove that something is bent or running out of truth. For example, there might be bright marks on one side of a piston, at the top near the ring grooves, and others at the bottom of the skirt on the other side. This could well be the clue to a bent connecting rod. Suspected cracks can be proved by heating the component in a light oil to approximately 100°C, removing, drying off, and dusting with french chalk. If a crack is present the oil retained in the crack will stain the french chalk.

4 In determining wear, and the degree, against the permissible limits set in the manual, accurate measurements can only be achieved by the use of a micrometer. In many cases, the wear is given to the fourth place of decimals; that is in ten-thousandths of an inch. This can be read by the vernier scale on the barrel of a good micrometer. Bore diameters are more difficult to determine. If, however, the matching shaft is accurately measured, the degree of play in the bore can be felt as a guide to its suitability. In other cases, the shank of a twist drill of known diameter is a handy check.

Many methods have been devised for determining the clearance between bearing surfaces. To-day the best and simplest is by the use of Plastigage, obtainable from most garages. A thin plastic thread is laid between the two surfaces and the bearing is tightened, flattening the thread. On removal, the width of the thread is compared with the scale supplied with the thread and the clearance is read off directly. Sometimes joint faces leak persistently, even after gasket renewal. The fault will then be traceable to distortion, dirt or burrs. Studs which are screwed into soft metal frequently raise burrs at the point of entry. A quick cure for this is to chamfer the edge of the hole in the part which fits over the stud.

5 **Always check a replacement part with the original one before it is fitted.**

If parts are not marked, and the order for reassembly is not known, a little detective work will help. Look for marks which are due to wear to see if they can be mated. Joint faces may not be identical due to manufacturing errors, and parts which overlap may be stained, giving a clue to the correct position. Most fixings leave identifying marks especially if they were painted over on assembly. It is then easier to decide whether a nut, for instance, has a plain, a spring, or a shakeproof washer under it. All running surfaces become 'bedded' together after long spells of work and tiny imperfections on one part will be found to have left corresponding marks on the other. This is particularly true of shafts and bearings and even a score on a cylinder wall will show on the piston.

6 Checking end float or rocker clearances by feeler gauge may not always give accurate results because of wear. For instance, the rocker tip which bears on a valve stem may be deeply pitted, in which case the feeler will simply be bridging a depression. Thrust washers may also wear depressions in opposing faces to make accurate measurement difficult. End float is then easier to check by using a dial gauge. It is common practice to adjust end play in bearing assemblies, like front hubs with taper rollers, by tightening up the axle nut until the hub becomes stiff to turn and then backing it off a little. Do not use this method with ballbearing hubs as the assembly is often preloaded by tightening the axle nut to its fullest extent. If the splitpin hole will not line up, file the base of the nut a little.

Steering assemblies often wear in the straight-ahead position. If any part is adjusted, make sure that it remains free when moved from lock to lock. Do not be surprised if an assembly like a steering gearbox, which is known to be carefully adjusted outside the car, becomes stiff when it is bolted into place. This will be due to distortion of the case by the pull of the mounting bolts, particularly if the mounting points are not all touching together. This problem may be met in other equipment and is cured by careful attention to the alignment of mounting points.

When a spanner is stamped with a size and A/F it means that the dimension is the width between the jaws and has no connection with ANF, which is the designation for the American National Fine thread. Coarse threads like Whitworth are rarely used on cars to-day except for studs which screw into soft aluminium or cast iron. For this reason it might be found that the top end of a cylinder head stud has a fine thread and the lower end a coarse thread to screw into the cylinder block. If the car has mainly UNF threads then it is likely that any coarse threads will be UNC, which are not the same as Whitworth. Small sizes have the same number of threads in Whitworth and UNC, but in the ½ in size for example, there are twelve threads to the inch in the former and thirteen in the latter.

7 After a major overhaul, particularly if a great deal of work has been done on the braking, steering and suspension systems, it is advisable to approach the problem of testing with care. If the braking system has been overhauled, apply heavy pressure to the brake pedal and get a second operator to check every possible source of leakage. The brakes may work extremely well, but a leak could cause complete failure after a few miles.

Do not fit the hub caps until every wheel nut has been checked for tightness, and make sure that the tyre pressures are correct. Check the levels of coolant, lubricants and hydraulic fluids. Being satisfied that all is well, take the car on the road and test the brakes at once. Check the steering and the action of the handbrake. Do all this at moderate speeds on quiet roads, and make sure there is no other vehicle behind you when you try a rapid stop.

Finally, remember that many parts settle down after a time, so check for tightness of all fixings after the car has been on the road for a hundred miles or so.

8 It is useless to tune an engine which has not reached its normal running temperature. In the same way, the tune of an engine which is stiff after a rebore will be different when the engine is again running free. Remember too, that rocker clearances on pushrod operated valve gear will change when the cylinder head nuts are tightened after an initial period of running with a new head gasket.

Trouble may not always be due to what seems the obvious cause. Ignition, carburation and mechanical condition are interdependent and spitting back through the carburetter, which might be attributed to a weak mixture, can be caused by a sticking inlet valve.

For one final hint on tuning, never adjust more than one thing at a time or it will be impossible to tell which adjustment produced the desired result.

WARNING

If, during any overhaul or service, it is necessary to extract any roll pins and/or circlips they MUST be discarded.

New pins and/or circlips MUST be fitted on reassembly. The refitting of used roll pins and/or circlips could result in failure of a component and possibly create a safety hazard.

NOTES

GLOSSARY OF TERMS

Allen key — Cranked wrench of hexagonal section for use with socket head screws.

Alternator — Electrical generator producing alternating current. Rectified to direct current for battery charging.

Ambient temperature — Surrounding atmospheric temperature.

Annulus — Used in engineering to indicate the outer ring gear of an epicyclic gear train.

Armature — The shaft carrying the windings, which rotates in the magnetic field of a generator or starter motor. That part of a solenoid or relay which is activated by the magnetic field.

Axial — In line with, or pertaining to, an axis.

Backlash — Play in meshing gears.

Balance lever — A bar where force applied at the centre is equally divided between connections at the ends.

Banjo axle — Axle casing with large diameter housing for the crownwheel and differential.

Bendix pinion — A self-engaging and self-disengaging drive on a starter motor shaft.

Bevel pinion — A conical shaped gearwheel, designed to mesh with a similar gear with an axis usually at 90 deg. to its own.

bhp — Brake horse power, measured on a dynamometer.

bmep — Brake mean effective pressure. Average pressure on a piston during the working stroke.

Brake cylinder — Cylinder with hydraulically operated piston(s) acting on brake shoes or pad(s).

Brake regulator — Control valve fitted in hydraulic braking system which limits brake pressure to rear brakes during heavy braking to prevent rear wheel locking.

Camber — Angle at which a wheel is tilted from the vertical.

Capacitor — Modern term for an electrical condenser. Part of distributor assembly, connected across contact breaker points, acts as an interference suppressor.

Castellated — Top face of a nut, slotted across the flats, to take a locking splitpin.

Castor — Angle at which the kingpin or swivel pin is tilted when viewed from the side.

cc — Cubic centimetres. Engine capacity is arrived at by multiplying the area of the bore in sq cm by the stroke in cm by the number of cylinders.

Clevis — U-shaped forked connector used with a clevis pin, usually at handbrake connections.

Collet — A type of collar, usually split and located in a groove in a shaft, and held in place by a retainer. The arrangement used to retain the spring(s) on a valve stem in most cases.

Commutator — Rotating segmented current distributor between armature windings and brushes in generator or motor.

Compression ratio — The ratio, or quantitative relation, of the total volume (piston at bottom of stroke) to the unswept volume (piston at top of stroke) in an engine cylinder.

Condenser — See capacitor.

Core plug — Plug for blanking off a manufacturing hole in a casting.

Crownwheel — Large bevel gear in rear axle, driven by a bevel pinion attached to the propeller shaft. Sometimes called a 'ring gear'.

'C'-spanner — Like a 'C' with a handle. For use on screwed collars without flats, but with slots or holes.

Damper — Modern term for shock-absorber, used in vehicle suspension systems to damp out spring oscillations.

Depression — The lowering of atmospheric pressure as in the inlet manifold and carburetter.

Dowel — Close tolerance pin, peg, tube, or bolt, which accurately locates mating parts.

Drag link — Rod connecting steering box drop arm (pitman arm) to nearest front wheel steering arm in certain types of steering systems.

Dry liner — Thinwall tube pressed into cylinder bore

Dry sump — Lubrication system where all oil is scavenged from the sump, and returned to a separate tank.

Dynamo — See Generator.

Electrode — Terminal, part of an electrical component, such as the points or 'Electrodes' of a sparking plug.

Electrolyte — In lead-acid car batteries a solution of sulphuric acid and distilled water.

End float — The axial movement between associated parts, end play.

EP — Extreme pressure. In lubricants, special grades for heavily loaded bearing surfaces, such as gear teeth in a gearbox, or crownwheel and pinion in a rear axle.

Fade	Of brakes. Reduced efficiency due to overheating.
Field coils	Windings on the polepieces of motors and generators.
Fillets	Narrow finishing strips usually applied to interior bodywork.
First motion shaft	Input shaft from clutch to gearbox.
Fullflow filter	Filters in which all the oil is pumped to the engine. If the element becomes clogged, a bypass valve operates to pass unfiltered oil to the engine.
FWD	Front wheel drive.
Gear pump	Two meshing gears in a close fitting casing. Oil is carried from the inlet round the outside of both gears in the spaces between the gear teeth and casing to the outlet, the meshing gear teeth prevent oil passing back to the inlet, and the oil is forced through the outlet port.
Generator	Modern term for 'Dynamo'. When rotated produces electrical current.
Grommet	A ring of protective or sealing material. Can be used to protect pipes or leads passing through bulkheads.
Grubscrew	Fully threaded headless screw with screwdriver slot. Used for locking, or alignment purposes.
Gudgeon pin	Shaft which connects a piston to its connecting rod. Sometimes called 'wrist pin', or 'piston pin'.
Halfshaft	One of a pair transmitting drive from the differential.
Helical	In spiral form. The teeth of helical gears are cut at a spiral angle to the side faces of the gearwheel.
Hot spot	Hot area that assists vapourisation of fuel on its way to cylinders. Often provided by close contact between inlet and exhaust manifolds.
HT	High Tension. Applied to electrical current produced by the ignition coil for the sparking plugs.
Hydrometer	A device for checking specific gravity of liquids. Used to check specific gravity of electrolyte.
Hypoid bevel gears	A form of bevel gear used in the rear axle drive gears. The bevel pinion meshes below the centre line of the crownwheel, giving a lower propeller shaft line.
Idler	A device for passing on movement. A free running gear between driving and driven gears. A lever transmitting track rod movement to a side rod in steering gear.
Impeller	A centrifugal pumping element. Used in water pumps to stimulate flow.
Journals	Those parts of a shaft that are in contact with the bearings.
Kingpin	The main vertical pin which carries the front wheel spindle, and permits steering movement. May be called 'steering pin' or 'swivel pin'.
Layshaft	The shaft which carries the laygear in the gearbox. The laygear is driven by the first motion shaft and drives the third motion shaft according to the gear selected. Sometimes called the 'countershaft' or 'second motion shaft.'
lb ft	A measure of twist or torque. A pull of 10 lb at a radius of 1 ft is a torque of 10 lb ft.
lb/sq in	Pounds per square inch.
Little-end	The small, or piston end of a connecting rod. Sometimes called the 'small-end'.
LT	Low Tension. The current output from the battery.
Mandrel	Accurately manufactured bar or rod used for test or centring purposes.
Manifold	A pipe, duct, or chamber, with several branches.
Needle rollers	Bearing rollers with a length many times their diameter.
Oil bath	Reservoir which lubricates parts by immersion. In air filters, a separate oil supply for wetting a wire mesh element to hold the dust.
Oil wetted	In air filters, a wire mesh element lightly oiled to trap and hold airborne dust.
Overlap	Period during which inlet and exhaust valves are open together.
Panhard rod	Bar connected between fixed point on chassis and another on axle to control sideways movement.
Pawl	Pivoted catch which engages in the teeth of a ratchet to permit movement in one direction only.
Peg spanner	Tool with pegs, or pins, to engage in holes or slots in the part to be turned.
Pendant pedals	Pedals with levers that are pivoted at the top end.
Phillips screwdriver	A cross-point screwdriver for use with the cross-slotted heads of Phillips screws.
Pinion	A small gear, usually in relation to another gear.
Piston-type damper	Shock absorber in which damping is controlled by a piston working in a closed oil-filled cylinder.
Preloading	Preset static pressure on ball or roller bearings not due to working loads.
Radial	Radiating from a centre, like the spokes of a wheel.

Radius rod — Pivoted arm confining movement of a part to an arc of fixed radius.

Ratchet — Toothed wheel or rack which can move in one direction only, movement in the other being prevented by a pawl.

Ring gear — A gear tooth ring attached to outer periphery of flywheel. Starter pinion engages with it during starting.

Runout — Amount by which rotating part is out of true.

Semi-floating axle — Outer end of rear axle halfshaft is carried on bearing inside axle casing. Wheel hub is secured to end of shaft.

Servo — A hydraulic or pneumatic system for assisting or augmenting a physical effort. See 'Vacuum Servo'.

Setscrew — One which is threaded for the full length of the shank.

Shackle — A coupling link, used in the form of two parallel pins connected by side plates to secure the end of the master suspension spring and absorb the effects of deflection.

Shell bearing — Thinwalled steel shell lined with anti-friction metal. Usually semi-circular and used in pairs for main and big-end bearings.

Shock absorber — See 'Damper'.

Silentbloc — Rubber bush bonded to inner and outer metal sleeves.

Socket-head screw — Screw with hexagonal socket for an Allen key.

Solenoid — A coil of wire creating a magnetic field when electric current passes through it. Used with a soft iron core to operate contacts or a mechanical device.

Spur gear — A gear with teeth cut axially across the periphery.

Stub axle — Short axle fixed at one end only.

Tachometer — An instrument for accurate measurement of rotating speed. Usually indicates in revolutions per minute.

TDC — Top Dead Centre. The highest point reached by a piston in a cylinder, with the crank and connecting rod in line.

Thermostat — Automatic device for regulating temperature. Used in vehicle coolant systems to open a valve which restricts circulation at low temperature.

Third motion shaft — Output shaft of gearbox.

Threequarter floating axle — Outer end of rear axle halfshaft flanged and bolted to wheel hub, which runs on bearing mounted on outside of axle casing. Vehicle weight is not carried by the axle shaft.

Thrust bearing or washer — Used to reduce friction in rotating parts subject to axial loads.

Torque — Turning or twisting effort. See 'lb ft'.

Track rod — The bar(s) across the vehicle which connect the steering arms and maintain the front wheels in their correct alignment.

UJ — Universal joint. A coupling between shafts which permits angular movement.

UNF — Unified National Fine screw thread.

Vacuum servo — Device used in brake system, using difference between atmospheric pressure and inlet manifold depression to operate a piston which acts to augment brake pressure as required. See 'Servo'.

Venturi — A restriction or 'choke' in a tube, as in a carburetter, used to increase velocity to obtain a reduction in pressure.

Vernier — A sliding scale for obtaining fractional readings of the graduations of an adjacent scale.

Welch plug — A domed thin metal disc which is partially flattened to lock in a recess. Used to plug core holes in castings.

Wet liner — Removable cylinder barrel, sealed against coolant leakage, where the coolant is in direct contact with the outer surface.

Wet sump — A reservoir attached to the crankcase to hold the lubricating oil.

INDEX

Buying Secondhand

Land~Rover

MAKING a complete survey of the enormous choice of secondhand Land-Rovers in the confines of one four-page feature is virtually impossible. Rover, in the past, have advertised the Land-Rover as ''The World's Most Versatile Vehicle'', which is a claim we do not dispute; one reason for this is that Land-Rovers are, and have been, sold in the most enormous variety of guises. There is a wide choice of engines, wheelbase lengths, chassis specifications, bodies and optional equipment.

Anyone looking for a secondhand four-wheel-drive machine at present must come to terms with the fact that in Britain at least there is really only one rival to the Land-Rover, and that is the smoother and considerably more expensive Range Rover. It is arguable that the Land-Rover is unique and effectively has no competitors. Even though there are Toyotas, Jeeps, Ladas and the like in this country their numbers are tiny, and they are not of commercial significance.

There are so many ways in which a Land-Rover could have been built when new that the customer would do well to remember these two facts:

a) There is no such thing as a ''standard'' Land-Rover.

b) The *precise* variant he wants will be extremely difficult to find.

If, on the other hand, he is prepared to compromise somewhat on optional equipment and perhaps even on body layout, there is a big choice in the market place.

Twenty-eight years of Land-Rovers — the first prototype (left) of 1948 and the millionth production model of 1976. At right is the 109in. Station Wagon Series III model

Defining the pedigree

The first Land-Rover, which had an 80in. wheelbase and a 1,595 c.c. engine, was sold in July, 1948. Ever since then there have been long waiting lists for the model, and sales have risen to keep ahead of production. The millionth Land-Rover was built in June, 1976, and more than 1,300 examples are built every week. There are big plans to double this rate by the early 1980s.

The Series I Land-Rover was built for ten years, and was replaced by the Series II range in 1958. The Series IIA vehicles followed in 1961, and the current Series III models in October, 1971. Because the oldest of these SIII models may be more than seven years old, and because more than a quarter-million have now been built, we confine our detail attention to the latest varieties. Much of what we know, however, can also be applied to the mechanically-similar SIIAs.

Since 1957, all normal-control Land-Rovers have been built on one of two basic chassis frames — one with an 88in. wheelbase, and one with a 109in. wheelbase. The 21in. extra length is all accommodated behind the front

seats, and this combined with a longer load platform means that the 109in. version has an extra 36in. overall length, all useful for carrying people or goods. The frames are mainly of massive steel box sections, on to which the no-nonsense bumpers are bolted.

There is a choice of engines — two petrol and one diesel — a rugged four-wheel-drive transmission by centre gearbox, transfer gearbox and propeller shafts to front and rear axles, live front and rear axles, and suspension at front and rear by hard half-elliptic leaf springs. All vehicles have drum brakes, steel disc wheels, and may have several types and sections of cross-country treaded tyres.

The nose, front wings, engine bay, screen and doors are common to all Land-Rovers, but there is a very wide choice of rear bodywork which ranges from the open ''Regular'' type to the fully-equipped (if utilitarian) 12-seater station wagon type. There is a huge range of factory-approved optional equipment, and every Land-Rover is built to special order to include these when first being assembled.

Chassis and transmission

The basic design of chassis frame, transmission and suspension has not changed in 30 years, but there have been many important changes. 88in. and 109in. wheelbase lengths have been standardised for more than 20 years. Each and every version has a generous ground clearance, and the hard suspension is designed to keep the rest of the vehicle in one piece with absolutely no thought to passenger comfort.

There is a two-speed arrangement in the transfer gearbox itself, and in all normal use a Land-Rover is driven with front-wheel-drive disengaged. The alternatives, therefore, are:

High (—gearing) range, rear-wheel-drive).

High (—gearing) range, four-wheel-drive.

Low (—gearing) range, four-wheel-drive.

It is not possible to have rear-drive only when Low Range is engaged.

Since 1974, a Fairey overdrive has been optional on Land-Rovers, and a good number have also been fitted

Seats — pretty basic in earlier models (above), but quite good seats were available as an option later (below)

No wasted space, as underseat stowage illustrates. Changing dashboard styles; at top, 1971 6-cylinder 109in. model. At bottom, 1973 88in. version

retrospectively to older models; the conversion is simple, and takes three hours when tackled by experienced mechanics.

The main gearbox has four forward speeds, all with synchromesh, so normally there is the possibility of eight forward speeds; with overdrive this rises to no less than 16 (and four reverses!).

There is not, nor ever has been, an automatic transmission alternative.

It is worth noting that tens of thousands of Land-Rovers have been built with "freewheeling" front hubs, which help minimise fuel consumption on the highway by not driving the front differential.

All Land-Rovers have the same axle ratios — 4.7:1 — but there are two sets of transfer box "step down" ratios. Those fitted to the heavy-duty "one-ton" payload Land-Rover (see below) have a much greater step down ratio to Low Range, to give even greater overall gearing than usual, and this set of gears is also optional on other Land-Rovers.

Engines

Since 1967, the Land-Rover range has boasted a choice of three engines, all of which have been fitted in large quantities; two are four-cylinder units (a petrol and a diesel), and one is a smoother and more powerful "six".

Both four-cylinder engines are

of 2,286 c.c. and are based on the same basic production machine tooling. The basic design stems from 1957 when a wet-liner diesel engine was first introduced, but both the modern versions have dry liners, are conventionally laid out, and very long-lived. The petrol engine develops 70 bhp (DIN) at 4,000rpm, the diesel 62 bhp (DIN) at 4,000rpm. Although the petrol engine was fitted to the Rover 80 private car for a time, it has not otherwise been shared with any other Rover (or British Leyland) model. The diesel unit has always been confined to the Land-Rover.

The "six" is the last derivative of the P3/P4/P5 family of engines introduced in 1948, and is distinguished by a unique valve gear/valve layout with an overhead inlet valve but an angled side exhaust valve. It produces 86 bhp (DIN) at 4,500rpm in Land-Rover form, and is confined to 109in. wheelbase models, not for engineering but for product planning reasons.

Body styles

Here there is a large variety. Basically, all engines can be found in all types of body. Apart from sub-divisions and export-only varieties, secondhand Land-Rovers may be found in these styles:

88in.
Regular (open cab, with hood)
Hardtop (open cab, van body)
Truck cab (with rear hood)
7-seat Station Wagon

Regular, with lightweight Military-type bodywork.

109in.
Regular
Hardtop
Truck cab
10-seat Station Wagon
12-seat Station Wagon

Hoods may be found with or without side windows, as can hardtops. Rear doors may be side-hinged or top-and-bottom hinged, and there are sub-variations on all these themes.

Quite a lot of ex-Military 88in

"half ton" Land-Rovers are now appearing on the secondhand market. These have an entirely different (and more basic) body style than the conventional machines, and do not have the smart full-width facia and instruments of civilian versions.

Optional equipment

Mechanical items which are often found on secondhand Land-Rovers include the overdrives, wide-ratio gears and free-wheel front hubs already mentioned, along with centre power take-offs and rear power take offs of various types, drum and capstan winches and other less expensive items. Depending on original usage. 15in. or 16in. wheels might have been specified, with 6.50, 7.00, 7.50, 8.20 or 9.00in. section tyres.

Above: Load area of 109in. model. Note spare wheel position — alternative position in some 88in. models is shown at top. Right: The 2,286c.c. 4-cylinder petrol engine, one of only three variations available

Model	2,286c.c. ohv 4-cyl petrol single carb	2,286c.c. ohv 4-cyl diesel fuel injection	2,625c.c. ioev 6-cyl petrol single carb
Power (DIN bhp)	70	62	86
88in. wheelbase, all bodies	1971-1979	1971-1979	—
109in. wheelbase, all bodies	1971-1979	1971-1979	1971-1979
109in. wheelbase, 'one ton' version	1971-1979	1971—1979	1971-1979

BODY AVAILABILITY

Model	88in. wheelbase	109in. wheelbase	109in. wheelbase "one ton"
2,286c.c. 4-cyl petrol engine	1971-1979	1971-1979	1971-1979
2,286c.c. 4-cyl diesel engine	1971-1979	1971-1979	1971-1979
2,625c.c. 6-cyl petrol engine		1971-1979	1971-1979

Note: The Series IIA models, built from 1961 to 1971 inclusive, were mechanically very similar to the current Series III models apart from their gearboxes (which had no synchromesh on second and first gears)

CHASSIS IDENTIFICATION

October 1971: Series III Land-Rovers introduced, replacing Series IIA models. No visual changes externally, but new interior, all-synchromesh gearbox, many other details. From following chassis number sequences:

Chassis numbers

88in. petrol	90100008A (station wagon = 921 . . . . . A)
88in. diesel	90600008A
109in. petrol	911 . . . . . A (pick up)
109in. petrol	931 . . . . . A (station wagon)
109in. diesel	916 . . . . . A (pick up)
109in. diesel	936 . . . . . A (station wagon)
109in. 6-cyl petrol	941 . . . . . A (pick up)
109in. 6-cyl petrol	946 . . . . . A (station wagon)

—all models have continued basically unchanged to 1979. For guidance:
January 1978: Chassis numbers of existing range at beginning of year:

88in. petrol	92142006A (regular = 901.)
88in. diesel	92622441A
109in. petrol	91176485C (pick up)
109in. petrol	93176237C (station wagon)
109in. diesel	91623060C (pick up)
109in. diesel	93623021C (station wagon)
109in. 6-cyl petrol	94122252C (pick up)
109in. 6-cyl petrol	94622224C (station wagon)

SPECIFICATIONS AND PERFORMANCE

	88in. W.B. 4-cyl petrol pick-up	109in. W.B. 6-cyl petrol truck cab
Tested in *Autocar* of:	28 Oct. 1971	18 Jan. 1973
Specifications:		
Engine size (c.c.)	2.286	2,625
Engine power (DIN bhp)	70	86
Vehicle length	11ft 7.5in.	14ft 7in.
width	5ft 6in.	5ft 6in.
height	6ft 7in.	6ft 7in.
Boot capacity	— not measured— (Note: No separate boot)	
Turning circle (kerbs)	42ft 0in.	49ft 0in.
Unladen weight (lb)	3.090	3,582
Max. payload (lb)	1.450	2,450
Performance:		
Mean maximum speed (mph)	68	69
Acceleration (sec)		
0-30mph	5.8	6.6
0-40mph	10.9	11.3
0-50mph	16.8	17.0
0-60mph	29.1	31.7
Standing ¼-mile (sec)	22.6	22.9
Consumption:		
Overall mpg	18.0	14.9
Typical mpg — easy driving	23.4	19.4
— average	19.8	16.4
— hard driving	16.4	13.6
Mpg at steady 60 mph	14.8	12.8
(70 mph not sustainable)		
Fuel grade	2-star	2-star
Oil consumption (mpp)	1,000	500

Payloads

Quoted payloads sometimes conflict with maximum recommended weights (diesel engines are heavier than petrol units, station wagons weigh more than "Regular" versions) but these may range from 1,500 lb for an 88in. petrol "Regular" to 2,450lb for a 109in. 6-cyl model. There is also the rather rare 109in. "one ton" model with heavy duty suspension, transmission, and lower overall gearing, which can carry up to 2,900lb. Although the Military version is officially known as a "half ton" this refers to the payload which can be carried *in addition* to driver and front passenger; its effective payload is the same as that of any other 88in. Land-Rover.

Our experience is that many Land-Rover owners cheerfully overload their machines, which do not seem to protest over-much about this treatment unless they are driven hard over rough ground when fully loaded.

Dealer Organisation

Land-Rovers are, and always have been, sold and serviced through what were traditional Rover private car outlets, though in recent years this has been modified to include rationalised Rover-Triumph outlets. Land-Rovers are very rarely sold through Leyland truck outlets in Britain, though this arrangement is more common on overseas markets. There are 158 distributors and 335 Land-Rover dealers in Great Britain and it is also a fact that almost any wayside garage, agricultural engineering establishment and vehicle repairer has a good working knowledge of the type.

There are several specialists in Land-Rovers who are not on British Leyland's lists, and we consulted Jake Wright Ltd, of Burley-in-Wharfedale, West Yorkshire, about the final section of this feature. Jack Wright Ltd specialise in the renovation and sale of ex-Military 88in. "half tons", and concentrate on all Rover 4 x 4 matters.

APPROXIMATE SELLING PRICES

88in. W.B.				109in. W.B.						Price Range
4-cyl Petl. Reg.	4-cyl Dsl. Reg.	4-cyl Petl. Truck	4-cyl Dsl. Truck	4-cyl Petl. Truck	4-cyl Dsl. Truck	4-cyl Petl. Statn. Wgn.	4-cyl Dsl. Statn. Wgn.	6-cyl Petl. Truck	6-cyl Petl. Statn. Wgn.	
1972	1972	1972								£1,350-£1,450
			1972							£1,450-£1,550
1973	1973	1973		1972	1972			1972		£1,600-£1,700
			1973							£1,700-£1,800
1974		1974		1973				1973		£1,850-£1,950
	1974		1974			1972			1972	£1,950-£2,050
							1972			£2,050-£2,150
1975		1975		1974		1973		1974		£2,150-£2,250
	1975		1975		1974		1973			£2,300-£2,400
							1973			£2,350-£2,450
1976		1976		1975		1974		1975		£2,550-£2,650
							1974			£2,650-£2,750
	1976		1976				1974			£2,750-£2,850
1977				1976		1975			1975	£3,000-£3,100
	1977							1976		£3,100-£3,200
					1976					£3,250-£3,350
		1977					1975			£3,350-£3,450
1978				1977				1977		£3,600-£3,700
	1978					1976			1976	£3,700-£3,800
			1978		1977		1976			£3,900-£4,100
				1978				1978		£4,200-£4,400
					1978	1977			1977	£4,400-£4,700
						1978	1977		1978	£5,200-£5,400
							1978			£5,500-£5,700

Note: Many other body types are also available

WHAT TO LOOK FOR

Mechanical

In spite of what some fanatics would have you believe, Land-Rovers are not indestructible. Although they have a largely corrosion-proof, light-alloy body, parts of it are pressed-steel and eventually rust away, while the state of the chassis frame of a secondhand Land-Rover depends very much on the type of use it has had in its early life. Any true working Land-Rover, which encounters mud, rocks and chassis wracking conditions has a hard life. The frames are not galvanised (though the Military versions are under-sealed when new) and eventually rust badly. Corrosion spots are to be found at outrigger/side member joints (5), rear spring rear hanger brackets (2), on the main side-members of 109in models (4), above the rear bump stop brackets (3), but — most serious of all — around the rear cross-member/chassis side member junction (1). This last condition is aggravated by excess towing loads on the rear of the chassis, so any Land-Rover fitted with a towing hook which has regularly been used for towing a heavy trailer or implement should be inspected very carefully.

Leaf springs wear, of course, go rusty, and occasionally break a leaf (6). Spring bushes and pins (7) must also be considered as consumables, but are very simple and relatively cheap to replace. Dampers have to be changed mostly because their casing rust through and expose the works, rather than because they lose their effectiveness (8).

Surprisingly enough, the exhaust pipe under the engine bay is not the most short-lived part of that system — that behind the offside rear wheel (9) is usually the first to rust away. The front pipe is known to loosen away from the exhaust manifold, then break (10).

The two Achilles heels in the transmission are rear half shafts on 88in. wheelbase Land-Rovers with the non-heavy duty axle, which occasionally snap at their inner ends (there is no way that this can be prophesied when buying one, so it has to be treated as a possible occurrence at some time in the future!), or the pitting and severe corrosion of the chrome plated front hub swivels (11). Rover list leather gaiters as optional extras to keep mud and grit out of these swivels, so they must be aware of the problem; Military Land-Rovers have these gaiters fitted as standard.

The clutch is good and big, and appears to be man sized for the job; Land-Rovers which have been abused, perhaps by not having the low-speed Low Range engaged for really heavy jobs, may suffer premature wear.

The all-synchromesh gearbox fitted to Series III models is not considered to be as strong as the earlier box which only had synchro on top and third gears; because of the nature of a Land-Rover's life, the synchromesh on first and second gears suffers first, and the first gear wheels eventually get noisy, and chip their teeth. Replacement is straightforward, but time-consuming and therefore expensive (19).

John Wright, of Jake Wright Ltd, told us that his customers seemed to be very happy with front free-wheel hubs, when fitted, but that reaction (on value for money terms) was still mixed regarding the Fairey overdrives, which are approved by Rover, and can be fitted in no more than three hours. Their cost is more than £200, and one has to save an awful lot of petrol or diesel (the bonus is between 2 and 3 mpg) to pay for this. The overdrive, incidentally, can be engaged or disengaged while the Land-Rover is moving, but is not a clutchless change.

Tyres may last up to about 20,000 miles, and it is noted that Range Rover radial-ply treads can be fitted, and that there is one light-commercial radial with a "road pattern" tread which can also be fitted if the machine is not to be used in off-the-road conditions.

Surprisingly, diesel engines (which make up about half the market, and are fitted to the Military "half ton" variety) wear out quicker than the very robust petrol versions. They exhibit their age by burning their oil, or by pushing it out through the breather; this may herald the onset of a major top overhaul (rings, valve guides, and a careful look at the cylinder head, which eventually cracks and starts pushing combustion gases into the cooling water). Six cylinder engines, found only on long-wheelbase 109in. machines are rare in this country, and not very common on export models either.

Body

Although the bodies are mainly made of Birmabright (aluminium alloy), important parts are made of sheet steel. This means that although most of a Land-Rover's body will last and last and last (the Birmabright even seems to be resistant to the attack of salt spray from sea water, or tidal streams), these steel items eventually give up the ghost. When inspecting a secondhand Land-Rover, look carefully at the front bulkhead/toeboard (14), the front door pillar near the door hinges (17) and particularly at the upper door surrounds (above the glass — 15) for signs of rust. Insist on a drive through water so that you can check for any misalignment and underbody damage, which manifests itself in the form of leaks (16).

We think the "De Luxe" seats very desirable — some SIIIs have the older flat-cushion variety. Believe it or not, some Land-Rovers even have radios fitted, though it is often difficult to hear these above the cacophony of engine, transmission, wind and tyre noise emitted by any self-respecting Land-Rover on a surfaced road. The heating and ventilation on these SIIIs is much better than on earlier models.

Lastly, don't forget that a Land-Rover, under law, counts as a dual-purpose vehicle, which means that it is not normally limited to commercial vehicle speeds unless carrying unwindowed van coachwork. There are, however, all manner of pitfalls regarding licensing and insurance, which will need advice from your brokers.

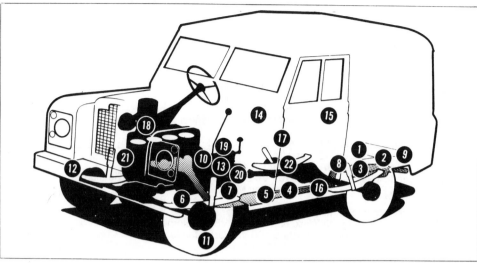

1. Chassis — rust around rear crossmember/chassis rail joints
2. Chassis — rust around rear spring rear hanger brackets
3. Chassis cracking above rear bump stop mount
4. Chassis corrosion in middle of 109in. side members
5. Chassis corrosion outrigger/side member joints
6. Spring leaf wear/broken leaves
7. Spring bushes and pins wear
8. Damper casings rusted through
9. Exhaust systems corrode behind rear wheels
10. Exhaust systems loosen near engine manifold joint
11. Corrosion/pitting of front hub swivels
12. Freewheel hubs very desirable
13. Overdrive fitment popular and effective
14. Steel bulkhead corrosion
15. Upper door frames (steel) corrosion
16. Water leaks, through floor, around door seals
17. Door pillars, rust near hinges
18. Oil burning/oil smoke from ageing diesels
19. Worn 1st/2nd gear synchromesh
20. Extra-noisy gearbox, first gear may have chipped teeth
21. Water loss from engine or pressurised system, suspect head (diesels)
22. Half shafts at rear (88in.) still susceptible to overloading

John Wright told us that prices paid vary enormously because the condition of a Land-Rover can also vary between spick-and-span and appalling. He quoted the instance of ex-military half-tons of 1972 vintage, complete with an MoT certificate and in good mechanical order, for about £1,850. Doubtful examples of the early civilian 88s may be rather cheaper. There is a Land-Rover to suit almost every taste and every pocket. Although the design is by no means infallible, take comfort from the reputation and experience that goes with production approaching the 1¼ million mark, and an order book already stretching into 1980. Can you really afford to be without one? ☐

LAND ROVER OFFICIAL FACTORY PUBLICATIONS

Land Rover Ser. 1 Workshop Manual	4291
Land Rover Ser. 1 1948-53 Parts Catalogue	4051
Land Rover Ser. 1 1954-58 Parts Catalogue	4107
Land Rover Ser. 1 Instruction Manual	4277
Land Rover Ser. 1 & II Diesel Instruction Manual	4343
Land Rover Ser. II & IIA Workshop Manual	AKM8159
Land Rover Ser. II & Early IIA Bonneted Control Parts Catalogue	605957
Land Rover Ser. IIA Bonneted Control Parts Catalogue	RTC9840CC
Land Rover Ser. IIA, III & 109 V8 Optional Equipment Parts Catalogue	RTC9842CE
Land Rover Ser. IIA/IIB Instruction Manual	LSM64 IM
Land Rover Ser. III Workshop Manual	AKM3648
Land Rover Ser. III Workshop Manual V8 Supplement (edn. 2)	AKM8022
Land Rover Ser. III 88, 109 & 109 V8 Parts Catalogue	RTC9841CE
Land Rover Ser. III Owners' Manual 1971-81	607324B
Land Rover Ser. III Owners' Manual 1981-85	AKM8155
Land Rover 90/110 & Defender Workshop Manual 1983-92	SLR621ENWM
Land Rover Defender Workshop Manual 1993-95	LDAWMEN93
(Covering petrol 2.25, 2.5, 3.5 V8 & diesel 2.25, 2.5, 2.5 Turbo, 200 Tdi)	
Land Rover Defender 300 Tdi Workshop Manual 1996-98	LRL 0097 ENG
Land Rover 110 Parts Catalogue 1983-86	RTC9863CE
Land Rover 90/110 Owners' Handbook	LSM0054
Land Rover Discovery Workshop Manual 1990-94 (petrol 3.5, 3.9, Mpi & diesel 200 Tdi)	SJR900ENWM
Land Rover Discovery Workshop Manual 1995-98 (2.0 Mpi, 3.9 V8i & 4.0 V8 & 300 Tdi)	LRL0079
Land Rover Discovery Owners' Handbook 1990 on (petrol 3.5 & diesel 200 Tdi)	SJR 820 ENHB 90
Land Rover Military (Lightweight) Ser. III Parts Catalogue	
Land Rover Military (Lightweight) Ser. III User Manual	608180
Land Rover 101 1 Tonne Forward Control Workshop Manual	RTC9120
Land Rover 101 1 Tonne Forward Control Parts Catalogue	608294B
Land Rover 101 1 Tonne Forward Control User Manual	608239
Range Rover Workshop Manual 1970-85 (petrol 3.5)	AKM3630
Range Rover Workshop Manual 1986-89 (petrol 3.5)	SRR660ENWM
Range Rover Workshop Manual 1986-89 (petrol 3.5 & diesel 2.4 - VM)	SRR660ENWM & LSM180WS4
Range Rover Workshop Manual 1990-94 (petrol 3.9, 4.2 & diesel 2.5 Tdi, 200 Tdi)	LHAWMENA02
Range Rover Parts Catalogue 1970-85 (petrol 3.5)	RTC9846CH
Range Rover Parts Catalogue 1986-92 (petrol 3.5, 3.9 & diesel 2.4 - VM, 2.5 Tdi)	RTC9908CB
Range Rover Owners' Handbook 1970-80 (petrol 3.5)	606917
Range Rover Owners' Handbook 1981-82 (petrol 3.5)	AKM 8139
Range Rover Owners' Handbook 1983-85 (petrol 3.5)	LSM 0001HB
Range Rover Owners' Handbook 1986-87 (petrol 3.5 & diesel 2.4 - VM)	LSM 129HB
Range Rover Owners' Handbook 1988-89 (petrol 3.5 & diesel 2.4 - VM)	SRR600ENHB

Engine Overhaul Manuals for Land Rover & Range Rover

300 Tdi Engine, R380 Manual Gearbox & LT230T Transfer Gearbox Overhaul Manuals	LRL 003, 070 & 081
Petrol Engine V8 3.5, 3.9, 4.0, 4.2 & 4.6 Overhaul Manuals	LRL 004 & 164
Working in the Wild - Land Rover's Manual for Africa	SMR 684 MI
Land Rover/Range Rover Driving Techniques	LR 369
Winching in Safety	SMR 699MI

Owners' Workhop Manuals
Land Rover 2 / 2A / 3 1959-83 Owners' Workshop Manual
Land Rover 90, 110 & Defender Owners' Workshop Manual

From Land Rover specialists or, in case of difficulty, direct from the distributors:
Brooklands Books Ltd., PO Box 146, Cobham, Surrey, KT11 1LG, England.
Telephone: 01932 865051 Fax: 01932 868803
e-mail sales@brooklands-books.com   www.brooklands-books.com
Brooklands Books Ltd., 1/81 Darley St., PO Box 199, Mona Vale, NSW 2103, Australia.
Telephone: 2 9997 8428 Fax: 2 9979 5799
Car Tech, 11605 Kost Dam Road, North Branch, MN 55056, USA
Phone: 800 551 4754 & 651 583 3471 Fax: 651 583 2023